Walter F. Mondale

The
Good
Fight

A LIFE IN LIBERAL POLITICS

WALTER F. MONDALE

With David Hage

SCRIBNER

New York London Toronto Sydney

Scribner
A Division of Simon & Schuster, Inc.
1230 Avenue of the Americas
New York, NY 10020

First Scribner hardcover edition October 2010

Scribner and design are registered trademarks of The Gale Group, Inc.,
used under license by Simon & Schuster, Inc., the publisher of this work.

For information about special discounts for bulk purchases,
please contact Simon & Schuster Special Sales at 1-866-506-1949 or
business@simonandschuster.com.

The Simon & Schuster Speakers Bureau can bring authors to your
live event. For more information or to book an event contact the
Simon & Schuster Speakers Bureau at 1-866-248-3049 or
visit our website at www.simonspeakers.com.

Book design by Ellen R. Sasahara

Manufactured in the United States of America

1   3   5   7   9   10   8   6   4   2

ISBN 978-1-4391-5866-1
ISBN 978-1-4391-7168-4 (ebook)

Photographs were provided courtesy of the author except for the following:
8, 13, and 14: Corbis.
9: University of Minnesota–Duluth/Michael Berman Archive.
10. Associated Press.
12 and 19. Robert Burgess.
15, 16, 17, 18, 20, and 21. Diana Walker/*Time*.
23. *Star Tribune*, Minneapolis St. Paul.

To Joan Mondale—
my lifelong partner of judgment and grace,
insightful author, gifted arts advocate, loving
mother to our lively family, my soul mate
for all seasons.

We rejoice in our family:
Ted and Pam, Louie, Amanda and Berit;
Eleanor—God bless her—and Chan;
William and our beautiful new granddaughter,
Charlotte.

CONTENTS

Taking Care

S OME YEARS AGO I was asked to give a lecture on political leadership at Rutgers University, and I found myself composing my remarks in the form of a letter to the next president. The year was 1987. Ronald Reagan, a popular president during his first term, had wandered into the swamp of Iran-Contra and was struggling to get back on solid ground with the American people. I had spent four years in the White House with Jimmy Carter, watching and working with the president at closer range than any other vice president in history, and I thought I knew something about leadership and integrity.

The advice I put in that letter was simple: Obey the law. Do your homework. Trust the American people. "The most cherished, mysterious, indefinable, but indispensable asset of the presidency is public trust," I wrote. "You don't get a bank deposit, but it acts like a bank deposit. You have only so much. You've got to cherish, to protect, and to nurture it, because once it's gone, you're done."

I pulled that letter out not long ago, after the election of Barack Obama. Not because I worried for Obama's leadership, but because I have watched the ebb and flow of public trust for fifty years, and I know that, at turning points in our nation's history, it can spell the difference between a society that slips backward into bitterness and frustration and a country that fulfills its greatest promise and highest ideals.

I came of age in a period when our country brimmed with hope and generosity. A confident people, following optimistic leaders, achieved a revolution in civil rights, declared a war on poverty, put astronauts in orbit, guaranteed health care for the elderly, reformed a bigoted and outdated immigration system, placed women on the path toward equality with men, and launched the movement known as environmentalism. I called it the "high tide" of American liberalism, and it left America a better, fairer nation.

But I also lived through a period of crippling cynicism and division. I watched one remarkable president, Lyndon Johnson, self-destruct because he could not level with the American people about a war he was waging in their name. I saw a brilliant politician, Richard Nixon, leave the White House in disgrace because he succumbed to the temptations of deceit and the conviction that he was above the law. I spent a year of my Senate career investigating conspiracies by the CIA and FBI to spy on American citizens and subvert the law—then watched another administration three decades later systematically violate the law we wrote and the Constitution they had sworn to uphold. More times than I hoped, I watched the cynicism and dismay that set in when Americans lose trust in their own government.

This is not, perhaps, the homily that most Americans will expect from me. They will remember me as the Democrat who carried the banner of liberalism against tough odds in 1984 and lost to Ronald Reagan. They will remember me, if they have long memories, as the heir to a progressive political tradition that put civil rights and economic justice on center stage in American politics. I spent a career fighting for those ideals and I believe in them today as passionately as ever.

Those battles, however, also deepened my appreciation for the political tradition we inherited from our founders, a constitutional framework that enshrined accountability and the rule of law. Our founders understood the value of high aspirations. Did the world ever see a more audacious band of idealists than that small group of colonial farmers and frontier lawyers who presumed to convert the philosophy of Locke and Rousseau into a working democracy? But the founders also understood the frailties of democracy and the dangers of power, noting, in Madison's famous phrase, that "men are not angels."

The Constitution they wrote more than two centuries ago contains a brief phrase that legal scholars call the "take care" clause. It's a simple sentence, contained in the passage setting out the duties of the three branches of government, enjoining the president to "take Care that the Laws be faithfully executed."

Time and again through my career I have taken inspiration from that phrase. In times that test our constitutional principles, the "take care" clause steers us back to the founders' wisdom and reminds us that ours is, after all, a government of laws, not men. In times that fray our conscience and compassion, it reminds us of the obligation to sustain and nurture the magnificent experiment they left us.

Our founders understood that a decent society, a society that can endure and prosper, needs leaders who transcend the politics of the moment and pursue the nation's long-term aspirations. These leaders will take care of the Constitution, understanding that they are only custodians of an ideal—stewards with a debt to their forbearers and a duty to their heirs. They will take care of their fellow citizens—especially the poor and the disenfranchised—understanding that a society is stronger when everyone contributes. They will take care of our children, understanding that a wise society invests in the things that help its next generation succeed. They will take care of politics itself, governing with honor and generosity rather than ideology and fear, understanding that a nation decays when its people lose confidence in their own leaders. They will remember that the Constitution enjoins them to promote the common welfare as well as the blessings of liberty.

I entered politics young, impatient, and full of confidence that government could be used to better people's lives. My faith has not dimmed. But I also came to understand that voters didn't simply put us in office to write laws or correct the wrongs of the moment. They were asking us to safeguard the remarkable nation our founders left us and leave it better for our children. This book is an effort to explain that philosophy, to chronicle the battles that taught me these lessons, and to describe the evolution of a man and the country he was lucky enough to live in.

1

A Progressive Takes Root

ONE DAY IN the spring of 1962, when I was finishing my second year as Minnesota's attorney general, I got a phone call from an old friend, Yale Kamisar. He was a law professor at the University of Minnesota and a respected constitutional scholar, and he was calling to ask if I had received a letter from the attorney general of Florida about a states' rights case that was headed to the U.S. Supreme Court.

I said, "Yes, I just threw it away."

"Could you fish that out of the wastebasket and tell me what it says?" Kamisar asked. "I think it might be important." The letter described the case of an indigent Southern drifter who had been arrested on suspicion of burglarizing a pool hall in Florida. He couldn't afford a lawyer, and at his trial the judge told him Florida law didn't require the state to provide one except in capital cases. After a brief trial, he was sentenced to five years in prison. From his jail cell he had written the Supreme Court asking the justices to review his case. His name was Clarence Earl Gideon.

At that time I was in touch with several of my counterparts around the country, people such as Tom Eagleton in Missouri, a great friend who later became a wonderful senator, and Eddie McCormack, the attorney general in Massachusetts. It turned out that several states provided counsel to felony defendants, but there was no federal guarantee. In 1942 the Supreme Court had ruled in *Betts v. Brady* that the Constitution does not flatly require states to furnish counsel. Now Florida's attorney general,

Richard Ervin, was asking his colleagues around the country to support the *Betts* decision and join the case on his side, arguing that this was a matter of states' rights. Kamisar, however, felt *Betts v. Brady* was bad law and thought the Court was ready to reverse itself. He asked me, "Is there any chance you would consider writing a response to Ervin and taking the other side?"

Kamisar's request made a lot of sense to me. At that time Minnesota already provided counsel to indigent defendants in felony cases, and I thought the due-process argument was clear. But it also appealed to me personally. The idea that a person could be convicted of a serious crime and spend years in jail, even if innocent, purely because he had no money, was an outrage to me. I told Kamisar I was with him, and the next day, with his help, drafted a reply to Ervin:

> I believe in federalism and states' rights too. But I also believe in the Bill of Rights. Nobody knows better than an attorney general or a prosecuting attorney that in this day and age, furnishing an attorney to those felony defendants who can't afford to hire one is fair and feasible. Nobody knows better than we do that rules of criminal law and procedure which baffle trained professionals can only overwhelm the uninitiated.

Eddie McCormack and I circulated a copy of the letter to every attorney general in the country, while Kamisar began drafting an amicus brief on Gideon's side. Within weeks attorneys general from twenty-two states had signed on, and we submitted our brief to the U.S. Supreme Court.

In March 1963 the court reversed *Betts* and handed down a landmark ruling, the *Gideon* decision, establishing the principle that indigent defendants have a constitutional right to counsel in felony cases. Attorney Abe Fortas, who represented Gideon and later became a Supreme Court justice, cited our work. "We may be comforted in this constitutional moment by the fact that what we are doing has the overwhelming support of the bench, the bar and even of the states." Justice Hugo Black, writing for the Court, concurred: "Twenty-two states, as friends of the court, argue that Betts was 'an anachronism when handed down' and that it should now be overruled. We agree."

The *Gideon* brief was probably the most important single case that I pursued in four years as attorney general, and it certainly represented higher stakes than anything a young Minnesota politician expected to handle during his first years in public office. But it typified the era in which I entered politics. A new generation of Democrats was breathing fresh energy into the party's progressive wing, and people were warming to the view that public office could be used to protect the disadvantaged and advance the rights of ordinary people. Around the country several pivotal figures were transforming the politics of their own states. In Iowa it was Harold Hughes, in Maine it was Ed Muskie, in Wisconsin it was Gaylord Nelson and William Proxmire. In Minnesota, it was Hubert Humphrey.

It was an exciting time, but only later did I grasp how dramatically politics was changing in the Midwest and around the country. In 1946, when I arrived in St. Paul to enroll at Macalester College, Democrats were dead as a political force in Minnesota. Republicans had been running the state for years, and they had the young candidates with talent and energy, people such as Harold Stassen and Elmer L. Andersen. In 1947 Republicans held eight of Minnesota's nine seats in the U.S. House, and the state hadn't sent a Democrat to the U.S. Senate for years.

My own politics were still rather vague, even though I had grown up in a household with strong values. My parents, both small-town Midwesterners, loved Franklin Roosevelt and Floyd B. Olson, Minnesota's great Farmer-Labor governor. My dad, the grandson of Norwegian immigrants, was a Methodist minister who spent his entire career serving small congregations in southern Minnesota. But he read voraciously, subscribed to progressive magazines such as the *Nation* and the *New Republic*, and followed the national conversations involving theology and public affairs; my brother, Lester, also a minister, later became a signer of the *Humanist Manifesto*, an influential document that made a moral case for racial tolerance, internationalism, and an end to poverty. Dad was a gentle man but stern. In my family you got a spanking for two things, bragging and lying, and we never knew which was worse. My mom was remarkable in her own way. She was not of the women's rights generation, which came later, but she was strong and determined. Having grown up poor in southwestern Minnesota, she somehow gained admission to Northwestern University and earned a music degree. She ran the Sunday school at our church and taught piano lessons to practically every kid in town. In Elmore, they talked about "Mondale weddings," where my dad presided, my mom played piano, and the Mondale boys sang. After my dad died, she moved to St. Paul and found a job as religious education director at Hamline Methodist Church to support herself and my younger brother Mort. She loved it and the church loved her.

My mom and dad were people of ideas, but they also knew the frustrations and modest hopes of working people in the rural Midwest. My dad had lost a farm in the land crash of the 1920s, and even though he had a series of successful small ministries, we never had a dime. Nevertheless, they tried to expose us to the world beyond the Minnesota prairie. In the summer of 1938, when I was ten, my dad fashioned a makeshift camper out of plywood boards and an old trailer, loaded it with canned goods and a couple of mattresses, and took us to Washington, D.C., for a family vacation. We saw all the sights, but my parents weren't impressed by the usual tourist attractions. We visited Senator Henry Shipstead of Minnesota; my dad lectured him for abandoning the Farmer-Labor Party, an early force in Minnesota's progressive politics, to become a Republican. When we left his office, we wandered through the Capitol until we found the marble bust of Senator Robert La Follette, the pioneering Wisconsin progressive. "There," my dad said, "is a great man."

For young people such as me, the late 1940s was a period of intellectual testing. Harry Truman was seen as old politics, the machine candidate. Some Democrats were flirting with William O. Douglas and some were still attracted to the Soviet experiment, on the theory that capitalism had failed disastrously in the Great Depression. For a time, I was drawn to Henry Wallace, who ran for president as the Progressive Party candidate in 1948. He was someone my parents admired—he had guts, he campaigned on national health insurance and civil rights, and he had what was probably the first racially integrated campaign in national politics. But then Wallace came to Minnesota for a big rally at the old Minneapolis Armory, and I went to hear him. At that time I had a professor named Huntley Dupre, a Czech-American citizen, who described the way democracy had developed in Czechoslovakia, deep and secure, until it was crushed by the Nazis and then a Soviet-backed Communist takeover. Wallace was campaigning on peace with the Soviets, and that night he defended the Communists by saying Czechoslovakia was having a rightist coup and the Soviets had no choice but to intercede. I left that night thinking, You cannot find common ground with governments that use police-state tactics. This is not where I want to be.

About this time my older brother, Pete, who had attended Macalester ahead of me, mentioned a hotshot political science professor named Hubert Humphrey. By that time Humphrey had left the Macalester faculty and was serving his first term as the young reform mayor of Minneapolis. People on campus still adored him, and one day my political science professor, Dorothy Jacobson, told us that Humphrey was speaking that night in Minneapolis and we should go hear him.

I've long since forgotten how I got across town that night, but I will always remember the scene. Humphrey was speaking in a ballroom at the old Dyckman Hotel, and the place was packed. Humphrey was only thirty-five at the time, but he already had a grasp of the big national issues and an intellectual stature that made people take notice. He also had that electrifying speaking style: the machine-gun delivery, the big crescendos, applause lines every few minutes. He hadn't been speaking more than ten minutes before he had that crowd on fire and the paint blistering off the walls. I remember thinking, This guy is really something.

When Humphrey finished speaking, I introduced myself to his campaign manager, Orville Freeman. Orv was only twenty-eight, but he was a former marine and World War II veteran with a commanding sense of organization. The next thing I knew, I was slogging through the slushy streets of Minneapolis, delivering leaflets and hanging posters for Humphrey's reelection campaign.

More than a year went by before I saw much of Hubert again. By the summer of 1948 he was running for the Senate, and Freeman had put me in charge of the Second Congressional District in southern Minnesota—my home territory but also a Republican stronghold. That summer the Farm Bureau was holding its annual picnic near Fairmont, Minnesota, and I asked if Humphrey might be their speaker. This was quite a gamble—the Farm Bureau represented the conservative wing of farmer politics—but they hadn't had a big-name speaker for years and I thought they would be receptive to Humphrey. For his part, Humphrey was eager to get his name known around the state, and I knew he would come to Fairmont if I could raise a big crowd.

The farmers who showed up that day weren't planning to vote for a Democrat, but within five minutes Hubert had them on their feet cheering. He had that knack for connecting with an audience, understanding what drove them, then speaking right to it. When he was finished, he came over to me and told me I'd done a good job. I was still a kid really, and I drank in every word. "Your work is needed," he said. "We have so much to do." After that day, I think I never stopped.

The campaign of 1948 not only launched Humphrey as a national figure, it transformed politics in Minnesota and created the state's modern reputation for progressive politics. In the 1940s, the state's Democratic Party was a kind of machine organization, mostly urban and rooted in St. Paul's Irish immigrant community. If you wanted to be postmaster or get some other patronage position, it was a good organization to join because Roosevelt was president. But it didn't groom strong candidates, and it wasn't the place to be if you wanted to win elections. To their left was the United Front crowd—political activists who leaned toward communism. They believed that even though American liberals had our differences with the Soviet Union, we shared the same ideals and could work together. But the Democrats and the United Front had no trust for each other and no issues in common. In fact, in 1944 Franklin Roosevelt feared that Minnesota's progressive wing would split in two and he would lose the state to a plurality Republican vote. He had heard about Humphrey through Americans for Democratic Action, a progressive, anti-

Communist branch of the party that Hubert had cofounded with Eleanor Roosevelt, John Kenneth Galbraith, and Arthur Schlesinger, and he encouraged Humphrey to rebuild the state party.

Hubert was the perfect choice. He was talented and ambitious and had no peer when it came to motivating a crowd. He also knew how to build coalitions. He understood farmers; he could speak their language on issues such as price parity and rural electrification, and he could convince them that he would be their advocate. He did the same thing with the labor movement. He would go over to the Minneapolis Labor Temple every other night and speak to union locals. He understood their goals, too, and he had dozens of ideas to advance the interests of working people. Then he started pulling together all the factions and convincing them that they needed each other to win, and that the old differences and suspicions were only holding them back.

In addition to his political skills, Humphrey had an energy that is hard to appreciate if you never saw him in action. When he was campaigning, he would barnstorm across the state, delivering ten or twelve speeches a day. His driver was Fred Gates, an old friend and longtime supporter, whom Hubert called Pearly Gates because he drove with such abandon. A car would travel ahead of Humphrey from town to town, with a loudspeaker to drum up a crowd, then Hubert would pull in riding in a flatbed truck, and he would speak from the back. Sometimes he would draw only ten or fifteen people, but he didn't care. When he hit his stride he could stop traffic and bring Main Street to a standstill. (Barry Goldwater, a political rival but personal friend, once described the effect this way: "Hubert has been clocked at 275 words a minute, with gusts up to 340.") Later, I traveled with Humphrey from time to time, and no matter how tired he was, you could see the color come back into his cheeks and his eyes brighten as he waded into a crowd. He could go for days without showing fatigue. "Don't spend too much time in bed," he told me once. "That's where most people die."

Because of his political skills and his tremendous energy, Humphrey attracted an entire generation of new talent in his wake. There was Orville, of course, who served three terms as governor and then became

U.S. secretary of agriculture. And Gene McCarthy, another political science professor, who became a congressman in 1948 and a senator a decade later. When Humphrey and McCarthy campaigned together, they were unbeatable. There was Gerald Heaney, an accomplished attorney who became a Democratic National Committee member and later a federal judge; Art Naftalin, a brilliant progressive mayor of Minneapolis; and Don Fraser, who was elected to Congress from Minneapolis in 1962 and became a distinguished leader on human rights and foreign policy. They were typical of that generation.

Between 1944 and 1948, Humphrey worked constantly to unify Minnesota's progressives, finding common ground between farmers and union members, intellectuals and business leaders—while gradually marginalizing the old United Front crowd. The result was the Democratic Farmer-Labor Party, or DFL, which would change the face of Minnesota politics for the next half century. But we got into some pretty rough fights along the way. In early 1948, hoping to earn the party's nomination for the Senate in November, Humphrey made one last push to consolidate the organization behind him. One of his first moves came at the convention of the Young DFL in Minneapolis. We met at the old Minneapolis Labor Temple. The room was divided right down the middle, the United Front supporters on one side and our group on the other, and you could have cut the tension with a knife. I was afraid we were going to be outnumbered if it came to an endorsement vote, so I brought a big crowd over from the St. Paul college campuses—Macalester, Hamline, and St. Thomas. We packed that place, and I think we caught the other side by surprise. The hard-left people got up and gave their speeches about how we were fascists, then Humphrey got up and brought the crowd to its feet. At one point, someone in the audience asked if he thought the United Front supporters were actually members of the Communist Party. He said, "Well, if they're not members, they are cheating it out of dues money." A lot of people in that room had worked with Humphrey in the past, and I think they were stunned at the hard line he took. But he was mesmerizing, and we had the numbers, and he carried the crowd overwhelmingly. At the state convention a month later he did the same thing. He had the numbers and he won the crowd, and after that the party belonged to him.

Some people never forgave Humphrey for what they regarded as a purge of the left in Minnesota politics. But it showed the rest of the party—and voters across the state—that he could be a unifying force, that he represented something new in Minnesota politics and demonstrated that we had an alternative to the Republican Party.

With Humphrey leading the charge, the 1948 election proved to be a turning point in Minnesota's political history. Humphrey won big, defeating the Republican incumbent, Joe Ball. Truman carried Minnesota, becoming the first Democrat apart from Franklin Roosevelt to carry the state in a presidential race since the Civil War. We elected three new Democrats to Congress, including Gene McCarthy. In a few other races, we just missed. But you could see the elements: a generation of new talent, highly motivated, and the foundation of a new political movement. I packed up my things in Mankato and drove back to St. Paul that night after the polls closed. It was a good feeling. The next morning, Minnesota was a different state.

From time to time around this country, an extraordinary political figure emerges—a candidate who has that unique power of leadership, who breaks the mold and leads his or her state in a fundamentally new direction. In Minnesota, that figure was Humphrey. Minnesota was a cloistered, isolationist place when Humphrey came on the scene in the 1940s; he gave it a worldly, internationalist outlook. It was a state of conservative, self-reliant people. He inspired them to think about social justice and the role government could play in expanding opportunity. He put civil rights on the agenda in a state with a long history of bigotry and anti-Semitism. He brought ambition and a flair for innovation to people who, by nature, were cautious and shy. He didn't simply establish himself as a leading figure in national politics, he built his state into an admired incubator of progressive ideas. Hubert brought out the decency and optimism in people, and he made Minnesota a different place.

Thirty years later, delivering Humphrey's eulogy in the rotunda of the

U.S. Capitol and reflecting on a friendship that lasted a lifetime, I ventured that Hubert would be remembered as one of the greatest legislators in our history, as one of the most loved men of his time, and even more, as a leader who became his country's conscience.

After the 1948 election I had to think about my own prospects for a while. When my dad died, we couldn't afford the tuition at Macalester, so I dropped out and finished my degree at the University of Minnesota. On graduating I joined the army and served two years at Fort Knox, then returned to the Twin Cities and enrolled in law school at the University of Minnesota on the GI Bill. By this time my mom had moved to St. Paul, so I moved in with her and became a full-time law student.

One evening in 1955 a classmate, Bill Canby, invited me over for dinner with his wife, Jane, and her older sister, Joan Adams. I suppose I should have been intimidated: Joan's father was the chaplain at Macalester College and came from an old Presbyterian family. She had studied history and art, had worked at a museum in Boston, and had an elegance that was quite outside my experience. But she seemed to think it might be all right to date a guy who was getting started in politics. Her mother wasn't quite so confident. She called one of my professors at Macalester, the great political scientist Theodore Mitau, and asked what sort of young man I was. He told her, Walter doesn't have much money, but he works hard and I think he has a future. After seven dates in six months, Joan and I were married in the Macalester College chapel.

But all the while, I could not shake the political bug. When Orville Freeman ran for governor in 1950, unsuccessfully, I worked on his campaign. When he ran in 1954, I worked for him again, and this time he won. When he ran for reelection in 1958, I was his campaign manager.

Then one day in the spring of 1960 the phone rang and it was Orv. The attorney general, Miles Lord, was planning to resign, and Freeman wanted to appoint me to fill the vacancy. I was stunned. I had graduated from law school in 1956 and was trying to build a law practice. Joan and I had just bought a house in south Minneapolis. We had one baby, Ted, at home, and our daughter, Eleanor, was on the way. I tried to talk Orv out of it: "You're going to be in a very close fight in November and you're going to have your hands full. I'm brand-new, not very qualified, and people in Minnesota don't know me. Why don't you pick someone established, a lawyer of prominence, a selection that reassures people." I remember mentioning George Hulstrand, a successful lawyer in Willmar. "George would love it and add strength to you." But Orv had been talking with other members of the party's younger generation—people such as Don and Arvonne Fraser—and he wanted to groom talent for the party's future. "No," he said, "you're the one I want." That spring, at age thirty-two, I became the youngest attorney general in Minnesota history.

In Minnesota at that time the attorney general's office was not a political springboard. The attorney general served chiefly as a lawyer to state government, someone who handled land condemnations for the highway department and wrote legal opinions for the governor. This had started to change under Miles Lord, a wily populist who loved to represent the underdog. Miles had started looking into the finances of a Minneapolis-based charitable foundation called the Sister Kenny Institute and attracted some press for the investigation. On his last day in office he pulled me aside and said, "Take a look at this. This is going to be big."

I was going to be up for election right away in November, and I knew I had to establish myself with voters. I was brand-new to public office, and I thought the Sister Kenny investigation would be a test case for Minnesotans who didn't know me—and most Minnesotans did not know me. So that first week, I assigned some of our best talent to the investigation. Miles had already dug up some irregularities that raised eyebrows, but I wanted to get a full sense of the evidence and the law, to see if we had a strong case. I assigned Syd Berde, who was my chief deputy and a talented guy, to conduct a series of depositions, and we hired an accounting firm to go into the institute's books.

We found a cesspool. In theory, the institute was a charitable organization that raised money for polio research and therapy. In practice, millions of dollars were being siphoned off for the benefit of one or two officers. Our auditors found that the institute had paid large sums to a Chicago firm that prepared letters and mailings, which then paid kickbacks to the foundation's top executive. The Chicago firm also sold phone directories to the foundation at inflated prices, with a cut going back to the foundation's officers. Then there were outlandish trips to Florida and other exotic destinations, all expenses paid. Meanwhile, the auditors were cooking the books so the board of directors couldn't tell what was happening. Little money was left to do any good for anybody.

This was a big scandal in Minnesota, where people idolized the institute and its mission. Minnesota had suffered terribly from the polio epidemic in the 1930s. Polio would strike, and the next thing you knew, you were in an iron lung. Years later I would still see old friends walking with crutches because they'd had polio as children. It was a horrible and frightening experience. Sister Kenny was an Australian army nurse who had developed a new form of polio therapy in the 1930s, then traveled to the United States, and eventually to Minnesota. The institute promoted her system and treated hundreds of patients, providing a source of hope when everybody was terrified by the disease. The board included distinguished people from the Twin Cities business and civic community, and the executive director was a former mayor, Marvin Kline. So it was a terrible shock when the public and the foundation's board learned that some of its leaders were corrupt.

The investigation consumed our attention for several months, while we completed our audit and deposed experts. Paul Ellwood, a distinguished doctor who went on to become one of the theorists of the modern HMO, was a Minneapolis physician who had done some work with the institute. He wasn't implicated in any way, but he helped us understand how the place ran. We also interviewed Bert Gamble, the chairman of their board. Bert was a prominent and successful businessman, a strong civic presence in Minnesota, and he didn't like that we politicians were raising questions about his foundation. That was an uncomfortable interview. But my idea was that we could excise the wrongdoers and save Sister Kenny so it could go forward as a healthy organization with public trust. I didn't want to antagonize the board. I knew if we missed, that could be the end of me. And if we missed, it *should* have been the end of me.

To make our case, I did three things. I wrote a report on our investigation and made it public. The *Minneapolis Tribune* printed the entire document. Next, I tried to save the Sister Kenny foundation by putting new people in charge and removing the officers who were responsible for the malfeasance. In everything we did, all the lawsuits and all the reports, the state of Minnesota worked with the board. Finally, we sued to recover assets for the institute and to terminate the state licenses of its accountants, then we brought criminal indictments against the principals involved. We got a conviction in every case.

The Sister Kenny investigation made headlines for months and gave my office a reputation. Soon people were coming to us with complaints about other kinds of fraud. Before long we began hearing about a Michigan company called Holland Furnace, whose salesmen were using deceptive tactics to sell heating equipment. They would send a salesman into the home of potential customers, and of course he would find something wrong with their furnace. They picked on old people, and they scared them. One salesman who had left the firm in disgust gave us an affidavit saying that the salesmen actually carried hammers in their briefcases; they would pound on the customer's furnace, then report that it had cracks. So we hired an investigator, a former FBI agent, who followed the salesmen from one home to another and examined the furnaces as soon as they left. He loved this—he was a real freight train. He would examine the same furnace as a salesman and write his own report: This furnace could last another twenty years. We sued Holland Furnace and got the court to pull its license to operate in the state of Minnesota. That case, too, made a big impact because they had defrauded a lot of people over a long time.

The Holland Furnace litigation taught me an important lesson about the attorney general's authority. The judge could easily have thrown out our case on the grounds that my office had no jurisdiction. It was a cutting-edge case because the law was not clear—we were depending on a common-law theory of public nuisance as well as innovative interpretations of statutory law. The powerful evidence and the affidavits made the case, and the court upheld our right to sue. Still, it wasn't entirely clear that the attorney general had the authority to pursue a broad range of consumer-protection cases.

That's one reason I felt I had to be really sure-footed. I wanted people to see that our investigations were correct and legal, not just the efforts of a young political hotshot. But I also thought it was important to clarify the powers of the office itself. When I first took office, I pulled down every volume of the Minnesota statutes that mentioned the attorney general. I read every law and every one of the case reports—cases that went back almost to territorial days. I wanted to get a clear idea of what I had. One of the things I discovered was common-law powers—powers not enumerated in the statutes—giving the attorney general authority to regulate "public nuisances," cases in which no one else had jurisdiction and individuals could not protect themselves. I saw that under common law—that is, the accumulation of court rulings—the attorney general was also considered the trustee of charitable trusts, such as the United Way or Sister Kenny, that is, the one who ultimately protected beneficiaries and the public. We had quite a few of these charitable and nonprofit groups at that time, which were technically fraternal benefit organizations but which went through a lot of money and had the potential for sizable fraud. The attorney general was the master of these disputes.

After all the publicity on the Sister Kenny case, I was starting to take some hits in the political arena from people who accused me of becoming a tyrant operating out of the attorney general's office. These are not lawsuits, they said, these are press releases issued by a young politician. One prominent lawyer, a friend of mine, actually said I was the only Joe McCarthy that Minnesota had ever produced. So I appointed an advisory council on consumer protection, and we wrote legislation that would clarify the attorney general's jurisdiction. It wasn't a perfect law, but it passed and modernized the office in important ways.

I didn't go into that job intending to redefine the attorney general's role or to advance a broad vision of activist government. But I did sense that consumers are always at risk of getting cheated by some shady operator, and that they often have no remedy. It's perennial, it goes to human nature. If there's a crooked way of doing something, someone sooner or later will try it. It's still with us today in the Bernard Madoff debacle, the Enron collapse, and other corporate scandals, where trusted experts defrauded their investors and their own employees. In the collapse of the subprime-mortgage market you find much the same thing, a regulatory failure that ruined people's lives and cost the economy billions of dollars. A lot of those mortgage brokers must have known there was no chance that their customers could pay back their loans. They offered funny teaser terms to make the loan attractive, collected a down payment, and took their fees, and the mortgage was sliced up and sold as a mortgage-backed security to parties unknown. When the poor homeowner can't make his monthly payment, he has nobody to talk to. There used to be a neighborhood banker, and you could go in and explain the problem and work something out. Now there's nobody, and before you know it, they've taken your money and your house.

This is not to argue that everyone is crooked. Quite the opposite. But greed lurks in any society; every era and every industry will have some reprobate trying to figure out how to game the rules and cheat the customer. This, I believe, is why markets need regulators. From time to time I caught heat from business leaders who didn't want some young politician going through their books. But I argued that no one loses more from business corruption than honest businessmen and women. It's not free enterprise anymore, it's a process corrupted by fraud. To say that if you believe in free enterprise you should stay the hand of government is a false choice. Sometimes you need the hand of government to ensure that honest people can carry on in business.

After a time, I noticed a pattern in the crimes we investigated. The crook who wants to steal money and get away with it commits a lot of little frauds—peddling phony magazine subscriptions, selling bad life-insurance policies, advertising phony trade schools and taking people's tuition money. He targets the elderly and the poor. No one customer has the incentive or the resources to mount an investigation and go after him. The result is a fraud without a remedy. That's where an attorney general can step in and do something.

Gradually I developed a theory that the attorney general's office would protect members of the public in cases where they couldn't protect themselves. We added a consumer protection unit to the office, and then, after investigating price-fixing by a company that sold gymnasium bleachers to school districts, we created an antitrust unit.

As attorney general I also served on the state Board of Investment, which oversees bank accounts in which the state deposits tax collections and other revenues known as idle cash. I discovered that the state treasurer was depositing millions of dollars of idle cash in non-interest-bearing bank accounts, often at banks whose officers had political connections. That practice cost the state thousands of dollars in lost interest income and, in effect, gave a subsidy to those banks. I wrote a change in board policy to require competitive public bidding by banks for the holding of idle-cash funds; it passed and remains state policy today, saving the taxpayers millions of dollars.

As a result of these activities, we transformed our little corner of the state capitol from a sedate, passive law office into an agency that would defend consumers and regulate market failures. It changed the way Minnesotans think about the attorney general and the role of government in protecting the public interest.

Those were busy years, not easy on a marriage and a young family. I was often gone five or six evenings a week, occasionally on weekends, and I sometimes wondered if Joan knew what she was getting into as a politician's wife. But of course she did. Some political spouses love the spotlight, some hate it. Joan was just extremely good at it—a real soldier and a great campaigner. Al Quie, a Minnesota congressman and later governor, told me about a League of Women Voters event in Northfield, Minnesota, where Joan substituted for me one night. During the Q&A a member of the audience stood up and started asking why the attorney general's office had so many lawyers and spent so much money—the standard Republican attack at the time. Well, Joan had memorized a long, detailed memo defending the size of the staff and describing every lawyer's function. She stood her ground and gave a precise five-minute answer that wowed the audience. Al, who was there, said it was the most extraordinary thing—people stood up and cheered.

Although consumer protection was the central thread in my tenure as attorney general, civil rights also became a priority in our work. I hadn't been in office long when I got a letter from Earl Battey, a catcher with the Minnesota Twins, a wonderful guy and a popular player. Battey, an African-American, wrote to complain that when he traveled with the team, he wasn't allowed to stay in the same housing as the white players. This seemed pretty extraordinary, but we looked into it, and sure enough, when the Twins traveled in the South or held spring training in Florida, they claimed that they could not get integrated housing for the players. Except, we discovered, they were the only team in Major League Baseball that had segregated housing. I was astonished and offended. I contacted the governor and notified the state antidiscrimination commission, and we fired off a letter to the Twins organization and put an end to the practice. After that, the Minnesota Twins were a fully integrated baseball team.

It might seem odd that civil rights would figure prominently in the politics of Minnesota, a northern state with a population that was overwhelmingly white. But many people of my generation had come back from World War II or Korea feeling the injustice of discrimination. We had seen black Americans fight alongside white soldiers, risking their lives, then come home to build a better life for their families—just like anyone else—and face obstacles that white Americans did not. We were determined to do something about it. We also had Hubert's example: his speech at the 1948 Democratic National Convention had put civil rights on the party's agenda and made his national reputation. Then, too, Minnesota had a tremendous history of leadership in the black community. Roy Wilkins, a legendary leader of the NAACP, had worked as a journalist in the Twin Cities and was a graduate of the University of Minnesota. So was Carl Stokes, who later became the first black mayor of a major American city, Cleveland. Clarence Mitchell, later the chief lobbyist for the NAACP, had worked for a time in the St. Paul Urban League.

This was also a big issue for me personally. My dad preached what might be called the social gospel—that our faith requires good deeds as well as good words. When I was young, it was common for black congregations in the South to send church choirs on tours through the North, and as we moved from one town to another in southern Minnesota, my Dad always made sure his church hosted one of the black choirs. It might sound old-fashioned, but he really said that we are all equal in God's eyes. I remember an evening in the early 1940s when we were gathered around the radio listening to one of those wartime propaganda programs, and the announcer caricatured the Japanese in demeaning terms. Dad turned off the radio and said, Let's talk about this. He said the people of Japan are human beings just like we are; don't ever get the idea that there's any difference. There are bad people in the world, he said, but don't ever make those judgments on the basis of someone's skin color or their religion or where they were born.

Not long after the Earl Battey case, I got a phone call from a friend who was active in the Minnesota NAACP. They were organizing a civil rights rally at the state capitol, and they were looking for elected officials to serve as speakers. I said of course I would do it. When you're a young person in elective office, you look for chances to get in front of a crowd, but this issue was also close to me. The day came and there weren't many public figures there after all. Even in Minnesota at that time, the civil rights cause left some politicians a little uneasy, and a lot of the elected officials just found it easier to be somewhere else that day. But I went and was the leadoff speaker, even though I was the youngest person in elective office in Minnesota at that time. Later I learned that the crowd was laced with FBI agents that day. That was the era of J. Edgar Hoover, who thought every dissident was a Communist subversive, and the Bureau apparently thought that a civil rights rally in Minnesota was suspicious. I thought about that once or twice over the years. If I had known the FBI was compiling a dossier on me, I might have had second thoughts. But I didn't know, and I was proud to be a speaker and I'm glad I did it.

By the summer of 1964, I was nearing the end of my second term as attorney general and counting myself a lucky man. The voters seemed to like my work, I was just inhaling the job, and I could happily have spent the rest of my career serving the people of Minnesota from an office at the state capitol. Fate had another idea.

In August the Democratic Party was scheduled to hold its national convention in Atlantic City, with Lyndon Johnson expected to get the presidential nomination. Johnson's poll numbers were strong, and everyone expected him to beat the likely Republican nominee, Barry Goldwater. But within the party, trouble was percolating. Johnson had begun to emerge as a genuine civil rights president—he had provided the crucial push for the Civil Rights Act of 1964—and Southern Democrats were unhappy about it. Everyone expected several of the Deep South delegations to arrive in Atlantic City supporting a segregationist such as Strom Thurmond, or even Barry Goldwater. Johnson wasn't particularly worried by this, but he didn't want the convention to blow up and embarrass him, and he was watching the preparations carefully.

Meanwhile, in Mississippi a group of civil rights activists called the Mississippi Freedom Democrats had begun operating as an alternative to the regular party. They had assembled an integrated slate of delegates they planned to send to the national convention, and they were planning to challenge Mississippi's regular delegation, an all-white slate chosen under rules that effectively and brutally locked black voters out of party politics in the state.

I was a young guy on the rise in the party, and someone had the idea of putting me on the Credentials Committee, which, in a normal year, handles routine disputes over seating delegates. But a few days before I left for the convention, Hubert called me with a warning. The Freedom Democrats had requested a hearing before our committee, he said, and we might well be called on to choose between their slate and the regular Mississippi Democrats. In a year when the whole country was watching the civil rights battles in Jackson, Birmingham, and other Southern cities, the credentials challenge could easily become a national flashpoint. I thanked Hubert, and a few days later, with my Minnesota colleague Geri Joseph, got on a plane for Atlantic City.

The convention was scheduled to open on Monday evening, August 24, and the Credentials Committee began its work on Saturday. It didn't take long for me to understand that Hubert's warning had been prescient. The Freedom Democrats came before us that first afternoon, and they had a powerful team of witnesses. Martin Luther King Jr. spoke on their behalf, as did Joe Rauh, the great legal counsel for the United Auto Workers union and a friend of mine, who had agreed to advise them. The knock-out witness was Fannie Lou Hamer, who started in life as a sharecropper, became a fearless volunteer in the movement to register black voters, and had now earned a spot as cochair of the Freedom Democrats' slate of delegates. She testified in the most powerful terms about the ordeals they had suffered; she herself had been arrested under phony charges, thrown in jail, and beaten severely—all for trying to register black voters. "If the Freedom Democratic Party is not seated now, I question America," she said. "Is this America, the land of the free and the home of the brave, where we have to sleep with our telephones off the hooks because our lives [are] threatened daily because we want to live as decent human beings? In America?" You could not help being moved by her testimony.

But when the committee recessed to deliberate, we quickly fractured. Several members from Northern states said this was simple: The Freedom Democrats had been excluded by blatant discrimination, our party did not stand for discrimination, and if we didn't seat them, we would be hypocrites. The white Southerners saw it differently: The Freedom Democrats were nothing more than a protest group; they hadn't been selected through official party nominating rules and had no legitimate claim to serve as delegates. These Southerners accused the Freedom Democrats of having Communist ties and said we would lose the South in November if we seated them. They threatened a walkout from the convention.

The longer we talked, the more we disagreed. One of the Southerners made what seemed to be a death threat against someone else on the committee. Edith Green, an influential congresswoman from Oregon, said the Mississippi regulars were no different from Nazis and that we were sellouts if we turned our backs on the Freedom Democrats.

When we quit for the day, the chairman of our committee, former Pennsylvania governor David Lawrence, was clearly at a loss. He was well into his seventies and though he had been a real force at Democratic conventions going back to 1948, we could see that this was not what he had bargained for.

By Sunday morning, the national press had caught wind of the Freedom Democrats' story. Fannie Lou Hamer's testimony had been compel-ling, and civil rights activists were beginning to organize sit-ins in support of the Freedom Democrats on the boardwalk outside the convention hotel.

By Sunday afternoon the Southerners were escalating their threats of a walkout, the committee was getting nowhere, and we were running out of time. When our committee convened again, I suggested that Lawrence appoint a subcommittee and empower it to find a compromise. Lawrence agreed immediately and named five members: Price Daniel, a former governor of Texas; Irving Kaler, an influential party leader from Atlanta; Charles Diggs, a black congressman from Michigan; and Sherwin Mark-man, an attorney from Iowa who would later become a special assistant to Lyndon Johnson. Knowing that I was close to Humphrey and Humphrey was close to the president, Lawrence put me in charge.

I took the assignment knowing that we didn't have much clout. In those days, a sitting president still called a lot of the shots at a convention, and Johnson was watching every step of the proceedings from the White House. The old-line white Southerners still held a lot of sway with party elders, so they were going to be heard. The leading civil rights figures, such as King and Bayard Rustin, were going to be heard as well. But we were an excuse to get negotiations going, and we had twenty-four hours to come up with a solution. We rented a hotel room where we could meet and make phone calls and began improvising.

We had more train wrecks than you could count on two hands. The Freedom Democrats saw an injustice—an internal party process that made it impossible for black citizens to participate—and they wanted their remedy right now. The old white crowd wanted to keep the sta-tus quo. They were playing by rules that the national party had tacitly accepted for decades, and they knew that integration of the Mississippi Democratic Party would bring an end to their reign. Johnson and Hum-phrey, too, had a lot at stake: Johnson worried that the convention would blow up over this issue, with an embarrassing walkout by the Southern delegations that would deliver the South to Goldwater. Because Hum-phrey had been Johnson's lieutenant in the Senate, word in Atlantic City was that Johnson wanted Humphrey to settle this without fireworks as a condition for becoming Johnson's running mate.

Johnson wouldn't arrive at the convention for another day or two, but he had his top aide, Walter Jenkins, on the phone to Atlantic City regularly. Through Jenkins, Johnson had proposed a nominal settlement—that the party give the Freedom Democrats a couple of at-large seats—and he wanted us to jam it through. But after talking it over with King, Rauh, and Edwin King, a minister who was head of the Freedom Democrats' delegation, we believed we had to proposes something more substantive. We worked through Sunday afternoon and into the evening, then late into the night, calling in one group or another, testing the grounds for a compromise.

Finally, early on Monday a group of us came up with a new proposal. The first part was symbolic: We would recognize the regular Mississippi delegation, but we would also give the Freedom Democrats two seats as at-large delegates. The second part was substantive and historic: We would change the national party rules to explicitly prohibit discrimination of any kind in state party operations. From that convention forward, the Democratic Party would not seat a state delegation chosen under discriminatory rules. Finally, as a condition of seating the Mississippi regulars, we also required that they take a loyalty oath—that is, that they would support Johnson as the party's presidential candidate. None of them would sign it.

I had no illusions that this compromise would mollify the competing camps. I was pretty sure the Freedom Democrats would find it inadequate, and I thought it quite likely that the Mississippi regulars would walk out regardless. But I did think it was an honorable compromise. I believed it would satisfy the party's major civil rights leaders and win support on the Credentials Committee. Most important, I thought it would redress the injustices of Southern politics that the Freedom Democrats symbolized. I took it to Hubert, who liked it, and he showed it to Martin Luther King Jr. and Bayard Rustin, who also endorsed it.

But now we had almost no time. Hubert agreed to present the compromise to the leaders of the Freedom Democrats, along with Walter Reuther, the president of the United Automobile Workers, who also had good credentials in the civil rights movement. Meanwhile, I called former governor Lawrence and asked for the opportunity to present the compromise to the Credentials Committee. All this happened simultaneously because the convention was scheduled to open that evening. It meant that the two sides—the Freedom Democrats and the Mississippi regulars—never got a chance to sign off on the compromise before the committee voted, but I felt we couldn't afford to lose more time in what were likely to be fruitless negotiations. Lawrence assembled the committee, I presented the proposal, and it was approved by an overwhelming vote.

I know that, to this day, that compromise generates criticism and controversy. The Reverend Edwin King, who is white, said it appeared to be one more exercise in white power: Party leaders were dictating a compromise and telling his group who would be seated. Others in their delegation felt it was trickery, that we were voting on the proposal even as they were reviewing it. The meeting with the Freedom Democrats was agony for Hubert. Fannie Lou Hamer accused him of putting his political ambitions above his commitment to civil rights. Hubert begged them to give him and Johnson a chance to prove their commitment to civil rights in the White House, but he was almost in tears by the time the meeting ended. Fannie Lou Hamer wasn't buying it. After that meeting broke up, she gave an eloquent interview in which she said, "We didn't come this far to get no two seats. We're all tired, and we all want to sit down."

The historian Taylor Branch has said that both sides—the Credentials Committee and the Freedom Democrats—made mistakes in those three days. He has argued that our committee failed to understand the emotional pull on the Freedom Democrats and the depth of feeling they brought to Atlantic City. They had begun to develop some trust in the political system and expected to be treated as serious participants, and instead they were all but shut out. He also thinks the Freedom Democrats were naive. This wasn't a political science convention, it was a political convention: We were there to nominate candidates and win an election. He believes, too, they didn't appreciate how the Atlantic City reforms would work in the long run to advance the cause of civil rights.

I'm proud of that compromise, and I think with the distance of time it holds up well. The white Mississippi delegates certainly didn't regard it as a victory. They knew we had repudiated their segregationist rules, and they promptly walked out of the convention, leaving just three delegates behind.

Martin Luther King Jr., Bayard Rustin, and Joe Rauh, the great national strategists of the civil rights movement at that time, also recognized our compromise as progress. They knew it was a bitter pill for the Freedom Democrats, but they thought the larger civil rights movement would be well served: We would have the symbolism of seating an integrated delegation at a national convention, a permanent change in the rules of the Democratic Party, and a party united behind Johnson and Humphrey, knowing that they had a strong civil rights agenda for Congress if they won the fall election. King and Rustin also saw how the political ground was shifting nationally. The GOP, the party of Lincoln, that year explicitly repudiated civil rights. Barry Goldwater had voted against the Civil Rights Act of 1964, and the GOP national convention in Los Angeles was almost entirely white. Black delegates were spat upon and verbally abused; moderates were pushed out of party positions. Baseball great Jackie Robinson attended the convention, but left in disgust, saying, "I now believe I know how it felt to be a Jew in Hitler's Germany." King and Rustin endorsed what we were doing because they were confident that, over the long term, the Democratic Party would be the party of progress on civil rights.

Nevertheless, we left Atlantic City with a lot of bad blood in the party. John Stennis, the powerful senator from Mississippi, a Democrat, would later chide me for meddling in the politics of his state. He was a real power in the party, someone not to be trifled with. Later, after I returned to Washington from a trip to Mississippi, he asked me what right I had to go into his state and talk about discrimination. "You have struck a powerful blow against the state of Mississippi," he told me. Other Southern Democrats told me we had destroyed the party in the South.

What they said had a good deal of truth. Just four years later, Richard Nixon rolled out his famous "Southern strategy," campaigning on the latent racism of the Southern states. He carried Virginia, Tennessee, South Carolina, North Carolina, and Florida—states that had once been part of the "solid South" for Democrats. In 1972 Nixon swept the South, and except for Jimmy Carter in 1976, no Democratic presidential candidate has carried the entire South since then. In Congress, too, those reforms triggered a backlash. Within a few years many of the old white segregationists—Strom Thurmond and Jesse Helms, to name two—had left the party to become Republicans. Control of Southern congressional seats shifted to Republicans, putting people such as Newt Gingrich, Trent Lott, and Mitch McConnell in charge of the House and Senate. In 1980 Ronald Reagan kicked off his presidential campaign in Philadelphia, Mississippi, just a few miles from the place where three civil rights workers had been murdered during the Freedom Summer of 1964.

The point is that we did this knowingly, understanding the risks and believing it was necessary. We were a hypocritical party in the mid-1960s. In Congress we were the party of civil rights. We had passed the Civil Rights Act of 1964, and when, as individual members, we went home to Minneapolis or Seattle or Dearborn, we spoke of integration and equal opportunity. But all the time we knew that Southern Democrats stood for segregation, and racism was a cornerstone of their political power. Roosevelt never challenged the South. Truman never challenged the South. William Jennings Bryan, a great populist Democrat, went along with Southern racism. We dodged that issue by looking the other way and keeping a quiet peace with the all-white delegations that came to our conventions. That ended after Atlantic City.

Although we paid a heavy price in the short run, the Atlantic City reforms yielded profound changes in the long run. We permanently changed the rules and the complexion of the Democratic Party that August. Just four years later, in 1968, Mississippi sent an integrated delegation to the Democratic National Convention; many of the Freedom Democrats were delegates, including Fannie Lou Hamer. Aaron Henry, a leader of the Freedom Democrats in 1964, became a close friend of mine and soon a member of the Democratic National Committee. By 1968, all the Southern states sent integrated delegations to the National Convention. Julian Bond was a potential candidate for president, and talented African-American candidates were running for office all over the country. When I attended the 2000 Democratic National Convention, Minnesota's delegation was seated immediately behind Mississippi's. I noted that twenty-six of Mississippi's forty-eight delegates were African-American, and that pattern of integration was true across the convention floor. Black delegates and white delegates sat side by side, working together as friends and colleagues. The nation had changed, and so had our party. It is not overstating the case to say that the events we sent in motion in 1964 helped clear the way for the election of Barack Obama in 2008.

Johnson's anxieties about the 1964 election proved groundless, and in November he crushed Goldwater in one of the biggest landslides of the twentieth century. As a political matter, I was thrilled that voters had repudiated the hawkish views of Goldwater and the latent bigotry of the GOP. As a personal matter, I was thrilled for Hubert, who would ascend to the vice presidency. But I also wondered what would become of Humphrey's Minnesota Senate seat. Appointing someone to fill the vacancy would fall to Governor Karl Rolvaag, a friend of mine and a member of the DFL family. I knew my name would be considered: I was the second-highest constitutional officeholder in the state, after the governor, and I had done well in the elections of 1960 and 1962. But I had competition. Representative John Blatnik from northern Minnesota was the senior member of the state's congressional delegation and would make a good senator; Rolvaag was also rumored to want the seat himself.

A few weeks after the election I got a phone call from Karl, who was vacationing in Florida. "Come down here and let's have a talk," he said, "but don't let anyone know where you're going." We knew that the sight of me boarding a plane for Florida would trigger a lot of speculation, so Warren Spannaus, my friend and state party chairman, got me out the back door of the attorney general's office and off to the airport. The conversation with Rolvaag went well, and in December 1964 I was named Minnesota's next U.S. senator.

Three weeks later the Mondale family was on a plane to Washington,

D.C., our lives moving so fast that I sometimes wonder how Joan and I ever kept up. The itinerary required us to change planes in Detroit, and in our distraction we failed to notice that Eleanor—already an adventurer at age four—had disappeared on her own personal inspection tour of the airport. We managed to find her before the next flight boarded and we arrived in the nation's capital with the family intact—Joan and the kids taking a taxi to our new house in the Washington suburbs and me heading straight for a news conference on Capitol Hill. It would begin one of the most productive periods of my career and one of the happiest times of our life as a family.

2

High Tide

O N THE EVENING of March 15, 1965, I left my Senate office and
walked over to the Capitol with my colleagues George McGovern of South Dakota and Gaylord Nelson of Wisconsin. Lyndon
Johnson was scheduled to address Congress that night on his civil rights
agenda, and as we took our seats in the House chamber, the great room
was buzzing. As a senator from the South, Johnson had earned a mixed
record on civil rights. But now he was president, a national leader, and
he felt the weight of John Kennedy's example. He had signed landmark
legislation the previous year—the Civil Rights Act of 1964—and I knew
from talking to Hubert that Johnson wanted civil rights to be his legacy.

We finally settled in and Johnson began. From his first words, I knew
this evening was going to be historic. That address has been described
as Johnson's greatest speech, as one of the great civil rights speeches of
all time, and I believe it was. Every phrase was beautifully crafted, every
line gave expression to something we all believed. When he got to that
signature line—"And we *shall* overcome"—the chamber erupted. It was
electrifying. To hear a Southern president say those words, to embrace the
credo of the civil rights movement, was a wonderful thing. It represented
a turning point in American history.

From today's perspective, it's easy to forget how different our country
was just five decades ago. Across the South, African-Americans couldn't
eat at a lunch counter, couldn't drink from a public drinking fountain,

often didn't dare to register to vote. Cities were badly divided, black from white, and black children mostly attended segregated schools, often in terrible conditions. Housing discrimination was commonplace and in many places legal.

Beyond discrimination itself, a politics of white rage prevailed in many parts of the country. George Wallace had stood in the schoolhouse door in Alabama, even when he knew he was defying the courts. Local sheriffs had beaten peaceful black demonstrators. Roving thugs and lynch mobs intimidated black citizens in many places. The entire nation knew of this boiling rage in the South and that something had to change.

Still, civil rights didn't quite capture the nation's attention while black protesters were bearing the brunt of the abuse. Sadly, it took white demonstrators to accomplish that. The previous year had seen what became known as Freedom Summer, a movement of white college kids who went down to Mississippi to register black voters. That summer three civil rights workers were murdered, two of them white, one black. That's when the North started realizing that something intolerable was occurring.

The nation's problems didn't stop with racial segregation. Nearly 20 percent of Americans lived in poverty. Thousands of children went to school hungry every day. Bobby Kennedy conceived the idea of field hearings in Appalachia and found children who went to school barefoot and got by on one meal a day. You saw photographs of skinny kids staring at the camera with hollow eyes.

Even so, these problems were often met with callousness. A few years later I was on George McGovern's Hunger Committee, and we conducted a field hearing in Immokalee, Florida. We visited a migrant labor camp and saw families living in hovels, children who never went to school. We had a series of meetings with local officials and county commissioners, one of whom told us, "This isn't our problem. These are federal people. We aren't going to use local resources to take care of them." In other words, he wanted migrant workers to pick oranges and perform other menial, back-breaking jobs—and then just go away.

It wasn't much different in the nation's capital. We conducted field visits there, too. We met families living in housing that was unsafe and unsanitary; we saw schools with ceilings caving in and without running water. Just blocks from where we did our work in the Capitol.

Of course, progressives in Congress knew all this. Humphrey had been hammering away at it for years. But until 1965 we couldn't get anywhere. The Supreme Court had been conservative in the 1950s; Congress passed several weak civil rights bills that didn't accomplish much. Congress was very much under the control of conservative Southern Democrats. Democrats from Northern states would come and go; they would win an election, then lose the next one. But the Southerners won election after election and built up seniority, and seniority controlled Congress. The "old bulls" had the powerful committee chairmanships: James Eastland of Mississippi had Judiciary. John McClellan of Arkansas had Government Operations, then Appropriations. Allen Ellender of Louisiana had Agriculture, which controlled most of the nutrition programs. Harry Byrd of Virginia had Finance. If they didn't want legislation to move, it didn't move. In the House, Howard Smith of Virginia was chairman of the Rules Committee, and a bill couldn't get to the floor of the House without going through his Rules Committee.

The result was a huge backlog of social progress waiting to happen. The historian James MacGregor Burns called it "the deadlock of American democracy."

Then, with the historic election of 1964, the impasse broke. Democrats picked up thirty-eight seats in Congress, so that in 1965 we convened holding a two-thirds majority in the House and a staggering margin of sixty-eight to thirty-two in the Senate. We had such numbers on the Democratic side of the Senate chamber that they had to add an extra row of desks. I was in that row, at the very back, sitting next to Bobby Kennedy, who had just been elected from New York, and Fred Harris of Oklahoma. We were closer to the men's room than to the Senate rostrum. Over on the Republican side it looked like a ghost town.

But it wasn't just our numerical advantage, it was the people and their aspirations. The new senators elected in 1962 and 1964 were progressive in their values and impatient in their outlook: Bobby Kennedy, Joe Tyd-

ings, Fred Harris, Birch Bayh, George McGovern. A lot of them were veterans, back from World War II, and they were eager to make a difference.
They wanted to change the world, and they thought they could.

Suddenly, after years of deadlock, the floodgates burst open. We had
a filibuster-proof majority in the Senate and the Old Bulls couldn't stop
us anymore. We had a sympathetic Supreme Court, with Earl Warren
as chief justice. After Kennedy's assassination, I believe, we had moral
momentum. And in the White House we had Johnson and Humphrey—
masters of Senate procedure and brilliant legislators. We could have
passed nearly anything we wanted.

The Senate has never moved so fast in its history. The Elementary and
Secondary Education Act, which established the first federal aid to poorer
children, was reported to the Senate floor on April 6 and passed on April
9. The Voting Rights Act—reported on April 9 and passed on May 26.
Medicare—reported in the Senate on June 30 and passed nine days later.
The Immigration Act of 1965—a landmark bill that did away with the
old country-of-origin quotas—was reported on September 15 and passed
seven days later. It was like driving in a hailstorm—Johnson kept hitting
us with one bill after another.

Altogether, Johnson proposed eighty-seven bills in the first session of
the Eighty-ninth Congress; eighty-four became law. At the end of that
year the editors of the *Congressional Quarterly* wrote, "The first session
of the 89th, starting early and working late, passed more major legislation than most Congresses pass in two sessions. The scope of the legislation was even more impressive. Measures which, taken alone, would have
crowned the achievements of any Congress were enacted in a seemingly
endless stream."

Johnson's economic program was equally ambitious. The 1950s had
been a pretty grim time for the nation's economy. We had gone through
two recessions, and the prevailing view in Washington was a sort of Cal-
vinist belief that we had to live within our means rather than strive for
something better. Johnson came in with a new generation of brilliant
economists, including Walter Heller from the University of Minnesota,
who never got enough credit, and Jim Tobin and Art Okun from Yale.

They had embraced and refined the Keynesian idea that an economy was not a fixed thing, with a sum of resources handed down by God. Their idea was that you could stimulate the economy to grow faster, to live up to its true potential. If the economy was growing, then the public would feel more affluent and the nation would have the resources to tackle its problems.

This idea seems obvious in retrospect; the Kennedy-Johnson tax cuts are today regarded as one of the great economic success stories. But it wasn't obvious at the time. I would go back to Minnesota and give talks to business leaders, and they were skeptical. The dominant idea at the time was that the government couldn't do much to improve the national condition. If you kept interest rates nice and low, then the economy would do just fine. When we approached them with this Keynesian idea—that the economy was underperforming and we could help it reach its capacity—they thought it was a trick, like getting something for nothing. But the tax cut of 1964 worked. The economy grew more than 6 percent the next year, a stunning performance, and it was healthy, noninflationary growth. Once the new economics started working, the skeptics came around. That ushered in an extraordinary period of affluence, which made people more confident about addressing the nation's challenges.

This was heady stuff for a kid from Minnesota. I was just thirty-six and still trying to figure out how to be a senator. I would call Hubert for advice and, from time to time, visit him at the Old Executive Office Building across the way from the White House. Humphrey had gone to Washington sixteen years earlier blazing away, giving speeches and telling his elders how to turn things around—and he advised me pointedly not to follow his example. Instead, he always emphasized the importance of relationships. Voters see a candidate running for Congress, and they think politics is about combat. But once you're in the Senate, it's often the opposite—everything depends on cooperation and comity. You might vote against a colleague today and then need his help on something else tomorrow. You learned quickly that your career depended on getting along with other members, especially the ones with seniority. I did get along with most of my colleagues. During breaks in committee hearings, I would go over and strike up conversations. If we were on the Senate floor waiting for a vote to conclude, I would go over and ask a colleague about his family or the latest polls in his home state. Even with the Old Bulls such as Richard Russell or John Sparkman, if you could find a way to do them a favor on an issue where you did agree, they would know that you weren't always going to be sand in their eye.

One of the best places to build these relationships was a little office just off the Senate floor known at that time as "Mansfield's hideaway." Technically, it was the office of the secretary of the Senate, a staff officer who coordinated the floor schedule, supervised the clerks and pages, and managed other Senate functions. The office's informal host was Stan Kimmitt; he was not yet secretary of the Senate, but he was an old and trusted aide to Mike Mansfield, the majority leader, and he was a good friend to young senators. One day Kimmitt invited me into the office and introduced me around. The office was popular as a place where senators could relax between floor votes, make phone calls, or rest up if we were headed for a midnight session. Sometimes two senators would be there, sometimes twenty. Sometimes Mansfield would be there, conducting a little business. Sometimes, after hours, you would just have a drink and swap jokes. Kimmitt was close with several of the Southerners and always seemed to have a supply of excellent bourbon. But in this place, the Senate's North-South divide did not hold. Elsewhere around the Capitol—in the Senate Dining Room, for example—the Southerners tended to keep to themselves, almost as if we had two wings of the Democratic Party. In Mansfield's hideaway those regional distinctions fell away. It was there that I got to know Jim Eastland and John Stennis and Herman Talmadge. Sometimes the conversation was personal and congenial; sometimes it was brutally candid. Here Talmadge lectured me that our civil rights revolution was destroying the Democratic Party in the South. Whatever the tone, you could get to know other senators personally and build friendships that transcended politics.

From time to time, I got my political lessons from the master himself, Lyndon Johnson. At that time, I was trying to get a judicial appointment for Lee Loevinger, a respected attorney in Minneapolis. I would make phone calls, send memos, try to figure out who could help me. Johnson wasn't going to do it, I soon discovered, but he was indirect about it and very diplomatic. He would return my calls and talk and talk until I was running out of time—and he knew I was running out of time—and then I would understand that he wasn't going to give Loevinger that appointment. But even when he wasn't giving you what you wanted, he made you feel good about yourself and left you feeling that you had received a fair hearing.

I didn't see a great deal of Hubert in those first couple of years; work, family, and campaigning consumed all our hours. But occasionally he would come up to the Capitol to have lunch with old friends, and I seldom missed a chance to remind him that the junior senator from Minnesota was keeping busy. One day in the summer of 1965 I was having lunch with a few colleagues when I noticed Humphrey eating with two other senators in another part of the Senate Dining Room. Raising my voice so I knew he would overhear me, I said to my friends, "You know, Humphrey's been in Washington all these years, giving speeches about Medicare and Food Stamps, funding for the arts and help for the farmers. I just got here six months ago, and we got it all done." He turned in his chair, stunned, then burst out laughing.

A freshman senator does not get glamorous committee assignments, and I wasn't enthusiastic about mine. I was a young Northern liberal, and the Senate Democratic Steering Committee, controlled by mostly older, more conservative members, wasn't going to give me much. I got Space and Banking and Agriculture, but these were the authorizing committees, not the appropriations committees, which meant we didn't control any money. Nevertheless, I found ways to pursue the priorities I had begun to develop in Minnesota. One day I was talking to Bill Mullin, a lawyer and a friend who had worked for me in the attorney general's office, who mentioned something I found outrageous. He had been on the highway one day when his brand-new car drove off the road due to a mechanical defect. Upon inquiring, he found out that the automaker knew about the defect and was quietly making repairs, but without ever giving consumers any warning. I drafted a bill, the Fair Warning Act, requiring automakers to notify consumers when defects were discovered in cars already on the road, and asked Ralph Nader to help. That bill became part of Lyndon Johnson's landmark auto-safety legislation the next year, the National Traffic and Motor Vehicle Safety Act of 1966, and millions of consumer warnings have since been issued.

About this time I made one of my great friends in the Senate, Gaylord Nelson. Gaylord had been governor of Wisconsin while Orville Freeman was governor of Minnesota, and I had run into him occasionally at regional governors' meetings. Gaylord was from Clear Lake, Wisconsin—a big man from a small town—and I liked him immediately. He had been elected to the Senate in 1962, and by the time I arrived in 1965 he was already establishing himself as a leader on conservation and the environment. He knew the subject, he had allies all over the country, and he had guts. He would become a valued colleague, a great teacher, and one of my best friends.

I hadn't been in Washington more than a week or two when Gaylord approached me to ask if I would cosponsor a new bill he had drawn up, the Wild and Scenic Rivers Act. It was written to restrict development and preserve wilderness along several beautiful and unspoiled rivers, and he was having trouble finding cosponsors. The environmental movement was still in its infancy, and most members of the Senate didn't know much about rivers and wilderness. But the first river he had on his list was the St. Croix, the boundary river between Wisconsin and Minnesota, so I was a natural ally. What he didn't know was that the St. Croix is where Joan and I had our first date, an afternoon of canoeing. I loved that river, and we became allies instantly.

Gaylord was older than I by about a decade and already a skilled legislator. One day we had to testify before Senator Allen Ellender's committee to get funding for a study of the St. Croix. At that time the Army Corps of Engineers was considering a plan to dredge the river and build a series of dams. Ellender, who was from Louisiana and worried a lot about flood control, was partial to the Army Corps. Opening the hearing, he noted that the Corps, too, was interested in the St. Croix and that he would have to balance their interests against ours. Gaylord replied, "Senator, the Army Corps of Engineers is always interested in a river. It is like the beaver. Any time they see the slightest trickle of water, they want to build a dam there. The difference is that the beaver does it himself at no cost to the public." We won the argument that day and we got our money.

In 1965 Gaylord was becoming a national apostle of environmental issues, and he saw that a handful of pristine rivers remained in the country—mostly away from the East Coast—that for one reason or another had been untouched by industry and urbanization. The St. Croix was one of them—clean, forested, winding, beautiful. But we knew that if we didn't act fast to protect these rivers, the developers would find them and they would be permanently lost as wilderness rivers.

The political problem with legislation of that sort is that you run into a buzz saw of local opposition, and that's exactly what happened to Gaylord and me. Every mayor and county commissioner along the river thinks you're trying to preempt his or her authority and destroy the local property-tax base. All up and down the river, on both sides of the St. Croix, the local Republicans said our bill was an outrageous assertion of federal power into local matters. And of course a lot of local commercial interests, including real estate developers and electric utilities, were well organized. They played hardball and stirred up a lot of fear, and pretty soon people along the river thought federal water protection might as well be an invasion by the Red Chinese.

One evening in the summer of 1966 I attended a meeting in Bayport, Minnesota, a beautiful town on the St. Croix about an hour east of the Twin Cities. The meeting had been organized by the St. Croix River Association, and I thought, naively, that it was a way of building support for our bill. I got there and found an angry crowd: local business owners, real estate developers, people who had owned family cabins on the river for years. They wanted to know what I was doing to their river and why I would do it without talking to them first. Our proposal got beaten up pretty badly in the local papers, which ran editorials with every scare story they could think of: We would destroy local government. We would condemn Andersen Windows, a big local employer. We would take away family summer cabins. Someone was handing out leaflets describing our bill as "Mondale's Monster." I drove home that night thinking, "We just lost Washington County." But the funny thing is, that November I carried that county by a bigger margin than ever. A lot of people liked that bill, even though they didn't come out to public meetings. It told me that noise and votes are not always the same thing.

It took us more than three years to pass the Wild and Scenic Rivers Act, but it was finally signed into law by Lyndon Johnson in October 1968. To this day it's one of the most satisfying things I've done. By 2006, after a series of amendments, the law protected 165 rivers in thirty-eight states, including the Snake River in Idaho, the Black Butte in California, and the Musconetcong in New Jersey. Alaska alone has more than three thousand miles of protected rivers and streams. It means that long stretches of the Missouri River still look much the way they did when Lewis and Clark explored them, and that the delicate environment of the Saline Bayou of Louisiana has been protected against navigation and commercial encroachment. Thanks to Gaylord, we got to those rivers just in time.

Gaylord Nelson became a friend and a hero to me, and working with him on that bill allowed me to see that environmental issues would take a special place in my public career. While I was growing up, we hadn't been an especially outdoorsy family, but my dad did take us camping in the North Woods of Minnesota, and we kids went away to Bible camp most summers. After Joan and I were married and I became attorney general, I always set aside one week a year for a fishing or hunting trip up north with a couple of buddies. I called those trips my "religious holidays" as a joke, but there was something almost spiritual about working on legislation where water and wilderness were at stake. It became one of the issues where I was willing to risk public opposition of the sort that could end a career. Apart from the immediate satisfaction of protecting a lovely river or cleaning up a polluted lake, the environmental issues reminded you of your place in a larger natural world and your obligation to care for it during your brief time. When the nation's founders wrote the "take care" clause of the Constitution, I'm sure they weren't thinking that an environmental movement would emerge one day in our country. But they did have a profound sense of history, of each generation's responsibility to the next, and whether explicitly or implicitly religious, a sense that they were stewards of some enduring value.

In addition to working with Gaylord on the Wild and Scenic Rivers bill, I became a sponsor of the Clean Air Act and the Clean Water Act, the landmark federal antipollution laws, authored the legislation that created Voyageurs National Park in northern Minnesota, and introduced the bills that would create the Upper Minnesota River Wildlife Refuge (now the nation's largest urban wildlife reserve) and the Mississippi National Scenic Riverway System. I also interceded on the side of environmentalists in an epic battle to halt the dumping of taconite-ore waste into Lake Superior by mining companies of northern Minnesota. We stopped that practice, saving the lake from a source of massive degradation, and struck an agreement that proved to be a model in balancing the needs of the environment and the state economy.

We were still in the early phases of the scenic rivers bill when a second major environmental battle came my way. In 1960 Orville Freeman had lost the governor's race to Elmer Andersen, but Orv helped Jack Kennedy carry Minnesota, and Kennedy, recognizing Freeman as a strong administrator, named him secretary of agriculture. For some years the Agriculture Department had been reviewing timber harvests in a pristine area of northern Minnesota known as the Boundary Waters Canoe Area, or BWCA, a spectacular swath of wilderness along the Canadian border. In early 1965 a department commission recommended that the area be given additional federal protections, and Freeman proposed a set of rules that would greatly limit the timber harvest and the use of motorized boats and vehicles there.

I had spent a lot of time canoeing in the Boundary Waters while I was attorney general, and I knew that Freeman's proposal would trigger a fight. I loved to go fishing with friends such as Fran Befera, a dear friend and businessman from Duluth, and Harry Munger, who was the brother of the great legislator and environmentalist Willard Munger. But I also took the opportunity to study economic development in northern Minnesota because we had a lot of friends in the labor movement there, and the local economy was heavily dependent on mining and timber. I had also become friends with Sigurd Olson, the naturalist and writer, a saint, who was one of the first advocates for what became Voyageurs National Park in an adjacent wilderness directly west of the Boundary Waters.

But the local politics of the Boundary Waters were brutal. Every commercial interest in the region lined up against Freeman, and they were effective at turning us into the enemy. The mining companies controlled a lot of jobs and a big tax base, and they were influential. So were the timber interests. In addition, the livelihood of a lot of resort owners and outfitters depended on traditional recreation, which meant boats and motors. Many local residents felt the same way. For the average guy in Ely, Minnesota, the dream was always to get enough money to buy a snow-mobile and go off into the backwoods, or to buy a nice fishing boat and go fishing. If you said you wanted to ban motors, it became class warfare— regular working folks against environmental elitists who lived far away, and the antienvironmentalists played on that. A resolution, passed by the Lake County Board of Commissioners in the fall of 1967, was typical of the local reaction:

> We favor management of the forest by trained professional forest-ers using approved forestry practices as has been done in the past and without interference from well-intentioned but misguided advocates of single-use concepts.
>
> We favor a BWCA policy permitting access to some of the presently-inaccessible lakes by the general public and not limiting the use entirely to the canoeist type of individual.

We were going to change their lives by tightening restrictions in the Boundary Waters and, later, creating the Voyageurs National Park. I got a lot of mail, some of it from friends, that said in so many words, Drop this issue or you will get hurt.

Compounding our challenge was that northeastern Minnesota had been a Democratic stronghold for years. The steelworkers' union had thousands of members in the taconite mines around Eveleth, Hibbing, and Ely. They had always turned out for candidates like Freeman and me, but they were suspicious of environmentalists who wanted to come into their part of the state and tell them what to do. Yet there wasn't a lot of room for compromise. The other side's slogan for the Boundary Waters was "multiple use," which sounded like a friendly compromise but was just a cover for gutting any restrictions whatsoever.

In many ways, that battle foreshadowed the culture wars that would break out in national politics a decade later. The commercial interests tried to pitch it as average working people against a group of loopy elitists from the Twin Cities who didn't understand them.

I think the people of northern Minnesota were, however, willing to listen to me. I wasn't just another outsider who flew in with ideas about using up the locals' land. As attorney general I had set up a body called the Northeastern Minnesota Development Association to study job creation, and that gave me an opportunity to go up often and listen to what was on people's minds. So I had a lot of friends in the area and they knew I was on their side. It was kind of funny: They would give me hell at meetings and in letters. They would threaten to tip over the boat for Democrats. But at election time, they pretty well left me alone. I suppose I had enough of a connection to the people and their values that they could write me off as some sort of fool but still consider me a friend.

As the Boundary Waters dispute unfolded, I found the most effective political strategy was just to listen. Where we could grandfather people in—let them keep their cabin or their resort for their lifetime—we tried that. Where we could delay the implementation of some rule, give people time to prepare and adapt, we tried that.

But at some point you simply had to take a deep breath, jump in, and vote the right way.

Historians who have written about the 1960s don't generally list environmentalism as a part of the Great Society. But I think it represented a parallel and equally important part of the country's emerging social conscience. When Gaylord and I started working on the Wild and Scenic Rivers Act, the environmental movement was not the force it is today. The Environmental Protection Agency didn't come into existence until

1970. We hadn't yet passed the Clean Air Act or major portions of what became known as the Clean Water Act. The first Earth Day—Gaylord's inspiration—wasn't held until 1970. In big swaths of the country people felt that the federal government had no constitutional right to intercede in their jurisdiction. The developers didn't want it. The mining companies didn't want it.

But the country's attitude was starting to change. People were beginning to realize that they were choking on smog, that their drinking water held health risks. Americans had begun to abandon the old Wild West mind-set, the attitude that there was always an open frontier. The new conviction was that, acting together, we could do something to protect our air and water.

Our argument was that effective environmental protection required federal action. Air and water don't respect state boundaries. Moreover, if you leave it to local leaders, they will always be outgunned by commercial interests. There's always somebody who wants a power line *right here* or a bridge *right there*.

Gradually we began to make the case that we had a responsibility as a nation to preserve something that had been given to us, something extraordinary, and that a failure to protect it would be a grave and permanent loss. Anyone who visits one of those wilderness areas today will understand what I'm talking about. You take a canoe out on the St. Croix and you feel healthier right away. You spend a day in the quiet of the Boundary Waters and you understand we've got something precious there. Gaylord died in 2005, but I saw his widow, Carrie Lee, not long ago. I told her every time I go over to Scandia or Taylors Falls and take a look at that river, I salute Gaylord and what he left us. I've kept that promise.

Some years later, in a talk at the University of Minnesota, I called that period of my career the "high tide" for American liberalism. It was as if we took the intellectual heritage of Franklin Roosevelt, the moral inspiration of John Kennedy, and a decade of pent-up demand for social change and converted them into a social reality. The laws we passed in that period changed America permanently—for the better—and set the stage for the pivotal battles of the rest of my career.

But I'm not sure that, at the time, we understood the significance of the moment. When you are that passionate about a cause, when you believe so deeply in a set of values, you feel it's only right that things are going your way, and you don't stop to think that you might be living at one of those rare periods when the stars are in alignment.

What I didn't see at the time, but understood later, is that when you move that fast, you can make mistakes. We would pass a bill on Monday and hold the success party on Friday. In our enthusiasm we probably hoped for too much and promised too much, and as a result we probably planted the seeds of some of the doubts that would later set in about the Great Society. We did an awful lot in a hurry, and some of it didn't work. Some of the legislation wasn't well designed. When we put those bills together, everybody had his favorite idea, and the result was sometimes a hodgepodge—something for the mayors, something for the counties, something else for the community activists. Some of the legislation didn't help at all, some of it helped quite a lot. But overall it gave the impression of a government overreaching.

Then, too, some of the challenges we took on proved harder than we anticipated. To really help poor kids perform better in school, to help them overcome the problems of growing up in troubled households—that is complicated and requires more than just spending money. People were bound to be disappointed, after all we had promised, when we got into the reality.

A third factor was money. If you look at the actual federal appropriations that resulted from the Great Society, you see that many of the most ambitious concepts were funded at modest levels, especially after we began facing up to the costs of the war in Vietnam. Some programs, such as Medicare, became immense. But most had to scrape along on rather lean budgets. The Legal Services program, for example, had a budget of only $1 million to open 269 offices in its first year, or less than $4,000 per office. Head Start, one of the best-known creations of the

War on Poverty, even today reaches only 40 percent of eligible three- and four-year-olds. In other words, we authorized dreams and appropriated peanuts.

A final factor was diminishing political will. When it became clear that some of these challenges were going to require a lot of money and a lot of time to produce results, the public began to lose patience. They grew skeptical about these academic experts and their grand ideas. Some wondered why the government was taking their money to help someone else with what I heard voters call "all this free stuff." Americans are compassionate people, idealistic people. But they're also pragmatists. If you're going to spend their money, you'd better show results.

Some of the warnings appeared immediately. Even as we were putting the finishing touches on the civil rights legislation, the country's cities started blowing up. Race riots occurred in Watts, Harlem, Detroit, Washington, even in Minneapolis. In place of our message that the country could finally go forward together, the riots spawned a belligerent, divisive rhetoric. For black Americans, the anger had been building a long time, and change wasn't coming fast enough. For white Americans the riots caused a backlash. We had promised to end poverty and hopelessness, and Americans saw their cities erupting in violence instead.

Then along came Vietnam. By 1967 casualties were rising and so was the war's cost. It was robbing us of the money we had planned for the domestic initiatives. Walter Heller told Johnson he needed to raise taxes to pay for the war. But Johnson didn't want to raise taxes. He was starting to worry about the war's unpopularity, and he didn't want to accentuate the issue. Worse, the war changed the subject and distracted people from the message of confidence and progress. It tore the country apart and embittered people about their government and their leaders.

The result of these setbacks was at least two decades of retreat from government activism and social progress. Richard Nixon attacked the Great Society as an assault on traditional, middle-American values and tried to dismantle it piece by piece. Ronald Reagan launched a more sweeping critique, advancing the idea that government can do nothing right. It's time we reassessed that philosophy and reconsidered the achievements of the Great Society: By any objective standard, they were enormous.

The education programs alone—Head Start, Pell Grants, Title One aid to poor school districts—constituted an entirely new federal effort to give opportunity to disadvantaged young people. Sometimes we had to go right past the states—as with Head Start and Title One—to mayors or school boards because many states were still officially discriminating. That was a revolution in itself, but we did it because we recognized the development of our nation's talent as a federal problem. Many young people who grew up in poverty could not serve in the military because their health was so poor and their skills were so weak. Others became wards of the state or wound up with chronic, costly diseases. We were wasting a big part of America's talent, and we needed to correct that for national reasons. You can argue the details—whether Pell Grants were the right size, whether Head Start had the right organizational structure—but hundreds of thousands of young people, maybe millions, have done better in school, and millions have been able to go to college, because of what we did in those years. Twenty years later, the social scientists Marshall Kaplan and Peggy Cuciti summed up the shift in national philosophy: "For one relatively brief period, the national government discovered poverty and assumed responsibility for ameliorating its burden and finding a cure. In doing so, the federal government affirmed the concept of America as a single national community, rather than as thousands of separate communities divided by class or caste."

We also revolutionized health care for the elderly and the poor with Medicare and Medicaid. In 1960, most elderly Americans had no health insurance. I remember one physician telling me, "Older people look at a major illness the way they would look at the atomic bomb. It would end their life." Their children would try to help out, but if they got ill, they no longer had an independent life. Today, older Americans do have independent lives and first-rate medical care. With these measures, improvements in Social Security, and the banning of age discrimination, the quality of life for American seniors was hugely improved.

Consider the hunger and nutrition programs. Today the critics say,

"Well, we still have poor people." Of course we do. But today people don't starve in America. When we started the hunger hearings with George McGovern and Bobby Kennedy, we found real malnutrition. Children in Appalachia and Texas and California were growing up with preventable illnesses, stunted growth, vitamin deficiencies, unable to perform well at school for sheer lack of adequate nutrition. A lot of poor people were simply left to the good graces of the local community. Some communities were generous and forward-thinking, but many were not. We embraced the idea that this was a national disgrace and a national responsibility. America's poor and elderly are measurably better off than they were when we started.

Finally, there was the civil rights revolution. People who dismiss what we achieved in the 1960s like to gloss over the way race relations have changed in our country. For 250 years or more, America could not confront the evil of official discrimination. It was this country's greatest moral scandal—our national shame. We changed that. We gave all Americans equal treatment in the workplace, in housing, at the lunch counter, and on the city bus. Access to the ballot box—the South had made it a mockery, we made it a reality. With the Civil Rights Act, we also banned gender discrimination, which would have a gradual but enormous impact in opening up the nation's workplaces and universities to women.

The Voting Rights Act was an astonishingly powerful bill because it allowed the Department of Justice to go right past the states, bypass the governors, and set up local voter registration operations, to get people registered and give them the right to vote. In the ensuing years, voter registration rates among Southern blacks soared, and before long you had distinguished black political leaders emerging from the South, such as Andrew Young and John Lewis. Historian Robert Caro said of the accomplishment, "Abraham Lincoln struck off the chains of black Americans. Lyndon Johnson led them into the voting booth, closed democracy's sacred curtain behind them, placed their hands upon the lever that gave them a hold on their own destiny, made them at last and forever a true part of American political life."

The important point to remember about the civil rights movement and the War on Poverty, often overlooked, is that they weren't merely about giving money to the poor or rights to the disadvantaged. They also empowered people who had been powerless. Justice is linked with power. For those who have the power to help themselves, America is quite a country. For those who do not, it is quite another.

This was the underlying philosophy in every aspect of the Great Society. It was the argument behind *Gideon:* In America everyone has the right to a trial, but if you're impoverished and can't afford a lawyer, good luck defending yourself in a court of law. It was a principle behind the Civil Rights Act: It not only banned discrimination, but made it easier for plaintiffs to move their cases from state courts, where they might face hostile judges, into federal courts, where they had some assurance of justice. It was also the strategy behind Head Start and other programs of the War on Poverty: They gave parents and local communities a big role in spending money and governing antipoverty agencies.

We wanted to set up structures so that when we were gone, people who had been powerless could continue to assert their place in society. They would have the skills and education to make it on their own, they would have the legal tools and political weight to demand that they be heard. We had to unravel the paternalism.

No program embodied this philosophy more profoundly than Legal Services, which started in 1965 as a series of federal grants to local legal-aid organizations. The creators understood that access to a courtroom, though guaranteed by our Constitution, isn't much use if you lack the legal tools to make your case. Poor Americans who faced big problems—a bad landlord, for example, or a consumer scam—could get their day in court, but a big law firm was almost always on the other side. The poor could lose their health care, their homes, their families, or indeed their liberty—wrongly—and not have a fair chance to be heard. Legal aid empowered poor Americans to have their cases heard.

But people who hold power understand when it is being transferred away from them, and legal aid created an immediate backlash. When he was governor of California, Ronald Reagan tried to block funding for California Rural Legal Assistance after its lawyers challenged his welfare and Medicaid policies on behalf of indigent residents. By 1970 the future of legal aid was in doubt because Richard Nixon began dismantling its parent agency, the Office of Economic Opportunity, and cutting funds for the various programs within it. Several of us in the Senate recognized that as long as legal aid was subject to direct control by the president, it would be vulnerable to attack by people who might be inconvenienced if poor people have access to a lawyer. In 1971, working with Ted Kennedy and Representative William Steiger, a Wisconsin Republican, I introduced legislation to create the Legal Services Corporation, removing the program from the executive branch and establishing it under an independent board. Our bill eventually became law in 1974 and has served the program well, giving it a degree of autonomy and a series of distinguished board members. Though Legal Services came under threat again under President Ronald Reagan, who tried to cut its budget and appointed his own board, it has survived and thrived; today it supports roughly 140 local legal aid agencies and handles roughly 1 million cases each year, providing millions of Americans the dignity of being treated like the rest of us.

At about that time, I got to know César Chávez, the great farmworker organizer. Chávez understood the dynamics of power. He once said, "It may be a long time before the growers see us as human beings . . . but we will win, we are winning, because ours is a revolution of mind and heart, not only of economics." In my Senate subcommittee on migratory labor, we held a hearing on power and powerlessness, and when the United Farm Workers then held a rally at the National Cathedral in Washington, I was invited to speak. I said, "It is a revolution against powerlessness; a revolution against that predicament which makes far too many of our fellow Americans totally dependent upon others. If we are to have a decent America, it is a revolution that must be won and a struggle which must be won wherever our fellow citizens lack the power to assert their rights."

To a younger generation, even to people of my age looking back many years later, these changes are easy to forget. We take it for granted that a woman can run for her party's presidential nomination, that an African-

American can be president of the United States, that every American should be able to participate fully in public life and make his or her best contribution to our country. That was not possible a few decades ago. We did that, and it was a stunning thing. When we had completed our work, America was a different, fairer, and far better nation.

3

The Fight for Equality

I N 1966, thinking that a young Democrat might be vulnerable after just two years in Washington, the Minnesota GOP nominated a veteran Republican, Robert Forsythe, to run against me. I worked hard that fall, visiting dozens of counties and shaking thousands of hands, and in November the voters of Minnesota were kind enough to return me to the Senate with 53.9 percent of the vote. But a number of Senate Democrats lost their seats in that midterm election. This was taken as a vote of no confidence in Lyndon Johnson, and some of my colleagues returned to Washington uneasy about pressing ahead with the president's program. Others of us were more impatient than ever to complete the Great Society agenda, and since I had won with a decent margin, I felt I was in a position to play a role.

When the Senate convened in January, a group of us who made up the Civil Rights Caucus sat down to discuss our priorities. After passing the Civil Rights Act of 1964, the basic charter, then the Voting Rights Act of 1965, we felt we had broken a long-standing deadlock and that the Senate could be persuaded to go further on issues of race and segregation.

The next frontier was fair housing. At that time, some states had laws that flatly prohibited housing discrimination, but the federal government did not. Johnson's attorney general, Ramsey Clark, had drafted the next civil rights bill, which included a ban on housing discrimination and additional voting rights enforcement provisions. But we weren't sure how hard Johnson was going to push for it. By this time Johnson was distracted by Vietnam, which was going badly and sowing doubt and anxiety in the country.

When we convened at the beginning of 1967, Mike Mansfield, the Senate majority leader, decided to break Johnson's civil rights legislation into five parts, to be passed as separate bills. He sensed that the Senate had lost enthusiasm for the issue. But it also was the leadership's way of shucking the fair-housing component, because everyone doubted that it could pass and people didn't want it to drag down the rest of the legislation. Many in Washington remembered that Governor George Romney of Michigan had embraced fair housing, with disastrous consequences. He had once talked about opening up the suburbs of Detroit to black homeowners, and his polls fell from 50 percent approval to something like 10 percent. So this issue caused a lot of fear. One day I ran into Ramsey Clark, a staunch civil rights supporter. He pulled me aside and said, "Fritz, I'd like to help you, but fair housing just won't pass and you have to understand that."

Clark understood, as we all did, that this was civil rights getting personal. The legislation we had in mind would forbid discriminatory practices for almost the entire housing industry, including apartment buildings and real estate brokerages, and open the door for minority families to move into white neighborhoods. It wasn't just some abstract cause down South, this was bringing desegregation into neighborhoods in Northern cities. Even Mansfield, our wonderful Senate majority leader and a supporter of the bill, thought it couldn't pass and would tear the Congress apart.

This was the backdrop that first afternoon when we convened the Civil Rights Caucus. Around the room sat a community of solid, pro–civil rights senators—Jack Javits from New York, Jim Pearson from Kansas, Ed Brooke of Massachusetts, and Cliff Case from New Jersey—all of them Republicans—and a strong group of Democrats, too. Phil Hart, a saint, was the chairman. We met every week or two and talked about the prospects for moving a bill. We would bring in people such as Clarence

Mitchell, then the NAACP's chief lobbyist in Washington. Clarence was a moderate, but he was really tuned in to the black community, and if he felt you were faltering, he would report you to his committee and you would feel the heat. Mitchell was so influential that we called him the 101st senator.

As we discussed strategy, looking around the room, it became clear that no one wanted to carry fair housing. So I volunteered. I was a young guy, I was ambitious, and legislation of this magnitude would let me learn how things are done in the Senate. But I also believed it was time for Congress to show leadership on the issue. Many black Americans were getting impatient with the nonviolent philosophy of leaders such as Martin Luther King Jr. I worried that an upsurge of violence in urban communities had the potential to rip the nation apart and destroy the Democratic Party. I felt that if we were going to give King the support he needed and give ourselves any credibility, we needed to show that the legal path, the nonviolent path, could produce results.

When I went back to my office that day and told my staff that I had volunteered to carry the fair-housing legislation—this is the story my staff tells—they just hung their heads and said, "Great. Thanks, boss." It was a long shot, but the staff was terrific and went right to work.

At that time I was on the Banking Committee, a very conservative committee. It had been chaired by Willis Robertson of Virginia, the father of Pat Robertson, and he once told me he never voted for a bill that came out of his own committee. By 1967 the chairman was John Sparkman of Alabama. Sparkman was a gentleman, but he could not be found supporting civil rights in Alabama. A few days after the meeting of our Civil Rights Caucus, I called Phil Hart, who had become a good friend and was wise about the ways of the Senate. "How am I going to move fair-housing legislation in the Banking Committee?" I asked. Phil told me this might actually work to our advantage. Such a bill would never move in the Judiciary Committee, the normal venue for civil rights legislation, because its chairman, James Eastland of Mississippi, was a staunch, very powerful opponent. But Phil said that the Banking Committee, because it had jurisdiction over housing, might just give us an opening. I drove home that night thinking maybe we could circumvent Judiciary and find a way to get this done.

Because I was brand-new, the older members of the Senate weren't looking at my future closely—not as closely as I was. This had disadvantages. But it could also work to your advantage because sometimes they didn't take you seriously enough to get in your way. After a couple of friendly conversations, I convinced Sparkman to agree that I could hold hearings on fair housing in the Banking Committee's subcommittee on housing. Sparkman had no enthusiasm for the issue, but he was decent to me and didn't interfere with our work. It wasn't much—it wasn't going to get TV cameras or a pack of reporters. But I hoped that it would allow me over three or four days to make a record, to show people just what a disgrace discrimination was in our nation, and perhaps to get the country thinking about the issue again.

When you're managing a piece of legislation in the Senate, you never quite know where your opposition will crop up, so you use hearings to make the broadest possible case. In the end, we assembled a spectacular group of witnesses. To address the constitutional issues we had some of the nation's top academic talent, including Dean Louis Pollak of Yale Law School and the Reverend Robert Drinan from the Boston College Law School. We recruited leaders from major industry groups, including the National Association of Real Estate Brokers and the National Association of Real Estate Boards. Their testimony was powerful because it documented the industry practices that kept black families out of white neighborhoods and showed that the industry itself wanted changes in federal law. We also invited top officials of the U.S. Justice Department and the Department of Housing and Urban Development, who documented the segregation of American cities in great detail and showed how discrimination sentenced African-Americans to living in substandard conditions.

The statistics alone were persuasive. In 1967 twenty-two states, plus Puerto Rico and the District of Columbia, had banned housing discrimination. But the statutes were uneven and enforcement was spotty. At the federal level, antidiscrimination regulations covered only projects built with direct federal assistance—not including FHA or VA mortgages—with the result that federal fair-housing laws covered less than 4 percent of the nation's housing supply. In 1965 the U.S. Commission on Civil Rights estimated that the nation's major cities had a "segregation index" of roughly 95 percent, meaning that 95 percent of whites and blacks lived in neighborhoods that were overwhelmingly of their own race. A survey by the U.S. Department of Housing and Urban Development found that nonwhite homeowners were four times more likely to live in substandard housing than their white counterparts of equal income. The U.S. Census Bureau estimated in 1960 that some 1.8 million nonwhite families lived in housing without plumbing or other standard utilities, and that more than 1 million nonwhite families in urban areas lived in overcrowded housing.

But we wanted to put a human face on this dilemma as well. To start off the hearings we called a remarkable witness, Carlos Campbell, a young African-American navy lieutenant. Handsome and accomplished, he appeared at the hearing in a crisp, white uniform. After a series of impressive assignments in the navy, he had earned a posting to the Pentagon, but, try though they might, he and his wife couldn't find an apartment anywhere nearby. He told of going to various homes and apartment houses with For Rent signs. Many of the landlords, he said, had been encouraging over the telephone. But when they saw him in person, they would go into excuse-land. He kept right at it. His wife would go with him. The Defense Department had a housing office that tried to help him, and even they couldn't find anything in white neighborhoods. They knew what the problem was. Some of them even encouraged him to look in black neighborhoods. It was a disgrace. Here was a person good enough to perform tough assignments for our country in the armed forces, but not good enough to find housing for himself and his family. Could this be possible in America? A lot of hard hearts on the committee started softening that day.

But that testimony alone didn't sway everyone. One afternoon after the hearing ended, I was walking back to the Russell Building with one of my colleagues, a good friend and a distinguished senator. He was suspicious of federal power and thought the federal government had no place regulating private housing. So I tried another argument. I told him a big struggle was taking place in the black community. This struggle created what I called the *civil* civil rights movement on the one hand—leaders who believed that law and reason could deliver justice—and on the other hand a movement of people who were so outraged that they thought only violence would work.

I was much influenced at the time by Martin Luther King Jr. and his steadfast support for the philosophy of nonviolence. He often said that once you get into "enemy thinking," you're lost: You turn your opponents into villains and you diminish their humanity. He said our actions must be based on our religious faith and the values of tolerance and law—it's why he so deserved the Nobel Peace Prize. But other leaders in the civil rights movement, and there were growing numbers of them, said King was a fool. They were getting beaten up and jailed, and worse, and they believed that only violence could turn back the bigots. This was a real struggle, and if King had ever gone down the violent route, America would have become a more bitter place, more like South Africa.

It wasn't always easy to make this argument. One night I stayed late in my office, reading mail from constituents. It was frightening and discouraging. White voters would write that they were fed up with black demonstrators. They didn't want black families moving into their neighborhoods. They didn't want the government telling them to whom they could sell their house. I pointed out that our bill, of course, didn't do that. All the standard reasons for rejecting a sale—financial ability, credit record, and so on—remained in place. What our bill prohibited was refusing a sale solely because of race. It's worth remembering that eminent members of the U.S. Senate opposed fair-housing legislation. My good friend Robert Byrd of West Virginia said our bill would violate a citizen's right to private property. He debated me on the *Today* show and called our bill "forced housing," not fair housing. It's hard to believe today. He later got over it, but it was more or less expected at the time. A lot of my constituents felt that way. Even when they didn't want to sign their name to a letter, if you moved around in public or went to big events such as the Minnesota State Fair, you would hear the fear and sometimes latent racism.

We completed our hearings in August, and I think they made an impact on other members of the Senate. We had made our case on the constitutional questions, we had rallied the business and the religious communities, and we had given everyone a palpable sense of the injustice. But in the end we never did move a bill that year. By the time we completed the testimony, Sparkman realized where I was going, and he was not about to let my bill out of the Banking Committee.

We were, however, able to make a strong record and establish the case for fair housing—and that would prove crucial just a few months later, when fair housing triggered one of the most remarkable floor battles in the Senate's history.

When we returned in January 1968, Lyndon Johnson was prepared to introduce a broad new civil rights bill, but the odds against us were mounting. I had spoken to Hubert, and he wasn't sure how much effort the president was going to put into fair housing. In the Senate a solid bloc of Southern Democrats, practiced hands at bottling up civil rights legislation, stood in our way. Typically, they would filibuster even the motion to proceed on a civil rights bill, so it was impossible to enroll your legislation and get it on the floor for a debate.

But this time we caught a break. Toward the end of 1967 the Civil Rights Caucus had quietly approached Mike Mansfield, a great leader and an absolute master of Senate procedure. Mansfield had an idea. The House had passed a version of Johnson's civil rights bill in the 1967 session and sent it to us. When we adjourned at the end of the year, Mansfield arranged the Senate calendar so that the House bill would be the first item of business on the Senate floor when we returned. This meant that the Southerners couldn't filibuster the bill's consideration by the Senate; if they wanted to stop it, they would have to debate the legislation on the merits. I remember being on the Senate floor in January with Richard Russell of Georgia, one of the Old Bulls and a great Senate strategist, but also an entrenched foe of civil rights. He stood up and said, "How did this get here?" But it worked, and away we went.

So in January 1968, the Senate commenced its next great civil rights debate. The key provisions of the administration's bill promoted fairness in jury selection and expanded federal authority to prosecute civil rights violations. Now the question was whether I should offer fair housing as an amendment. This was a tough call, so I took it up with my civil rights colleagues. Mansfield remained unconvinced. I was young and untested; the Southerners had already started to filibuster the main civil rights bill, and Mansfield was afraid my amendment would only intensify the opposition. More than anyone else, Phil Hart made the call because he had such a good feel for the Senate. He doubted that the fair-housing amendment could pass, but he let me run with it. I teamed up with Ed Brooke, a Republican from Massachusetts and the only black member of the Senate, and we prepared to introduce the fair-housing amendment.

Even at this stage we weren't sure how much help we would get from the White House. Johnson supported the bill, at least publicly, and mentioned it in one of his State of the Union messages. But Ramsey Clark was still skeptical, and Hubert told me that the administration as a whole was lukewarm and distracted. I was pretty confident, however, that once we got a little momentum, Johnson would put his authority behind it. Others in the White House, such as Joe Califano, who was a domestic-policy adviser to Johnson, supported it from the beginning, and I thought they would gain leverage within the administration if we made progress in the Senate.

On February 6 Ed Brooke and I introduced the fair-housing amendment and we opened the debate. The battle would test whether we were up to managing a major piece of legislation through a skeptical Senate and whether a young Northern liberal could take on the Old Bulls and a big group of skeptical elders.

Thanks to our work in the Civil Rights Caucus and the work of Clarence Mitchell, we had a list of colleagues whom we knew to be solid supporters. Then we had a long roster of undecided senators. We would work on them over lunch or in the hallways and have constituents write them letters, and if we couldn't persuade them, we would call local newspapers and community groups who might send people to visit them in person and make our case.

The Southern Democrats, however, were digging in for battle. They would stand up on the Senate floor and give their speeches about states' rights and their unique culture. I understood that we were repealing their way of life. Already, we were sending federal registrars to every precinct in the South and registering black voters. We were sending FBI agents throughout the South to investigate violent incidents. We were changing the party rules so they couldn't send segregated delegations to the national political conventions. We were knocking the pins out from underneath their world. But I had a theory. I remembered that Humphrey, when he was managing the Civil Rights Act, showed the greatest respect for the Southerners. He was always generous in the floor debates and magnanimous in his language. So, although they were angry about the bill, they weren't angry at Humphrey. It helped pull the institution together. I believe we did things the same way: We didn't make everyone like the bill, but we didn't leave people angry at us.

Now, too, I could invoke the record we had built in our subcommittee hearings the previous summer. We had statements from the leading civil rights organizations. We had had the attorney general of the United States and the secretary of housing and urban development. Prominent law school deans had testified that the Constitution was on our side. A panel of real estate executives had said discrimination was destroying their industry. We had George Meany and Andy Biemiller of the AFL-CIO, and John Doar, another saint, of the Civil Rights Division of the Justice Department. These were all big names in those days. We had the American Bankers Association, the Synagogue Council of America, the American Civil Liberties Union, the American Jewish Committee, the Anti-Defamation League. Roy Wilkins, who was then executive director of the NAACP, had been magnificent: "One of the burning frustrations Negro residents carry with them in city ghettos is the knowledge that even if they want to and have the means to do so, very often they cannot get out," Wilkins had testified. "The white sections of the cities and the suburbs are, to a great extent, shut against them." Ramsey Clark, despite his doubts about the political prospects, had been eloquent on the merits: "We must show a doubting world that different races can live together in a free country with equality and justice."

Having a good bill and a good case, however, wasn't going to suffice. We also had to win a war of Senate procedure. Southerners such as James Eastland and Richard Russell were not happy that this issue had even come to the floor, and they were determined to kill it with delaying tactics. To get past them we would need a two-thirds majority—sixty-seven votes, if all senators were present and voting—the supermajority required to invoke cloture and end their filibuster. That was a high bar, and seldom had it been crossed on a civil rights bill.

At first, the prospects looked bleak. My Southern colleagues started their speeches, and we debated fair housing for two entire weeks. On February 20 we forced the first roll call on cloture, and the vote came up 55–37 in our favor. This was about ten votes short of what we needed, yet I was encouraged because I could see another five easy votes out there, maybe eight.

At that point, too, I think we were beginning to carry the argument on the merits. The segregationists weren't conceding, but their objections were beginning to take on a mad-dog tone—irrational and mean. As I went through the vote tally that evening, I saw that if you subtracted the Southerners, not many senators were left opposing our amendment. I could tell that day that our cause was becoming bipartisan and national.

But by this time we were starting to test Mansfield's patience. As someone who aspired to maintain some comity in the body, he was afraid that fair housing would tear up the Senate. In his eyes we had lost our first cloture vote decisively, and the debate had dragged on into its third week. A lot of smart people had concluded that this was a lost cause.

On February 21 Mansfield scheduled a procedural test. He and Everett Dirksen, the Republican minority leader, offered a motion to table fair housing for the year—to separate it from the main civil rights bill and set it aside. In part, they thought we had failed and they just wanted to get it off the floor. But I also believe that Mansfield wanted to take the measure of the Senate. He supported our amendment, even if he doubted that it could pass. He understood that if the majority leader offered a motion to table the amendment and a majority voted against him, it was the Senate's way of saying, "Keep this issue before us, let's work on it some more."

When they called the roll that day, it was 58–34 against the motion to table. I was thrilled. It still wasn't the two-thirds majority we would need to break the filibuster, but it was significant. For one thing, it suggested that Mansfield and Dirksen had identified a large bloc of senators who supported us. For another, it proved that we were starting to get public support, because we had senators who were up for election who didn't want to be on the wrong side of this issue. They were troubled by the violence in our country, by the struggle between the violent crowd and the nonviolent crowd, and they were thinking, All right, how do we get out of this? All the civil rights groups were engaged by now. They were in Washington, calling the senators and getting others to call. The newspapers were all starting to editorialize about it, too. Now we had a tailwind.

On February 26 we had the second cloture vote. I stood on the Senate floor, checking my list and talking with my colleagues as they came down to vote. It was one of the most tense days of my life. When they called the roll, we picked up one vote but came up short again, 56–36.

This was agony. We had a majority of senators behind fair housing. But we couldn't shut off debate and conduct the vote. Meanwhile, I was testing the patience of my fellow senators. As I walked back to my office that afternoon, I was wondering, How do I pick up eleven votes? Most Northern Democrats were holding with me, along with a number of Republicans from the Civil Rights Caucus. But I just couldn't pick up the remaining Republican votes.

That afternoon, at Phil Hart's suggestion, I called Everett Dirksen. I knew he was not philosophically opposed to housing desegregation; he and his colleagues just had to be comfortable with the details and the implementation. Hart told me, however, that Dirksen never voted for a civil rights bill unless he had authorship. I knew that if I could swing the Republican leader, I could probably swing the Senate. His support would legitimize the issue with Middle America. In addition, I knew four or five Senate friends of Dirksen's would want to support him personally. Earlier in the week I had called Hubert to see if he had any advice, and he told me that Dirksen had signaled to him and to Ramsey Clark that he would like to find a way to get behind our cause. There were a lot of ifs, but I could see how it could be done.

On the evening of February 27 Dirksen called me with a proposition: If I could agree to scale back the scope of the amendment on one or two points, he would introduce his own version and offer it under his name. I hung up the phone and thought, This is a miracle. It was a compromise, of course; he wanted to place limits on the authority of the Department of Housing and Urban Development to enforce antidiscrimination regulations because some of the Republicans still opposed a broad expansion of federal power. And he wanted to exempt single-family, owner-occupied housing if it was sold by the owner and not through a broker. He felt he needed these concessions to bring around some members of his caucus, and they effectively scaled back the reach of the amendment, from 91 percent of the nation's housing supply under my amendment to about 80 percent under his. But having the name of the Senate's top Republican on the amendment was a huge victory. It meant we would almost certainly pick up enough Republican votes to break the filibuster.

On February 28 Dirksen introduced his version of the amendment as a substitute for mine, and I thought that perhaps we had turned the tide. The third cloture vote was scheduled for March 1, and I went to the Senate floor that day full of confidence. That proved to be misplaced. Several moderate Democrats who had voted with us on the first two cloture votes, including Senator Albert Gore Sr. of Tennessee, were piqued by all the changes in the Dirksen substitute. It wasn't the compromise itself, but that they felt caught by surprise and hadn't had enough time to read the new bill before the vote. "I'm not voting for cloture," Gore told me. "I don't know what's in this bill." We picked up a handful of Republican votes but lost two of our Democratic allies, and we came up short for a third time, 59–35.

By now, Mansfield was extremely restless. We had been debating civil rights for seven weeks, and all the while he had been trying to move the nation's business through the Senate. By now we were on our way to holding more cloture votes than on any other bill in the history of the Senate.

At the end of the day on March 1, Mansfield pulled me aside and said, "All right, I'll give you one more vote." So this was it, but I still couldn't see where we would get the last eight votes. That night we had a skull session in the office, and at eleven thirty I called Hubert. I said, "We're not getting enough help from the administration and this is our last shot." He paused a moment, then said, "Call the president."

The next morning I called the White House. They told me the president was on *Air Force One*, flying back from a trip to Puerto Rico. My heart sank, but the White House operator said, "No, I can patch you through." The next thing I knew, I was on the phone with Lyndon Johnson. I told him, "Mr. President, we need some help here. Mansfield is going to give us one last shot, and by my latest head count, we only need to pick up one more vote." Johnson asked if there was anyone who could vote for us and not hurt himself with his constituents. I told him, when I looked over the holdouts, there was one, Bob Bartlett from Alaska. But I told Johnson, "He comes from a small state and he hates to vote for cloture."

Bartlett, a Democrat, had no particular reason to oppose fair housing. But at that time the senators from small-population states rarely voted for cloture; the filibuster was their defense against the power of the big-population states of the East and West coasts. "It's a principle of my career," Howard Cannon of Nevada once told me. "I'm not going to bargain that away." By this stage of the fair-housing debate, most of these senators had come around, and Bartlett was the last holdout. Bartlett had told a lot of people that he had to stand up for Alaska, but I knew something else: He badly wanted a certain federal construction project for Alaska, and I told Johnson.

After a moment's silence, I heard the president say, "Thank you." And a click.

Two days later, the day of the final cloture vote, the galleys were packed and the roll was called. Senators started coming down on the floor to vote and wait for the tally. I was watching the clock and checking names from my list. It was excruciating. It didn't take us long to get to thirty ayes. Then forty. Then fifty. But we still weren't over the top, and we were starting to run out of time on the roll call. With only a few senators left to vote, and only a few minutes left, we were still four votes short. Then Howard Cannon came down—he had voted no on cloture the previous times—and cast his vote, "Aye." Then Jack Miller of Iowa, who also had voted no before, came in from the Republican cloakroom and voted "Aye." Only minutes remained. Then Frank Carlson, a Republican from Kansas, came down. He had voted no on all three previous cloture votes, and my heart was in my throat. "Aye," he said. Now you could hear visitors stirring in the gallery. We were just one vote short, with time almost gone. I looked at the roll call and my list of names, and saw that Bartlett hadn't yet voted. Then I realized he must be holding back. He was an "if needed" vote—a colleague who agrees to vote your way, but only if his or her vote is needed to win. In the meantime, the senator may wait in the cloakroom rather than be seen, undecided, on the Senate floor. Bartlett was apparently still hedging his bets and wanted to be off the floor. As I was wondering, Where is he? I turned around and here was Bartlett coming from the cloakroom. He strode down to the front of the Senate chamber, raised his hand, and said, "Aye." We had it and the place blew up.

I will never forget that moment, never forget that day. As a personal matter, it was the first time that I was able to show, not only to the public but to myself, that I could manage the procedural traps, stay on my feet, and carry a tough bill through the U.S. Senate.

But above all I realized we had turned a page in our nation's history. Northerners who thought civil rights could only go so far, who told me, "Hell, Fritz, this isn't going to pass," realized the country was ready to change. The Southerners, who had been through so many civil rights battles, finally understood that their time had come and gone. They had to go down to the Senate floor and give their speeches, but they knew this country had turned a corner. That was the last big civil rights bill of the 1960s, and it completed the list. When cloture passed that afternoon, Richard Russell, the legendary Georgia senator, came up to me, shook my hand, and said, "Congratulations, sir."

4

Lost Trust: Vietnam and the Election of 1968

ETWEEN EARLY 1967 and early 1968, enthusiasm for Lyndon Johnson's Great Society began giving way to dismay over his policy in Vietnam. Polls showed that Johnson was losing the confidence of the general public, and the launch of the Dump Johnson movement by a group of antiwar Democrats made it clear he was losing control over his party, too. On March 31, 1968, Johnson scheduled a national television address to discuss his strategy in Vietnam, an address that led to a stunning turn of events.

On the evening of Johnson's speech, I was in the studios at NBC television in Washington with Scoop Jackson, my Senate colleague from the state of Washington. Scoop was one of the Senate's leading authorities on defense and foreign policy, and I suppose they asked me because I was close to Humphrey and, through him, close to the White House. My neighbor Bill Bundy, an assistant secretary of state, had gone over that day to see the president and get advice on what I might say. We had no inkling that Johnson was about to drop a bombshell. But as Johnson came to the end of his text, his tone suddenly shifted and he announced that he would not stand for reelection. That night he uttered that famous line "I shall not seek, and I will not accept, my party's nomination."

I was astonished. Just a few weeks earlier, Johnson had invited a group of state Democratic Party leaders to have cocktails with him at the White House. The group included my old friend Warren Spannaus, who was then chairman of the Minnesota DFL. Johnson had asked them for support on Vietnam, and he insisted he wasn't going to "cut and run."

Yet, in retrospect, Johnson's announcement shouldn't have come as such a surprise, given the military and political developments of that year. Johnson had bet his stack on the troop escalation of 1965 and 1966, and then it failed. Negotiations with the North Vietnamese weren't getting anywhere. He knew that the war was not winnable and was very losable. His polls were sagging; by late 1967 his approval ratings were well below 50 percent. I think he saw a lot of dispiriting realities and calculated that only by announcing that he planned to step down could he get outside of politics and reclaim some public trust, which he could then use to try to resolve the war before he left office.

Then, too, Johnson was a human being. I'm sure the daily death toll tore at him. He saw those antiwar rallies, with young demonstrators chanting, "Hey, hey, LBJ, how many kids have you killed today?" and I'm sure that pained him.

The political landscape was shifting, too. Gene McCarthy, my Senate colleague from Minnesota, had entered the race late in 1967, challenging Johnson from within his own party, and within weeks Gene had attracted more support than anyone anticipated. Johnson did win the first contest, the New Hampshire primary in March, but it was close and all the excitement was with McCarthy.

No love was lost between McCarthy and Johnson. McCarthy had expected to be Johnson's running mate in 1964, and when Johnson chose Hubert, Gene felt Johnson had toyed with him. Gene was quirky—you could never tell what was principle and what was personal. But his opposition to the war was genuine, deep, and persuasive. He stepped into the race and opened that issue up.

Then Bobby Kennedy entered the race, and I think Johnson saw Bobby as an even bigger threat. He had all the Camelot charm and the Kennedy organization, and people were heartsick over the death of his brother. Bobby had tremendous emotional pull with the public, and that must have gnawed at Johnson, too.

Meanwhile, on Humphrey's behalf, I had gone out to Wisconsin, the site of the next Democratic primary. After the close outcome in New Hampshire, the Johnson-Humphrey ticket had to do well in Wisconsin. The party leaders I met with, old friends of mine, told me it was hopeless. One poll showed that McCarthy would get 75 percent of the vote. They said it was over, that the White House could do nothing to stop him. I believe Johnson knew about that poll and timed his withdrawal to avoid an embarrassing primary loss.

Lyndon's thinking had a personal side as well. Johnson had often complained about his standing in Washington to Humphrey. LBJ had more than a little self-pity, a feeling that he was a poor kid from the South and the elite that ran the country never respected him. He had a string of landmark achievements, such as Medicare and civil rights, and he felt he didn't get credit for them, and he hinted that he was simply going to go home to Texas. That night, in effect, that's what he did.

So there we were in the NBC studio, and what was going to be a discussion about Vietnam and the president's speech instead became a discussion about who should run in Johnson's place. I said, "I certainly hope Humphrey will think about it. He's just what the country needs."

Humphrey was out of the country that night, in Mexico City, at a dinner for Mexican president Gustavo Díaz Ordaz. One of his aides, Bill Connell, called me right away, and I talked to Humphrey early the next day. By today's standards it was already late to start a campaign; McCarthy and Kennedy had a big jump on Hubert, but I had little doubt that he would enter the race. Humphrey had wanted to be president all his life. He was the sitting vice president, a seasoned politician, and a leader with an extraordinary record in the Senate. He was the most gifted orator in America, the most sought-after speaker, and he saw no reason why he couldn't make it to the presidency. Even before Johnson's speech was over, I felt that Hubert would run. The key Humphrey staff members were on the phone immediately that night talking to dozens of Democrats around the country, asking their advice and gauging their support.

Within a few days I got another phone call from Humphrey. He wanted Fred Harris and me to be cochairmen of his campaign. I was a little surprised because Hubert had plenty of veteran people around him, people who had gone through a lot of campaigns with him. But I thought it was a good idea. By this time Hubert was being labeled as old politics. He was still young by the standards of national politics, just fifty-seven, but he had been around a long time, a visible figure in American politics for more than twenty years. The younger generation of voters thought of him as part of the establishment, for which they had no affection. Now he was associated with Johnson and the old wing of the Democratic Party, while Bobby Kennedy and Gene McCarthy seemed to represent something young and different.

Hubert also had an organizational problem. Only five months remained until the Democratic National Convention, and he had to raise money, organize a staff, and secure commitments from party leaders. He had to get around to a lot of states quickly, to make his case to young people and introduce himself to voters who didn't know him, and I think that is why he turned to Harris and me. Fred and I had come to Washington at the same time. Fred was young, smart, well liked in the Senate, and progressive. He was from Oklahoma, which gave him a kind of Western patina. He was a good speaker, and his wife was of Comanche descent, a beautiful woman; they made a great couple. Harris had some national ambitions himself. I believe he wanted to be vice president, so this was a way for him to make the national scene. The Kennedys wanted him, too. They courted him. But I knew Fred well, and I knew he wanted to be with Humphrey. It was a big coup for us.

But for Hubert nothing was going to be easy that year. He and his staff needed a few days to prepare a formal announcement. He had to consult a lot of party leaders around the country, people such as Richard Daley in Chicago, and he had to see if he could raise the money for a national campaign. He remembered the campaign of 1960, when he was chronically short of funds for travel and advertising.

Humphrey scheduled his announcement for the first week of April; then, on April 4, Martin Luther King Jr. was assassinated in Memphis. My

God, what a horrible night. That evening I was attending a big Democratic Party dinner at the Shoreham Hotel in Washington, a black-tie
fund-raiser, and the news spread through the room with whispers and
gasps. The master of ceremonies went to the microphone and said a tragic
event had occurred, but the dinner would go on. Humphrey immediately
sensed that this wasn't right. He stood up, politely stopped the proceedings, and asked for the microphone. He said the country had just lost a
magnificent American, that this was a sad moment in American history,
and that it would be a good idea if we stopped right there, said a prayer,
and went home. And that's what we did.

More than may be realized now, King held the country together in
those years: He was an apostle of nonviolence, a man respected by black
and white Americans alike, a source of optimism for people who had cause
to doubt their hopes. Now he was gone. We were in shock, the country
was coming apart at the seams, and Hubert had to step into that chaos
and try to make his case to voters. For people who admired Humphrey,
this period was agonizing. He had waited for years to make a proper run at
the White House and had given it a good shot in 1960. Now, finally, his
moment had arrived, and it came under the worst possible circumstances.
Vietnam was going to hell. The country was frustrated. The great Pandora's box of civil rights had opened and wasn't going to be closed. And suddenly, the black community's greatest leader, the preeminent civil rights
leader of our time, was killed and the cities exploded.

A few days later I went down to Atlanta for King's funeral. It drew
a huge crowd of dignitaries. Humphrey was there, and Jacqueline Kennedy. A big delegation of senators flew down together. Most of us wound
up watching the funeral from a garage, a place where they greased cars,
because there was no room in the church. Then we walked behind the
casket, and half a million people must have been there. A mood of mourning fell over the entire nation.

For the next several days all the candidates suspended their campaigns.
Hubert told us he was not going to go around giving speeches while the
nation was in mourning, and no one would have heard him if he tried. But
there was tension, too, because before long the candidates all wanted to

get started again. The primaries and the delegate-selection calendar were not going to wait, and the convention was just a few months away.

But now the agenda had shifted. Up to that point the race had been a referendum on Johnson and the war. Now the whole painful range of social issues opened up. Black people and many whites were incredibly frustrated by the slow progress on civil rights. The cities were volatile—we forget that now, but it was on everyone's mind back then. The mayors were worried, and so were we in Congress. The Kerner Commission had issued its landmark report on violence in our cities, and all the dilemmas of poverty, education, and social justice demanded attention from the candidates. It placed another heavy burden on the candidates and the voters.

By May we had opened a Washington campaign office and formed United Democrats for Humphrey. Then, just as the country was starting to recover from King's assassination, just as the presidential campaign was regaining momentum, Bobby Kennedy was shot in California. I was home in Washington that night, talking to Hubert on the phone and watching returns from the California primary on television. I watched as Bobby gave his victory statement at the Ambassador Hotel in Los Angeles, then made a little joke about Mayor Sam Yorty wanting him to leave, then made his way out through the hotel kitchen. Then he was shot and lay bleeding on the floor. That night of pandemonium was followed by a day of dread as the nation held out for word that he might survive. But he didn't, and it was crushing. Even though we were rivals at that point, I was heartbroken. Bobby had been a friend and a fine senator and a source of hope to millions of Americans who felt disenfranchised. I worried about the rage and despair that were setting in.

Now the campaign was at another turning point, an agonizing one. We had the war. We had the death of King and the death of Kennedy. We had cities erupting in riots and the nation on edge. And we had Humphrey and Nixon. A lot of Americans felt that they had been cheated by the assassinations, that the system no longer offered them the leaders they revered or the solutions they desired. Americans are levelheaded people; they are not conspiracy-minded. But at this extraordinary time in the country, the suspicion, alienation, and anger were frightening. It was a strange, dangerous time.

In the middle of all this stood McCarthy, who might have been able to reassure the disaffected and speak to all these alienated young Americans. Gene was an appealing candidate—elegant, articulate. He knew the classics and would recite them on the stump. He had great aspirations and great confidence in his talent. But Gene also had a way of fading when it came to the heavy lifting, as if he were tuned out from the expectations of the people around him. He was also something of a lone wolf. I had seen that side of Gene years earlier, when I was managing Orville Freeman's campaign for governor and Gene was running for Senate. Our campaign offices were in the same building, and I had wandered down to his headquarters one afternoon to chat with his staff and sit in on a strategy meeting. Gene simply looked at me and said, "Why don't you leave now?" Not mean, but cold. I saw it again later, just a year or two after the 1968 campaign. Gene was a member of the Foreign Relations Committee, and we ran into each other in the hall one day. He was midcareer and had seniority, and rumors were that he might run for president again. But he told me he was losing interest in the Foreign Relations Committee and might quit. I said, "Gene, don't get off that committee. You could run for president on the foreign policy issues. You're highly respected, and if you leave that committee, people will wonder what you are doing and why they supported you." He muttered something about his colleagues on the committee and shrugged his shoulders as if he had simply lost interest.

Humphrey knew McCarthy was unpredictable, but it only compounded his dilemma. That spring, with the entire country teetering on an emotional brink, perhaps waiting for a signal from McCarthy, Gene seemed to vacate the scene. He took a short trip to Europe and his campaign went into sleep mode. When he returned, not long after Kennedy's assassination, Gene met with Humphrey and acknowledged that Hubert would win the nomination. "I should endorse you," he said. "You're the only one who can beat Nixon." But he didn't. I've always wondered how the 1968 campaign—indeed, the next decade—might have turned out if they had reached some sort of truce. The Humphrey-McCarthy team had been a tremendous asset for Democrats and progressive causes for more than a decade, but over time tension seemed to develop between Gene and Hubert. Within a week of that meeting, McCarthy's people were out pushing for delegates again and the fight was on.

Now, in the third week of June, we were in the middle of a campaign with more distractions, confusion, and tragedies than any other I can remember. Because he entered the race so late, Hubert hadn't raised enough money to compete in the California primary, thus the largest state in the union had supported someone other than the sitting vice president—and this candidate was now dead. The party was deeply divided. The kids were all with McCarthy. The Democratic convention was less than two months away. Worse, the Humphrey campaign was broke. Contributions dried up when Kennedy was shot. Apparently much of the money flowing to Humphrey was conservative money, to help him defeat Kennedy. According to one poll, they turned us off and went to Nixon. It was going to be a witch's brew all the way through.

The one great asset we had was Hubert Humphrey. He was vice president of the United States. He was well-known in most states and much loved in many. He was a fabulous orator and a great campaigner when he hit his stride. He had a lot of supporters in America—in the general public and among the party's leaders. We had a system that, although challenging, still permitted us to line up delegates even though it was late in the season. At that time the Democratic Party didn't have the string of early primaries through February and March, and dozens of delegates were still uncommitted in late spring. Most states used a precinct caucus system, leading to state conventions, to select their delegates to the national convention. This meant that state party leaders played a big role, and most of those leaders were close to Humphrey and Johnson. A large share of the convention delegates were what would be called superdelegates today—mayors, governors, state Democratic Party officers, precinct leaders, and party activists. Humphrey knew them all. He had worked with a lot of them, done favors, raised money—he had a lot of chits to call in. They knew him and trusted him, and most of them thought that after

Kennedy's death Hubert had the best chance to beat Nixon. As a result, by the beginning of June Humphrey had rounded up commitments from 561 delegates, even without entering primaries, compared to 393 for Kennedy and 258 for McCarthy.

I thought that Humphrey, despite all the challenges, could still win the election. But we had one intractable problem: Vietnam. By this time, the war was the black cloud hanging over Democratic politics. Our young people were dying, the South Vietnamese were not reliable allies, and the violence against the Vietnamese people was unspeakable. We had tried one military and diplomatic option after another, and none was working. At home, our campuses were on fire. The White House had no more good options. The war had destroyed Lyndon Johnson's presidency, and my Democratic friends were telling me it would destroy Hubert.

By this time I was struggling with the war myself. In the 1966 campaign, when I ran to retain my Senate seat, the war came up only occasionally. It was starting to turn sour but hadn't bitten yet in public opinion. Thoughtful people, however, were starting to have doubts. About three days after the 1966 election I had gone over to the Minnesota Church Center in Minneapolis, where a few pastors had invited me to meet with them once the campaign was over. Some four hundred clergy and professors were gathered there, and they gave me hell. They said, We kept our mouths shut during the campaign, but we think your position on the war is wrong. We don't know what you are doing and don't understand it, but we expect you to be our senator now. I didn't know what I was walking into, and I was a little offended. But in retrospect I know it was a helpful warning. I needed the cold shower.

I had gone to the Senate almost completely unshaped on Vietnam and foreign policy in general. I had read William L. Shirer's *The Rise and Fall of the Third Reich*, and like many in my generation I took the lesson that we had failed to stop Hitler soon enough and that the world had paid a terrible price. I looked at Vietnam in much the same light. I thought, here come the Communists, and the sooner we stop them the better off we will be. A lot of Democrats felt that way. We were in John Kennedy's thrall: Being a liberal meant fighting communism. As for the strategy of the war, I listened to Humphrey, of course, but I also got the formal Senate briefings. I believed that all those veteran experts, in the Defense Department, in the State Department, and in the White House, must know more about it than I did. It might seem naive today, but many people in Washington trusted that the old hands would furnish expertise and sound judgments. I soon became a much more skeptical person.

As I tried to formulate my own position on Vietnam, I had a two-track system. I did my own reading and attended the Senate briefings. But I was trying to help Humphrey, who had been extremely supportive of Johnson's Vietnam policy, at least in public. I was hoping it would work out for Hubert. I really believed then and believe now that Humphrey would have ended the war expeditiously and that he was the best of the candidates. It was almost like a father-son relationship. We had been together so long. He was now the vice president and I had taken his seat in the Senate, and it was thick blood.

During my first year in Washington, it was all happiness because you could still believe that the war might succeed. Then, in December 1965, I went to Vietnam and spent a week visiting our military installations. I went to Saigon and Cam Ranh Bay and Da Nang. I spent some time getting the official briefings, which were always encouraging. But occasionally I would pick up things around the edges, too. At a U.S. military outpost north of Saigon, we got a briefing that was all optimism and progress. But on the way out, the officer in charge, Brigadier General Russell Sutton, pulled me aside and said, "You know, it's not all perfect around here." He said that just up the road the Vietcong collected taxes from everyone who tried to pass. "We try to stop them, and we can't. We are in a position where we don't know who the people are."

Then I went to Cam Ranh Bay, a huge base, and received the same official briefing, upbeat and hopeful. Afterward, I asked the briefing officer if he thought any Vietcong were working on the base itself. He said yes. I asked how many, and he said, "We figure twenty to thirty percent of our employees are Vietcong." I asked how he knew this. He said, "First of all, we can't go anywhere. Any sortie, any march that we take, the Vietcong are always waiting for us. So we figure that everything that happens here is being monitored." That troubled me. If this is such a good war, I thought, why are we so ineffective?

I went home from that trip still inclined to support the war but harboring new doubts. Then I started to read more deeply and ask for more briefings, and I became more and more skeptical. When I gave a speech at Macalester College, my alma mater, I didn't break with the war, but I tried to signal that I was troubled, and I started talking about bringing dissident Vietnamese groups into the peace talks.

Some months later, in early 1967, I attended a meeting with Defense Secretary Robert McNamara and five or six senators. McNamara insisted things were going fine. I said, "Mr. Secretary, why is it that if you have a unit made up of South Vietnamese soldiers, with our uniforms and our equipment, trained by our best people, fighting their conationalists who are Vietcong or Pathet Lao, in their black pajamas with no equipment, that their fighters are the best in the world and ours are the worst? What is going on here?" He said, "I'll go into that next week," and got up and walked out. That made an impression: I didn't think he had an answer. By the end of that year, McNamara had announced his resignation from the Pentagon because he didn't think the war was winnable. He must have had private doubts even while he was assuaging ours.

Joan was another important influence on my thinking. She was no more a pacifist than I was, but she had friends in the peace movement. She hated the war and encouraged me to speak out about my doubts. Joan came from an old Presbyterian family with a missionary history, which, I think, brought a strong moral sense to the way she thought about foreign policy and a philosophy that concerned people have to step back and hold their government to account.

So I was beginning to feel that Vietnam was a sinkhole, and I was getting restless. A few months later I finally called Humphrey and said, "Hubert, I think I'm going to have to get off this." He urged me to be patient and said things were really a lot better than they seemed. "Call Arthur Goldberg and he'll tell you," he said. So I called Arthur Goldberg, who was our ambassador to the United Nations. Before long, he, too, would fall out with Johnson over the war. But at that point he said, "I'm glad you called. Don't move now; things are fine. Talk to Joe Sisco," who was one of the top aides to Dean Rusk in the State Department. I called Sisco and he bullshitted me for about twenty minutes. I heard him out, but it was clear to me that they had no answers.

These doubts had been gnawing at me for a long time, and now here we were in the thick of a campaign and closing fast on the Democratic National Convention. Humphrey couldn't speak on college campuses without having students heckle him, and worse. McCarthy was still holding big, successful rallies. Some of my friends back in Minnesota, including Don Fraser from our congressional delegation and Maurice Visscher at the University of Minnesota, were telling me Hubert had to speak out against the war or the campaign was lost. Fred Harris and I were young, and we hadn't been in national politics as long as some of Humphrey's other advisers, but we kept trying to find a new way for Humphrey to talk about the war. In a May 11 note to Don Fraser, I wrote, "I have a copy of your very fine letter to the Vice President. I think it is extremely well taken. I hope you will not let it drop there, but arrange for a group of sensitive and creative Viet Nam critics to meet with the Vice President and talk with him about it. If you have the time, I have it, and we will work together on this matter."

Still, a tug-of-war continued in the campaign. Some of Hubert's old hands argued that a shift on Vietnam would appear disloyal to the president and raise doubts about Humphrey's judgment; others said we needed Middle America to defeat Nixon, which meant remaining tough on communism. But I think that Harris and I gradually exerted some pull on Humphrey's thinking. Journalists certainly thought so. "Prodding here, pushing there, [Mondale and Harris] moved Humphrey back toward the leftish regions of his political origins," the columnists Rowland Evans and Robert Novak wrote. "Mondale and Harris probably synthesize the future of the Democratic Party and its hope for revitalization."

As we drew closer to the convention, I joined with the group that was pushing for a peace plank in the party platform. I told Hubert, We've got to change your position on the war. We've got to get away from this because all your friends are changing. We've got to show that we can bring this to an end and that you can be independent from Johnson.

After one of those meetings, Humphrey worked up good language for a speech about stopping the bombing in North Vietnam. McCarthy had called for that, and it was the key objective for many antiwar Democrats. I said, "This is terrific. But has Johnson approved it?" Humphrey said that Rusk and some others thought it was all right. When I heard that, my heart sank. I knew Johnson hadn't approved it and it would never happen.

A few weeks later Hubert and I discussed Vietnam again. I told him a lot of our friends were saying the Democratic candidate could not win without making a break from Johnson. He told me he was going to see the president again and would bring up the subject. But a week later I asked him about the meeting, and he said he didn't want to talk about it.

In retrospect I'm convinced that it was Vietnam—and the inability to break with Johnson—that finally destroyed Humphrey's best chance to be president. But making that break was difficult. Humphrey had lived through the period when communism was a serious threat, when you had Senator Joe McCarthy asking, "Who lost China?" A lot of the most prominent Democratic senators—Scoop Jackson, John Pastore, and of course Jack Kennedy—had in their own way promised they would never get on the wrong side of communism again. It's important to remember that the nation was still badly divided on Vietnam in 1968. We remember Gene McCarthy and the antiwar rallies. We forget that many Middle Americans still feared communism and believed in loyalty to the president and the military. They were turned off by the radicals and the demonstrations. Nixon was successfully playing to that constituency. I would look over Humphrey's campaign mail—he got hundreds of letters on the war, much of it supporting Johnson and calling McCarthy a traitor.

Then, of course, Hubert was loyal to Lyndon, and Johnson had an extraordinary ability to hold people in his sway. Many people have recounted the way Johnson belittled the people who worked with him, and I occasionally saw it happen myself. One evening our class of senators was invited to dinner at the White House. We were standing in a circle, having a drink with Johnson and Hubert. Lyndon seized the stage and waved an arm at Humphrey, who had been a dear colleague of most of us, and said, "I've got to say that Hubert Humphrey as vice president has been"—a long pause followed—"okay." It was mortifying, a deliberate insult, just Johnson's way of going over someone with rough sandpaper.

Johnson's mean streak wasn't the only force that put Hubert on the defensive. In an important episode between them in February 1965, Humphrey had written a memo to Johnson raising tough questions about what could go wrong in Vietnam—all of which came true. Johnson was furious, and after that he froze out Humphrey for months, completely isolated him. Imagine, you're vice president of the United States and you're out of the loop on the biggest decisions being debated in the administration. After that, Humphrey's tried to be a cheerleader for the war to repair the damage.

Another factor that played into Humphrey's dilemma was the draft. Every elected official in America understood that young Americans were in harm's way and grasped the need for national unity in decisions that would affect their safety. By the spring of 1968 peace talks had begun in Paris. Johnson was trying to negotiate an end to the hostilities, and Hubert genuinely worried that if he announced a new position, he would undercut Johnson's negotiating position and the military itself. Anytime Johnson heard doubts about the war from Humphrey, he would accuse him of helping the enemy—an argument that you often heard in those days. Humphrey told me Johnson would say to him, "This will undermine the peace talks. It will destroy my presidency and your vice presidency. It will strengthen communism, and, by God, you can't do that to me and you shouldn't do it to yourself."

All that spring Humphrey kept trying to find a way to break with Johnson, to make a fresh statement on Vietnam. He would meet with his advisers and develop a different position on Vietnam and get all enthused, then he would run it past Johnson and it would disappear. One afternoon Hubert drove over to the White House with a draft position paper on Vietnam, and one of Johnson's aides came out and said the president couldn't see him. Humphrey said, "But I have an appointment." And the aide said, "No, the president just can't do it." So the vice president of the

United States could not see the president to discuss the most important issue before the American people.

My own theory is that Johnson had suffered his share of humiliations as Kennedy's vice president, and he couldn't help inflicting some of the same on Hubert. I also believe Johnson was crestfallen about leaving the presidency. He was bitter that Humphrey had to break with him on Vietnam—and would be highly popular for doing it. For whatever reason, this went on right into the summer of 1968, and it was crushing for Hubert.

For those of us who were close to Hubert, this was hard to imagine—one of the most spirited and inspiring leaders of his century, diminished that way by the treatment he received from his president. But then it's hard to understand the sway Johnson held over people if you didn't experience it yourself. Later, Humphrey told me about one of his final meetings with Johnson, when he was trying to get a little flexibility to speak his mind on Vietnam. He went to the White House and made his case for a peace plank and a halt to the bombing of the north. He said Johnson sat down and moved up close and reminded him that two of Johnson's sons-in-law were in Vietnam. Johnson said, "Every day of this war the enemy comes down the Ho Chi Minh Trail with new equipment and new weapons, and they want to kill my sons-in-law. This happens every day, and it puts our boys in danger, and anybody who calls for a halt in bombing I'm going to call a murderer."

By July we were confident that Humphrey had the delegates to secure the nomination. But on the eve of the convention we still didn't know where the party would come down on Vietnam.

In truth, it was really Lyndon Johnson's convention right to the end. In those days the Democrats were still very much a top-down party, with the White House wielding enormous influence. Only a few states held primaries, where rank-and-file Democrats or younger activists could choose delegates. Most of the state delegations were run by the governors, who were close to Johnson out of party loyalty. Many of the Southerners remained bitter from the civil rights battles, which made them resent Humphrey and the way he had turned the party around in 1948. Meanwhile, many of the Northern delegations were run by the old urban machines, such as Richard Daley's operation in Chicago. They saw Humphrey as too liberal and acted as if they were holding out for somebody else. A lot of White House staff were on the convention floor, working people over to stay loyal to Johnson on Vietnam. I was working the floor, too, trying to squeeze out commitments on the opening day of the convention, and even then many of the older machine guys wouldn't commit to Hubert. Humphrey was clearly going to be the nominee, and the direction of the convention was our responsibility, but right to the end Johnson and his friends kept up the pressure to deliver for the White House.

Absent a deal between Humphrey and Johnson, I thought the best hope to resolve our internal tensions on Vietnam was to adopt a peace plank in the party platform. It would set out a new policy for the rest of the campaign, and it would let Humphrey run as his own man. I was convinced that we could craft the plank in such a way that it would link the two factions. It wouldn't bring everybody back into the fold, but it would build a bridge so that a lot of the old Humphrey friends who were alienated could walk across. That might allow us to put the convention together and let Humphrey come out with the party unified behind him.

We had been working on the peace plank for two months going into the convention. I had spent hours going over the language with David Ginsburg, a brilliant lawyer. We also worked hard on key delegates and party leaders. Ted Sorensen had been contacted, as had some of the other moderates in the antiwar wing, including a lot of the Kennedy people, and they had told us they thought they could go for it. We had our people check with Averell Harriman, Johnson's chief negotiator in Paris, and Dean Rusk, the secretary of state, and we went all through the party leadership to check the traps to be sure we weren't going to get hit from behind. Finally we met with Hale Boggs, the congressman from Louisiana, a huge power in the party. He was chairman of the Platform Committee and had been picked by Johnson. He, too, approved our language, so it looked as if we had the Platform Committee ready to go, and it could have been a wonderful moment.

Then, just as the convention was getting under way, Johnson called Boggs. He told him there was an emergency, that Boggs had to come to

Washington immediately, and that a plane was being sent to pick him up. Boggs flew back to the capital, and Johnson told him that the nation was close to World War III. He said the Russians had just invaded Czechoslovakia, the situation was dangerous, and it was absolutely essential that America appear strong, with no doubts about our Vietnam policy. Johnson had to be seen as the leader. He said, "You've got to go back there and this convention has got to stand behind me in order to preserve our nation." In one night, Johnson got back into play and changed the party position on the war. We lost the vote and the peace plank failed.

As miserable as events were for us inside the convention hall, they were even worse outside on the street. Thousands of young people had poured into Chicago for antiwar demonstrations. Some were angry over the way we had locked up delegates and taken the nomination away from McCarthy. Some were disappointed at the failure of the peace plank. I think hundreds more were there just because it was the time and place to express opposition to the war and their outrage at the events of 1968. In those few days, a year of rage boiled over.

Daley, who was worried about negative news coverage of his city, had seen it coming and had erected storm fences all around the convention hall. That only made the press corps more critical, and then, because of an electricians' strike, the television networks had trouble getting extra phone lines installed in the convention center for up-to-the-minute coverage. They were not happy. The day before the convention opened, David Brinkley came to see me and said, "We know what your party is up to, and we're not going to let you get away with it." I protested that we had nothing to do with the strike or the storm fences. I pointed out that we wanted coverage because this was going to be Humphrey's convention. But Brinkley didn't believe it—none of the news editors believed it. They thought Johnson, through Daley, was trying to suppress coverage of the protests, so they were determined to do an even better job of covering them. It was extremely frustrating: Night after night great Democrats gave powerful speeches loyal to Hubert, and they would get ten seconds on the newscast before the cameras cut to the chaos in the streets.

That week was one of the most frustrating of my life. My great friend and mentor had the presidency within his reach, yet the convention was turning into a nightmare. I could look down from my hotel window at the Hilton and see police officers chasing young people through the streets, beating them with nightsticks, and attacking them with dogs. When you stand in your own hotel lobby and get a whiff of tear gas, you don't soon forget it. The whole country could watch the spectacle on television every night.

On the final day of the convention, Johnson's forces finally relented and the delegates formally nominated Hubert. But it felt hollow and late. The party's liberals were furious with Daley. Daley was furious right back. The antiwar camp felt deflated. Humphrey felt demeaned. Instead of celebrating, we were licking our wounds.

After the election, I once asked Humphrey, "Why did Lyndon Johnson want to defeat you?" Hubert said, "No, that's not true." I said, "Of all the things he could have done to hurt you, name one thing he didn't do." In the end, Johnson tried hard to help Humphrey carry Texas, but up to that point he had made it a difficult path.

One of the extraordinary subtexts of that convention is the way that two Minnesota Democrats, Humphrey and McCarthy, politicians descended from similar traditions and longtime allies, contended bitterly for the presidency. At the finish we begged McCarthy to come up onto the stage with Humphrey to make some gesture of reconciliation, but he wouldn't do it. He wanted to be outside with his supporters. I've spent hours with old Minnesota friends wondering how that year might have played out differently if McCarthy had reconciled with Hubert before the convention ended. The left, knowing that they should support Humphrey against Nixon but unsure if they wanted to, might have been swayed by McCarthy. He might have made the difference. We were praying for it. A few weeks later we organized a national telethon where people called in with endorsements and explained their support for Hubert. We did it in part because we thought McCarthy was ready to come around. He did eventually call in, but he gave such a tepid statement that it probably did

Humphrey more harm than good. Humphrey and I spent many hours dissecting that campaign. I've concluded that I never understood McCarthy. I asked Hubert if he was angry with his old ally, but he always said there was no point in being angry at people after the fact.

As a result of these many conflicts, the convention left many voters with questions about our party. To conservatives, we were the party of radicals and demonstrators; others saw us as an organization that trampled the antiwar movement. Some simply figured if we couldn't control our own convention, how could we govern the country? It was a disaster for Humphrey and a disaster for the party. I later told a friend, I didn't leave Chicago, I escaped.

As we entered the fall stretch of the campaign, we were looking for a break that would give us momentum for the final weeks. By this time Hubert had hoped to be pulling even with Nixon, but a poll released in mid-September showed him trailing by something like fifteen points, and he was beginning to wonder what he could possibly do to catch up. Many of our old friends in Minnesota insisted that the war was the key. I went back to Minnesota for a couple of speeches at college campuses to signal that we were getting the message on Vietnam. But even Humphrey's staff was still divided on the question, which was only a reflection of the entire country. A lot of people were saying Humphrey simply had to break with Johnson. They felt that the young people, the demonstrators, had the pulse of the nation and that the country had turned against the war. But another group, including Bill Connell, who was close to Humphrey and was an old friend of mine, were hardliners on Vietnam. They thought the central issue was law and order, and that if Humphrey was going to beat Nixon, if he was going to hold Middle America, he had to look tough.

In the end, Humphrey decided the only way to save the race was to make a dramatic break with Johnson. The campaign bought television time for a major address on Vietnam, and Hubert began working on a text. The speech was scheduled for the last day of September, to be delivered from Salt Lake City. Even then, pulling it off was torture. Humphrey went through draft after draft, getting ideas from all his foreign policy experts, all his speechwriters, all his political advisers, trying to find something that would show he was serious about ending the war without undercutting Johnson and the American negotiators in Paris. When he finally had something he liked, he showed it to me, and I said it was terrific. It called for a halt in U.S. bombing of the North, the core position of McCarthy and Kennedy, with only one precondition—that the Communists honor the demilitarized zone between North and South Vietnam. It was careful, but it contained the peace message that voters wanted to hear.

Humphrey called Johnson, and, of course, Johnson said it wouldn't help. He said it would hurt the party and that he hoped Hubert wouldn't deliver it. But Humphrey, God bless him, gave that speech, and it was exactly what people wanted to hear. It got tremendous coverage in the press and favorable reviews in the days that followed. It opened up his candidacy again. Suddenly, the rallies started drawing bigger crowds. Money started coming in again, and volunteers, too. Humphrey started to hit his stride again. The heckling ended.

Looking back, it's heartbreaking to think how close we came at the end. Humphrey was getting jubilant crowds and great press. The old Humphrey, the machine-gun orator, was back. One pollster said that after that speech Humphrey was picking up 250,000 votes a day. We asked ourselves a hundred times how history might have been different had Humphrey given that speech even a few days earlier. But in the end, it wasn't enough and it was too late. On November 5 Nixon carried 43.4 percent of the popular vote to Humphrey's 42.7 percent, and George Wallace finished with 13.5 percent.

In the years since 1968 I've spent a lot of time thinking about the legacy of Vietnam. From time to time this country goes through a period when, as a people, it changes its mind about something big. I believe that's what we were watching in 1968. The country went into that year supporting the war and came out opposing it. Yet, as a party, we just couldn't manage the break with our past.

It took Democrats years to recover from Vietnam—not just the military debacle, but the erosion of public trust. An entire generation grew up understanding that their government had lied to them; an entire generation held less respect for their leaders and their generals. The war, and

Democrats' division over it, probably elected Nixon—and Nixon only accelerated the corrosion of trust. Finally, the war divided our society in a way it had not been divided in a long time. A lot of Americans were offended by the antiwar protesters and street demonstrations. They vilified their opponents and turned to law-and-order candidates running in Nixon's wake. The national discourse grew more bitter. The constructive, civil dialogue that we had been able to carry on over issues such as Medicare and poverty policy turned angry. After Vietnam, everything was poison and distrust.

Mistaken wars are tragic not only for those who pay the greatest price on the battlefield but also because they crush our hopes for reform and justice. The historian Robert Dallek told Barack Obama, "War kills off great reform movements." The Korean War ended Truman's Fair Deal and Vietnam sabotaged Lyndon Johnson's Great Society.

Vietnam is also a story of recuperation in America. Every president is an antidote for the previous one, and I think the war still exerted an influence eight years later, when Carter and I ran. Voters were disheartened and disgusted by the lack of integrity after Johnson and Nixon, and in Carter they saw an honest leader.

What breaks my heart, however, is that as a nation we failed to learn the lessons of Vietnam. The Pentagon Papers tell us that in 1965 and 1966, when we senators were still getting upbeat briefings in the field, the generals knew better. The White House was hearing doubts that it didn't share with Congress or the public. Rather than coming clean and changing course, the administration buried the facts and got in deeper. Thirty years later we made many of the same mistakes in Iraq and Afghanistan. Where were the skeptical voices asking, Is this war going to be as easy as the generals predict? Are we really fighting terrorists there or are we producing terrorists? Do we understand this region and its history? Americans had deep questions, and the administration was not being straight about the answers, and the public's cynicism eventually grew deeper and deeper. In 2003 General Eric Shinseki, the army chief of staff, told Congress it would take hundreds of thousands of soldiers to pacify Iraq—a forecast that proved correct—and he was denounced by Defense Secretary Donald Rumsfeld. I felt I was dreaming the nightmare of Vietnam all over again.

When a president is not straight with the people on an issue as fundamental as war, it knocks the supports out from under a democracy. Making mistakes is okay. Changing the subject is okay. The people understand that. But lying on the big things is not okay. Pretty soon you are building power for cynics—people who argue against the entire system, argue against elections, argue against a government that is, after all, theirs— and you poison a generation. In the years after Vietnam I found myself quoting what Lincoln said about public sentiment: "With it, everything is possible. Without it, nothing is possible." Once you break that trust, you have broken something that takes a long time to fix.

5

Poverty and Opportunity

O NE MORNING TOWARD the end of 1968, the *Washington Post* published a story about a little boy, Freddie Joiner, who had been run over by a truck while crossing the street on his way home from school. The further I read, the sadder it got. He had a little brother, a toddler, who stayed home during the day while their mother worked. She was a single parent and couldn't afford day care or a babysitter. They were so poor that Freddie would go home on his lunch break, take part of his school lunch to his younger brother, and look after him for half an hour. That's how he was killed—taking lunch home to his little brother.

This happened not far from the Capitol; many of the neighborhoods near Capitol Hill were terribly poor in those days. I could practically see the site of the accident from my office window, and some days I would stand at the window and wonder, How could this happen in America?

I had been in Washington for four years, and for four years we had talked about eliminating poverty and giving people a better chance in life. I was about to join George McGovern's Hunger Committee, which conducted field hearings in communities of terrible deprivation. We visited places where malnutrition was rampant. We talked with teachers who told us children were listless in school because they had nothing to eat. I was struck by the unfairness, but I also thought about the tremendous potential these children represented if we could find a way to give them a fairer start in life.

This was personal for me. In southern Minnesota, when I was growing up, some of my friends came from poor families. One of my best friends was "Guts" Reifer. He was the son of a German immigrant and one of twelve kids. They had nothing. Once I was in their home at dinnertime and I saw that they didn't even have enough chairs for all the kids to sit down at the same time. They would have one huge loaf of bread and some modest main course that they would hand around the table. A lot of hands were reaching. My family didn't have much money, but this was different from anything else I had ever seen.

Guts left school sometime around eighth grade to help his parents. Most of his siblings had to go to work, too, because the family desperately needed the money. They couldn't finish high school, even though some of them were bright, and that always struck me as unfair. I had a lot of friends in the same situation. They were farm kids, and a lot of them were good students, but everyone knew they would never have the chance to go on to college. I was haunted that one of my best friends wasn't going to have much of a life. My family wasn't rich, but I knew I would graduate from high school, attend college, and make something out of my life. It seemed to me that other kids should have that same chance.

For the second time, those words from the Constitution, "take care," came into my Senate work. One of the traits of Minnesota politics in the 1950s and 1960s was steadfast faith in education and children. It wasn't just a DFL issue; progressive Republicans and Democrats competed with each other to invest in public schools and higher education, especially the University of Minnesota. The unspoken sentiment was that this was not *my* state or *your* state, but *our* state. You could not prosper in Minnesota politics unless you demonstrated a commitment to leaving the state a better place; the plainest measure of that commitment was, in the words of Governor Elmer Andersen, a progressive Republican, investment in the institutions that would help Minnesota build its future. A philosophy like that was comfortable, almost automatic, in a stable and homogeneous state such as Minnesota, where generation after generation grew up with the assumption that they would stay there and raise a family. Establishing that sense of common obligation was not so easy on the national stage in a country that, even in the late 1960s, was sprawling, mobile, diverse, and suspicious.

I had been unhappy with my committee assignments early on, and after Bobby Kennedy's death opened a spot on the Labor Committee, I asked if I might have that. The Labor Committee had a broad reach, including issues such as education, health, poverty, and employment. There, I could dig in on the issues I cared about.

When we began the Senate field hearings, I felt I was seeing my childhood friends all over again, only in even more dire circumstances. Edward R. Murrow's great documentary "Harvest of Shame," had come out a few years earlier and had a big influence on us, especially the way we thought about migrant families and low-wage workers. After I was appointed to chair the Senate Subcommittee on Migratory Labor, I took one trip to California at the invitation of César Chávez, who was starting to organize a union for farmworkers. We visited people in their homes and saw appalling conditions—crop dusters flying low and spraying pesticides on fields where migrant workers were picking crops; women giving birth in the fields; children living in homes without plumbing or running water. We made a trip to Brownsville, Texas. I put on khakis and went out in the fields to see how migrant workers sneaked across the border. Apparently I asked too many questions because, before long, some U.S. border guards came along and told us we had to move on. I suppose I didn't look like a U.S. senator. Here again, we saw children living in shocking conditions—no shoes, bad schools, little medical care, one or two meals a day. You thought, This can't be America.

Yet after the 1968 election, I knew the politics of social policy had shifted, and I knew that Democrats had to find a new way to talk about poverty. Nixon had tapped into a deep skepticism about the progressive agenda, and George Wallace, running on an implicitly racist agenda, had won more than 13 percent of the popular vote. The politics of poverty had turned volatile. Marian Wright Edelman, a friend at that time and later the founder of the Children's Defense Fund, wrote, "Support for whatever was labeled black and poor was shrinking, and new ways had to be found to articulate and respond to the continuing problems of poverty and race, ways that appealed to the self-interest as well as the conscience of the American people."

I had also come to see how conservative the Senate could be, now that Lyndon Johnson was gone and Nixon occupied the White House. We could still pass legislation in the authorizing committees to help poor families. But creating a new program didn't go far unless you could get the appropriating committees to fund it, and the appropriating committees were still dominated by older, more conservative senators. Not only did the appropriators control the money, they also found informal ways to control the implementation of new laws. For example, they would write instructions into their committee reports that could, without the benefit of a vote or formal legislation, speed up or slow down the pace of funding. We had managed to pass a bill creating a new public housing program for low-income families, but when I saw the Appropriations Committee report, a line read, This committee expects only modest amounts of housing to be built. The next day I went down on the Senate floor and let them have it. "Mr. Chairman, is this an amendment to our bill? Is this something where the committee intends to consult the Senate as a whole? Or is this a case where one or two members feel they can speak for the Senate as a whole?" I learned, to my dismay, that it was the latter.

At that time, Mike Mansfield and others in the Democratic leadership had the idea of giving every member of our caucus a subcommittee of his or her own, so even if you were a younger senator and weren't going to be handling major legislation, you could begin to make a mark. I went to Harrison Williams of New Jersey, who was chairman of the Labor Committee, and asked if I might have a subcommittee on children and youth. Williams agreed. But Peter Dominick, a senator from Colorado who was the ranking Republican on the committee, didn't want me running off with too much authority. He suspected he wouldn't approve of anything I came up with, and he wanted any legislation I produced to come back to the full committee for review. The compromise we reached was that my subcommittee would have no legislative authority—we couldn't write a bill—we would just conduct hearings and

· 94 ·

make recommendations to the main panel. But this was fine with me because I knew we could lay the groundwork and use hearings to make our case.

As a result of the McGovern Hunger Committee and my travels to field hearings, by 1970 I was starting to change the way I talked about poverty. I realized that I had been relying on guilt as a rhetorical device. I would say, How can America do this? We say we love children, but look at the reality. I soon decided that this approach wasn't working and wasn't right. Most families were working hard and had plenty to do without worrying about solving poverty, and the last thing they needed was someone like me telling them they should feel guilty.

Beneath the choice of language lay a philosophical debate. In the late 1960s a lot of ideas were floating around about the best way to help disadvantaged families. Even Nixon, though he didn't like the War on Poverty, was experimenting with antipoverty policy. He was considering an idea called income maintenance—using the tax code, specifically, a negative income tax, to simply guarantee every family a basic level of income. The idea was to forget all the developmental services for children—preschool, medical clinics, nutrition—and just give every family an allowance and let them figure out how to raise their children. That strategy actually looks quite progressive today, compared to some of the punitive welfare legislation that has since come through Congress. But even though it had a certain elegance, I believed that it was not going to sell with the public. After the backlash against the antipoverty programs of the Great Society, I knew that voters were skeptical of giveaways. You had to be careful or you would be accused of just giving people "free stuff." For a lot of Americans working hard and on a limited income, income support would look as if some people were deciding to work and some were not. Americans believe that if people can work, they should.

Apart from the politics, I thought a simple income-support model—Nixon's idea—was the wrong way to improve children's prospects in life. As I attended committee hearings and heard the evidence, I became convinced that a focused, intensive preschool effort would work better. It would give those I called the "cheated children" the skills and resources to do better in school, and in this way it would pay a dividend to society. As the science increasingly shows today, this would pay off. In other words, shortchanging children was not just immoral, but counterproductive from society's standpoint.

About this time, I began talking about the difference between "custodial child care programs," programs that just kept children on ice, and "developmental programs," which improved children's academic and social skills. I was trying to be on the opportunity side of the politics. Everyone agreed that kids, whatever their circumstances, weren't to blame for their parents' failings. Improving opportunity for children stripped away the overhang of so-called welfare. You could say, We are just helping children and their families do their work.

Fritz Hollings of South Carolina, a liberal guy from a conservative state, supported my approach and had a nice way of framing the issue. When he spoke to meetings of local business leaders, people who were often skeptical of federal early-childhood programs, he would ask for a show of hands by those who had attended nursery school. Typically a large number would raise their hands. Hollings would say, "So did I, and all we are talking about is making it possible for poor children to have the same opportunities we had. It's like kindergarten."

In recent years scholars have developed a whole research literature on early-childhood development and the value of quality preschool. But at that time it was quite new and we didn't have much to go on. Congress had created Head Start, which took a comprehensive approach by giving disadvantaged kids preschool, meals, and medical care. But the closer I looked, the more I became convinced that we were just skimming the surface. We weren't dealing in numbers of families or amounts of money that would make a difference, and we didn't have the comprehensive strategy we needed to provide hope. I also thought a lot of the federal programs were paternalistic, and in some ways insulting. If you are poor, that doesn't make you wrong. Those parents were trying to do a good job and deserved to be treated respectfully. Gradually, a new approach to child poverty began to take shape in my head.

In 1969 I hired Sid Johnson, a brilliant guy who had worked under Secretary Wilbur Cohen at the Department of Health, Education, and Welfare, and Ellen Hoffman, who had covered social issues for the *Washington Post,* to help prepare hearings and draft legislation on child development. We spent most of the next year researching the topic and looking at the various models. In our earlier hearings we had listened to a number of experts in child development, including Edward Zigler of Yale, who was known as the father of Head Start; Robert Coles at Harvard; and Urie Bronfenbrenner at Cornell. They all underscored the idea that disadvantaged children needed a comprehensive package—not just free lunches, but high-quality preschool with trained teachers, health care, even family counseling for their parents. We thought we had a pretty good approach in Head Start—it was showing results and communities understood it— so we took that as our model. By this time I was working occasionally with Marian Wright Edelman. She was married to an old friend of mine, Peter Edelman, who had worked for Bobby Kennedy. She hadn't founded the Children's Defense Fund yet, but she had worked in Head Start and the civil rights movement, and she knew a lot about child development and disadvantaged children. Those two were tenacious and made a tremendous team. They would go around to various federal agencies, proposing new strategies for helping children. Marian would make the moral case about our responsibility to children, and when some agency official would balk, there would be Peter, knowing every detail of federal law and telling them they had all the statutory authority they needed. They were a big help.

We held a series of hearings in my subcommittee, and the next spring I introduced the Comprehensive Child Development Act of 1971. The idea really was to build on Head Start—to establish a national network of locally managed preschool centers that would also offer medical care and nutrition programs to needy families. We aimed to ramp up the funding so that we could reach every family that qualified under the poverty guidelines and some working families above the poverty level. Head Start already had a good track record, but it wasn't anywhere near reaching all the families who qualified. We authorized $2 billion in our bill for 1973,

$4 billion for 1974, then up to $7 billion by 1975. In other words, real money.

Because the focus was on children and the emphasis was on opportunity, I assumed this would not be a controversial bill. The politics of family policy then were not what they are today. We had enthusiastic support from Republicans such as Richard Schweiker of Pennsylvania and Jacob Javits of New York, and for a time we even had the Nixon administration on board. Nixon was trying to win passage of a welfare overhaul called the Family Assistance Plan, which aimed to move poor mothers into the workforce and so projected the need for more child care. Elliot Richardson, Nixon's secretary of health, education, and welfare, conducted several quiet meetings with my staff and Representative John Brademas, the lead sponsor in the House, to find common ground. (I came to respect and like Richardson, even though, as the heir to a distinguished New England family, he came from a background very different from mine. During one of our meetings I noticed that he wouldn't take off his suit jacket and kept tugging at the lapel, as if to hide something. His pen had sprung a leak and was dripping into his shirt pocket. On his way out I pointed to the ink stain and said, "Elliot, now I know why they call you people blue bloods.") In June 1971 Richardson sent me a letter outlining the administration's general support for legislation to consolidate and coordinate federal child-care programs, and Ed Zigler, who then ran the Office of Child Development, was sent to Capitol Hill to testify in support of our work.

By November 1971, without much debate, the bill had passed both houses of Congress with large, bipartisan majorities. I thought, All right, we've cracked this, we've found a new strategy to attack poverty and open up opportunities for children, and we can do it in a way that wins broad public support. All we needed was Nixon's signature.

Yet even then, conservatives were beginning to harbor doubts. Among the moderates, Richard Nathan, who worked in Nixon's Office of Management and Budget, worried that our legislation would undermine support for the main goal of Nixon's welfare reform—that is, increased work among single mothers. Among Washington's conservative intelligentsia, a deeper hostility was taking root. The columnist James J. Kilpatrick was one in a group of ideological conservatives who opposed any expansion of the federal role in family policy. Kilpatrick, a skillful writer, would later describe our bill as a "far-reaching scheme for the essential Sovietization of the American family."

This theme was soon embraced by "family values" conservatives outside the Beltway, who gave us a preview of the culture wars that would dominate left-right politics in the 1980s. Before we knew it, people affiliated with Bob Jones University, the ultraconservative Christian school in South Carolina, and the Christian Crusade, an anticommunist organization in Oklahoma, had picked up the argument and were organizing opposition to our bill.

In early December, back in Minnesota for the holidays, I was paying a visit to Rabbi Bernard Raskas and his wife, Leah, both old friends and influential voices in the Twin Cities ecumenical community. When I walked in the door, Rabbi Raskas said, "You have a phone call. The president just vetoed your bill." I stopped in my tracks and asked him to repeat what he had said. "You just got a phone call. Nixon vetoed your bill." I can't say I was entirely surprised. Despite friendly words from Richardson and HEW, we had always wondered if, in the end, Nixon would support our approach and the money we were seeking. Even so, my heart sank. Months of work were now frustrated, and a rare opportunity was gone. Worse than the veto was the harsh language Nixon used in the veto message. He accused us of "Sovietizing" American youth. He said our bill would take the responsibility of child rearing away from parents. It was plainly designed to scare people, poison the conversation about helping families, and dip into the nation's stew of cultural resentments. Even for Nixon, it was surprising.

Within days social conservatives in Congress picked up on Nixon's veto language and attacked my bill as antifamily. I knew the charge was fraudulent and challenged it whenever I could. In mid-December I found myself on the Senate floor, debating the issue with Senator James Buckley, a New York Republican, who had spoken favorably about Nixon's veto message:

> Mondale: On two occasions, the senator has said this measure threatens to undermine the family. Will he refer to the provision he had in mind?
> Buckley: I refer to section 501(a) of the bill, which establishes the premise of parental inadequacy, which states that most of the nation's children are, in effect, inadequately brought up.
> Mondale: Would the senator read the language to me that says families are inadequate?
> Buckley: It implies that, in many places, families alone are somehow unable to handle their tasks.
> Mondale: Is that the best on which the senator can base his charge that this bill threatens the family?
> Buckley: I certainly do—that and the whole thrust of this legislation and the pressure that we know will be brought to bear to encourage women to put their families into institutions of communal living.
> Mondale: Communal living? What section is that?

In time, we learned the full story behind Nixon's veto. Pat Buchanan, then Nixon's chief speechwriter and a shrewd guy, latched on to the issue. He advised Nixon that if he was going to oppose the legislation, he might as well use the issue to rally cultural conservatives. The other piece of the puzzle was that Nixon had announced his groundbreaking trip to China, which was not popular with his conservative base. I always thought that vetoing our bill, and casting himself as the defender of traditional American values, was his way of mollifying the conservatives and creating a little maneuvering room to make the China trip.

Whether Nixon and Buchanan knew it or not, they had tapped into deep currents in American society. Families were changing, as was the role of women in the economy, and resentment was stirring against the liberal establishment that seemed to threaten traditional values. The abortion rights and antiwar movements had already prompted a backlash among conservative Americans, who saw in them contempt for their values and the nation's institutions. Voters were also growing more skeptical about what they saw as grand social engineering by us in Washington—a feeling that the government was using their money to promote ideas they didn't like. Few observers picked up on those early threads—only a handful of reporters were writing about child and family issues, and political scientists weren't paying much attention. But I believe that episode helped launch the religious right as a political movement and Nixon's veto was one of the triggering events for the culture wars that would consume American politics for the next three decades.

America was undergoing two social revolutions in those years, equally profound and equally influential. One was the civil rights movement, which was highly visible and well understood. The other was the change in women's roles, which was less visible and less well understood. People forget, but the Civil Rights Act of 1964 had contained a ban on gender discrimination in addition to the provisions on race, so before long the American workplace began slowly opening up to women. Women were starting to attend college in greater numbers and to assert some economic independence. By 1971 nearly one in every three mothers of preschool children was in the workforce, a historic shift. As a result, the roles of women, parents, and families were about to undergo a sea change.

A lot of American men were caught off-balance in this transition. We had grown up in institutions dominated by men, and that was reflected in our thinking and even our language. In the household where I grew up, respect for women was never in question; because of my upbringing, the women's movement felt natural to me when it came along. Nonethless, men of my generation often said the wrong thing or got trapped in old thinking. Joan and I spent a lot of time talking about this issue, and she was eloquent. She belonged to a generation of women who had tremendous talent but not a lot of economic or professional opportunities. Joan was accomplished—she had built a considerable reputation as a ceramics artist and cultural advocate. But she saw the imbalance in our society—that women had far fewer options outside the home and far more responsibilities inside it—and she thought that the next generation of women, our daughter's generation, should have a broader range of opportunities. She also saw the advantages our kids had enjoyed—a stable, loving family and economic security—and felt, as I did, that all children deserved the same thing. Joan also helped me think and speak more rigorously on gender issues. The big problem for men of my generation was vocabulary—we thought it was gracious to use such phrases as "lovely lady"—and Joan quickly set me straight on that.

This would prove to be a huge transformation in American society over the next two decades. You could feel the social change building, but you could also feel that people were confused and uneasy about it. I spoke to many audiences about my legislation, about the importance of quality preschool and economic opportunity for women, and the response often was hostile. People would say that these women were taking a man's job, that they didn't know their proper role. Later, when the right wing attacked my bill for Sovietizing American youth, they were really saying that the woman's place is in the home.

Much the same thing happened with the law known as Title IX, a provision of the Education Amendments of 1972 designed to give young women equal footing with men in high school and college athletics. I strongly supported that legislation, yet when we held hearings, we saw how fiercely some people resisted change. Coaches from every corner of the country wrote angry letters accusing us of stealing resources from the boys and predicting the end of collegiate athletics if we prevailed. Billie Jean King, one of the greatest tennis players of all time, testified that her high school coaches encouraged her to practice—as long as she used facilities and equipment the boys weren't using. Nevertheless, that law revolutionized sports in the United States. Over the next three decades, the number of women competing in varsity collegiate athletics grew fivefold, to nearly 170,000, and the number competing in high school sports grew tenfold, to more than 3 million. In 1984, at the Summer Olympics in Los Angeles, American women earned more than one-third of the medals on a U.S. team that dominated the competition, and female athletes such as Mary Lou Retton and Jackie Joyner-Kersee became international stars. By opening doors, we not only changed U.S. Olympic competition, we set a better example in the world. I understand that pockets of resentment remain. But I think the argument is settled among the millions of women—to say nothing of their fathers, brothers, husbands, and children—who saw how Title IX corrected a long injustice and opened new horizons for women in sports, academics, and society itself.

In the early going, the economic pressures on working families were mostly invisible to middle-class Americans. The women's movement hadn't touched them personally, and they could brush it off with demeaning phrases such as "bra burners." People with marginal incomes, working families, felt it first. But by the mid-1970s, middle-class aspirations required two incomes, and soon families found themselves trapped with not enough money and not enough time. Before long, these pressures touched Americans of all incomes. For professional reasons, for stature, or from simple economic need, more and more women wanted a career. They saw what happened in case of a divorce or the death of the "head of the household." Women could see that they would be left holding the bag, and they wanted to have some alternative, some economic security, for themselves and their children.

In time, the country's attitudes toward working women changed. Soon a lot of fathers wanted the best for their daughters. Before long employers joined the club, too. They saw that recruiting and hiring women served their own best interests. It was the same way with the civil rights movement: It really started to click when the business community renounced discrimination and recognized the advantages of attracting minorities into the workforce.

But in 1970 or 1971, most Americans couldn't quite comprehend this revolution. In those days only a brave, unusual woman would speak up about it. If a woman was struggling to get a better job or a fair wage, many people would say, She should be taking care of her children. Before long, people were talking about the "good old days." To them, we looked like arrogant social scientists telling people how to live their lives, moving in on the backward families and saving them from their traditional ways of doing things. Soon evangelical preachers—Jimmy Swaggart, Jerry Falwell, and Pat Robertson—picked up on the resentment and made it a steady theme in their televised sermons. They accused us of being pointy-headed bureaucrats who lacked respect for the values of Middle America and vowed, by God, to take revenge.

I understood why people felt that way. One of the institutions that had worked well for Americans over the years, even in the midst of utter poverty, even in the Depression, was the family. It was the shock absorber, the institution that gave love and confidence. So people of my generation didn't regard child rearing as an issue of money or law. A lot of people felt we didn't need a new government program. They felt we just needed to go back to those better days that were idealized in their memories. In 1974, when we passed my Child Abuse Prevention and Treatment Act—the first federal legislation to address child abuse—we held hearings on family violence. We pointed out that this wasn't a debate over whether parents should spank their children. This was about criminal neglect and violence; the evidence showed abusive parents burning their children with cigarettes and fathers forcing sex on their daughters. Even so, we got mail that seems incredible today—people who said our bill represented a government effort to undermine parental authority and subvert traditional American values.

Underneath this ambivalence toward women and their changing roles was tremendous guilt in American society. People tend to feel guilty about their families in any case. Parents are always asking themselves, Did we give the children enough? Were we fair to them? Should we have stayed home? Parents have always asked these questions. Now the country was going through a massive change in social norms, and the anxiety only deepened. No one knew what the new rules were, what the right balance was—responsibility to children, equity for women, economic opportunities for families. The nation was drowning in family guilt, and we walked right into the middle of it.

It took me some time to recover from Nixon's veto. Sid, Ellen, and I would stay late in the office, discussing the way Nixon had framed the issue and cast liberals as enemies of the family. We spent a lot of time thinking about how we could get the issue back. I was not about to give up on the issue—I just knew we had to be smarter about it.

For my legislation, however, it was back to the drawing board. I wanted to reintroduce the bill in 1972, but I knew we would have to do a better job of fending off the conservative attacks. The first thing we did was to rework the language, which the right-wingers had so effectively used against us. They had used phrases like "substituting government for parents," which had nothing to do with us. Our bill was completely voluntary. It was an effort to give parents more choices—the antithesis of state control over families. But those arguments had aroused suspicion, and we knew we had to come to grips with them or lose a big chunk of Middle America. First, we dropped the word *comprehensive* from the title of the bill. By *comprehensive* we meant the entire package of services a family might need—preschool, medical care, nutrition—but opponents made it sound like Big Brother. We also began to stress the word *voluntary* when we talked about the bill to make it clear that we were trying to help families, not substitute for them. We also added a family tax credit to make it clear that we were trying to support families, not undermine them. We renamed the bill the Child and Family Services Act of 1972.

The second priority was to renew Republican support. Humphrey once told me you get the big things done in the Senate only when you work with the minority, and that had been my experience on the fair-housing legislation. In those days, luckily for me, it wasn't hard to get Republicans on a bill like this. Friends such as Jim Pearson of Kansas and Richard Schweiker of Pennsylvania understood these issues and weren't afraid to work with a Democrat. Sid and Ellen spent hours working with their counterparts on the staffs of my Republican and Democratic colleagues, hammering out language and working up compromises. You worked across party lines to give your bill the best chance. If you got the work done at the staff level, these senators would help you, Republicans or Democrats.

When I introduced the new bill in 1973, we brought in the top academic talent from around the country for a second round of hearings.

Ed Zigler testified again, as did Robert Coles. Coles was a fascinating researcher who became good friends with Joan and me. He had started as an MD and took an interest in the health of migrant children. He went into the field and asked children to make little drawings of their world. He found that, in one way or another, every child felt rootless, lacking in family stability and hope. Then Coles interviewed the children. When listening to this unfiltered information about life in poverty, unless you had a lead heart, you could not help responding. We also called in an economist from Stanford, Henry Levin, who had compiled data on academic achievement by socioeconomic quartiles. He examined how kids performed on high school achievement tests, then checked how many went on to college. He had found, predictably, that kids from the top economic quartile were most likely to go to college. But he also found a lot of kids in the lowest economic quartile who had strong test scores, yet never went on to college. They never got the chance. We used these studies many times to prove the potential among these cheated kids, potential that we thought the country could tap.

In all these proceedings we were very careful with the witnesses. Conducting a Senate hearing is an art. We urged the witnesses to be precise, not go off into family planning or welfare or the other touchy issues that could scare away potential supporters. This was about opportunity for children and strengthening the family. We even called Margaret Mead to testify. In those days, few people in Washington followed this issue, and we couldn't get reporters to cover the hearings. But we figured if we led off with Margaret Mead, that would get some attention. And it did.

Nevertheless, the attack on us actually intensified. In the spring of 1975, when we were making our third attempt with the legislation, an anonymous leaflet started circulating in congressional districts all across the country. Its charges were astonishing: We wanted to transfer parental authority to the government; parents would no longer have the right to discipline their children or pass along their religious beliefs; children would have the right to sue their parents if they were disciplined or raised improperly. The leaflet said the bill "smacks of Communism" and quoted us, falsely, as asserting, "We recognize that not parental, but communal forms of upbringing have superiority over all other forms." We never did figure out who produced the flyer. But it had the desired effect because outraged mail started pouring into congressional offices, and some of my colleagues, Democrats and Republicans, got pretty nervous.

But this time we were ready. The committee staff assembled a document responding to that leaflet. It had everything—the charges, our answers, letters from respected academic experts, and testimonials from religious leaders that our bill was profamily, not antifaith. The Catholic archbishop in St. Paul, John Roach, issued a statement in support of the bill. The Catholic Conference of Bishops gave us their support. So I asked, If this was such an assault on family values and moral life in America, why were the clergy behind us? I think this had some effect because about that time I got a letter from a Republican in Oklahoma, a pretty right-wing guy. It ought to be pinned up on every senator's wall to remind us of another day, another era, in American politics. It said, "I don't think I'm for your bill, but I don't agree with these attacks that are being heaped on it and I think it hurts the Senate." That's what we had in those days, people actually trying to keep politics civil.

After all that work—two years of hearings, drafting legislation, and battling to hold our supporters—we passed the new bill in the Senate in 1973 and again in 1975. But we never got it through the House again. "Family values" politics had already grown too hot. Nixon's critique was starting to poison the conversation, and it was too hard to compete with "Let's go back to the good old days." It would be twenty years before Congress again came to grips with the issues of child poverty and early-childhood development.

Because most journalists in Washington did not cover children's issues at that time, and because Americans were still just coming to understand the changes in the American family, I think the importance of that episode has widely been overlooked. Mainstream America took another decade to confront the issues of working women, and years passed before business and civic leaders got serious about early-childhood development.

In her remarkable book *When Everything Changed*, *New York Times* columnist Gail Collins discusses this anomaly:

American women had shattered the ancient traditions that deprived them of independence and power and the right to have adventures of their own, and had done it so thoroughly that few women under thirty had any real concept that things had ever been different.

The feminist movement of the late twentieth century created a United States in which women ran for president, fought for their country, argued before the Supreme Court, performed heart surgery, directed movies, and flew into space. But it did not resolve the tensions of trying to raise children and hold down a job at the same time.

We tried to ease those tensions for working mothers, while seeking to help the millions of young children who are denied the stimulation and emotional support all children need. We passed that legislation in the Senate three times, and it's an enduring frustration to me that it never became law.

I do think the country's attitudes have changed since that period. Americans have finally understood that increasing numbers of women have to work—are going to work—and realize that instead of decrying that, we ought to figure out how to make it work. That was not the common wisdom when I took on this issue. A lot of people knew these changes were happening in their own lives, but they didn't see it as a social phenomenon, a national phenomenon. Today, if you gave a speech and used some of the same arguments our opponents used against us—that these jobs are needed by men and women should give them up, that we should stop giving school lunches to poor children, that a law against child abuse weakens family authority—an audience would boo you off the platform. And not just the women. The men would boo you, too, because they have wives and daughters who are working and know in their own lives that the world is different. That is a big change in America.

Nevertheless, our national response remains far behind the reality and the need. In 1997 Congress created S-CHIP, the State Children's Health Insurance Program, to extend medical care to more kids. Minnesota,

Florida, Georgia, and other states did some good work with preschool education. Respected economists such as Arthur Rolnick of the Federal Reserve Bank of Minneapolis have made the case that early childhood education is the best investment a society can make. We've made a little progress, but I wish we had made more. In 2000 the Harvard sociologist Theda Skocpol noted that the United States had by far the highest child poverty rates of any developed nation and wrote, "American children have not enjoyed generous help through government. As the authors of the Luxembourg Income Study put it, 'there is much less in the way of public support for both working and nonworking parents in the United Sates than is found in other nations,' and this is what accounts for most of the greater poverty experienced by American children today."

My frustration is that we missed two decades of opportunity and lost a generation of children who grew up in poverty. I don't say my bill would have worked perfectly. It might have cost more or done less than we hoped. But I believe we could have made a big difference in the way life starts for millions of kids, and I think we'd all have felt better about it. It would have given us a generation in which, for the first time, everyone had an equal chance in America. We lost a generation, and it breaks my heart. I hope that the next generation of American leaders will pick up where we left off and find a way to tap the talents and promise of our youngest Americans—while we do a better job of reducing the "tensions of trying to raise children and hold down a job at the same time."

6

The Battle for a
More Responsive Senate

O N THE DAY of Richard Nixon's second inaugural, in January
1973, I was sitting with the other young senators on the West
Front of the Capitol and feeling rather glum. Nixon had crushed
George McGovern in the 1972 election, sweeping aside questions raised
by the Watergate investigation, and seemed to have discovered a formula
for capturing the votes of Middle America. I remember leaning over to
Ted Kennedy and saying, "If he can hold the momentum he's got now, I
don't know how Democrats are ever going to get the White House back."
Four years later, I would be standing in the same spot, ready to be sworn
in as vice president of the United States. The intervening years gave the
nation an extraordinary constitutional drama, turned our politics upside
down, and also worked a profound change on the way I thought about
power in government.

By the spring of 1973 I had become deeply troubled by Nixon and
Watergate. I had watched his first term skeptically, of course, because I
still was certain that Humphrey would have made a better president and
because I found myself opposed to so much of Nixon's agenda. But as his
second term began, I was becoming alarmed by the results of the Watergate investigation. The White House had clearly used federal agencies to
manipulate a presidential election, punish political opponents, and frus-

trate the legitimate inquiries of the Congress and the public. As Nixon's mendacity deepened, I felt American democracy was at risk.

Because Watergate has become part of the received national lore— with heroes, villains, and the comforting moral that crime does not pay— we forget that its outcome was not foreordained and that those two years were very suspenseful. For weeks after Bob Woodward and Carl Bernstein began covering the Watergate burglary, few other news organizations took the story seriously, and the White House tried to wish it away. Nixon gave a series of speeches on the investigation, and though each one was riddled with improbabilities, I thought the American people wanted to give him the benefit of the doubt and felt, deep down, that the president of the United States could not be a felon.

As late as the summer of 1973, I was conferring with Bill Fulbright, my Senate colleague from Arkansas, one morning and I ventured the opinion that Nixon might just survive the scandal. Fulbright said, "I thought so, too, but did you hear that someone told Judge Sirica this morning that there are tapes of all those conversations in the Oval Office?" I was stunned, and I remember thinking, This might be Nixon's smoking gun.

Even so, the investigation took another year to fully unfold. One afternoon in August 1974 I was on the Senate floor when I saw Barry Goldwater. By this time, a number of prominent Republicans, including Howard Baker and my friend Jim Pearson of Kansas, recognized that Watergate was real trouble and had distanced themselves from Nixon. I went over and asked Goldwater what he thought. "We're going down to the White House today," he said. "We're going to tell him he has to go."

On August 9, the day of Nixon's resignation, I was in the Senate cloakroom with several of my colleagues. We gathered around a television set and watched Nixon's resignation—that strange speech and his references to his mother. I thought that after all the months of suspense and revelations I might feel a sense of victory, or at least vindication. But instead I felt let down and sad. You hate to see anyone destroyed so completely, yet we all knew we had to end it.

But that evening, as I drove home to our house in Cleveland Park in D.C., I felt something else—a tremendous sense of relief that the system had worked. We had addressed a great national crisis, and no one could say it was partisan: Democrats and Republicans had worked together to get to the bottom of Nixon's crimes. Congress had stood up to the White House and exposed an abuse of power. The courts, too, had upheld their place in the constitutional system of checks and balances—Judge Sirica, a Republican appointee, had ruled against Nixon, and the Supreme Court, which was full of Nixon appointees, nonetheless sided with Congress. The American people saw through the fog that Nixon had tried to spin around the White House and knew that their president had behaved in ways that were unacceptable.

I left that experience with a new respect for the balance of powers created by the nation's founders, but also a new sense of responsibility for the branch of government in which I served.

By the beginning of 1975, as the Ninety-fourth Congress convened, I had begun to feel that the Senate was my home. I liked the drama of a committee hearing and the collegial atmosphere of the historic Senate chamber. Colleagues such as Gaylord Nelson, Ted Kennedy, and Ed Muskie had become good friends. Senators such as Mike Mansfield had become wonderful teachers. (Mansfield, who was gentlemanly but stern, had taught me more than one lesson about Senate procedure. During a vote on aircraft carriers for the Nixon administration in 1971, I challenged some of my elders, including John Stennis of Mississippi and John Pastore of Rhode Island. Both had shipyards in their states and both thought the navy needed more aircraft carriers than I thought it did. I stood my ground during the floor debate—rather effectively, I thought—before losing. As we walked off the floor, Mansfield took me by the arm and said, "C-plus.")

But perhaps the most striking lesson I learned about the Senate was the power of the individual. By design and tradition, the body grants great deference to its members. A single senator can put a "hold" on legislation, an informal practice that temporarily keeps a bill off the Senate floor. A single senator can block the nomination of a federal judge over differences of judicial philosophy—or for no reason at all. A senator who really masters the parliamentary rules can, during an important floor vote, tie the place in knots with procedural maneuvers and delaying tactics. And then there is the filibuster: Senate rules grant an individual member, once recognized to speak, almost unlimited latitude to stay on the floor and talk an issue to death.

In the 1970s, the master of all these tactics was Senator James Allen of Alabama. Jim Allen had been a state senator, then lieutenant governor under George Wallace. Though a Democrat, he was probably the most conservative member of the Senate. Allen was also a guy who had spent his life studying the rules. He had come to the Senate in 1969 and, unlike most senators, had mastered the fine points of procedure. Point of order? Substitute amendment? Quorum call? He knew them all—every way you could use the rules of procedure to frustrate your rivals and tie the Senate in a snarl.

As a result, Jim Allen had made himself *the* guy among the conservative Southerners. By this time the Southern segregationists had lost the major battles over civil rights, but Allen still stood for a small reactionary bloc that continued to fight rearguard actions against almost all social justice legislation. We had bipartisan support for an array of progressive projects—consumer protection, legal services, subsidized housing, child and family services—but he opposed them, usually with great skill and tenacity.

I had arrived in the Senate a decade earlier impatient to reform these tactics. I knew that the Southerners had used filibusters to frustrate Humphrey on one civil rights bill after another. Strom Thurmond held the Senate record at that time, a filibuster against the 1957 Civil Rights Act during which he spoke continuously for more than twenty-four hours while his staff brought him sandwiches and glasses of orange juice. For me the tactic had come to symbolize the reactionary politics that were binding the country to its worst traditions.

Until the early part of the twentieth century, filibusters were rare and the Senate had no formal way to end them. Then, in 1917, recognizing that endless talk was paralyzing the nation's response to German aggression in World War I, the Senate adopted Standing Rule 22. It allowed the body to invoke "cloture" to close off debate, but it set a high standard:

It required a two-thirds supermajority of senators present and voting—generally sixty-seven votes. This meant that a disciplined minority of senators—thirty-four or fewer—could keep debate going indefinitely and control the Senate in defiance of the majority. The *Congressional Record* showed the results: In the years since 1917 the Senate had taken 102 votes to invoke cloture, or about 2 per year, and only 23 had succeeded.

I felt the filibuster was allowing an embittered minority to hold the country back from correcting long-standing injustices, and at first I supported a radical reform—cloture with fifty-one votes. In time, however, I became more sympathetic to the Senate traditions of deliberation and debate. I was in the progressive wing of the Senate, and we had used filibusters periodically to stop some of the excesses of the Nixon administration and to kill ill-considered antibusing legislation when the country was in a panicky backlash against school integration.

Beyond these specific issues, I had gained a deeper respect for the Senate's tradition of deliberation and its role in the constitutional system of checks and balances. The Watergate scandal had deepened my appreciation for Senate procedure—not the filibuster per se, but the Senate's ability to slow things down, to demand explanations, to ventilate an issue and give complex issues careful scrutiny. As the war in Vietnam dragged on and as Nixon's abuses of federal agencies came to light, his administration had no interest in explaining itself to Congress, and by the time the Watergate episode concluded, we saw that the unrestrained exercise of executive power had produced a dangerous moment in American history. It was a glimpse of what our founders feared—an imperial government that would place itself beyond the law and the reach of the American people unless a countervailing force in another branch of government could call the president to account. The Senate is just such a force.

The founders did not base our government on goodwill and benevolent human nature, although they surely hoped for that. The model they gave us is based on a distribution of authority among the branches of government so that each must account to the other and power is shared. Even today you can read the Federalist Papers—the magnificent essays by the framers of the Constitution—and see that they knew exactly what they were doing.

I had also come to see how unusual the Senate is among the world's legislative bodies. No other institution is like it. The House of Representatives, for example, is designed for speed. If you hold the majority, you get your way. The Rules Committee decides what legislation will come to the floor and under what conditions: how many hours of debate, how many amendments (if any) can be offered, how quickly the vote must be concluded. It's like a freight train coming down the track; you can't possibly slow it down. A president is always in a hurry, and if his or her party also controls the House, they can pass things quickly, no matter how bad.

The Senate can set a more deliberate pace and demand that an administration account for itself. Only the Senate permits extended debate. Only the Senate can stop a doctrinaire president from appointing extremists to lifetime positions on the federal bench. One courageous senator alone can do this, and at times in our history this proved crucial—when the national mood was such that Congress was ready to legalize torture, for example, or write a loyalty oath into law. The Senate, Washington supposedly told Jefferson, is the saucer where the hot ideas of the House are poured to cool off.

I believe it was the Senate that brought the Vietnam War to an end, by finally forcing Lyndon Johnson and then Richard Nixon to explain what was happening on the ground. I believe the Senate finally brought Nixon to account on Watergate, finally investigating and exposing how he had abused presidential power. Time and again the Senate has saved the country from extremist nominees to the federal bench—extremists who appeal to a president at one political moment but would then be in a position to undercut justice for a lifetime. The Senate finally pulled back the curtain on intelligence abuses at the CIA and the FBI—abuses that threatened our constitutional system of checks and balances.

The Senate has also performed a grand and largely unappreciated role as the nation's mediator. It demanded regional compromises at crucial junctures in American history when the country was on the verge of splitting apart. Because one senator can insist on being heard, and because sparsely populated states such as North Dakota and Vermont have equal weight with big states such as California and New York, the Senate demands that the majority respect the minority. When Congress created a new tariff system in 1816 to nurture the young manufacturing sector of New England, senators from the East pledged some of the resulting tariff revenue for roads and canals to serve farmers in the Midwest because they understood that every region of the country had to gain from industrialization. When we passed new trade legislation in 1974, opening foreign markets to computers and electronics from America's high-tech states, we built in provisions so that a president could protect the rust-belt states from a flood of manufacturing imports. Because the Senate represents states, not just people, it creates the conditions for regional and national compromise.

My friend Tom Eagleton, a great senator, was eloquent on this point, arguing that the Senate guided America through its most difficult transitions—the closing of the frontier, the evolution from an agrarian society to an industrial nation. It has carried us through wars, droughts, depressions, McCarthyism—and only once, during the Civil War, was the nation unable to resolve its differences amicably. Eagleton wrote, "Government's life force, what makes it work and endure, is our capacity to accommodate differences and to find a way, beyond parochial, partisan and ideological concerns, to live together in a free nation. We remember the poet Yeats' very gloomy assessment: 'Things fall apart; the center cannot hold.' Well, in the United States, with the tragic exception of the Civil War, the center has held. It has held without religious or racial homogeneity. It has held without the reassuring and unifying symbol of a King or Queen. It has held without the built-in assurances provided by a parliamentary system." The Senate, time and again, forced us to confront our differences and find a compromise that would let the nation endure.

I had been in Washington more than a decade, and I had also come to take a larger view of the role of a senator. When you serve in the chamber where Daniel Webster and Henry Clay served, you can't help but be sobered by the responsibility. You are no longer just a young politician from Elmore, or a Democrat from Minnesota, you are a trustee of a nation's traditions, the steward of its past and its future.

This led me to decisions that sometimes surprised my friends, and sometimes surprised me. In 1974, confronting the troubling inflation that followed Lyndon Johnson's guns-and-butter budgets, the Senate established a new committee to oversee federal spending, the Budget Committee, and I asked for a seat on it. We had suffered through a dangerous price spiral toward the end of the Vietnam War, then we had seen Richard Nixon impounding the budgets of any program that he didn't like. A small group of us said, Someone has to get responsible. Someone must take the larger view of federal spending. We were not big taxers, but we felt we had to be honest with voters: If you're going to promise better education or better roads, you must show how you will pay for them. In 1974 we passed the Congressional Budget Act, which created the House and Senate Budget Committees and the Congressional Budget Office, bringing new rigor to the way Congress raises revenue and spends money.

In passing the Congressional Budget Act we understood that Congress's budget process needed more transparency and discipline. We understood, as liberals, that government *can* spend too much, and that getting the federal deficit under control would be infinitely harder without an overall budgeting framework. These tools have not always saved Congress from imprudent budgets, but they brought tremendous new transparency and accountability to its decisions.

I also served on the Senate Finance Committee, where I began to take a greater interest in foreign trade. The topic was new to me because I had spent most of my time to that point on domestic issues. But a new round of world trade talks had commenced in Tokyo in 1973, and upon succeeding Nixon, President Gerald Ford had asked Congress for authority to negotiate market-opening deals on behalf of the United States. In the Senate, that legislation would have to originate in the Finance Committee, and the Trade Reform Act of 1974 soon became our preoccupation.

Imports hadn't emerged yet as a major threat to American workers, as they would a decade later, but my friends in the labor movement and in the Farmers Union were wary of international trade, especially the way that countries in the European Union subsidized their industries and exports. On the other hand, Minnesota was beginning to emerge as a high-technology state with companies such as Control Data, the early computer manufacturer, and I thought the entire country had much to gain from access to export markets. We were on the cusp of an era when America's industrial preeminence would be challenged, and I was coming around to the view that vigorous competition in world markets would make our economy stronger, not weaker. Then, too, a number of us worried that the global trading regime established after World War II, which had brought some stability to international relations, was under threat as countries withdrew into protectionism. Finally, our committee chairman, Russell Long, made a convincing case that granting trade privileges to poorer countries could be an important tool to build their economies and reduce poverty. It's now mostly forgotten, but a group of like-minded Democrats and Republicans crafted a bill that gave the president authority to negotiate new trade deals while giving the administration tools to make sure our trading partners acted fairly. It wasn't the sort of issue that I had expected to tackle when I went to Washington, or the sort of priority that my friends expected of me, but I began to see that it was an important contribution to America's economic competitiveness and a stable world economy.

For all these reasons, after a few years I had gained a deeper appreciation for the Senate's role as a sober, deliberate body, an institution that could stand back from the pressures of the moment and consider the country's long-term interests.

By late 1974, however, I came to believe that the power of deliberation was being abused by Jim Allen and his allies. While the filibuster had been used in the 1960s mainly to block civil rights legislation, Allen and his group were now using it to bottle up anything they didn't like. We had good legislation to create a federal consumer protection agency—they filibustered it. We were trying to create what is now the Equal Employment Opportunity Commission—they filibustered it. An international genocide treaty, the Legal Services Corporation, electoral college reform—Allen's crowd blocked all of it. Even when Allen couldn't kill a bill outright, he could force other senators into the sort of debilitating compromises that are required when you are trying to round up the last vote or two to invoke cloture. He had developed a way of blocking anything he didn't want, of trumping the majority and paralyzing the country.

Allen was not unlikable. He and I got along well. But he was tireless, he was a parliamentary magician, and his reputation had reached the point where other senators were afraid of him. He had used his procedural mastery to humiliate them on the Senate floor, and they were afraid to go toe-to-toe with him. Even the leadership was intimidated because he didn't care what they thought of him.

Standing with him were a small bloc of Allen-like senators—enough to sustain a filibuster time and again. Some were Southerners still trying to defend their old way of life. Others came from the small-population states of the West and Midwest, who felt the filibuster enhanced their power in contrast to the House, where the big states had the votes. There is this idea that Wyoming is still equal to New York, or should be, and that's pretty powerful in the mind of a senator who feels he or she is upholding constitutional principles.

Jim Allen had also perfected what I called the postcloture filibuster. That is, even when we'd rounded up enough votes to end debate, he would still carry on with quorum calls and points of order and so many other delaying tactics that your head would spin. Soon Allen and his group didn't have to actually conduct a filibuster, only threaten one, and they could get the leadership to back down. All it took was a grunt from Jim Allen or John Stennis, and you knew: We're not going to get this done.

After a year or so of watching this, I believed that a substantial number of my colleagues, on both sides of the aisle, agreed with me. The rules were being abused. The Senate was unable to work its will on anything Jim Allen didn't want, and it was a crisis. We needed to change the Senate rules.

But here is the paradox we faced: How could we change the rules of the filibuster when our opponents would simply filibuster any effort to make a change? If they could muster thirty-four votes to block a consumer bill or Legal Services, and they always did, they would certainly round up enough votes to block filibuster reform and retain their power.

That's when I started to talking to my colleague Jim Pearson. Pearson was a nice guy, a farmer and lawyer from Kansas, and a smart senator. He was a Republican, but the old kind—we agreed on practically everything, from civil rights to budget reform. I knew he had the courage to take on Allen's crowd, and I knew that making this a bipartisan enterprise was the only way we might succeed.

Pearson and I had participated in two previous attempts at filibuster reform, in 1969 and 1971. On both occasions, reform proposals had attracted more than fifty votes in the Senate, but not the two-thirds supermajority necessary to halt a filibuster. So we felt we had substantial support, but we knew we needed a new strategy to circumvent Jim Allen.

Reviewing the two previous attempts and reading Senate history, we came up with a plan. In our reading of the Constitution, Article I gives the Senate, at least at the start of each new session, the right to establish its own rules of procedure. Article I, Section Five, states, "Each House may determine the Rules of its Proceedings, punish its members for disorderly Behavior, and, with the Concurrence of two thirds, expel a Member."

This question had been debated periodically over the years, and it wasn't clear if the majority accepted our reading. Some traditionalists argued that, since only one-third of senators are up for election at a time, the Senate is a continuing body with continuing rules. But that line of thinking, we argued, implied that rules adopted in 1875 would still bind all of us a century later, no matter how much the Senate and the nation had changed. We thought we could win that argument. Since Rule 22 was one of the rules established by our predecessors, we thought the Constitution gave us the right to change it at the start of a new session of Congress.

And so on January 14, 1975, Pearson and I introduced Senate Resolution 4, which would change the Senate's standing rules on cloture. We didn't propose reducing the threshold all the way to fifty-one votes; I didn't like the idea, and we knew that would never prevail with our colleagues. Instead, we proposed reducing the threshold from two-thirds to three-fifths—that is, from sixty-seven votes to sixty, if all senators were present. It meant that when a minority wanted to sustain a filibuster, they would have to muster forty-one votes instead of just thirty-four. It's a small shift, but in the Senate, seven votes make a big difference.

When we opened this debate, no one thought we would win. We thought about fifty of us believed change was overdue. But a significant bloc of older senators, moderate but cautious, were quite skeptical of our effort. I'm sure they thought we were being a little uppity, that rules changes were the business of the old whales, not us little minnows. And then the hard core, twenty-five or thirty senators, liked the rule the way it was—and the way it was being abused. A lot of the old guard were angry about our proposal because minority control was the basis of their power.

On the morning we offered our resolution, a funny thing happened. Pearson went first and introduced it, then I gave the second speech. When I finished and looked up, Jim was gone from the Senate floor. I stood there thinking, Where did he go? In about two hours he turned up again and came over to me. "I made my opening remarks," he said, "and suddenly I realized I wasn't sure I was ready to answer the first question they were going to throw at me." He had got cold feet and left the Senate floor.

But we were prepared. We had a gifted staff to prepare the amendments, research the parliamentary issues, and guide us on the rules. A young attorney had just joined my staff, Robert Barnett, a genius who had clerked at the Supreme Court and later became one of Washington's most prominent lawyers. He came in completely green on the Senate as an institution, but he dug in on the procedural issues and within a month he knew as much as the Senate parliamentarian. We shaped our resolution carefully, we alerted the leadership about our plans, and we had a series of strategy meetings to anticipate the kind of parliamentary traps we might encounter. We also rounded up a substantial bipartisan team of younger senators, including Pat Leahy of Vermont, Alan Cranston of California, Gary Hart of Colorado, Mac Mathias of Maryland, Robert Stafford of Vermont, and Jacob Javits of New York, so that we would never leave Jim Allen alone on the floor. The key was to load up the Senate's "amendment tree"—the menu of pending business—so fully that Allen would not have an opening to introduce any diversionary measures of his own. We knew that if we left him alone for a minute, he would find a way to take control of the chamber and hijack the debate.

A few days after we offered Resolution 4, Allen came down to the Senate floor with a preview of the counterattack. He argued that the Senate had a right to debate our resolution once it became the business of the day and that, since standing rules required a two-thirds majority to end debate, he should be able to debate it until we mustered a two-thirds majority to stop him. In other words, he planned to filibuster. He also made the constitutional argument that the Senate is a continuing body, so its rules, too, should continue from one session to the next.

Allen had an elegant, courtly style—he always referred to himself as "the senator from Alabama"—and he was masterful, as shown in this excerpt from his floor remarks on January 30:

> Mr. President, I have been somewhat intrigued at some of the statements that have been made by those who are supporting this change in the Senate rules, both as to comments on precedents that have been set and pretty liberal quotations from the Constitution. I believe the distinguished senator from Kansas spoke of the Constitution's saying that by a majority vote, the Senate could amend its rules. I believe that the distinguished senator from Minnesota and the distinguished senator from New York spoke of the Constitution's providing that at the beginning of a new Congress, a new session, a different rule applied in this regard.
>
> Let us refer to the Constitution itself to see just what it does say. I believe that would be the highest and best evidence of what the Constitution says.
>
> Article One, Section Five, Subsection Two: "Each House may determine the Rules of its Proceedings."
>
> That does not seem to indicate to the senator from Alabama that a different situation exists every two years, at two-year intervals, in the continuing Senate.

For four weeks our group and Allen's bloc engaged in preliminary skir-mishes, circling each other like wrestlers in the ring, each of us trying to let the Senate conduct other business without allowing our opponent to gain a procedural advantage on Rule 22.

Then, on Thursday, February 20, the battle was joined in earnest. Pearson and I secured time on the Senate floor and argued in a series of long speeches that the Constitution gives the Senate the power to change its own rules, by a simple majority, at the start of a new session.

By prearrangement, Mike Mansfield took the floor next to challenge our premise, arguing that standing rules of the Senate do carry over from one session to the next. Essentially, he was arguing Allen's position. Next, he offered a point of order that a two-thirds majority should be required to halt a filibuster if Allen started one. This was a crucial tactic: A point of order can be rejected by the Senate's presiding officer; then the whole Senate, by a simple majority vote, can sustain the presiding officer's rul-ing. If we could table Mansfield's point of order with fifty-one votes, we would in effect vitiate the two-thirds requirement.

Vice President Nelson Rockefeller, in his capacity as president of the Senate, was presiding that day. We had conducted some brief consulta-tions with Rockefeller's staff during our preparatory work, but we couldn't predict if he would be presiding when the crucial day came, and we simply didn't know how he would rule. It was the first of many tense moments. Rockefeller asked for order, picked up the gavel—and sided with us, rejecting Mansfield's point of order. Allen's group roared, but Rockefeller banged the gavel again. His decision was appealed, and the appeal was voted down, fifty-one to forty-two. For the first time in its history, the Senate had voted that Senate rules could be changed by majority vote.

For a moment we thought we had won. But we had been careless, and we paid for it.

Our resolution had been drafted in two parts. The first simply called on the Senate to begin debating our rules change. The second asserted that the Constitution gives the Senate the right to change its own rules. But Allen immediately noticed a flaw: A resolution that does not contain a constitutional question can be debated—that is, filibustered—and he asked Rockefeller to divide our resolution into two parts so that he could debate part one. Rockefeller consulted the Senate parliamentarian, and although the parliamentarian had told our staff that he would not advise the chair to do so, Rockefeller assented to Allen's request. To groans from our side, Rockefeller divided the resolution into two parts and turned the floor over to Allen. Allen, who never missed an opportunity to gloat, stood up and said, "The senator from Alabama would like to advise all senators who do not want to hear a further discourse on this motion that they can leave the chamber." His filibuster was under way, and we walked off the floor in dismay.

On Monday, February 24, we resumed. Allen had won the right to debate our motion, and we knew he would propose that it be debated under the existing Rule 22. If he won that motion, we knew he had the votes to block cloture and that he would be able to talk us to death.

But we had spent the weekend poring over the Senate rules and drafting a new strategy. It hinged on our side being prepared to shut Allen down immediately when he asked to be recognized, and on the presiding officer recognizing us before Allen got control of the floor. Both sides came spoiling for a fight, and that's exactly what ensued. Here's the opening of the debate from the *Congressional Record*:

> Mr. Allen: Mr. President, I move that the Senate proceed to the consideration of S. Res. 4. And I further move that, the "beginning" of the 94th Congress having now ended, and no constitutional question now existing, if in fact one ever existed, debate on this motion may continue until brought to an end as provided by the provisions of Senate Rule XXII.
>
> Mr. Mondale: Mr. President—
>
> Mr. Allen: Mr. President, the Chair recognized the Senator from Alabama.
>
> Mr. Mondale: Mr. President, I have the floor in my own right.
>
> Mr. Allen: The Chair recognized the Senator from Alabama.
>
> The Presiding Officer: The Senator from Minnesota has been recognized in his own right.

Mr. Allen: I understood the chair recognized the Senator from
Alabama.

Mr. Mondale: May we have order, Mr. President?

The Presiding Officer: The Senate will be in order.

Mr. Mondale: Mr. President, I renew my motion. Under article
I, section 5 of the U.S. Constitution, I move that debate
upon the pending motion, to proceed to the consideration of
Senate Resolution 4, be brought to a close by the Chair—
by immediately putting this motion to end debate, without
debate and with no intervening motions and without amendments, to the Senate for an immediate vote; and, upon the
adoption thereof, by a majority of those Senators present and
voting, a quorum being present, the Chair shall immediately
thereafter put to the Senate, under article I, section 5 of the
U.S. Constitution, without further debate, the question on
the adoption of the pending motion to proceed to the consideration of Senate Resolution 4 for an immediate vote.

Behind the flurry of words the choice was plain. Allen was demanding that this debate be conducted under Rule 22, so that we would need
a two-thirds majority to silence him. I was asking that the presiding officer—Senator Bill Hathaway of Maine, at that point—bring debate to a
close and order a simple vote on our resolution. It all hinged on a favorable ruling from Hathaway.

The test, once again, would be a motion by Mike Mansfield that my
proposal was not in order. If Hathaway let us table Mansfield's point of
order and a majority of senators upheld his ruling, we knew we would gain
the advantage. We thought our chances were good. So did Allen, because
immediately a donnybrook broke out.

Mr. Mansfield: Mr. President, I make a point of order that the
motion by the Senator from Minnesota is not in order.

Mr. Mondale: Mr. President, I move to lay that point of order on
the table, and I ask for the yeas and nays.

[Several Senators address the chair.]

Mr. Mondale: I ask for the yeas and nays, Mr. President.

The Presiding Officer: Is there a sufficient second? There is a sufficient second.

[The yeas and nays were ordered.]

Mr. Allen: Mr. President, I raise the point of order that the whole resolution is out of order, which would supplant the point of order and the motion to lay on the table.

The Presiding Officer: The chair states that the proceeding is in order and the point of order is not sustained.

Mr. Allen: That the resolution is in order?

The Presiding Officer: That the proceeding is in order. That the motion to table is in order.

Mr. Mondale: Regular order, Mr. President.

The Presiding Officer: The question is on agreeing to the motion to lay on the table the point of order of the Senator from Montana. The clerk will call the roll.

Mr. Allen: Mr. President, I suggest the absence of a quorum.

[A quorum was confirmed.]

Mr. Allen: Mr. President, point of order.

The Presiding Officer: The Senator will state it.

Mr. Allen: Mr. President—

Mr. Mondale: May we have order, Mr. President.

Mr. Allen: I must express my disappointment—

Mr. Javits: Mr. President, we cannot hear anything.

The Presiding Officer: The Senator from Alabama will suspend.

Mr. Allen: Mr. President—

The Presiding Officer: The Senate will be in order. The Senator from Alabama will not proceed until the Senate is in order.

Mr. Allen: I must, Mr. President—I must express my disappointment with the fact that the Presiding Officer, on the Senator from Alabama having risen and immediately asking for recognition, failed to recognize the Senator from Alabama. I do,

Mr. President, raise the point of order that the entire motion is out of order.

Mr. Harry F. Byrd Jr.: I move to table the motion just made.

The Presiding Officer: The chair already ruled the point of order raised by the Senator from Alabama is not well taken.

Mr. Allen: I appeal the ruling of the chair.

Mr. Mondale: Mr. President, the yeas and nays.

Mr. Javits: Mr. President—

Mr. Mondale: Mr. President, I move to table that point of order.

Mr. Allen: I call for the yeas and nays.

The Presiding Officer: The Senator from Minnesota moves to table the appeal.

Mr. Mondale: I ask for the yeas and nays.

Mr. Allen: I suggest the absence of a quorum.

The Presiding Officer: The clerk will call the roll to establish a quorum.

Mr. Allen: Mr. President, I move that we recess for one hour.

Mr. Mondale: Mr. President, I object.

Mr. Mansfield: Mr. President, we do not know what is going on. Will all Senators be told to take their seats so we can at least hear?

So unfolded the most chaotic day I have ever seen on the Senate floor. Before it was over, we would go through five separate quorum calls—one of Allen's favorite delaying tactics because each one required every member of the Senate to leave his office and come down to the Senate floor—and eight time-consuming roll-call votes, a marathon. The procedural exchanges grew so dense that at one point we were voting on the following: a motion to table a motion to reconsider a vote to table an appeal of a ruling that a point of order was not in order against a motion to table another point of order against a motion to bring to a vote the motion to call up the resolution.

As the day wore on, however, Allen gradually began losing ground. By midafternoon, Rockefeller had stepped back into the presiding officer's chair. Allen quickly made a new motion for the Senate to recess. Rockefeller gaveled him down, and shouting began again. After several attempts to restore order, we voted on Allen's motion to recess. It was rejected. After more motions and confusion, we voted on Allen's appeal of Rockefeller's ruling. It was rejected. One by one we cleared away the underbrush that Allen kept throwing in our path and moved closer to a real vote.

By the time we adjourned that night the Senate was exhausted, and so were we. But for the second time in a week, our colleagues had adopted our basic premise: that the Senate could change its own rules—including Rule 22—by a simple majority vote.

More important, I could feel the emotional tide of the Senate beginning to shift. Senators who had come to think of Allen as a bully were finally seeing their chance to silence him. Those who had admired him for his tenacity and floor skills were beginning to find the tactics tedious, even embarrassing. Most important, Mike Mansfield was growing impatient. He had important business to move through the Senate: a rescue bill for the Penn Central railroad, which was on the brink of failure, and economic stimulus bills proposed by the Ford administration. He had started out skeptical of our reforms and a defender of Senate tradition, but now he saw something else—that he was losing control of his own chamber. In addition, Mansfield had seen the Senate vote twice, by solid margins, to support the theory that it could change its own rules by majority vote.

A day or two after the marathon of February 24, Mansfield called me over to his office in the Capitol. He had been talking with Robert Byrd, his majority whip and a master of Senate tradition in his own right, and Russell Long of Louisiana, chairman of the Finance Committee and one of the most powerful members of the Senate. They were traditionalists, all three of them—senators who feared rule by a simple majority and revered the Senate's tradition of deliberation and minority rights. But I think they were also getting nervous. They could see the tide turning toward reform, and they were looking into the abyss—a move for cloture by simple majority. This frightened them. But they were also sick and tired of Jim Allen and the way he had hijacked the Senate and caused so much frustration. Mansfield was a great strategic thinker, aware of his historical obligations. He saw that the Senate was on the verge of fracture, and he wanted something that would unify the body again. Meeting in Mansfield's office, they had drafted a compromise: Instead of lowering the cloture threshold to three-fifths of senators present and voting, as we proposed, they would place it at three-fifths of the constitutional membership, that is, of all one hundred senators. This meant that the Senate would always need sixty votes for cloture; under our resolution, the number needed for cloture might be as low as fifty-four or fifty-five if several members were absent. They were also badly rattled by the assault we had mounted on the tradition of the Senate in changing its standing rules. The second part of their compromise held that cloture on a *rules change* would still require a two-thirds majority.

I thanked Mansfield and told him I needed to talk it over with Jim Pearson, but as I walked back to my office, I could think of no good reason to reject the compromise. A sixty-vote cloture threshold was a big victory. It would in some ways make it easier to round up votes for cloture: You could tell a colleague that you had, say, fifty-eight votes and absolutely needed his or her vote to get to sixty. Under current rules, the actual threshold was unknown until you saw how many senators had showed up to vote on a given day, and it became harder to collect votes. I also knew that if I spurned the leadership, I might lose everything. I knew that with the support of Mansfield and the Republican leadership, and with Byrd and Long—respected Southerners—we would carry the day.

Early the next week Mansfield circulated the basics of the compromise, and we prepared for what we hoped would be the final round of battle. We knew we had more than fifty votes for our rules change, but we still weren't sure we had the sixty-seven votes to stop Allen if he tried to filibuster the Mansfield compromise.

On Wednesday, March 5, Mansfield introduced his compromise and called for cloture. This was crucial. He wasn't asking senators to vote on the resolution. He was merely asking if they wanted to end this marathon debate and proceed to a vote. When the roll was called, his motion carried the day, 73 to 21. Mansfield then moved to make the compromise the next order of business. That motion passed 69 to 26.

Then a curious thing happened, something I'll never forget. I got a signal from Mansfield to go into the Democratic cloakroom. Allen was there, with Mansfield and one or two of our staff. Allen looked like a broken man. He was on the verge of physical collapse and his face was ashen. But it wasn't just exhaustion. He knew he was losing the procedural battle, something new to him, and worse, that he was losing stature among his allies. Allen feared that they might abandon him. He was, in a word, asking us for mercy. He was pleading with Mansfield to give him a way out of his quandary, to craft a deal that might leave him the appearance of winning. I thought he was actually on the verge of tears. I shrugged my shoulders, said I thought the sense of the Senate was clear, and gave Mansfield a look. He turned to Allen and said, No. It's over.

On Friday, March 7, with cloture invoked and our resolution the pending order of business, we moved to the final votes. Bob Byrd sat in the presiding chair. He called the Senate to order at eight thirty—three and a half hours earlier than normal—and vowed to keep us there until Senate Resolution 4 was finished. Mansfield opened the proceedings with a stern talk, concluding, "We cannot allow a member or a small group of members to grab the Senate by the throat and hold it there."

Yet Jim Allen could not go down without one more fight, and the result was one of the saddest spectacles I had ever seen in the chamber. In the Senate, when you ask for a roll call vote, the presiding officer will ask if there is a "sufficient second," that is, a sufficient number of colleagues who support your request. The rules say 5 percent of members present, and it's almost a formality. But on that day, as Allen began asking for roll call votes and other time-consuming formalities, the seconds began drying up. Allen would ask for a quorum call. No hands would go up. He would make a point of order and ask for a vote. No seconds. He would challenge the reading of yesterday's Senate prayer. He would propose a recess. He could not get a second. A lot of people were on the Senate floor waiting to vote and watching the proceedings. A lot of them were friends of Jim Allen's and were reluctant to embarrass him. But he would not relent and would not go away, and in the end they just shut him down. Not one senator would second his motions. It was the strangest moment. When you lack a second in your request for a roll call vote, the motion is dispatched with a voice vote and it happens fast. That afternoon we voted down eighteen Jim Allen amendments in twenty minutes. I doubt the Senate has ever seen it since. This was the Senate saying to Jim Allen, No, this is over. You have lost.

We stayed in session that evening until almost nine o'clock, but at the end we passed Senate Resolution 4 by a vote of 56 to 27. It was only the third time in American history that the Senate had changed the rules of the filibuster.

When that fight was over, we thought we had restored balance to the Senate—retaining the filibuster as a tool to require debate and deliberation, yet removing the power of a small, stubborn minority to paralyze the chamber. We believed that reasonable senators from both parties would end debate if that course made sense. I still believe those changes were essential to subsequent progress on issues of national importance, and I can't imagine how our country would have handled the major challenges it has faced in recent decades—tax reform in the 1980s and deficit reduction in the 1990s, to name two—if the Senate required sixty-seven votes on every difficult issue. Without diluting the Senate's tradition as a deliberative body, our reforms broke the hold of a reactionary minority and signaled that when the nation is ready for change, the Senate can act. My friend Pat Leahy would later say that our effort "brought the Senate into the twentieth century."

Nevertheless, I'm deeply troubled by the Senate's recent history. Today almost every major bill that comes before the chamber faces a filibuster—from health care to global warming to financial regulation—so that sixty votes are required to address any important issue. In the 1979–80 session, the Senate held just four cloture votes. In 2007–8 there were more than one hundred. The pernicious "hold" on bills and nominations also means that one senator can hold up the whole country, often for undisclosed or irrelevant reasons.

We have returned to the sort of crisis that forced the rules changes of 1975: The Senate is paralyzed.

The new crisis, however, is not a creation of the Senate rules, but the product of a toxic political mood—the rule-or-ruin polarization that grips Congress today. During my time in the Senate, we were always able to get Republicans and Democrats to work together on the major issues of the day, including civil rights, education, and environmental protection. We passed our reform of Rule 22 with forty Democrats and sixteen Republicans; ten Democrats and seventeen Republicans voted no. Leaders such as Howard Baker, Bob Dole, and Hugh Scott were good Republicans, but they also had a feel for the Senate and a sense of obligation to the nation's larger interests. Today the center aisle of the Senate is like the Great Wall of China. The vast cleavage between Democrats and Republicans has made compromise impossible and allows delaying tactics to be used without any penalty.

I can't say that I know for sure what has made us such a fractious society, or what has made the two-party system so divisive. But I believe it has something to do with the success of the right wing in using religion as a political weapon. After all, if an issue is not a civic disagreement but a basic question of good and evil, how can you compromise? Beliefs are important, but you have to work out your differences for the good of the country. That doesn't seem to be in the minds of many senators today.

I also believe that the ideas that gained force under Ronald Reagan—the idea that the market is all-powerful, the idea that America can decide by itself through the use of power how to resolve the world's problems—created a new generation of Republican leaders who have no interest in resolving differences.

Finally, the country has seen an enormous increase in the influence of big money and activist groups at both ends of the political spectrum, which increases the pressure on lawmakers of both parties to take more rigid and reflexive positions.

For all these reasons, I believe the Senate needs a new debate on the rules. Simply repealing the filibuster is not the answer. We must always ask ourselves these questions: What institution can confront a runaway presidency? How does Congress protect the nation from a cheapening of the federal courts? How do we force an open, national debate on crucial issues such as Vietnam or abuses of the Geneva Convention? The best bulwark we have is a strong, independent Senate. Nevertheless, the rules must be shaped to strike a balance between careful deliberation and abuse by the minority. Senator Tom Harkin of Iowa has proposed a reform whereby the number of votes required for cloture would decline slowly over, say, a month of debate, until only a mere majority is required. I worry about such an approach: I think senators would simply wait out the clock and the Senate would become more like the House, where the leadership can force anything through and the body becomes a tool for deliverance, not deliberation. Maybe the magic number should decline slowly over a month, but no further than fifty-eight or fifty-seven votes.

I would also prohibit the "hold" strategy that allows one senator to block a judicial nomination or a bill. I think that much power, placed in the hands of one senator, humiliates the Senate and makes a farce of the nominating process. Perhaps the Senate needs a rule allowing the leadership to call up issues by majority vote under certain circumstances. Despite what the rules now say, it's important to remember that the Senate can, with the clear mandate of the Constitution, adopt new rules by majority vote, at least at the outset of a new Congress. We made history and established that precedent during the pivotal week in 1975.

I also wish that American voters would ask whether the candidates seeking their support will contribute to this impasse in Washington, this divisiveness that grips our nation, or whether they can be a force for reason and progress. I spent many years of my life in the Senate, and I deeply believe in its capacity for compromise. I've been in the Senate when it really worked, and I believe it can work again. But we have to take care that we make it work.

7

Spies, Security, and
the Rule of Law

URING MY SENATE years I liked to set aside several hours every
Sunday for reading—books on public affairs, journals of opinion,
and three or four Sunday newspapers. I always found something
that bore on my work in the Senate or deserved attention from Congress, and I would usually arrive at the office on Monday morning with
a briefcase full of clippings, notes, and ideas for the staff. But one Sunday
in late 1974 stood out from the others. On December 22 the *New York
Times* published a front-page story by Seymour Hersh detailing a massive
and long-standing government campaign of illegal spying on American
citizens. Hersh wrote that the CIA had conducted illegal surveillance,
surreptitiously opened thousands of pieces of mail, conducted illegal
break-ins, and infiltrated dozens of domestic dissident organizations—all
in violation of its charter.

In the Senate we had been hearing rumors of this sort of thing for
months, but even so, the story came as a shock. Within a few days my colleagues started making their way down to the Senate floor to talk about
it. My friend John Pastore of Rhode Island gave an elegant speech asking, How could these things occur without anyone in Congress knowing about them? Who's watching these agencies? What's happened to our
country? That day he and Mike Mansfield began drafting a resolution to

establish a special Senate committee to investigate the behavior of the intelligence agencies—a committee whose work would dominate my life for much of the next year.

When Hersh's story broke, most members of Congress were feeling numb on the issue of trust and deceit in government. We had spent most of 1971 reading the Pentagon Papers and absorbing their lessons—how generals and presidents had lied to the public about Vietnam. Then we had gone right into the morass of Watergate and the trauma of Nixon's resignation.

Even so, the CIA revelations stunned us. We had come of age assuming that we were a nation of laws, and that the intelligence agencies existed to protect the American people. It will seem naive today, perhaps incredible, but when I first came into government, Americans still presumed that government experts were generally right and public leaders were generally honest. Most of my colleagues, and most of the voters we represented, believed our country had enemies overseas who were dangerous, and criminals at home, and that we needed strong, aggressive security agencies to protect us. We also generally agreed that if these agencies were going to do their work properly, they had to operate in secret. I knew few people in Congress who would have argued otherwise.

This attitude was reflected in congressional oversight of the intelligence community. No congressional committees had full, formal authority over those agencies, nor did any committees have unambiguous power to compel testimony from them. If the heads of the agencies did come up to the Hill to report, theirs was just anodyne testimony. The embarrassing activities—the risky operations, the secret projects—would be disclosed to only two or three people on Capitol Hill, maybe the head of Appropriations because he controlled their money, or the head of Judiciary, who knew how to keep a secret. Moreover, these generally were members whom the agencies themselves chose to brief.

This was fine with most members of Congress. Americans had a lot of fear in the mid-1960s and early 1970s, and most people, I would say, believed that the Communists were bent on destroying us. We had lived through World War II and Korea. The Soviets and the Chinese were regarded as frightening forces, and patriotic Americans never doubted that we had to protect ourselves at home and abroad. John Stennis of Mississippi, often called Judge Stennis, chaired the Armed Services Committee, and I once heard him say that he had told the director of the CIA, You just go do your work, and you don't have to come back to me with all this information.

So although some of my colleagues, including Gene McCarthy, had started raising questions about the CIA, even if we had wanted greater scrutiny of these agencies we would have faced institutional barriers. We would have had to change the way Congress was structured and the way it compelled information from these agencies, and we probably couldn't have passed such changes in those days.

As for the FBI, no one could touch it as long as J. Edgar Hoover was in charge. Even when he was senescent and behaving erratically, he still intimidated people. This stemmed in part from his reputation as a crime-fighter, a guy who knew how to keep criminals off the street. But Hoover was also rumored to keep secret files in his personal office—embarrassing material, which his agents around the country were supposedly encouraged to call in to him directly. Later, when we were investigating the foreign assassination plots, for example, our committee uncovered evidence that John Kennedy was having a liaison with Judith Campbell, who was the girlfriend of Sam Giancana, a mafioso who was also working with the CIA to assassinate Castro. Our evidence showed that on the very day Hoover heard about this affair, he wrote a letter about it to Bobby Kennedy, then later went to see President Kennedy after getting an FBI memo describing the affair. No one knows what they talked about, but Hoover's approach, when he found something ugly, was to go to that someone and say, "Don't worry about it. Trust me. It's here and it's under wraps and nothing is going to happen to it." Maybe that's why Lyndon Johnson refused to fire Hoover. Johnson, who had an earthy Texas way of saying things, used to say, "It's better to have Hoover inside the tent pissing out than outside the tent pissing in."

For all these reasons—patriotism, the fear of genuine security threats, intimidation by the people who ran these agencies—Congress's attitude had for years been hands-off, leave them alone and let them do their jobs.

That attitude began to change after the release of the Pentagon Papers. That had been a cold shower, a story of deception and manipulation that ran from the Pentagon right up to the White House. The generals and the intelligence experts had lied to us, had kept vital information from the public and even leading members of Congress—and in addition had made some extremely poor military calculations. Vietnam had failed and the country was now skeptical.

By the mid-1970s, many Americans presumed that the government was wrong much of the time. Nixon had left office in disgrace, and people understood that a president of the United States had commandeered and politicized agencies that were supposed to protect the rest of us. A public opinion survey at the time asked, "Do you think government officials tell the truth most of the time or do they lie most of the time?" Shocking percentages said they lie most of the time. So when Seymour Hersh's exposé came along, it stirred the cesspool of public cynicism.

To make matters worse, shady behavior within these agencies was starting to undermine the broader justice system. Frank Johnson, a distinguished federal judge from Alabama, later told me that, over the years, he noticed that juries granted less and less credence to the testimony of FBI agents. The word was out that they were playing games. He said this troubled him because agencies that were so important to the criminal justice process had begun to lose the public's confidence.

The Seymour Hersh stories and a lot of fine subsequent reporting brought all this to a crescendo. The old guard, the hands-off crowd, started giving way to the younger senators, and to a new idea that while these agencies are essential to our security and must operate in secret, they must also operate under the law and make themselves accountable to the legislative branch and the courts. The general feeling was that the Congress had to take responsibility for these agencies, to find out what it didn't know—and hadn't wanted to know. As Mike Mansfield observed, "It used to be fashionable . . . for members of Congress to say that insofar as the intelligence agencies were concerned, the less they knew about such questions, the better. Well, in my judgment, it is about time that attitude went out of fashion. It is time for the Senate to take the trouble, and, yes, the risks, of knowing more rather than less."

In the first week of January 1975 Washington was on fire over Hersh's allegations about the CIA, and President Ford appointed a commission to investigate, with Vice President Rockefeller as chairman. Ford probably thought that would calm things down and pacify the skeptics in Congress, but he was wrong. Pastore had raised a lot of serious questions, and a number of senators felt we had simply not been doing our job. In addition, some felt that the Rockefeller Commission wouldn't get to the bottom of the matter for fear of embarrassing Nixon and the people who had worked in his administration.

Three weeks later, acting on a resolution by Pastore, the Senate voted 82 to 4 to establish a select committee to conduct its own investigation. Frank Church, who was on the Foreign Relations Committee and had been in the Senate almost twenty years without chairing a major committee, was Mansfield's choice as chairman. William Miller, a former Foreign Service officer and a talented Senate staff member, was appointed staff director. The other Democratic members were Phil Hart of Michigan, one of the deans of our delegation, and three relatively new senators: Robert Morgan of North Carolina, Walter Huddleston of Kentucky, and Gary Hart of Colorado. The Republican members were all respected senators of great integrity: John Tower of Texas, Barry Goldwater of Arizona, Charles "Mac" Mathias of Maryland, Richard Schweiker of Pennsylvania, and Howard Baker of Tennessee.

I also asked to be on the committee. I had been shaken by the loss of public trust after Vietnam, and I was still offended by Nixon's abuse of public office. I had written a book, *The Accountability of Power*, which made the case for greater accountability of the presidency to the other branches of government and to the public. I still believed in government as a force for good, but I wasn't sure how long we were going to be able to hang on to the public's confidence. This wasn't just a matter of a few little spy capers. This was a question of whether large, powerful agencies of the executive branch and even the White House were going to obey the law and make themselves accountable.

Everyone on the committee understood that we had a volatile assignment, but when we first convened we weren't sure how to proceed. The mandate was immense. We were supposed to examine every federal intelligence agency, including the CIA, the FBI, the Defense Intelligence Agency, and the National Security Agency, over a span of forty years of activity. We had a staff of 135, including 53 investigators. We had to develop document requests, draw up witness lists, write chronologies of the abuses we knew about, and investigate whether there were others. Pastore had told reporters he assumed the committee would meet exclusively in "executive session," that is, behind closed doors. Church, on the other hand, said he hoped to hold a number of hearings in public. There was no precedent for our work. We had a profound investigation, perhaps never to be repeated. We were going to be looking at the files and classified documents of our most secret agencies, and that had never happened before.

The committee itself had different theories on how to proceed. Some Republican members, John Tower and Barry Goldwater among them, didn't want to do an awful lot at first. Many clung to the idea that we shouldn't be digging around in the operations of secret intelligence agencies. I'm sure some also worried that this would just be a Nixon witch hunt. Bill Miller, for whom I developed great respect, thought we could conduct our investigation mainly through interviews with agents and agency officials, then put the story together without digging around in the sewer for facts. That view was not shared by the committee's chief counsel, F. A. O. Schwarz Jr., who came down from New York to join the committee's staff. Fritz, as he was known, was an heir to the toy-retailing empire but was a successful trial lawyer and later head of the respected Brennan Center for Justice at the New York University School of Law. He was a Harvard Law graduate and a partner at Cravath, Swaine & Moore, who had advised the New York Police Department on difficult issues such as use of deadly force and handling of public protests. Schwarz was a litigator at heart, an investigator, and he felt we had to see the files, get the documents, start digging, then draft the questions and call witnesses. Fritz argued that without exposing specifics we couldn't document a case for genuine reform.

Most of us endorsed Schwarz's strategy, but President Ford was reluctant to let us get too close. In February, we had private sessions with Edward Levi, Ford's attorney general, and William Colby, the CIA director, to set ground rules for the investigation. In early March, Church, Tower, Miller, and Schwarz went to the White House for a meeting with Ford and his secretaries of defense and state, Jim Schlesinger and Henry Kissinger, to specify the sort of documents they planned to request. In 1973 the CIA had been implicated in Watergate, and Schlesinger, then CIA director, asked his staff to compile a list of all activities conducted outside the agency's charter, a list that became known as "the family jewels." We wanted that. We also wanted a copy of a report that Colby had prepared for Ford on alleged CIA involvement in overseas assassination plots. In addition, Church asked for a series of classified White House documents and memoranda from the National Security Council.

For several weeks we sent document requests of this nature over to the White House and got the stall treatment—"We can't find that" or "It will take us some time to produce those documents." Fritz Schwarz and Frank Church even met with Rockefeller to pry loose the documents being delivered to his commission. Schwarz told me later that Rockefeller charmed him, mentioning the family toy store, but he didn't give up the documents.

Some members of our committee were fine with this. They didn't want to embarrass Ford and they weren't sure about the scope of our mandate. But after this went on for a few more weeks, we knew we were getting stonewalled by the executive branch. If this continued, we would just be wasting our time and perpetuating the original problem—an executive branch unaccountable to Congress.

Meanwhile, the story continued to unfold in the press. In late February, Daniel Schorr of CBS News reported, for the first time, that the CIA was alleged to have developed plots to assassinate foreign leaders. Over the next month, additional details on alleged assassination attempts continued to trickle out. At the same time the CIA, or agents acting on their own, had begun a counteroffensive. They said our investigation, and a parallel investigation in the House, threatened to expose covert work and cripple the nation's intelligence gathering. One even told a columnist that he was prepared to lie under oath before our committee if that's what it took to protect national secrets. That was the start of a conservative drumbeat against our work that would continue for the rest of the investigation.

Originally we planned to complete our work in eight months. Generally when senators establish a select committee on a topic, they are anxious that it not turn into a permanent committee. But I soon saw that our deadline was unrealistic, and that if we set ourselves an artificial timeline, the Ford administration would have no trouble waiting us out. Finally, at a committee meeting on April 23, we argued it out. Gary Hart said we needed a backup strategy in case the White House continued to stall. Goldwater thought we should scale back the document requests; he was afraid we would get something sensitive and someone on the committee or the staff would leak it to the press and embarrass us. But Phil Hart seemed to speak for most of us when he said, "The White House has just given us two 'go to hells.' What is our response going to be?" I was not as senior as Phil Hart or Barry Goldwater, but I did have some experience conducting investigations and working with reluctant sources. I lit a cigar—senators often smoked in committee meetings in those days—pushed my chair back, and said, "We will have to wait them out." We had to get in a position where the White House knew we were going to be around as long as necessary. My colleagues agreed, and in May we voted to extend our timetable.

In today's environment I don't believe that would work. The partisan divide is so deep that, unfortunately, a president can usually count on members of his own party in Congress to protect him. This is precisely what we saw in 2007 and 2008, when Congress tried to investigate the intelligence failures that led to the war in Iraq. Bush and Cheney knew they would be out of office by January 2009 and figured they could string out the investigators until then. But it was different for us. Bill Miller, our committee staff director, had been a staff aide for Senator John Sherman Cooper, a Republican. We had Republicans such as Dick Schweiker, Mac Mathias, and Howard Baker, who had demonstrated a good deal of independence from the White House on Vietnam and Watergate. We had John Tower, the committee cochair, who ultimately earned considerable prestige by making this committee work. These people were moderates, senators for whom these issues were really not partisan matters. The intelligence abuses had occurred under both parties—we documented abuses under every administration from Franklin Roosevelt to Richard Nixon— and people who believed in the law and accountability, Republican and Democrat, were troubled by what they heard. They all were serious about the Senate's constitutional responsibility to oversee the executive branch, and they insisted that the White House produce what we needed.

In addition, the Republicans had just come through the embarrassment of Watergate. They had supported a president who let them down and humiliated them. I remember Goldwater telling me that he had once told Nixon, "The only time you ever had me up to the White House was when you got your ass in a crack." So the Republican side had a mood of self-preservation, a sense that they would be loyal to the White House in their fashion.

Then, too, our Republican friends began to realize that the investigation was playing well with the press and the public. As our committee began uncovering a series of far-fetched CIA espionage plans, Goldwater called a news conference one day to discuss a bizarre gadget developed by the agency, a "bio-innoculator" that was supposed to inject poisons into targeted victims from long distances. He drew a big crowd of photographers, and the next day his picture ran on the front page of newspapers around the world. I teased him, saying that he had staged a publicity stunt. "Of course I did," he said with a big smile. "I learned it from Hubert."

Eventually Ford came around. He was a loyal Republican, but he was not an ideologue. His attorney general, Edward Levi, a distinguished former dean of the University of Chicago Law School, understood the gravity of the abuses. And the politics were with us. People were confused and angry about what they read in the newspapers. Members of Congress were under a lot of pressure to do something on this. They couldn't just walk away from their responsibilities, as they tried to do later with the intelligence failures on Iraq.

But we made accommodations on our side, too. We didn't want the investigation to seem partisan, or to embarrass employees of these agencies. I insisted that we get key documents, but I also argued that we should limit the degree of detail we asked for. We wanted only to learn about what happened and how it happened. We were not out to get individuals. I knew that if it looked like we were undermining America's security, we were going to get shut down—and probably deservedly.

In addition, we knew that our inquiry had little precedent in the Senate's long history. During the Civil War, a Conduct of War Committee had made Lincoln's life miserable. Then in the 1920s some hearings were held on the Palmer Raids on suspected anarchists. But before, during, and after World War II, nobody wanted to interfere with intelligence operations. This was the first time—and maybe it would be the last time—that a congressional committee would be able to operate the way we did, conducting a deep, broad, and unrestricted investigation of our nation's secret agencies. Fritz Schwarz and Bill Miller spent a lot of time figuring out how to slice this watermelon so we could get what we needed without hurting the agencies or risking our country.

These questions generated no little friction in the Senate, with some of our colleagues charging that the probe would help the enemy and expose agents to risk. In December 1975, the CIA bureau chief in Athens, Richard Welch, was gunned down on his way home from a party, an incident that shocked us all. A few months after that, my colleague Milton Young of North Dakota gave a speech on the Senate floor implying that we were responsible for revealing Welch's identity and, thus, for his death. Fortunately, the facts were on our side. I went right down to the floor myself and pointed out that the committee had never been given his name. We insisted on that rule—we never received names and couldn't have leaked any. I also pointed out that a Greek newspaper had published the address of the CIA office in Athens. Nevertheless, we had to step carefully because those accusations circulated frequently.

Eventually Ford's stalling tactics failed and the administration began making witnesses available. On May 15, behind closed doors in a windowless, bunkerlike room high up in the Capitol, we conducted our first formal hearing, and William Colby presented a history of CIA covert actions. A week later he confirmed to our committee that the CIA had sponsored several foreign assassination plots, including a plan to kill Fidel Castro and a bungled attempt on the life of Patrice Lumumba, prime minister of the Congo.

When members of the Rockefeller Commission saw the assassination files, they realized that they couldn't handle the inquiry on their own. The topic was so full of explosive allegations that, I think, they decided they had to have some sort of understanding with the Congress, particularly with the Senate. At the end of that month, they concluded their investigation rather abruptly and began turning their files over to us.

In September we began our public hearings, and people began to grasp the gravity of the investigation. We produced evidence of a series of embarrassing CIA activities, including outlandish programs to develop shellfish toxins and other poisons. We also examined the Huston Plan, a strategy developed by a Nixon aide named Tom Charles Huston to use the FBI and the CIA to conduct illegal burglaries and open the mail of thousands of American citizens.

At this point, a second dynamic began working in our favor. Many of the CIA's career professionals were offended by the illegal operations and were willing to say so. For the good agents, the professionals, that was Looney Tunes time. One agent in particular stood out—he had an Irish surname, although in our reports we used pseudonyms to protect agents' safety. We asked him to testify about the effort to assassinate Patrice Lumumba. He thought the project was shameful. He said, "When the agency wanted to do something like that, they always picked an ethnic like me. That's the kind of work we do. The nice guys up in the front shop—the Waspy Ivy League guys—don't do that sort of thing." The image of classy professionalism began to crumble pretty quickly.

Clearly, these doubts ran straight up and down the CIA, to the point where intelligence-gathering had become dysfunctional. We learned that the head of counterintelligence, James Angleton, whom the other agents called Mother, was so wary of corrupted intelligence that he simply stopped reading the agency's own intelligence reports. Even Bill Colby, who had been involved in some pretty brutal stuff during the Phoenix counterintelligence program in Vietnam, came to feel that the secret projects were destroying the agency. People such as Colby, who were still rational, understood that the agency had run off the rails and could not correct course internally. Colby later wrote in the *New York Times* that congressional oversight would "strengthen American intelligence."

In November our focus turned to the FBI, and we saw the same pattern. By now we had divided our work between two subcommittees, one for the foreign intelligence agencies and one for the domestic agencies, and I was asked to chair the domestic task force. I thought we had a top-notch investigative staff, and I happily dug into the documents and ran the hearings. We produced evidence that the IRS had shared confidential taxpayer files with the intelligence agencies, and that the FBI had conducted "black bag" jobs—that is, burglaries—against alleged domestic subversives all the way back to the 1940s.

All this was deeply embarrassing—infuriating to people on both sides of the aisle—and it suggested that this cancer had spread beyond the foreign intelligence agencies into domestic operations. William Sullivan, the number three official in the FBI, testified that J. Edgar Hoover had, in his later years, completely politicized the agency. As a result, all the things that are important to an FBI agent—his professionalism as an investigator and as a fact finder—were given second place to the political activities Hoover wanted to pursue. Sullivan said they had spent more time pursuing Hoover's enemies than they did catching crooks.

It was at this point that we made one of our great investigative breakthroughs, a set of discoveries that broke the domestic inquiry wide open. I was concerned about intelligence abuses directed against American citizens, and I was pushing our staff hard. I wanted witnesses and documents, not vague rumors. One day one of our staff investigators, Mike Epstein—a brilliant guy, unbelievably tenacious—came into my office and said, "Senator, I have something you'd better look at. They're called COINTELPRO files, and you won't believe what's in here."

The acronym COINTELPRO was FBI slang for "counterintelligence program," the Bureau's own program for fighting subversive activity—or what it considered subversive activity—inside the United States. What we read in those files is well known now, but at the time it was astonishing. In its paranoia, the FBI had kept secret files on one million American citizens. Hoover had designated twenty-six thousand individuals to be arrested and jailed in any national emergency, including Martin Luther King Jr. and Norman Mailer. The FBI had conducted hundreds of burglaries at offices of political groups. It had investigated half a million "subversives" without ever obtaining a court order. It had engaged U.S. army intelligence agents to infiltrate meetings of various progressive organizations, including the NAACP, environmental groups, and women's rights organizations. The CIA, with the cooperation of the U.S. Post Office, had illegally opened the mail of hundreds of American citizens for more than twenty years, including the personal mail of John Steinbeck, Hubert Humphrey, Arthur Burns, and even Nixon himself. There was utter contempt for the idea of accountability, and it was all there, in official agency documents that couldn't be denied.

Worst of all was the persecution of Martin Luther King Jr. FBI memos showed that Hoover considered King a "black hate leader" and believed that King had conspired with the Communist Party. Hoover hoped to replace him with someone else of Hoover's choosing. The Bureau had tried to prevent King from meeting with the pope. It tried to keep him out of the better hotels in Memphis by writing anonymous letters that asked, "What is a Negro doing in a high-class hotel like this?" It even tried to prevent him from attending the ceremony at which he received the Nobel Peace Prize. It bugged his hotel rooms—he had girlfriends, and the FBI made sure that Mrs. King knew about that. And of course agents wrote the notorious anonymous letter, mailed with a set of tapes, that seemed to suggest that King commit suicide: "King, there is only one thing left for you to do. You know what it is. You are done. There is but one way out for you. You better take it before your filthy, fraudulent self is bared to the nation."

After going through these documents we called Andrew Young, who had been second-in-command at the Southern Christian Leadership Conference and King's lieutenant in the early 1960s. Young testified that he and King knew all along that the Bureau was watching them. He said they felt safer when FBI agents were around because, in some of those mean counties in the Deep South, the Ku Klux Klan behaved itself when federal agents were in the vicinity. Young told us they learned to identify FBI agents. An agent always drove a green Plymouth sedan and always wore a black suit with a black tie, white shirt, and a hat—even in hundred-degree weather in Alabama. "We knew who they were because they always had a whip aerial on their car," Young told us.

Testimony of this kind was almost comical, but also sad and infuriating. After Young testified, we started calling FBI agents, and their stories revealed that the agency had gone haywire. Hoover ordered the agency to celebrate several occasions every year—the thirtieth anniversary of the FBI, for example, or the thirtieth anniversary of the day he became director—and on these days the agents were expected to bring him presents. One day a story appeared in the *Washington Post* revealing that Hoover was manipulating the agency to get presents. Hoover called in his key people and said, "This is offensive to me. How many times have I told you that I do not want any gifts?" Then the next day he sent word around he would like an ice-making machine.

Much more serious, it became clear that the people running these agencies were incapable of resisting political pressure and drawing a line between the legal and the illegal. We traveled to New Hampshire to interview Sullivan, and under cross-examination he admitted, "Never once did I hear anybody, including myself, raise the question, 'Is this course of action, which we have agreed upon, lawful? Is it legal? Is it ethical or moral?' We never gave any thought to this line of reasoning because we were just naturally pragmatic."

We got a similar response later when I questioned Benson Buffham, deputy director of the National Security Agency, about one of its surveillance programs:

Mondale: Were you concerned about its legality?
Buffham: Legality?
Mondale: Whether it was legal.

Buffham: In what sense? Whether that would have been a legal
    thing to do?
Mondale: Yes.
Buffham: That particular aspect didn't enter into the discussion.
Mondale: I was asking you if you were concerned about whether
    that would be legal and proper.
Buffham: We didn't consider it at the time, no.

My approach to the domestic subcommittee hearings, as in all my
work, was to prepare intensively—reading documents, interviewing
experts, debriefing our staff. In these hearings that was crucial because the
issues went layers deep and the witnesses' testimony was often baffling.
We asked FBI director Clarence Kelley to testify on the COINTELPRO
activities. I asked him which activities were inside the law and which
were outside. He answered by saying that sometimes you have to give
up some rights to protect others. I said, "That's fine. Would you tell me
which rights you are willing to give up?" "Well," he said, "I didn't mean it
that way." This sloppy thinking prevailed in the agencies—the idea that
a higher purpose allowed them, with the encouragement of the White
House, to disregard the law.

I found a second pattern equally troubling. We would ask some low-
level agent, Who gave approval for these activities? He would say, Well, I
don't know—you'll have to ask someone higher up. We would go straight
up the chain of command, and they all said the same thing, none of them
knew who had authorized anything. The process was clearly designed for
fog—to hide responsibility and prevent anyone from ever being called to
account.

In December our work came to a head in a final public hearing. Kelley was still trying to stonewall us, insisting that the illegal activities had
long since stopped. But we had been told that Elliot Richardson, when he
was Nixon's attorney general, had ordered the FBI to compile a list of all
illegal activities over the years. I knew that if we got Richardson's list, we
could verify when this activity started and when it ended. So we called
Attorney General Levi to testify, and I asked him to produce that list.

When the hearing got under way, however, Levi headed off in a different direction. He wanted to argue that the Justice Department deserved a kind of legal escape hatch to do preventive investigations, a kind of penumbral area where the law didn't apply. I asked him the legal basis for such an argument, and to explain why his agencies couldn't simply obey the law. He went off into what I thought was a filibuster, a long answer to avoid addressing the question. You could see he was slipping all over. He didn't have an answer. He was one of the most respected legal scholars in America, but he had an impossible position to defend, so I brought him back to the issue of the document we had requested. This was our exchange:

> Mondale: I am asking you, as the head of the Justice Department, if we could get those reports.
> Levi: Well, I do not know if you can or not, but we will certainly consider it.
> Mondale: Why not?
> Levi: Because I think that it is one thing to give reports of that kind in confidence to a committee of this kind and another thing to make them public.
> Mondale: The CIA gave theirs to us. Why can't you?
> Levi: Well, I am not in the CIA. I do not care to be. I do not wish to be.
> Mondale: Do you consider that a good answer?
> Levi: I—yes, I consider the answer as good as the question.
> Mondale, to Senator Church: Well, I think that kind of arrogance is why we have trouble between the executive and the legislative branch. Thank you, Mr. Chairman.

I later regretted that testy exchange. I sounded like a smart aleck, when all I was trying to do was to underscore the importance of the rule of law. But I didn't want that colloquy to misrepresent what I thought of Levi. He was a first-rate scholar and a good person. I think he realized that the agencies he supervised had gone off in a direction that could not be defended, and he went back to the Justice Department and began looking for ways to get them back on course. In fact, Levi became indispensable to our reform efforts: He wrote a good set of operating guidelines for the FBI, which banned "preventive action" and other civil liberties abuses, and he helped convince Ford to accept proper congressional oversight. He did a great deal to bring integrity back to those agencies because he, too, believed that they should obey the law.

By early 1976 we had called eight hundred witnesses, reviewed more than 110,000 pages of classified documents, and documented a long history of abuse. We had issued one public report, on the CIA foreign-assassinations program, and were about to publish a powerful second volume, *Intelligence Activities and the Rights of Americans*, which detailed the findings of our domestic task force. The staff was finishing work on several more committee reports, which would include more than eighty recommendations to reform the intelligence community—some of which were quite hard on Congress itself. Loch Johnson, a University of Georgia political scientist who served on the committee staff, later summarized that aspect of our work: "In a political system based on checks and balances, Congress had provided too few checks and permitted a shift in balance from the overseers to the overzealous. The supervisors in the executive branch had failed to perform any better."

Now our challenge was to write a law that would prevent these abuses from happening again. At first we tried to use the common-law method. We took actual cases from the files and the testimony and tried to discern which activities must be off-limits, which were truly necessary, and which could have been conducted legally. We forced ourselves, through the discipline of dealing with facts and events, to come up with a series of guidelines, which we thought might then be enacted into a law. We spent days—twelve-hour days and more—for a couple of weeks. But the issues were simply too complex. Any guideline we wrote was too detailed and too long, and the agencies felt it would just tie them in knots.

In the end we kept running into the same two conundrums: We couldn't write rules broad enough to anticipate every contingency in a national security crisis, and we couldn't see how to impose public oversight on agencies that must operate in secret. Our answer was a piece of legislation that became the Foreign Intelligence Surveillance Act, or FISA. Since we couldn't write guidelines to cover every possibility, we created a new foreign-intelligence court where federal judges presided in secret to hear applications for surveillance warrants. We wouldn't tie the agencies' hands in advance, but we would require that they make their case before a court of law. That was some creative work, but I think it was a good answer, and by the spring of 1976 we had draft legislation.

By the time the FISA legislation started advancing in both houses of Congress, I was in the White House as part of the Carter administration. Now I was on the other side of the table, in the administration and seeking pragmatic solutions with the people who ran the FBI and the CIA. But that was fortunate, I think, because I could recommend to President Carter and the attorney general ways to make FISA work; I could make the argument that the FISA court was good for us. When we got into a quandary, I was able to bring in Fritz Schwarz, then in private practice, or committee staff from the Hill, to give us their reading on the law and congressional intent.

A measure of the difficulty of this issue is that even people working for the same administration often had differing points of view. Carter had established a special White House coordination committee consisting of representatives from the CIA, the NSA, the Departments of State, Defense, and Justice, and the National Security Council, and often I was the main advocate for tough court oversight of the surveillance. On a few points, such as whether the law should protect American citizens when they were overseas, only I and perhaps Griffin Bell would be arrayed against Zbigniew Brzezinski, Stansfield Turner, the NSA, and others. On a few of those topics Carter himself had to call the final compromise. Yet on the whole, we helped Congress write a good law and it proved to be an exceptional example of sophisticated, legislative-executive cooperation to bring about reform.

After three years of investigations, hearings, and debate, the FISA bill passed the Senate in 1978 by a vote of 95 to 1. In addition to the FISA law, Congress placed a ten-year term limit on the director of the FBI to prevent another J. Edgar Hoover from emerging and created a permanent panel, the Senate Intelligence Committee, with authority over the federal intelligence agencies.

I think it was a historic achievement, not just fine investigative work by our staff, and not just resourceful work in drafting the legislation, but proof that our political system is strong enough and wise enough to confront a threat to our constitutional framework, make corrections, and leave the democracy stronger. Americans understood that leaders of their government had abused the powers of office, and they saw that we had transcended partisanship to investigate those abuses and had rallied public support for dramatic and far-reaching changes to the way our intelligence agencies work. Loch Johnson would later write:

> The intelligence investigation of 1975 must surely rank as one of the most significant inquiries conducted by the United States Senate. It represented the first serious examination of the "dark side" of government since the establishment of the modern intelligence bureaucracy in 1947; it unearthed more information (much of it highly classified) from the executive branch than any previous congressional inquiry had done; it set in motion forces that would revolutionize the approach to intelligence policy on Capitol Hill and, consequently, within the intelligence community.

The new system changed behavior at our intelligence agencies. When I swore in William Webster as FBI director in 1978, I gave him a copy of our committee report and told him to read it before he did anything else. I think it had an impact on his tenure. Stansfield Turner, the CIA director under President Carter, came to feel the same way; he wrote that strong congressional oversight "ensures against our becoming separated from the legal and ethical standards of our society." George Tenet later told me the same thing. When he ran the CIA, he said, his agents liked the FISA system because they knew the authority of the courts stood behind them. It professionalized the agency again. That law worked well through Carter, through Reagan, through Bush I, through Clinton. They all worked with it, and I began to think: Now, at least for our generation, this issue is settled.

Then came the Bush-Cheney administration. They took a horrible set of events—the attacks of 9/11—and used them to create a climate of fear that would justify their drive to reinterpret the Constitution and arrogate unlimited power to themselves. They threw out a constitutional and legal framework that they were pledged to protect and that had survived through four administrations and more than two decades. They deliberately defied the FISA law and undertook illegal surveillance without seeking court approval. They commissioned legal memos justifying torture, then kept those memos secret from the very authorities with the most expertise. They destroyed tapes that documented their own torture practices—in plain contempt of the 9/11 Commission, which had legal authority to review evidence. At the core of all these activities was the same dangerous premise we investigated in the Church Committee: that the president can, unilaterally and in secret, do as he chooses despite the law.

The defenders of these activities said our nation faced a great threat and that they had a constitutional duty to protect the American people. But no one denies this. We argued that point, and settled it, during our Senate hearings more than thirty years ago.

The question we considered in the Church Committee is not whether America needs strong intelligence agencies and secret surveillance activities, which we do, but whether the president, and the president alone, gets to decide what is legal and what is not, what violates the Constitution and what does not.

In creating the congressional intelligence committees and enacting FISA, Congress voted, with large bipartisan majorities, that the answer is no—the president cannot arrogate these powers to the executive branch or decide, in isolation, to reinterpret standing law. As Frank Church told the *Washington Post* in 1976, "The lesson to be learned is not just that illegal actions were justified. Rather it is that once government officials start believing that they have the power and the right to act secretly outside the law, we have started down a long, slippery slope which culminates in a Watergate."

What I found most galling after 9/11 is that the Bush administration could have asked Congress to update the intelligence laws and make them current with developments in technology and the terrorist threat. But they had no interest in making the law work or in cooperating with Congress. They were trying to build their theory of the "unitary executive," a commander-in-chief privilege that would allow them to set policy without answering to anyone but themselves. It was different, in tone and depth and breadth, from anything this country had seen before.

A president who is accountable to no one—not the Congress or the courts—is a president who will be tempted to interpret the law for his own convenience, to decide who is an enemy of the state, to violate constitutional protections of our liberties. A system of government cannot operate this way. That defines the imperial presidency, the rise of tyranny, that gave our founders nightmares.

There will always be threats to our national security, and there will always be someone who argues that shortcuts are necessary to keep us safe. But that is no argument to subvert the law. If you want to adapt to new circumstances or new threats, then you amend the law. There is no evidence that Bush and Cheney accomplished anything by stepping outside the law that they couldn't have accomplished within its boundaries. A lot of evidence suggests that their policies did in fact weaken America. When you violate the Geneva Accords, when you operate Abu Ghraib and Guantánamo, when you use extraordinary rendition to torture people who later turn out to be innocent, you lose respect in the world. You create anger against the United States and you spawn violence and empower terrorists.

When you abuse the tools of our military and intelligence agencies, you subvert democracy itself. Americans wonder why they should support a foreign policy whose rationale is kept secret from them, or participate fully in their democracy if the tools of their own government can be turned against them when they dissent. The quality of your decisions deteriorates because you are afraid to test them in open argument.

A reassuring cycle of self-correction runs through American history, of citizens recognizing a problem in their midst and demanding that their leaders address it. But we can't trust our civil liberties to some abstract theory of history. We need to take care of them every day. The founders left us a great gift, an elegant but durable democracy that gives expression to the wishes of the majority while protecting the rights of the minority. Events will test that structure from time to time—a civil war, a terrorist attack—and we cannot simply assume that it will survive the challenge.

The lesson of American history is that, in threatening times, fear can overtake our better judgment. It happened with the Alien and Sedition Acts at the end of the eighteenth century, with the Palmer Raids after World War I, with the internment of Japanese Americans in the 1940s, with J. Edgar Hoover's abuse of power in the 1960s. We have strayed from our values time and again in our history, always in times of fear, and we were almost always ashamed of ourselves when we recovered our senses.

8

Meeting a New Democrat

I N 1973 AND 1974, having heard the call that many senators hear, I took a test run at a campaign for the presidency. By that time I had worked on a number of national issues in the Senate, and I wanted to see if I could have a national impact with voters. That turned out to be a tough period. I was on the road every weekend for more than a year, raising money and putting myself before audiences in states where I was not well known. It was time away from my family, from Minnesota, and from my work in the Senate. After more than a year of constant travel, constant fund-raising, and constant speeches, I had pulled about even with "None of the Above" in national opinion surveys, and I dropped that bid—to widespread applause.

On the day I announced I was ending that experiment, I felt huge relief. After that I had no intention of going back into the presidential arena. I felt I had found my sweet spot in the Senate.

Then one day in May of 1976, my chief of staff, Dick Moe, suggested that we have coffee with Humphrey, who was back in the Senate representing Minnesota. Governor Jimmy Carter of Georgia had come out of nowhere with a superb campaign for the Democratic presidential nomination, and the newspapers were starting to speculate about possible running mates. My name was on all the lists, along with those of Ed Muskie, John Glenn, and several other Democratic senators. When the political writers began calling me, I wasn't too excited because I didn't know Carter well and I was happy in the Senate. But I agreed to Dick's suggestion, and a few days later we met Hubert in the Senate Dining Room, a beautiful, quiet old room where I had spent many hours talking with him over the years. I knew the vice presidency had been hard on Hubert, and I expected some cautionary words. He said, "I did have some tough times with Johnson. There were days when the job was very difficult. But the vice presidency broadened me. I learned more about how our nation works." We must have talked for most of an hour, and as we spoke, Hubert's enthusiasm grew. Finally, as we were getting up to leave, I could see a spark in his eye. He said, "Fritz, you must do this. You'll get more done down there in two days than you will up here in two years."

Later I teased Hubert for trying to get rid of me so he could be the senior senator from Minnesota again. But the meeting rattled me, and I went back to my office that afternoon weighing Hubert's words. A few days later I had my staff start pulling together everything they could find on Jimmy Carter.

Although I didn't know Carter well, I was drawn to the idea that we could have a president of the United States who was from the Deep South yet fully committed to civil rights. The issue had dominated much of my career, and much of what happened in America during the 1960s and early 1970s. We had paid a terrible price for the way civil rights divided Democrats and the country, North against South. I had seen it in the 1968 presidential campaign, when George Wallace exploited latent racism so skillfully to damage Humphrey. I had seen the same rift during my work in Washington, where the North-South standoff paralyzed the Senate and impeded the business of the country: You just couldn't get big things done because the Southerners would never go along. I saw the lingering tension over racial issues during my own national campaigning, too. It's a big challenge to vault over the palpable differences between the regions and somehow put together a national coalition.

As a result of all three experiences, I worried about civil rights leaving a vestigial mark on our country and having the power to divide us for a long time. So when Carter won the Florida primary in March 1976, I was impressed. He pushed racial politics to the sidelines, kept Democrats with him, and, by appealing to voters' better instincts on issues of tolerance, made George Wallace the goat. I admired the political skill that required, and I admired Carter's principles and courage. One of the reasons Democrats ultimately chose Carter that year, I believe, is that he offered a promise to reunite America around civil rights instead of having the issue forever be used to divide us. Race had been America's greatest curse. Perhaps we could finally put it behind us.

Because Carter's tenure as president was so brief, I'm not sure people understand the way he realigned American politics. Ever since the mid-1960s Democrats had struggled to gain traction in the South. Lyndon Johnson had warned us about that when we passed the great civil rights bills, even though he thought they were right and essential. After the 1960s, when Republicans traveled South to campaign, they often went to Philadelphia, Mississippi, or some other place synonymous with segregation and would give their audience the old wink, wink. We wouldn't do that, so it was hard for Democrats to carry those Southern states. But Carter could. He was one of them and had proved himself. He combined many traits—being a Southerner, growing up in the countryside, and having been elected governor—that gave him a credibility that Northern Democrats couldn't achieve.

Carter's religious faith also set him apart. He wasn't afraid of religion the way some Democrats were, or seemed to be. He understood evangelicals and appealed to them, and he didn't hesitate to talk about his faith and how it influenced his thinking. A lot of evangelical Americans and religious thinkers—not just political conservatives—liked a candidate who seemed ethically and religiously committed. They respected that in Carter, at a time when many Democrats were ceding the appeal to so-called family-values Republicans.

Finally, Carter's temperament was the perfect counterpoint to Watergate. By 1976 the Nixon legacy wasn't white-hot anymore, but it wasn't just embers either. People remembered the lies, the dirty tricks, and the break-ins, and they remembered that Nixon had been pardoned by Ford, and they weren't happy about it. Carter offered an antidote to a long, poisonous period in American politics. That also appealed to me.

After a year investigating intelligence abuses and an executive branch run amok, I was developing some doubts of my own about the power of government and the lack of accountability. I wondered how we could restore people's trust in their government. People sensed that Carter had honor and integrity, and they found it reassuring after what had been an unsettling time.

Many Northern Democrats, however, were still skittish about this Georgian. They weren't sure he was a real Democrat. He was a fiscal conservative; he was unknown to unions; he hadn't really spelled out his position on sensitive issues such as abortion and gun control. But I read his speeches and studied his record as governor, and I came to feel that, while he was a Southern Democrat, he was also a national Democrat. He wasn't one of these Dixiecrats, the ones who are Democrats in name but have no interest in the national Democratic Party. If you read Carter's book *Why Not the Best?* or his campaign materials from the primaries, you could see that he was a genuine progressive: a committed environmentalist, a champion of civil rights, an advocate of human rights, a big believer in education and equal opportunity. Today, most national Democrats would look at that record and say it's fine. Also, I thought I could influence him. I thought that once he was in office, the pull of Congress and national politics would nudge Carter to the left.

A final trait that impressed me about Carter was his methodical approach to decisions. When it became clear, sometime in June, that he was serious about me as a running mate, Carter's people sent Charlie Kirbo up to Washington for a visit. Kirbo was Carter's friend, a wonderful old Southern gentleman and a shrewd lawyer. About ten of us were still on Carter's list, and the campaign assigned someone to take each of us to the woodshed and ask tough questions. Vetting running mates has since become a major industry, but in those days they just sat you down and put you through the ringer for several hours. They wanted to know if there was anything embarrassing about me—money problems, personal problems, law problems, health issues—that sort of thing. It was pretty grueling. But it ended with a funny story. Apparently Kirbo was on the phone back to Plains, Georgia, just before he came into my office, and he told them, "I think I can get rid of this guy pretty fast." When he came out, somebody said, "Well, Charlie, did you get rid of him?" And he said, "No, I don't think I ever will."

A week later Carter's staff called to say that he would like to meet me in person, and that Joan and I should arrange to fly down to Plains. I was excited about the possibilities, but worried that there might be some incompatibilities. I read Carter's book and a collection of his speeches so I knew where he stood on the issues, but I also placed a big emphasis in my preparation on what kind of working relationship we would have. That's where meeting Carter proved decisive.

July 8, 1976, turned out to be a big day in my life. Joan and I flew to Atlanta the night before and stayed overnight at the airport, where Chip Carter met us the next morning. From Atlanta we got in a little six-seater and flew to what everyone called Plains International Airport—a little grass landing field on the edge of town. They drove us through the tiny town of Plains to the Carter home, where we arrived about ten o'clock in the morning. We introduced ourselves to Jimmy and Rosalynn and spoke casually for a few minutes, the four of us, then Carter introduced me to his mother, Miss Lillian. Then he took me into his office, a converted garage, for a long, serious get-acquainted conversation. First we discussed what he called the "litmus paper" issues, including a balanced budget, which he supported, and forced school busing, which he did not. Then we talked about the primary campaign and what I thought of the state of the Democratic Party.

After a couple of hours we went out to see Joan and Rosalynn again, and the four of us had lunch together. Neither Joan nor Rosalynn were enthusiastic about cooking, but Joan allowed that her husband could roast a nice Thanksgiving turkey. Then Carter and I went back into his office and talked some more. We talked about his book and I asked him about his views on the party. We talked at length about civil rights because I thought that could be one of the bust-up points. I had a strong civil rights record in the Senate, of course, and I thought he might not know all of it. But he knew all about my record and said he agreed with every bit of it. That made a big difference to me.

The turning point in our conversation came when we talked about the role of the vice president in a Carter administration. I had spoken again with Hubert, and I had called Nelson Rockefeller for advice. I was determined to be blunt with Carter. I told him I thought the Humphrey vice presidency had been tragic and that I didn't want anything like that. I said I understood that I wouldn't be the president, but that I wanted a significant role in the administration. I told him it's demeaning for a vice president to be kept out of the information loop and that it's a waste of a public resource for a vice president to spend too much time on ceremonial functions.

Much to my surprise, Carter had been considering the same questions. He said, "That all sounds correct to me. I'd like to use the vice president in a way that hasn't ever happened before." Then he added something interesting: "I think some presidents in the past were uncomfortable with the presence of their own vice president. They were worried about their mortality, and their vice president only reminded them of it. But that doesn't bother me. I know I could be comfortable with that." He said he wanted a much more active vice president, and that was when I thought this might actually work.

After Carter and I finished talking he said, "Would you like to see Plains?" We took a walk through downtown—it doesn't take long—to the old train depot that he had converted to the Carter campaign head-quarters. Every other store in downtown Plains is a Carter this or a Carter that—a Carter worm shop or a Carter peanut warehouse. Then we walked out into one of the peanut fields. He's a farmer, after all, and loves the land. He picked up an old bottle and we talked about history. He collects bottles. In retrospect, I suppose it was a test—this was his community and these were his people and he wanted to see how I reacted. I never felt as if I were on the witness stand, but I'm sure he was trying to figure out if we were compatible.

While we walked, we talked about his upbringing. His religion is important to him, and he was interested to know that I also had a strong religious background. Then of course both of us grew up in small towns. As we were walking back up to the Carter home, he asked me what I thought of Plains. I said, "Gee, it's pretty big." That got a laugh. So despite a big regional separation, a lot of things came naturally between us.

After we finished walking, Carter and I held an impromptu press conference at the railroad depot. Eventually one of the reporters asked a question that had regularly come up since I'd ended my own presidential bid in 1974: whether I had the drive to pull off a presidential campaign. Carter said he had no doubts and made a few polite comments. Then, when one of the reporters helpfully reminded us that I had once said I didn't want to "spend the rest of my life in Holiday Inns," Carter looked my way and handed me the microphone. I paused for a minute, then said, "I've checked, and they've all been redecorated. They're marvelous places to stay."

By the time Joan and I left that afternoon I was pretty well decided that, if asked, I would run with Carter. I thought the day had gone well, and I thought Carter and I would make a good team. But I was exhausted and assumed that Carter's interviews with Muskie, Glenn, and the others were going well, too, so I had no idea where I stood. As we got on the plane, Joan said, "He'll pick you." I said, "Really?" She said, "You two get along perfectly. This is going to work out just fine."

Joan was right, of course, but we didn't know it yet, and we wouldn't know it until four days later, when the Democratic National Convention opened in New York City. Dick Moe, Mike Berman, and Gail Harrison from my Senate staff all went to New York ahead of me. When I arrived, reporters knew that Carter had interviewed Muskie, Glenn, and me in Plains, so I was in the spotlight. The press and all the networks also knew where I was staying during the convention, and they did their best to get us in the middle of a big story. I figured that commenting on Carter's choice could only be trouble—at least look like self-promotion—so I told Joan, "Let's disappear from here for a while." My friend Herb Allen had a nice room over at the Carlyle Hotel and he offered that to us, so we went there to hide out for a day or so. It worked pretty well, except that we ran into Charlie Rangel in the hotel lobby and he said, "Oh, there you are!" I said, "Please don't tell anybody," and I just slipped off the earth for a while. Then one hitch occurred to us: What if Carter's people didn't know that we had changed hotels? What if Carter did choose me and called the wrong room? So we had Gail Harrison stay behind in my room to watch the phone, which led to one of the funniest stories out of the convention. She wound up calling her parents to let them know where she was. She told them, "I'm in Walter Mondale's bedroom—but it's not what you think."

Waiting for Carter's decision turned into a rather anxious twenty-four hours. I wasn't sure I would be his choice, but I knew I had to be prepared. Carter was supposed to announce his choice on the morning of July 15, then his running mate would have to give a speech that night or the next night. That would be an important speech, with a big, hot audience in the convention hall and millions of people watching on television. I had a speech that I had given to the DFL in Duluth a few weeks earlier, which I thought would make a good starting point, so I went off privately with a pen and a pad and went to work.

The morning arrived, and through some miracle, we had given Carter's staff the right phone number. Joan and I got up at dawn, dressed, and had breakfast; then there wasn't much to do except read the newspapers and watch the telephone. It rang about eight thirty. I picked it up and it was Carter.

"Good morning, Fritz," he said. "Would you like to run with me?"

I thought it over carefully—for about two seconds—and said yes.

About two minutes after I put the phone down, there was a knock at the door. Mike Berman opened it, and four Secret Service agents walked into the room. They had been downstairs hiding and knew when the phone call was placed. I would have them as companions for the next four and a half years.

Then—and this is one of those moments that doesn't wind up in the history books—Joan and I realized we should prepare the kids, who were still down in Washington at our house. We hadn't brought them along because I knew New York would be hectic and they had things to do at home. Our oldest, Ted, had a job in the produce department of the local supermarket, and Eleanor was babysitting. When we called, they sounded scared. They said the house was surrounded by cameras, and they were hiding inside, not knowing what they should tell all those reporters. I didn't dare tell them that I had spoken with Carter. It had just happened and I thought Carter deserved the chance to issue the announcement, rather than three nervous teenagers. So I said, "You'd better get ready to come up here to New York, and maybe in about fifteen minutes I can call you and give you more news." Joan and I conferred for a while, then we called them back and I said, "I'm going to be nominated. Get right on that plane." Then it dawned on us that they didn't have anything proper to wear—kids don't have suits, or at least they didn't in those days. I turned Ted and William over to Herb Allen and said go get them some suits, and Eleanor had to get her hair fixed. The very next night, they were onstage with us, looking wonderful. They didn't know what had hit them, but they were great.

After the phone call that morning, Carter wanted me to appear at an afternoon news conference at his hotel across town. Joan and I went downstairs and got into a car. The next thing we knew we were in a long motorcade—Secret Service, Carter staff, and a lot of police. We had to go fifteen or twenty blocks downtown and it was sirens all the way. As we pulled up to Carter's hotel, crowds were already gathering. There must have been two hundred people, with cameras as far as you could see. There we were, Joan and I. We looked at each other before we climbed out of the car, and we just had to take a deep breath and take the plunge.

When the convention ended, Joan and I flew back to the Twin Cities for a few days to relax with the family and share our excitement with the people of Minnesota. I also wanted to spend some time with Hubert, to thank him, to get his advice, and, I suppose, to acknowledge that we were turning a page in our own history. We arrived at the beginning of Minneapolis's signature summer festival, the Aquatennial. The organizers had asked me to ride in the opening-day parade, with a big banner reading WELCOME HOME, MR. VICE PRESIDENT. But if you look at pictures of that parade, you'll see they added an *s* at the last minute. I had called the grand marshal and said, Hubert will be riding with me today.

In his nominating speech for me on the closing night of the convention, Hubert had invoked thirty years of Democratic Party history and had reminded the delegates of the party's long struggle over civil rights. He said with some authority that the Carter-Mondale team represented a milestone for Democrats and added, "This ticket represents a final reunification of North and South."

I think Hubert was right, and that's one reason I headed into the fall campaign with a special sense of hope and vindication. I was confident that Carter and I could deliver a victory for Democrats in November, but I also thought we would, over the long run, start to redraw the nation's political map. We were coming out of a long period in American history when the Deep South created vexing problems for Democrats and the nation. For a candidate such as me—a Northern liberal with a known record on civil rights—campaigning in Alabama or Mississippi was like going into hostile territory. Wallace had hurt Humphrey there in 1968, and even now he might run again as a third-party candidate, rip the Democrats apart, and cost us the national election. Then, too, a lot of white Southern voters were starting to look at the Republican Party for the first time. If we could not win the South, we could not win national elections. Someone who could change that dynamic would be a real asset to the Democratic Party, and Carter was the guy. He wasn't one of those pointy-headed Northerners coming in and giving Southerners a lot of unsolicited advice about how to behave. He was well respected and was one of theirs. Moreover, a lot of Southern voters liked the idea of a Southerner in the White House and Carter spoke to that tinge of regional pride. Humphrey and the other prominent Democrats who might have run that year, for all their strengths, could not do what Carter did—to utterly marginalize Wallace and the politics of segregation—and everyone understood that. It was a big asset for Carter and for our country.

I also thought that a ticket combining a Northern liberal with a Southern progressive had the potential to restructure the Democratic Party and give it a new future. Most states of the Deep South had two Democratic parties—one white, one black. They would meet together from time to time, but the structures were separate. In a way, that was a microcosm of the national party. Across the North, from New England through the Midwest and down the West Coast, we were a progressive party, the party of civil rights and enlightened social views. In the Deep South, we were still mostly a party of the nineteenth century, a party of white men. If Carter and I could break that pattern—and I think we did, over the next twenty years—we would be the party of opportunity, of inclusion, a party that opened doors and threw away the old distinctions of race and gender, a party with a future. If the Democratic Party was limited to white males, as this party once was, we wouldn't be winning today.

Shortly after the convention, Hamilton Jordan wrote a long memo mapping out the fall campaign and developing these themes. Jordan was a brilliant political strategist—underappreciated, I think, because he hit it off poorly with the Washington press corps and was never taken seriously by some in the political establishment. He was the mastermind of Carter's primary-election strategy—a strategy that stunned the more prominent national Democrats—and he could look into the party's future.

My role was to take our campaign to the traditional Democratic strongholds of the North and West, and my itinerary carried me repeatedly along the same arc: from New York through New England, west into the industrial states of the Midwest, then over the mountains and down the West Coast. We had to carry these states, but some Democrats there weren't quite sure about Carter. I believe I was trusted in those places. I had been in their union halls. I had campaigned for their candidates. I was close to Humphrey and they loved Humphrey. By now I knew Carter well and I could tell them what sort of president he would be: He was going to be honest, he was going to be competent, he was going to be a reformer. It was a good message, a message people wanted to hear. They just needed to hear it from someone they knew. During that campaign they heard it from me seven days a week, fourteen hours a day. We joked that I spent more time in Ohio that fall than the average county commissioner.

Of course we also had to make our case against Jerry Ford and Bob Dole, and there we worked along two tracks. The first was that we were the progressives, the empathetic party that cared about people in their daily lives, while Ford and Dole represented an older form of cold conservatism. Ford was an honorable guy and at heart a moderate, but both of them had records we could run against. Dole had opposed the creation of Medicare, for example, and many other elements of the Great Society that were now widely accepted as part of a progressive society. For his part, Ford simply seemed ineffectual in leading the country out of the 1975 recession. People were ready for a president who would create jobs and restore prosperity.

The second track went a level deeper and tapped into the doubt and frustration left over from Watergate. Polls showed that people were turned off by government and politicians, but were ready for someone who might restore personal integrity in Washington. While Ford was an utterly decent man, people remembered that he had pardoned Nixon, and they didn't like it, and the pardon somehow carried the taint of Watergate onto Ford. When I addressed rallies, nothing got a crowd revved up like Ford's pardon of Nixon.

We came out of the Democratic convention with a huge lead over Ford—one of the Gallup polls showed us up by thirty-five points—but by September the margin narrowed. Ford had given a good speech at the Republican convention, then Dole began attacking Carter as someone who could not be pinned down on the issues, and familiarity with the incumbent gave voters comfort with Ford. By the first week in October several polls put the gap at single digits, and I would wake up in the middle of the night wondering, Is this race slipping through our fingers?

Then two events broke our way. The first was Ford's performance in the second presidential debate, on October 6. We prepared carefully because we knew that some voters still had questions about Carter's abilities, whereas Ford was seen as the steady incumbent. But then, well into the debate, Ford was asked a question about containing the Soviet threat. To everyone's amazement, he said, "There is no Soviet domination of Eastern Europe, and there never will be under a Ford administration. I don't believe the Poles consider themselves dominated by the Soviet Union." We couldn't believe our ears. Max Frankel, then associate editor of the *New York Times* and one of the panel of questioners, reframed the question and let Ford take another shot, but he repeated what he said. Worse, he continued to repeat it for the next five days. People knew that Ford was well traveled and reasonably experienced in foreign affairs. If he had simply taken it back the next day, said he had misspoken, it would have blown over as an issue. But by letting it stand, Ford reinforced the stereotype that he was not astute and left people deeply puzzled about his judgment.

The second turning point came when the League of Women Voters decided to sponsor a debate between the vice-presidential candidates, the first ever. Our campaign accepted instantly because I was still trying to introduce myself to a national audience and because, in a debate setting, I thought we had the more sympathetic case. In those days we didn't do the elaborate debate rehearsals that candidates conduct today, but I did ask my staff for memos on the issues we should emphasize and the themes that Dole had been using on the campaign trail. One member of our debate prep team was Thomas Hughes, an old friend from Minnesota; he had been a Rhodes scholar and a diplomat and was then head of the Carnegie Endowment for International Peace. As one of our meetings broke up, Tom said, "You know, I'll bet Dole will use that line about 'World War II and all those other Democrat wars.'" I said, "You're crazy, he wouldn't say that." But Tom reminded me that the Republicans had been repeating that line since Nixon, and that Dole had been using it on the stump.

The debate was scheduled for October 15 in Houston, and I had a feeling going in that I could handle Dole. I had known him for a long time in the Senate. We were friends, but I knew how he thought and how he spoke, and I thought his acerbic style, which worked well in a press conference or on the Senate floor, would come off poorly in a debate. Dole is smart and funny, but if you read a transcript of his jokes that night, you see there's a rock at the center of every snowball.

As the debate began, I could see Bob was tense, and he tried to cover for it with a sarcastic delivery. It wasn't working for him and he could tell, and as the debate went along, he kept getting tighter and tighter. I was pretty sure that all I had to do was keep my cool and let him make a mistake. Sure enough, toward the end of the debate, Walter Mears of the Associated Press asked Dole what he thought about Ford's pardon of Nixon—a pardon Dole had criticized at the time. Dole tried to change the subject by taking a shot at Carter and me with a reference to all the blood and money spent on "Democrat wars" in the twentieth century. He said, "I figured up the other day, if we added up the killed and wounded in Democrat wars, all in this century . . . it'd be about 1.6 million Americans—enough to fill the city of Detroit." I thought that was a blunder and that no one watching that night would go for it. When the moderator, Jim Hoge of the *Chicago Sun-Times*, asked for my response, I replied, "I think Senator Dole has richly earned his reputation as a hatchet man tonight, by implying and stating that World War II and the Korean War were Democratic wars. Does he really mean to suggest to the American people that there was a partisan difference over our involvement in the war to fight Nazi Germany? I don't think any reasonable American would accept that."

I felt good when I came off the platform, but when you're up in front of the cameras, it's impossible to tell how the debate is going over with people in the audience. I asked Jim Johnson, then my deputy campaign manager, "How'd I do?" He said, "Fabulous." The overnight surveys confirmed it. We got a big bounce in the polls in the next few days and started drawing much bigger crowds at our campaign stops. Carter quickly commissioned television ads showing pictures of Dole and me and saying, "What kind of men are they? When you know that four of the last six vice presidents have wound up as presidents, who would you like to see a heartbeat away from the presidency?" I had emerged, the *Washington Post* wrote, as "Carter's No. 1 asset in this campaign."

Nevertheless, the polls still showed the race to be extremely close, with margins of as little as 1 percent in some surveys. In the campaign's final days I blitzed the states with big blocs of electoral votes—Illinois, New York, New Jersey, Pennsylvania, and Ohio—and on the last day Carter and I rendezvoused in Flint, Michigan, for one of our few joint campaign rallies, on the gamble that we could take Ford's home state.

When the polls closed on election night, I was back in Minneapolis, with Joan and the kids and my staff at the old Leamington Hotel, where the DFL had held its election parties for years. Network anchors were calling the states one by one, but neither ticket could quite pull ahead. At eleven o'clock it was still too close to call. California came in, then the rest of the West Coast. At midnight, the networks had still not called the race. We were exhausted, but we stayed next to the television and the phones. Finally, with only a few states undecided, after 2 a.m. Mississippi reported its results. It had gone for Carter-Mondale and put us over the top. A state where the white power structure regarded me as their nemesis, a state that hadn't gone Democratic in a presidential race since 1956, was the key to victory for a Northern liberal and a Southern civil rights governor.

After the election I went down to Plains frequently to help Carter with the transition and to discuss my role in the administration. I was part of a steady stream of visitors—economists, diplomats, energy experts—organized by Stu Eizenstat, who would become Carter's top domestic aide, to brief the president-elect and, I suppose, interview for cabinet positions.

Carter asked me to refine our ideas about the vice presidency and put them down in writing. Dick Moe and I had been thinking about it since that first conversation with Hubert, so I asked Dick to draft a memo for me to send to Carter, and that memo laid out the key elements of our thinking.

First, I worried about being excluded from the information loop. After Hubert's experience with Johnson, I knew that if I didn't see everything Carter saw, even the classified material, I could not be an effective adviser. Then I thought about ways I could help the president, not only in policy discussions within the administration, but up on Capitol Hill, where I had a lot of friends, and out around the country, where I had done a lot of campaigning.

I submitted the memo to Carter on December 9 and didn't know how he would react. A few days later Jim Johnson and I flew down to Atlanta to meet with Carter at the governor's mansion. While we were waiting, Ham Jordan came out to say hello and asked us into the kitchen for a cup of coffee. I had copied him in on the memo, of course, and I asked him how he thought the president-elect would react. "Oh, the memo?" Ham said. "Just double-space it, and he'll agree to everything."

Jordan was right about Carter's reaction—as usual. I had expected to spend hours going over the memo with Carter, reviewing each recommendation and negotiating. But he simply looked over the whole document, put it down on his desk, and said, "This is fine." I was startled, and it must have shown in my face. He elaborated, "I want you to be in the chain of command—a vice president with the power to act in the president's place." Then, in an afterthought that took me completely by surprise, he said, "I also want you to be in the White House." That had never happened before and it wasn't in our memo. But it proved to be one of the most important decisions Carter made.

I didn't know that Carter had already given a great deal of thought to the role of the vice president. We later discovered that Ham Jordan had drafted a series of memos on the topic that were uncanny parallels of the memos Dick Moe had drafted for me. My interest was in making the job meaningful; Carter, as I came to see over the following months, arrived at the same conclusion but for different reasons. In his concept the president was a trustee on behalf of the people—someone above ordinary politics who would make government work in the broad public interest—and he wanted a vice president who would make full use of the office in the same mission of public service.

People have called Carter a "new Democrat," meaning that he was more conservative than some of us on the budget and the economy, more hawkish on military questions, and less connected to the liberal interest groups. But he was new in another way: He had a different conception of the role of government and the way a president could use the tools of office—not for his own power but on behalf of the public. In this, the Carter presidency looks better with every passing year.

Before our administration, the job of vice president had a terrible reputation. I had talked to Nelson Rockefeller and knew he was a lonely guy in the job. Though an accomplished politician and an outgoing fellow, he was generally ignored by Ford. People in the Nixon administration told me Spiro Agnew had it even worse: Nixon wouldn't even eat lunch with him. Then, poor Hubert. Johnson had gone out of his way to humiliate him. If Hubert wanted to use one of the White House airplanes, he had to submit a memo, with two boxes to check, Yes or No. Sometimes he would get the memo back checked No—personally by the president, with no explanation whatever.

Carter had a different idea. He felt that the vice presidency was an underused asset. He wanted someone who would develop real expertise, do real work on his behalf, and be a genuine adviser. I agreed, and I think we developed a model that "executivized" the office, according to presidential scholars, and that subsequent administrations have used. The details differ, but the broad principles are the same.

The vice president can be a lot of help to the president and, because of that, to the country. The president needs an independent source of advice, a separate set of ears that are not connected with any federal agency, so he can get governmentwide, objective counsel. If you are secretary of state, you're going to look at administration policy from the perspective of diplomats. If you are director of legislative affairs, you will always be thinking about how a particular decision will play on Capitol Hill. The vice president isn't tied down to any one of these constituencies when it comes time to balance priorities across the government and advise the president. Moreover, every president has a lot more to do than he can do. He can't begin to take on all the compelling international assignments he would like to, but the vice president can do these things, and in so doing he can extend the influence and prestige of the presidency.

Another element, which you can't quantify, is that a president gets the hell kicked out of him every day. He (or she) has critics in the press, rivals on Capitol Hill, political enemies looking to pounce at every turn. To have somebody around feeling the same kick and being able to understand it and measure it—someone who is also accountable to a national electorate—and talk it over with the president is valuable. Often I would just walk down to the Oval Office and tell him, "Mr. President, this is what I'm hearing and this is what I make of it."

Some years later, the constitutional scholar Joel Goldstein, a law professor at Saint Louis University, captured our thinking well: "It is surely in our national interest for our Vice President to be fully engaged in the work of the Executive Branch. The Mondale model helps assure that the constitutional successor is fully conversant with the issues our government faces. It provides a high-level official to help shoulder some of our nation's business. And it provides the President with counsel on a range of issues from a seasoned public official who is not distracted by having to administer an agency of his own."

I think the job description that Carter and I negotiated that fall has held up well over time. Indeed, most administrations since ours, regardless of party, have adopted the model, and it has resulted in a government more useful and more accountable to the public.

The exception is the Bush-Cheney administration. Some have argued that Dick Cheney's tenure was a natural extension of our effort to expand the role of the vice president. I couldn't disagree more. Cheney's philosophy of the office, and of government, was exactly the opposite of ours. First, I never felt that Carter delegated presidential authority to me. I may have influenced Carter's decisions, but we always understood that the decisions were his. Bush, by contrast, seemed to delegate constitutional authority to Cheney, who seemed to take power into his own hands as a matter of course. As Jane Mayer has written in her excellent book *The Dark Side*, Cheney's office became a secret government within the White House, which he used to manipulate information and influence decisions in the executive branch. For example, the 9/11 Commission concluded that Cheney issued the first air force shoot-down order on the morning of September 11, 2001—apparently before he had spoken to the president. The theory that a president could neutralize legislation with his "signing statements" also seems to have originated in Cheney's office, as did the deliberate effort to flout the Foreign Intelligence Surveillance Act, and the secret strategy to render torture legal.

Cheney's office also played a central role in the unconscionable propaganda campaign to stampede America into the war in Iraq. He implied, falsely, that Iraq contributed to the 9/11 terrorist attacks on our country. He insisted that Iraq was developing weapons of mass destruction. He predicted that the Iraqi people would welcome our troops with joy and flowers. He overruled all of the administration's skeptics and led us into the biggest, costliest, and most mistaken war in American history. Then, when these falsehoods began to unravel, his office directed the effort to suppress the truth and silence the critics. His staff has been implicated in the effort to destroy the reputation of Joseph Wilson, an honorable public servant who challenged the administration's assertion that Saddam Hussein was buying nuclear materials from Niger. His chief of staff, I. Lewis "Scooter" Libby, was convicted in federal court of lying to a grand jury and an FBI agent in connection with the Wilson affair, and the trial record left no doubt that Cheney's office tried to shield the White House from the consequences of its own dissembling.

The second departure from our precedent, even more troubling, was the way Cheney operated in secret. His refusal to cooperate with the Government Accountability Office in a routine inquiry about his energy task force in 2001 was one of the best-known examples; his claim that he didn't have to cooperate with National Archives guidelines on classified information because he wasn't part of the executive branch—the first vice president to refuse—was probably the most outlandish.

Carter expanded the role of the vice president in an effort to make the government more responsive to the public; Cheney seemed to do the opposite. Joel Goldstein was on the mark when he wrote, "Cheney's approach was antithetical to that Mondale followed. Cheney's office did not simply avoid meaningful Congressional oversight. It structured decision-making within the executive branch in such a manner as to avoid debate. The Cheney vice presidency reflected a culture of political unaccountability which transcended the separation of powers debates regarding presidential power."

My earnest hope is that the Cheney model was an aberration—one since repudiated by the voters. That said, the American people pay more attention to the vice president and expect more from the office as a result of the changes that Carter and I initiated. But we were just feeling our way along at the time. It was all new. One day in November 1976, between the election and the inauguration, Carter came to Washington to pay a courtesy call on President Ford. Carter was staying at Blair House, the guest quarters across the street from 1600 Pennsylvania Avenue, and we had breakfast before he went over to see Ford. Just before he left to walk across the street, Carter turned to me and asked, "What's it like?"

"What are you talking about?" I asked.

"The White House."

"You've never been in the White House?" I had been there many times during my years in the Senate, but he had never been inside. I just shrugged. "It's a pretty nice place. I think you'll like it."

9

Our First Year in
the White House

THOUGH I HAD visited the White House many times, nothing quite prepares you for moving in. On Inauguration Day 1977, Joan and I were sitting in the reviewing stand on Pennsylvania Avenue with our kids and the Carter family, watching the inaugural parade go by. The University of Minnesota marching band performed, of course, along with a little high school band from Elmore. Thousands of friends and well-wishers turned out. It was a thrilling day for all of us. As the parade wound down, an aide from the White House staff came up into the risers and said, "Would you like to go to your office now?" It took me by surprise. After all those weeks on the road, concentrating so intently on the campaign, it had never quite sunk in that if we won, I would wind up with a new job and a new office. I said, "Sure." Two Secret Service agents took Joan and me out of the parade stand, through an opening in the fence, and across the White House lawn into the West Wing. When we reached my office, the walls were bare and a few boxes sat on the floor. It was all new, unknown, fun, and absolutely scary. I said, "Okay, what happens next?"

We didn't wait long to test my new role in the administration. In February 1977 the U.S. Supreme Court agreed to hear an explosive affirmative action case, *Regents of the University of California v. Bakke*. Allan

Bakke was a young white student—from Minnesota—who had unsuccessfully applied to medical school in California. He had sued, alleging
that the University of California used an unconstitutional preference system that admitted lesser-qualified minority candidates ahead of him.

I knew that our administration would be expected to take a position on this landmark case. A few weeks later, Stu Eizenstat, the head
of Carter's domestic policy staff, stopped into my office and said he was
worried about the way we were handling it. Stu said that Attorney General Griffin Bell had asked his staff to begin drafting an amicus brief
and that the draft came out on Bakke's side, with serious reservations
about affirmative action. Bell, Stu said, had not instructed his staff on
the argument of the brief, but he was an old friend of Carter's and a former federal judge from Georgia, so his views would be influential with
the president.

I hadn't known Stu well before the campaign, but he had worked on
Humphrey's 1968 race, and I quickly learned that we shared the same
values. He was a wonderful public servant, and over the next few months
we would become good friends and steady allies in the West Wing. I felt
much the way he did about *Bakke*. Civil rights had been one of the cor-
nerstones of the Carter-Mondale campaign. I had supported the concept
of affirmative action my entire career. Carter had said supportive things
about it, too. It was, I thought, a basic foundation of our administration,
and the idea that we would come out for the *Bakke* position scared me. It
scared Stu, too. Quite apart from the politics, he thought the brief was
poorly reasoned and poorly argued. He thought it was a weak case to test
such a big social principle, and he thought the Justice Department had
the wrong interpretation of the Constitution.

So we went to work. I had Mike Berman on my staff contact university
officials around the country to explore the consequences of a dilution of
affirmative action standards. University presidents and admissions officers told him that if the court rolled back affirmative action programs, we
would probably see a reduction in the number of minority students graduating with degrees in law, medicine, and other professions. Mike argued
that this could, in turn, cause reductions in medical and legal services in

minority communities. We also felt it would set back efforts to integrate these professions and open the door for young people of color in our society. Then I asked Ham Jordan for advice on broaching the subject with Carter and Bell. I often consulted Ham if members of Carter's inner circle might be in disagreement. He understood Carter's thinking better than anyone else, always gave me good counsel, and, though utterly committed to collegiality within the staff, had the courage to force decisions.

Meanwhile, Stu made some phone calls to the Justice Department to determine how they reached their position. Griffin Bell had told Carter that he assigned the drafting to "the best black lawyer in America," a reference to Wade McCree, Carter's solicitor general. McCree was a distinguished jurist, but when Stu called Wade, McCree said he had not been deeply involved and had left the drafting to Frank Easterbrook, a Justice Department holdover from the Nixon administration, who later became a federal judge. Nothing was wrong with this per se; we respected the work of career professionals in cabinet agencies, and Carter was wary of political meddling at the Justice Department. But Easterbrook plainly didn't understand the administration's thinking on affirmative action and was advancing arguments we didn't support. A little later I called a meeting in my office with McCree and representatives of the Congressional Black Caucus, and it seemed to me that the brief contained a number of arguments that McCree hadn't reviewed or couldn't defend.

I went to see Carter a few days later. I was just down the hall from the president and could walk into the Oval Office whenever I needed to. Carter had promised this kind of access and he kept his word. I didn't like to deal through memos—I would send them, but I preferred just to go in directly and talk through the politics with him. I told Carter I thought his attorney general was making a mistake. I said, "This is something that's fundamental to you. You've made a commitment, and if we break it, we're going to pay a big price. People aren't going to believe us anymore." He saw what I was saying and agreed with me. He had read the draft brief and had doubts of his own. It was tough for him because Griffin Bell was an old friend. It was delicate for me because Bell prided himself on the independence of the Justice Department; to him, anybody who meddled there was a politician, not a lawyer. But I thought this was public policy as well as politics, and that's what I argued to Carter.

I also argued that, although it was early in our administration, we had to think about this case strategically. I knew that this administration was going to run tight budgets and would not have a financial solution for every domestic problem. So on issues that turned on basic fairness and principle, as opposed to spending money, I thought we had to be seen as standing for opportunity. Carter agreed, and a few weeks later encouraged Stu, himself a lawyer by training, to join in drafting the administration's brief. In a memo that Stu prepared for Carter and me a few weeks later, he argued:

> The brief which the government files in the *Bakke* case will not simply be a legal document. Rather, it will be seen as a statement of this administration's policy on an issue—affirmative action— which is an integral part of large numbers of Federal programs.
>
> Your policy in this area is and has been that you vigorously support affirmative action as a necessary tool in the effort to overcome the legacy of discrimination, but that you oppose rigid quotas. The brief should say that.

As Stu argued in his memo, we did not support racial quotas, but we did think the Constitution permitted reasonable affirmative action programs that allowed universities to consider race as one factor in the overall admissions mix. That's the brief we wound up submitting, in September 1977. In June 1978, that's exactly what the Supreme Court ruled. The justices remanded the case to the lower court, agreeing that the California affirmative action policy was too rigid, but also affirming the broader right of universities to take race into account in their admissions programs. That proved to be a landmark ruling on affirmative action, and I think we helped guide the country to a good outcome, one that has held up well over the years.

The *Bakke* case was an important test of my working relationship with Carter. No vice president had ever done what I was doing—attending every meeting, reading every memo, walking into the Oval Office whenever necessary. It also signaled to the rest of Washington that something had changed in the White House. Members of the Congressional Black Caucus knew right away about the case and about where we were headed. The decision we reached made me stronger, later, when I went up to the Hill to work with them. Word of the president's and my relationship got around to cabinet officers, key members of Congress, and even world leaders, and that allowed me to have a different relationship with them. I was the junior partner, to be sure, but it was a partnership, unlike any other in American history. The press corps was skeptical, naturally, and before long they were writing stories saying that nothing had changed in the vice presidency. Later that year press secretary Jody Powell got word that Jack Nelson of the *Los Angeles Times* was working on a column to that effect. He was calling various officials in the administration to ask if Carter really listened to Mondale. Carter was great. He told Jody, "Get me Nelson's phone number." That was the end of that column.

One reason the new relationship worked is surprisingly simple: proximity. The West Wing is a very small place. You bump into each other all the time. Ham Jordan was three feet from me on one side, Zbig Brzezinski was about the same on the other. Stu Eizenstat was just upstairs. The president was just fifteen feet away. All the same materials were handed over our desks. I got the president's schedule every day and I was invited to every meeting. Some days Carter and I would be together four, five, six hours. Many times I simply walked down the hall to the Oval Office with problems, such as the *Bakke* case, and talked to Carter alone.

A West Wing office hadn't even occurred to me. Previous vice presidents for some years were billeted across the street in the Old Executive Office Building, where much of the White House staff actually works. It's a magnificent place—high ceilings, big windows, vast offices—whereas the West Wing is rather ordinary and cramped. But a hundred yards is a long way when crises blow up and blow over every five minutes. I used to joke with my staff, if you're in the Old Executive Office Building, you might as well be in Baltimore.

In addition, we integrated my staff with Carter's so we didn't suffer the usual us-versus-them divisions. Staff rivalries are legendary in Washington, and they can subvert the best of plans. I brought over Gail Harrison, Mike Berman, Bert Carp, and David Aaron from my Senate office, as well as Dick Moe and Jim Johnson. David Aaron, my foreign policy adviser in the Senate, became Brzezinski's chief deputy; Bert Carp, my adviser on education, desegregation, and other domestic issues, became Eizenstat's deputy. It was unconventional, but it worked. The day I called Stu about Bert, he said, "Mr. Vice President, I already have a deputy, David Rubenstein." I said, "That's fine. Now you have two." I think Stu never regretted the arrangement.

One of the things for which Carter never gets credit is picking great staff—bright and decent human beings. Ham Jordan had become a good friend during the campaign; his staff and my staff practically lived together in Atlanta for most of the fall. He made sure I was always in the loop. Charlie Kirbo, a cornpone Southern lawyer but bright and close to Carter, was always open to my views. This reflected Carter's basic decency, but was also the key to an effective White House. I used to joke, "Nothing propinques like propinquity."

Goodwill at the staff level, however, did not mean that I won every argument inside the White House, and we had our share. In February 1977, while making revisions to the federal budget left by Ford, Carter announced that he planned to veto nineteen federal water projects in more than a dozen Western states. It shouldn't have come as a shock on Capitol Hill. Carter had come to Washington with a reputation as a conservationist and had promised during the campaign to reform federal spending. In addition, the projects had been recommended for a veto by the Interior Department and the Office of Management and Budget because, measured honestly, they didn't meet federal cost-benefit requirements. People forget how deeply Carter felt about wilderness and natural resources. He saw these dam and irrigation projects as cheap politics and bad environmental policy. He'd had experience with one of them in Georgia, which he vetoed as governor. He was going to take that experience and show that in Washington, too, there could be a public dimension to federal infrastructure spending that cut across the special interests.

But water politics was still powerful in the West, and congressmen from the Western states were allergic to outside interference, which is how they regarded Carter's veto. Suddenly we had a rebellion on our hands. They said we had declared "war on the West." Within days, our detractors were circulating various lists around Capitol Hill about projects that were alleged to be doomed. Of course everyone added his or her own project to the lists to build the opposition, and within a month we had a big, organized region of the country putting the brakes on everything the president tried to do.

This was exactly the sort of fight where I was supposed to be helpful to Carter. I told him we were organizing our own opposition in Congress. Every Western state has two senators and one or two powerful congressmen, and every one of them was being alerted to stand in our way until we relented on the water projects. My advice was that we should pick two or three of the most egregious projects and go after those. I thought we were letting the politics get away from us, and that pretty soon we would face nothing but roadblocks on Capitol Hill.

But Carter felt deeply about the matter. He had developed the veto list in consultation with environmentalists and budget experts whom he trusted, and he felt it was part of his promise to govern in a new way—to represent the broad public interest instead of cobbling together the special interests. Carter's first reaction in the face of this rebellion was to turn the screws some more—to go over the heads of the caucus leaders and prepare lists of congressmen to call. He was tireless at that. Eventually we rounded up enough votes to sustain a veto, but House Speaker Tip O'Neill called the president and proposed a compromise—to suspend the projects rather than cancel them. Carter agreed, but that only infuriated several members of Congress who, at some risk to their congressional friendships, had promised to support us. In the end, a year later, Carter finally did sign a bill canceling several of the projects on his list. So we won a little on the merits, but we lost a lot on the politics.

Over time, however, I believe Carter changed the way people think about those federal infrastructure projects. The *New York Times* editorial page came around to our side, noting the environmental hazards and the international frictions caused by diverting rivers. Environmental groups raised their level of scrutiny on dam and diversion projects, and voters applied a more balanced view to the benefits and costs.

My new job also meant big changes for the Mondale family. We moved out of our house on Lowell Street in Northwest Washington to the vice president's residence at One Observatory Circle off Massachusetts Avenue. Ted, Eleanor, and William, now teenagers, found themselves in the media spotlight from time to time and handled it impressively. Joan, who had begun to establish herself as an arts advocate of national stature and had written a book, *Politics in Art,* soon found new venues for her skills. Thanks to President Carter, she became honorary chair of the Federal Council on the Arts and Humanities, where she established herself as a champion of art in public spaces and helped establish a set-aside for arts funding in the construction of new federal buildings. Although she missed our house and neighbors on Lowell Street, she soon transformed the Vice President's residence into a showcase for prominent American artists such as Claes Oldenburg, Louise Nevelson, Frank Stella, Audrey Flack, and James Rosenquist, and before long she was known around Washington as "Joan of Arts."

The water projects veto was only one of several power struggles that unfolded during our first months in office. In the early days of any administration it's normal for Congress and the new president to test each other: How do they fit? What is the role of the Congress with this president? Where are the powers? Even when they come from the same party and the congressional leadership wants to support the president, members of Congress will be looking for small issues and personal priorities where they can test their pull with the administration. They sort of stare and grunt and snarl, suspicious of each other, and try to find out what kind of equilibrium there will be.

In our case the suspicions ran even higher—on both sides. Some people assumed that, after eight years of Republicans in the White House, it would be all light and happiness with Democrats at both ends of Pennsylvania Avenue. But many of the lawmakers I called the old whales, the powerful veteran committee chairmen, had little interest in

My home town, Elmore, Minnesota, gave me a love of sports and competition—and the nickname "Crazy Legs" Mondale. It also taught me an appreciation for community and the idea that neighbors take care of each other in times of need.

1

My father, a farmer turned Methodist minister, and my mother, a music teacher, grew up in small towns and modest circumstances. But they read widely and instilled in us our faith and the values of compassion and service. This portrait, with my older brother, Pete, was taken in 1937 on the lawn of the Heron Lake Methodist Church in southern Minnesota.

2

3

I was a student at Macalester College when I first met Hubert Humphrey, shown here with Macalester president Charles J. Turck and me. Humphrey electrified students as a young political-science professor. He would soon electrify the voters of Minnesota with his vision for a new political organization, the Democratic Farmer-Labor Party, and became one of the most influential progressive leaders of his time.

Balancing work and family was tricky for a busy young attorney general, but from the beginning, Ted, Eleanor, and William were a source of joy and energy for Joan and me. Eleanor, shown here at age four, hadn't yet had her great adventure in the Detroit airport.

4

In 1960, I chaired John Kennedy's presidential campaign in Minnesota. We carried the state for him in a close election, and I later saw him periodically at the White House while serving on the president's consumer advisory council. Kennedy inspired many young Democrats of my generation with his charisma, optimism, and tremendous intellect.

5

6

A thrilling day: Governor Karl Rolvaag (*left*) named me to fill Minnesota's vacant Senate seat in 1964 when Hubert became Lyndon Johnson's vice president. Rolvaag and Miles Lord (*center*) were stalwarts of the DFL family that gave Minnesota its reputation for enlightened, progressive politics.

Humphrey taught me invaluable lessons about being an effective senator, and we became key allies in Washington. One result was that Minnesota's style of progressive politics had a big influence on the country's direction in the 1960s and 1970s.

7

The Fair Housing Act of 1968 was one of the first major bills I carried in the Senate, and it became the capstone of the great civil rights legislation of the 1960s. Lyndon Johnson, shown signing the legislation, made a crucial last-minute phone call that enabled us to break a filibuster by Southern segregationists and pass the bill.

8

9

Mike Berman, who had been on my staff since the attorney general days, could handle any assignment, from the most complicated legal question to a tailoring emergency. Jimmy Carter presented me with this photograph, scribbling in the corner that he was proud to work with such a humble populist.

The 1976 election was the first to feature a debate between the vice-presidential candidates. I didn't look forward to facing off with Bob Dole, an old friend from the Senate, but the debate went well for our side and gave the Carter-Mondale ticket a big boost in the polls.

10

Jimmy Carter and I shared a new vision of the vice presidency—and many happy moments, as this informal photo suggests—and together we redefined the job with lasting consequences.

11

12

My arrangement with Carter gave me unrestricted and unprecedented access to the Oval Office, to staff meetings, and to every document that crossed his desk. We were often together four hours a day, and it gave me a deep appreciation for his integrity and political courage. We remain close friends.

Indochinese refugees, known throughout the world as the "boat people," were subject to horrific suffering and dangers when the Vietnamese government began expelling them after the fall of Saigon. Organizing a successful multinational rescue mission was, to Carter and me, both a humanitarian imperative and a measure of our commitment to human rights in foreign policy.

13

The Iran hostage crisis, which started when student radicals stormed our Tehran embassy in November 1979, was a shattering experience for America and the Carter-Mondale administration. It also signaled the emergence of a new, nihilistic style of Islamic extremism that is still with us today.

14

15

Ted Kennedy and I had been good friends and political allies since our days as young senators, and though we clashed in 1980 when he challenged Carter for the Democratic nomination, he campaigned hard for me in 1984 at rallies like this one in Boston.

I went into the 1984 presidential race as front-runner for the party nomination but wound up battling Jesse Jackson and Gary Hart in a contest that forced Democrats to define what they stood for in the 1980s.

16

Geraldine Ferraro was an effective running mate—smart, spirited, and energetic. In choosing her, I think I opened doors and changed the way women—and all Americans—thought about power and opportunity in America.

17

18

Reagan campaigned with a series of finely crafted television commercials, a strategy I called "puppy dogs and picket fences." I preferred to get out in front of voters and reporters every day, and I consider it a privilege that I got that chance to make my case for values I believed in.

In the first presidential debate of the 1984 campaign, Ronald Reagan seemed distracted and confused, a performance that underscored voters' doubts about his faculties and gave our campaign a lift. But he disarmed those doubts with a crisp one-liner in the second debate. He had a sunny self-confidence that suited voters during a difficult decade.

19

During the Carter and Reagan years, politics in our country underwent a sea change, as Americans came to doubt many of the values I had worked on for two decades. I spent a lot of time thinking about ways to rally disillusioned voters behind a progressive agenda.

20

21

We were campaigning in Florida during the 1984 presidential race when I spotted this fellow and said, "Stop the bus." We talked about fishing, my favorite subject. With all the bedlam, I'm not sure he knew what had hit him.

22

The Japan-U.S. friendship is the most important bilateral relationship in the world, bar none, and I hoped my years as U.S. ambassador in Tokyo would help bring stability to a region of the world that can be very unstable. Prime Minister Ryutaro Hashimoto and I, shown here in the study of the ambassador's residence, worked together to revise the agreement covering U.S. military bases on Okinawa, greatly strengthening the friendship.

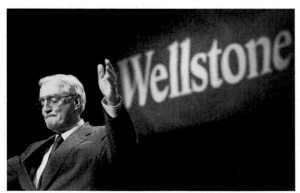

I had retired from politics by 2002, but the tragic death of Senator Paul Wellstone in a plane crash just eleven days before the November election created a unique challenge for the party, the state, and the nation, and I agreed to take his place on the ballot.

23

seeing us succeed. They were profoundly skeptical of this Democratic outsider, and they were scheming right from the start to find ways of testing and diminishing him. They were almost as happy with a Republican president as a Democratic president because the big point was getting their own way. To complicate matters, the Ninety-fifth Congress didn't embrace the old party protocols. Of 292 Democrats in the House that year, more than 100 had been elected since 1974; many were swept in on the reform tide after Watergate, and many were skeptical of traditional loyalties to the White House. For his part, I think Carter was suspicious of some of the national Democratic leaders. Carter felt many of them were just doing business for the interest groups and not the broader interest of the American public.

So we ended up, almost immediately, with a struggle over whether the president would have any stroke on Capitol Hill. Another test arose over missile negotiations with the Soviets, what became the SALT II Treaty. When we started negotiations, Scoop Jackson insisted that our negotiating team include Lieutenant General Edward Rowny. Rowny was a distinguished veteran of World War II, Korea, and Vietnam, but also a real hawk with respect to the Soviets. We were new and we wanted to accommodate Scoop; he was an expert on weapons systems and an influential member of the Senate, and he had his own presidential ambitions. But Rowny just threw sand in the negotiations. He briefed anyone who asked, generally describing the talks as hopeless, and he gave Scoop a direct pipeline into the negotiations, which Scoop used to his own ends. The idea was, in effect, to grab that steering wheel away from Carter.

Another project that became tough for us was economic stimulus legislation. The country had gone through a painful recession in 1975 and wasn't feeling much better as we campaigned in 1976, so Carter wanted to send a jobs bill to Congress right away. In late January we introduced legislation with several components—a jobs program, some public works spending, and a $50 per person tax rebate. Carter had put a lot of thought into it and had consulted some fine economists, including Charlie Schultze, the head of his Council of Economic Advisers, and Art Okun from the Brookings Institution. But from the beginning we were probably somewhat divided ourselves. The rebate was one of my ideas. While I was in the Senate, we had passed something like it, a tax credit aimed at low-income working families. I recommended a family rebate to Carter because I wanted to find a tax policy that would bring help to average families and children. It wasn't much, but I felt it was symbolically important to give something to every family.

But we quickly collided with the congressional barons. A lot of the public works characters wanted stimulus funds to pay for bridges and highways. They didn't want to put money in the hands of ordinary people. The tax committees had their own ideas about who should get tax relief, and they thought they had better ideas than simply giving the average family $200. Then we ran into the budget crowd—the House and Senate Budget committees—which had always been skeptical when I tried to sell the rebate.

Now we were getting into the spring, and the congressional committees with jurisdiction over spending and taxes were thoroughly reworking the stimulus package—especially the public works component. Meanwhile, the economy was starting to recover on its own, and Carter was afraid the tax rebate would look unnecessary and bog down the whole package. I don't think he was ever enthusiastic about it. He was more aware of the inflationary pressures building in the economy than I was, and he wanted to avoid stimulating the economy excessively. I think he believed this $50 per person would take a lot of work to get through Congress, then later would be blamed for aggravating inflation, so he unilaterally pulled it from the economic package. But that only caused more trouble for us. Ed Muskie, who was chairman of the Senate Budget Committee, had worked hard to make room in the Senate budget for the rebate, and then Carter dropped it without warning him. Muskie was furious. We did finally get an economic stimulus package, one that was limited and sensible, but that episode hurt us.

I had hoped I might help Carter navigate these shoals, or at least avoid collisions with our friends. I spent a lot of time up on the Hill with senators and members of the House picking up information that I would bring to the president. I also spent a lot of time traveling around the country attending fund-raisers and talking to various constituencies—labor, minority groups, teachers, environmentalists—consulting them, listening to them, and giving Carter reports on what I heard.

I would typically bring these reports to Carter at a private lunch we had each Monday. That proved to be one of our most valuable ideas—just the two of us, no staff, no fixed agenda, totally honest. I often used those lunches for politics because Carter didn't like to bring politics into our meetings with cabinet officials and agency staff. This was my chance to tell him what I was hearing and how I interpreted it.

After one or two of those early struggles with Congress I told Carter, "Before this is over, you are going to find that people like Tip O'Neill are your best friends. They might seem alien to you right now—creatures of Washington, of the party—but they want you to succeed. They can deliver with this constituency, if they want to, in ways others can't."

In the end he would concede that Northern Democrats such as Tip were often on his side. But we had plenty of misfires along the way. At that time the president traditionally invited the congressional leadership down to the White House for working breakfasts from time to time. Now we were in the White House and Carter wanted to do it his way. Out went the big, elegant breakfasts and instead we just served sweet rolls or croissants—Carter's way of signaling a new era of restraint. Carter also changed the format. He did not want to get into a bartering relationship with Congress. He wanted to describe the world as he saw it, and he took these sessions as an opportunity to spell out his agenda. Well, that's not the way members of Congress think about it. Most of the leadership wanted to help Carter be a good president, but they wanted to approach the relationship as equals, and they wanted some of their own ideas in the mix. Most of them, after all, had a good deal of expertise after years of drafting legislation and conducting hearings. At the very first breakfast, as we were leaving, Tip O'Neill pulled me aside in high dudgeon. He said, "Look, I've waited years to see a Democrat in the White House, and when I come down here to confer with the president, I expect a real meal." It sounds petty in retrospect, but it illustrated the way that Washington is constantly gauging egos and testing power. We were able to change the menu, but not all of the attitudes.

Carter came to Washington with a novel idea of presidential power. He was not going to conduct his presidency through interest groups, by balancing one constituency against another and engaging in the customary horse-trading on the Hill. He wanted to be the trustee of the public will and ride above the old politics. He thought that is why he had been elected president. He had run against the Hubert Humphreys and Scoop Jacksons in the Democratic primaries, and he mowed them all down because the public wanted something new. He thought he had a responsibility and an obligation to govern differently.

To be fair, I'm not sure the congressional leadership ever understood Jimmy Carter. He was president of the United States, a national Democrat, but he was also a moderate Southern Georgian. He believed in eating your peas and beans. He thought everything you did in Washington should be something you could clearly and honestly explain to your neighbors back home. He was an utterly honorable guy—he never embarrassed me, no matter how intense the pressures got within the White House. I think that Carter figured, in the final analysis, it's what the folks back home think of you that is the measure of your qualities as president: Do you tell the truth, do you keep your word, do you live by your principles?

As the first year progressed, I argued in our Monday lunches that he needed to be more political. I said we had people who elected us—minorities, working people, farmers and teachers and so on—and while we hadn't made any promises to them, we had an obligation to hear them out. As we put our budgets together, they needed to feel that we were empathetic, that the government was responsive to their concerns even in the midst of adverse circumstances.

But that is not where Carter was. He was a nuclear engineer, an empiricist, and believed in the value of evidence. He didn't understand why you would support a government program if you didn't have proof that it was effective and efficient. He wanted groups and organizations to take most responsibilities upon themselves, and he thought government should help only around the edges. He could be charming and he certainly heard me out. But if he had some objective in mind and thought he was right, he could be direct—laserlike.

But contrary to what some have concluded, Carter was not one-dimensional, or inflexible. Quite the opposite—he had a clear sense of the possible and the realities of governing. Early in our administration he had appointed a staff working group to study what we called the Dooms-day Question—the massive financial liabilities of future pension obligations to public employees. He put Charlie Kirbo in charge and told him to report back in a couple of months. The task force spent some weeks studying the issue, and almost every expert they consulted doubted that federal revenues could ever keep pace with the ballooning pension liabilities. The day arrived for Kirbo to present the group's recommendations, and Carter gathered us all around the big table in the Cabinet Room. Kirbo had by this time realized that the issue was a terrible can of worms. He began: "Mr. President, there are some people who think these obligations are an absolute crisis. There are some who think the system actually is working pretty well. There is another group who think that the best solution is to do away with all these pensions and let those people fend for themselves. And then"—here Kirbo paused—"there is a group who think the best solution for now is to just . . . let it sit."

After a moment's silence, Carter said, "What?"

Kirbo repeated, "Let it . . . sit."

Carter paused as if digesting something, then smiled and thanked us all and adjourned the meeting, and I never heard him bring it up again.

Carter could also be humorous, in a way that is not captured in the earnest profiles that appeared in the newspapers at that time. During our second year in office we were preparing for a state visit by Imelda Marcos of the Philippines. She visited the United States frequently and always made sure the White House was on her itinerary. Carter had asked me to take the meetings on Marcos's first three or four visits, and on this occasion he asked me to receive her again. About an hour before she arrived, I went into the Oval Office and protested, "Mr. President, this isn't fair.

She's not coming to see me, she wants to see you. She's the first lady of her country and she expects to see the president. Moreover, I've seen her four times in a row. Maybe you should just poke your head in and say hello this time." Without really looking up from his desk, Carter said, "Fritz, I wasn't going to tell you this, but we have certain ways of learning things, and we've discovered that Imelda *really* likes you." Then he looked up and flashed a grin. Needless to say, I hosted that day's meeting.

Carter also had a deeply thoughtful and compassionate side. One day I was on the phone with Humphrey, who by this time was quite ill with cancer, describing a meeting held at Camp David. Hubert asked, "What's it like?" I said, "Camp David? You've never been there?" I mentioned it to Carter the next day. He picked up the phone, called Hubert, and said, "Rosalynn and I would be honored if you and Muriel would join us for a weekend at Camp David." Hubert and Muriel loved that weekend, and I will never forget seeing, some months later, Hubert's now weakened signature on the Camp David guest book.

Looking back on our first year, I think there's no question that we misread the politics from time and time and sent too much up to Capitol Hill, as many of our critics charged. It was not a mistake, strictly speaking. Carter had campaigned on a broad range of issues—energy conservation, budget reform, job creation, military modernization—and he felt he owed action to the people who had voted for him. By any objective measure, the year saw significant accomplishments. We proposed, and Congress adopted, the creation of a federal Department of Energy; we passed an economic stimulus package that finally got the economy out of its doldrums; we prevailed with the Supreme Court on the *Bakke* decision; and we passed a budget that would, within a year, cut the federal deficit in half. But there's no question that, as Dick Moe put it, we "overloaded the circuits" in Congress. The public appearance, I'm afraid, was of an ineffective administration being diddled by a stronger Congress. For that, I blame myself in significant measure.

Before the year was over, Ham Jordan, Stu Eizenstat, and I had all made our case to Carter that our legislative program had been too ambitious. Carter didn't disagree—a point he later made in his memoirs—and toward the end of 1977 he asked me for a new blueprint. I turned to Gail Harrison, who had done a marvelous job of coordinating our legislative program during the transition, and she mapped out a new approach. Toward the end of 1977 each cabinet secretary submitted a list of legislative priorities for the coming year, which Gail compiled and submitted in a memo to the senior White House staff. They winnowed it down, separating essentials from wish lists, then Gail and Stu summarized them in a memo to me. We all went over them again, red pens in hand, and in the end we produced a matrix of priorities showing which issues required Carter's personal lobbying and which could be left to cabinet staff or our congressional office.

The result was a more tightly focused legislative program and better use of Carter's time, and our agenda fared well in Congress the next three years.

If Carter had to learn certain lessons about Washington, however, he was also in a position to teach some. By the mid-1970s we had entered a new era for the American economy, a period of slow growth and rising prices known as stagflation. This would have profound long-term consequences that most of us did not anticipate at the time. A slowing economy generated fewer jobs and less tax revenue, which meant we couldn't fully afford the ambitious government social programs of the 1960s. Slower productivity growth caused wages to stagnate and produced the squeeze on the middle class that caused so much economic anxiety over the next two decades. Inflation would cause jitters in the financial markets and bring higher interest rates.

Carter saw the implications before most people did. Nixon and Ford had wrestled with inflation—Nixon using temporary wage and price controls and Ford printing those WHIP INFLATION NOW buttons. But neither approach worked, and by the time we took over, inflation was well above the comfort range.

This wasn't just an American problem. Prime Minister James Callaghan had 20 percent inflation in Great Britain. The unions staged a series of strikes, trying to get wages that would keep pace with prices. Margaret Thatcher ran against the unions, against the social-democratic programs, and she beat Labour. All across Western Europe, governments were dropping like flies.

Carter recognized the challenge from our first days in the White House. He spent a lot of time with good economists, and he knew that the deficit spending of his predecessors had overheated the economy. He insisted on tight budgets, not only as a signal of prudent leadership but also as a way of taking money out of the economy and cooling off inflation. He wanted to disabuse people of the expectation that government would solve every problem. In our second budget, for the fiscal year that would start in the fall of 1978, he set a deficit target of $30 billion—down from more than $70 billion recorded in 1976. This was not an illusory struggle but a challenge he set before our administration every day.

But this only intensified our struggles with members of Congress who were supposed to be our friends. We were dealing with Democrats who came out of the Great Society, in better economic times. We had a Congress full of people like me, who had high expectations for what was possible under a new Democratic president, and a lot of backlogged expectations—only we didn't have the economy that would pay for it.

In time, I moved closer to Carter's view. The inflation rate was going up, not down. The budget deficits were not going to evaporate by magic. All the solutions were going to be unpleasant. My friends didn't expect to hear this message from me. But I had spent some months on the inside of government, and I saw how inflation could frustrate our plans. You would set a budget for health care programs or the schools or military salaries, and before you knew it, inflation was eating it up and everybody was coming back for more. I heard the same thing as I moved around the country, visiting communities and giving speeches on behalf of the administration. You could see the way inflation was creeping into people's psychology—their savings were shrinking, they were worried about next year's bills. The great economist John Maynard Keynes had observed the same thing, warning, "By a continuing process of inflation governments can confiscate, secretly and unobserved, an important part of the wealth of their citizens."

I knew we were headed for a showdown with a number of our allies—

in the labor movement, in the antipoverty movement, in city halls across the country—and I felt it was best to confront them out in the open. In February 1978 the United Auto Workers came to Washington for their national legislative conference—four or five hundred union activists and some close friends of mine. Victor Reuther had been a great ally going back to the civil rights era, and UAW president Doug Fraser had been an early supporter of Carter. In those days the UAW was a public-minded union, and its priority was national health insurance. I also knew that Ted Kennedy was going to address its conference. He was carrying a national health insurance bill in the Senate, and he was already growing restless with Carter. So I went to see them and explained what the Carter-Mondale administration was trying to accomplish and the ways we were working with the labor movement. We had submitted a good bill to improve labor's organizing rights in the workplace, and I had worked the Senate hard to round up support. We really sweated for that bill, but we came up two votes short, and it's the closest Congress has since come to enacting labor law reform.

At the end of my speech, an old friend of mine stood up and said, "Oh, yes, Mr. Vice President, but you didn't mention national health insurance. You have always told us you support our legislation, and now you are in office and not getting anything done. What can you possibly say?"

I said, "That's a good question. I do like that bill. But how many times has that bill been introduced in Congress? Into the most liberal committee in the Senate? How many years?" I knew the answer. I had been on Kennedy's committee, and we had been trying to move that bill for six years; most members of the Senate simply weren't prepared to vote for a national single-payer insurance system, and they foresaw a lobbying shoot-out that could tie up Washington for months. "How many markup periods have they had over these three Congresses, and how many times has it been reported out of that subcommittee, which Senator Kennedy chairs, in all these years?" I asked. "Not once. Not once, from the most liberal committee in the Senate."

It would be thirty-two years before Congress finally passed health care reform. It was a great achievement for President Obama and the country, but even then, with big Democratic majorities in the House and Senate, Congress didn't come close to creating a national single-payer system.

But the big showdown over Carter's economic policy didn't occur until ten months later, at the Democrats' midterm party conference in Memphis. I knew that Ted Kennedy was going to speak there, too. It was no secret that he found Carter too conservative and was considering a nomination challenge. Ted gave his famous "sail against the wind speech," which argued for ignoring the economic headwinds and following the old compass of 1960s liberalism. This fine, powerful speech was full of values I admired from a guy I considered a close friend. But I had to go up against him.

My talk that day was, in many ways, the most important speech I ever gave. I spoke as an old Democratic progressive among friends, arguing that we had to look at the world with new eyes. It was my speech, not something the staff produced. It was a distillation of everything I had been hearing as I had moved around the country for eighteen months and everything we had been struggling with in the White House. I believed that we had to confront inflation as our problem, as a monster that was riding on our backs. I mentioned the UAW conference and the exchange about national health insurance. I described the tough choices Carter had to make, and I said some things are realistic and some are not. Then I asked the delegates what they were hearing as they went around talking to voters. I said, What do you hear when you go down the streets in your communities? It's inflation, isn't it? What are people worried about? It's the price spiral, isn't it? What does that tell you? I told them inflation was not just a preoccupation of central bankers, but was something that could crush our agenda as liberals. If you get a raise, it will be gone. If we get an appropriation, it will disappear. If you want college for your children, it will be beyond your reach. Everything will be gone. The public will not tolerate it and they will turn us out of office, just as they did with Vietnam. It was a tough speech. But I knew that if we Democrats did not deal with the problem, voters would get somebody else who would.

After Memphis, I hoped I had opened a little room for Carter on the left, but I still hoped that we could steer a middle course on fiscal policy and domestic priorities. Over time, we learned to craft the president's budget by balancing these tough economic realities with the political values that brought us into office. Carter had a smart, conservative budget team—Bert Lance, until unproven allegations about his banking career led him to resign, then Jim McIntyre—and they were intent on producing a balanced budget before our first term ended. We would hear their presentations, usually with cabinet officers and department heads, then the president would make his mark. That was usually a conservative figure. Then we were allowed to come in and make our case to the president. Our little cabal, as Stu Eizenstat called it—Stu and me and maybe Gail Harrison or Bert Carp from our domestic staff—would have one final meeting with Carter and make a case for restoring some of the items that had been cut. My argument would be, "Mr. President, we are not talking about big money here. The fact is, none of our economists think it makes any difference whether the budget deficit is thirty billion or thirty-one billion dollars on pure economics. We are talking about modest gradations of funding, decisions at the margins that could help sustain decency for the people that are the most vulnerable, opportunity for kids who won't have it, and say to the American people that even in these toughest of times we're trying to help as best we can to make life better." The president would listen sympathetically, but every once in a while he would just say no, his mind was made up. I always tried to avoid being a scold. Once he made his decision, I lived with it. It was a profoundly sobering case study for Democrats about what you do when the economy won't support all the things you've hoped for.

Every developed nation was struggling with the same economic challenges—stagflation, the spike in world oil prices, competition from low-wage countries of the developing world. All across Western Europe, our counterparts were looking for ways to make their economies more competitive and efficient. The difference is that they had a tradition of social insurance and robust social safety nets—including universal health insurance, generous unemployment benefits, and strong family policies—to cushion the middle class against the blows of economic change. It made me all the more frustrated that Nixon had blocked our efforts to complete the Great Society agenda of the late 1960s and early 1970s, because a stronger antipoverty policy and a better social safety net could have braked the sharp increase in economic inequality that ensued in America.

By the end of our first year in office, the economy was beginning to recover and by our second budget, for fiscal 1979, we had cut the federal deficit almost by half, to $40 billon. But then the trade-offs got rougher. As inflation boomed along, all the costs soared—energy, health care, the Pentagon, the cost of delivering government services. Every budget we wrote bought less and less. The political demands got bigger and the trade-offs got worse.

Later it became apparent that we were up against economic forces that had been building since long before we took office, including the Vietnam guns-and-butter inflation and the spike in oil prices caused by the OPEC oil embargo of 1973. But by that time we were up for reelection, and we had run out of time to propose good answers that would produce reassuring results. Had I seen it earlier and prepared a strategy, we could have done better. We could have argued that we had inherited the problem, then immediately announced a combination of tight budgets, tighter monetary policy, and tougher jawboning—and right from the start we might have broken the psychology that was runaway inflation. I might have proved more effective for Carter. I didn't see it in time, and it's partly my fault.

The prevailing account of our first year in office is one of missteps and frustration. Certainly that's how Washington reporters wrote about Carter at the time: a political naif who clashed with Congress, a reformer who failed to understand Washington's realities.

I think that view obscures a deeper narrative whose significance has emerged over time: The realignment of the Democratic Party and the way it is viewed by the American people.

Carter understood before most Democrats the skepticism and distrust that had taken root among Americans in the late 1960s and early 1970s. As a businessman he had a practical streak that kept him in touch with the realities of ordinary people; as a former governor he knew the challenge of balancing budgets and making government more effective. As a Southerner and a man of faith, he had an abiding belief in individual responsibility and social responsibility. I think all these enabled him, before most Democrats, to understand the doubts that Americans were feeling about Washington and government toward the end of the Great Society—doubts that would erupt into full-blown hostility toward government in the Reagan era. Carter saw that government has to choose its undertakings carefully and execute them effectively.

Carter also saw before most Democrats that the world economy was changing, and that the United States would soon face competition unprecedented in the post–World War II era. He knew that our economy had to be more nimble and efficient to compete against new powers in Europe and Asia, which is one reason why he put such an emphasis on deregulation. For all of Reagan's talk, later, about reducing the burden of government, it was Carter who deregulated the airline industry, the trucking industry, and the prices of oil and gas. He saw, after the first OPEC embargo, that our economy was vulnerable to outside shocks and that energy conservation would be one way of improving our economic resilience in an unstable world.

These challenges would dominate America's economic discussion for the next twenty years, and Carter saw that Democrats needed answers.

10

Showing the World
a Different America

IN JANUARY 1977, before we had even settled into our West Wing offices, I proposed that I make a quick overseas tour to introduce the Carter-Mondale administration to our major allies, and over the course of a week I stopped in Brussels, Paris, London, Berlin, Bonn, Rome, and Tokyo. I met the leaders we would work with for the next several years, asked for their cooperation in coordinating a series of economic stimulus measures, told them that we hoped to operate in an atmosphere of close consultation, and got home without touching off any major international incidents.

Before long Carter had a second foreign assignment for me, one that wasn't going to be so congenial. During the campaign Carter had pledged to break with the foreign policy of Nixon and Ford, the Henry Kissinger realpolitik that emphasized a nation's strategic self-interest at the exclusion of other values. Carter had emphasized this point in a moving passage of his inaugural address: "Because we are free, we can never be indifferent to the fate of freedom elsewhere. Our moral sense dictates a clear-cut preference for these societies which share with us an abiding respect for individual human rights." A few weeks later, after receiving a letter from the Soviet dissident and human rights activist Andrey Sakharov, Carter wrote a warm reply, a step that infuriated the Kremlin but signaled Carter's sincerity about human rights.

Now we wanted a concrete example of the way human rights would figure in our foreign policy. Carter and I came into office opposing the apartheid regimes of South Africa and Rhodesia, and we both felt that this would be a good starting point to vindicate the human rights themes of the campaign. Cy Vance, Carter's secretary of state, was already working on some ideas to help Rhodesia make the transition to majority rule, and Carter asked me to approach the government of South Africa with the same idea.

The administration wasn't unanimous about this effort. Zbigniew Brzezinski, the head of Carter's National Security Council, felt, I think, that I was setting off without clear objectives and that a meeting with South African leaders was unlikely to produce tangible results. George Ball, a veteran diplomat in the State Department, was harshly critical.

But I thought desegregation had been one of the great American achievements of the twentieth century, and that, having embraced civil rights at home, we had standing to press for it overseas. That Carter and I had personal track records on the issue was liberating: It meant we could promote the ideal abroad without seeming to be hypocrites, unlike some of our predecessors, which had made them reluctant to take on the issue. Nevertheless, we spent a lot of time thinking about how to deliver this message to the South Africans and what might be the appropriate forum. We knew, for example, that if I traveled to South Africa, that would throw a spotlight on the mission and put the South African government on the defensive. We decided on neutral territory instead, Austria, and sent the South Africans an invitation.

In May 1977 I flew to Vienna for three days of consultations with South African prime minister John Vorster. Carter's idea, and mine, was that we had finally put an end to official discrimination in our country after 250 years and that we needed to adjust our relationship with South Africa to reflect the new reality at home. We wanted the Vorster government to end apartheid at home and exert its influence for progress in Rhodesia and Namibia as well. I also called on the South African government to release Nelson Mandela from prison. I wasn't to make any diplomatic or economic threats, but I was to assure Vorster that this would be a permanent change in American policy.

On the night before my first meeting with Vorster, I gathered our staff in my hotel room. I told them that, however difficult the talks might prove, we should be proud of our work. No one had insisted that the United States take on this task. There were no political rewards. We were doing it because our values demanded it. Then I pulled out a set of remarks written by the Namibian independence leader Herman Toivo ja Toivo. He had been arrested for political activities and tried in 1967 before an all-white South African court, then sentenced to twenty years on Robben Island, the notorious South African prison redoubt. I read my staff this excerpt from Toivo's statement to the court:

> I do not claim that it is easy for men of different races to live at peace with one another. I myself had no experience of this in my youth, and at first it surprised me that men of different races could live together in peace. But now I know it to be true and to be something to which we must strive. We are not looking forward to our imprisonment. We do not, however, feel that our efforts and sacrifice have been wasted. We believe that human suffering has its effect even on those who impose it. We hope that what has happened will persuade the whites of South Africa that we and the world may be right and they may be wrong.

I didn't go into the next day's meeting with any illusions that it would be a pleasant conversation. I had read about Vorster and knew he was a hard-liner. During World War II he had joined a group of Nazi sympathizers, and on one occasion he had actually praised Hitler. So this was not hopeful material. I also knew that many Dutch Boers such as Vorster resented Britain and the West, a legacy of the Boer Wars, and I think he brought some of that suspicion to Vienna. In person he confirmed my expectations. He was correct and stiff. He told me his people had been pushed around and martyred under British rule and they weren't going to have that happen again. He didn't want to leave anything in the record that would open him to criticism when he went back home, or to produce any recommendations from our meeting that would imply that he had compromised.

From our first session together, Vorster raised all the reasons why South Africa couldn't change, and I did my best to explain why it must. He insisted that his government was fighting communism and that if we wanted to keep the Soviets out of Africa, we had to support him. I said the way to defeat communism is to give people justice. If you treat people fairly, I said, you take the crowd away from the zealots. He tried to draw an analogy between South Africa and segregation in the United States. I agreed with him but said we had ended official segregation in America and we were stronger for it. Then he invoked the history of American Indians and their mistreatment at the hands of European settlers. I agreed with him again, but again said we had made progress—underlining that the goal should be progress.

For three days we went round and round, with Vorster's conversation proceeding like a choreographed dance. He insisted that his government encouraged political participation by all the relevant subgroups of the South African population and explained why apartheid was a perfectly fair way to run a country. His government had a painful, contrived nomenclature to avoid defining people by color, that is, black and white, which was the reality of their society. They would disaggregate the population into the different tribes and other phony categories in order to avoid the main message that we were bringing: majority rule. Though a small share of the population, the whites were running everything.

I doubt that American and South African officials ever had another conversation so substantive and so frank. At times Vorster would get angry with us, and sometimes I got angry with him.

In retrospect, the Vienna trip was probably an impossible mission. If Vorster and I had gone in agreeing that South Africa had to eliminate apartheid, I think we could have worked it out. It would have been a matter of pace and tactics. Carter and I had a slim hope that, because South Africa was such a pariah nation, meeting them in this way would cause them to budge a little in an effort to get some credibility in the world. They were paying a steep price in international trade and in the exodus of their young people, so we had some modest faith that we would see change. But that wasn't the case. Vorster was a nasty character. There was no agreement on anything.

When we concluded our conversations, Vorster and I held a final news conference, and what had been a private disagreement suddenly made headlines around the world. In our face-to-face talks, we had spent a good deal of time dancing around the language of democracy and enfranchisement. We had used the phrase "where all must participate." The South Africans wanted to fudge that. They wanted to use their own definition of "all," which would be themselves and some tribal representatives—all designed to dilute the voting power of nonwhite South Africans. At the news conference, however, one of the reporters asked what I thought would represent genuine political participation for South Africa's nonwhite population, and I used the phrase "one man, one vote." Well, that set off fireworks: It was much too specific for the white South Africans. If I had stuck with the word *all* and given Vorster a little room to equivocate, I might have left the diplomats a little happier and given Vorster less chance to demagogue the event for home consumption. But I said what I believed, and it is where South Africa ultimately went.

In a way, the doubters in our administration were right about the Vienna meeting. We went home without any breakthrough, and by the end of our term in office we didn't have much to show for our efforts. But I do think that meeting made a difference in the long run. It disabused the South African government of any notion that apartheid was selling abroad, and thus that they could shed their pariah status without putting an end to it. Just as important, it signaled to people throughout Africa and to millions around the world that the United States was a different country and a more hopeful nation. To the leaders within South Africa who wanted change—both white and nonwhite, fighting bravely—it sent a message that they had support from the United States and from the West. Over time, we did see the changes we hoped for.

Our emphasis on human rights often drew skeptical reviews from the realpolitik crowd, but our diplomatic corps was more receptive than people expected. When I arrived in Vienna for the meetings with Vorster, I was met by our ambassador to South Africa, Bill Bowdler, a career diplomat. I remember telling him, "Mr. Ambassador, I'm sorry to come over here and complicate your job this way." He said, "No, it's the happiest day of my life. We have been playing a cynical game with South Africa. My instructions were to keep it off the front pages and not have any discussions about what's happening down there. This is the first time I really felt good about my job."

The Vorster encounter was the first in a series of missions I carried out overseas for Carter. Sometimes my job was to deliver a tough message on behalf of the administration, but sometimes I was building or rebuilding an alliance. That's how I wound up going to Israel in the summer of 1978, a trip that would have much more tangible results than the South Africa meetings.

Carter had come into office wanting to pursue a peace settlement in the Middle East. The 1973 Arab-Israeli War had shaken everyone—it triggered the first OPEC oil embargo, which had shattering effects on the economies of the West, and it reminded the world how fast a war could flare up in the region. Moreover, Israel had fought two wars in six years, and four since its founding. Carter felt we could serve our security interests—and Israel's—by building a better relationship between Israel and the moderate Arab states in the region. In addition, he had a long-standing interest in justice for the Palestinians and wanted to begin moving Israel toward some agreement with them.

Our first initiative on this front was to revive the Geneva Summit process that had started in 1973, a multiparty meeting cohosted with the Soviets. I suppose the goal was to keep moving ahead on détente with the Russians, with the idea that they could bring pressure on some of their Arab friends to make peace with Israel. I didn't like Soviet involvement because I knew the Israelis would be suspicious—with good reason. Russia had a long history of stirring up trouble in the Middle East, with a cadre of experienced diplomats who would work with the rejectionist Arab states to keep pressure on Israel. Our experts at the State Department described the Soviet policy as "no war, no peace." But Anwar Sadat didn't want the Soviets around either. He hadn't liked their patronage and had thrown them out of Egypt, and he feared that they would use the Geneva Summit to regain influence in the region. In fact, we didn't make any progress on the Geneva track—it only alienated the Israelis.

But Carter didn't give up. When Sadat made his historic trip to Jerusalem in November 1977, Carter saw a new opportunity for the United States to play peacemaker. By now, however, the Israelis were skeptical. In May of that year, Israeli voters had installed the first non-Labor government since the nation's founding, giving a majority to the conservative Likud Party. The new prime minister was Menachem Begin, a religious nationalist who took a harder line than Labor toward the Arabs. Carter and Begin had held a cordial meeting in Washington later that spring, but Likud members remained skeptical of Carter because, more than any previous American president, he had expressed interest in the rights of the Palestinians. Begin was a fierce Zionist who believed in Israel's ancient right to biblical lands. He was suspicious of American motives generally and was extremely angry about Carter's statements to the effect that Israel should dismantle its settlements in Arab territory it had occupied during the 1967 war.

Over lunch one day shortly after the Israeli elections, Carter asked me to pay a personal call on Begin and Sadat. As an interim step toward peace, he wanted to convene the foreign ministers of Israel, Egypt, and America in Leeds, England, to discuss common ground for negotiations. Because I had a good relationship with the American Jewish community, and through them with some of Israel's leaders, Carter thought I might be able to build Begin's confidence in such a meeting. We chose the summer of 1978 because it was the thirtieth anniversary of Israel's nationhood and we could use a ceremonial visit as a cover for my conversations with Begin. I asked a group of prominent American Jewish leaders to go with me, in addition to Stu Eizenstat, who knew a lot about Arab-Israeli relations.

Once again, our administration had internal disagreements. Cy Vance looked on my visit the way a lawyer looks at negotiating a contract; he wanted to see the fine print. Brzezinski's predisposition was to announce the outlines of an agreement in advance so we wouldn't wind up with an embarrassing disappointment. I felt the first requirement was simply to win the confidence of Begin and Sadat so they would come to the table. Once that happened, we could start thinking about the details.

Confidence building was, however, going to be a steep climb. Carter was getting advice from some quarters to go hard on Israel, that a threatened Israel would be more likely to make concessions. I thought the opposite. When Israelis felt threatened by events, the brakes went on and the hard-liners took over because the question of national survival is always first on Israelis' minds. In addition, Begin was getting pressure from Israeli conservatives to resist any concessions to Egypt or the United States, and a steady stream of skeptical commentary appeared in the Israeli press before and during our trip.

The terrain was full of diplomatic land mines, and one quickly emerged as we planned the trip: whether I should visit the Western Wall in Jerusalem, the great religious and architectural site that was the remaining part of King David's temple. If I went there as a government official, I would be recognizing occupied territory—Israel had seized that part of Jerusalem in the 1967 Six-Day War. That would represent a major shift in American policy, and the State Department was not about to let that happen. But the wall is one of the holiest sites for the Jewish people, and many Israelis felt it would be a diplomatic slight not to visit. So a couple of weeks before our trip, I sent an old friend of mine, Max Kampelman, a former aide to Humphrey and a very savvy guy, on a trip to Jerusalem. He consulted friends and worked out a solution. Joan and I would visit the wall as private citizens and everybody would be happy.

On July 1 I arrived at Ben-Gurion International Airport outside Tel Aviv, only to get another reminder that this would be a tense visit. The whole government turned out on the tarmac, Begin gave the welcoming statement, and I went down the line shaking hands. But every Israeli official who spoke pointed out that relations between our countries were not good. Israel has serious security problems, they said; Israel is a proud nation and will stand up for what it needs, whatever the pressure.

But I had prepared carefully for the trip, and these sentiments came as no surprise. I knew that public occasions call for one kind of remark and that private conversations often take a different tone. That's why I had asked if Begin and I could ride together privately from Tel Aviv to Jerusalem. That's a long drive, maybe forty-five minutes, and I hoped I could use it to take his measure in a more relaxed setting. I asked him about Gaza and the Palestinians, and he told me about the border threats to Israel. I asked about his own history; I had read about it but I wanted to hear it in his own words. He grew up in Eastern Europe and was descended from a distinguished family of rabbis. His family had gone through hell during World War II and he had lost relatives in the Holocaust. He had been a member of the Irgun, a militant Zionist organization whose members believed that violence was a legitimate tool to create the independent nation of Israel. He believed that the Diaspora, which had destroyed Israel centuries earlier, had given the Jewish people a rightful claim to the land as a Jewish state. This was a religious argument, not a diplomatic exercise. Nonetheless, I got a better feel for Begin on that car ride. I was numb from the long overseas flight, but I think we established some trust. It seems he thought so, too. He later told Wolf Blitzer, who was then a correspondent for the *Jerusalem Post,* that the car ride turned him around and started him on the path that led to Camp David.

The next day consisted mostly of ceremonial visits. We visited the Western Wall in Jerusalem, and Beersheba, then made a trip to the Golan Heights. But ceremonial visits matter in Israel because history, ancient and recent, is so important there. That night we had a state dinner at the Knesset and I delivered my formal address. I talked about the special relationship between Israel and the United States, our shared values of freedom and democracy, and underscored America's unshakable support for a secure State of Israel. But I also tried to invoke a sense of history, the momentum of events that had brought us to a point where peacemaking might be possible.

On our last day in Israel I had a second private meeting with Begin, at his office in Jerusalem. I knew this would be a crucial conversation, and I knew I couldn't rush it. Begin was a very proper man. He always wore a suit and tie, even though casual attire is the norm in Israeli business and politics. I think he was skeptical that I could say anything that would allow Israel to go forward in negotiations with the Arabs. I told him I could understand his doubts. I assured him that Israel had the support of our government, but I also told him honestly that our administration was weighing different approaches to peace in the Middle East. Reporters and columnists in the United States were speculating about what the United States expected from the Leeds conference, but I said the final line was whatever we could negotiate. "We are not going to insist on prenegotiation settlements," I told him. "What you agree to is whatever you find, over the course of some days, that you can agree to."

I also said, "I understand it's not easy for you. It's not easy for us. But it's essential because we have to find some way of diminishing the threat to Israel. You've been through four wars in thirty years. You're trying to build a normal life for your people, you've got Egypt ready to go to the table. Maybe the United States by doing this can help Israel in the most important way, by giving you a chance to live a reasonable life."

I can't honestly say that I converted Begin in those three days. But I could sense the slightest change of heart. When you are around someone and the mood changes and he starts smiling, you feel that the nature of the meeting has changed. By the end, I think Begin thought it was worth an attempt.

By the time we got on the plane to depart for Egypt, we were all exhausted. I had made progress with Begin, but the visit had been arduous and delicate. Meanwhile, my staff had spent the entire three days batting down skeptical press reports and cynical critiques from anonymous critics who thought the mission was doomed—or wanted it to be. We were all desperate for some encouraging development. Our next stop was Alexandria, where Anwar Sadat kept a vacation home. We landed in the city, then helicoptered out to the coast and alighted on the broad lawn of Sadat's seaside villa. Sadat was waiting, with a crowd of aides and photographers, and when I descended the helicopter steps, he beamed, embraced me, and said simply, "Mr. Vice President, what can I do to make this trip a success for you?" I have seldom felt so relieved in my life, and I had a warm spot for Sadat from that day on.

Sadat reviewed what he had made clear with his trip to Jerusalem months earlier. Egypt had fought four wars with Israel in thirty years, and being constantly on a war footing was, he felt, destroying the soul of his country. "I want peace with Israel so I can work on the future of Egypt," he said.

After the visit with Sadat, I returned to Washington and wrote Carter a memo recommending that he go ahead with the Leeds conference and a summit meeting with Sadat and Begin. But I made two recommendations: He should insist that Begin and Sadat participate personally, and he should hold the meeting in a private, secluded place. After getting a feel for Sadat and Begin, I felt the issues were so grave and the necessary compromises were so difficult that lower-level diplomats could not achieve them. I also told Carter that private conversations would permit more flexibility than public meetings. In the volatile environments that both Sadat and Begin faced at home, the slightest compromise was likely to get shot down before anyone had a chance to explore it.

My visits with Begin and Sadat were even more productive than we'd hoped. At the end of July, they agreed to a meeting of their foreign ministers with Cy Vance in Leeds, England, to explore common ground for peace negotiations. Five weeks later, on September 6, Carter welcomed Sadat and Begin at Camp David, and the historic twelve-day peace talks began.

Carter's original plan was that, after being on hand to greet Sadat and Begin on their arrival in Washington, I would stay at the White House, freeing him to conduct the negotiations at Camp David. But about two or three days into it, Carter called and asked if I would come up. Both leaders were still extremely uneasy, and after the first meeting Carter decided that it hurt to have Begin and Sadat together in the same room. The talks had ground to a halt.

When I arrived the next day, I didn't have a specific assignment from Carter, and I thought I would simply to try to set people at ease and reduce some of the tension. I knew Ezer Wiezman, Israel's defense minister, from my time in the Senate, and after my trip to Alexandria I felt I had a cordial relationship with Sadat. I came to like him a great deal, and toward the end of the summit we spent an evening together watching the Muhammad Ali–Leon Spinks heavyweight boxing match. But Carter also asked me to deliver messages from him to the two leaders. The first message was sobering: Carter threatened to shut down the summit in a day if he didn't get some movement from them. I didn't deliver that in a threatening way; I merely said that nothing was happening and the president felt he was wasting his time, and wouldn't it be a terrible missed opportunity if they both went home without accomplishing anything for their people. Both said they were willing to stay and listen. The next day Carter asked me to go back to Begin and broach the subject of giving up territory in the Sinai Peninsula and some settlements near Gaza in exchange for Egypt's promise of peace.

The great thing about Camp David was that everyone had his own cabin, so we had a certain amount of privacy and could talk things over informally if that seemed best. After my conversations with Begin in Jerusalem, I knew he placed great weight on the history of the Jews. He would go on for twenty or thirty minutes with Carter, recounting that history and saying, "We cannot accept this. This is the reason for Israel's existence." The biblical history was important to him as well. If you had listened to his speeches you knew he couldn't leave Judea and Samaria, as he called them—the land we know today as the West Bank.

I understood this, and I concentrated on Israel's presence in the Sinai, the vast peninsula between Israel and Egypt. Israel had two military bases there and some resorts on the Mediterranean, at a place called Yameet. These all tended to be favorite places for Labor Party leaders, like a mini-spa just north of Miami. I said, "We are not talking about Judea and Samaria. I know your feelings on that; we are talking about places that have no significance to Israel. They are not essential to your defense, to your security, to your economy, to your history. It's just a pile of sand." If he would give on those points, I said, we would agree to have American protection where Israel was vulnerable, we would demilitarize the Sinai and pay for new bases to secure Israel's border.

I also tried to call upon Begin's sense of history. My argument was that we had a nonrecurring opportunity, that we would never get back to this place again. I said it was his chance to accomplish something for the State of Israel and take his place in Israeli history. He didn't buy it at first, but I could see that he was thinking it over.

In the end, it was Carter's persistence—sheer persistence—that caused the talks to succeed. He knew every line on every map. He understood the military stress points and the political aspirations of Begin and Sadat. He refused to give up until he found a way to get them on common ground. It was an extraordinary testament to Carter's resolve. When the summit concluded, we made history: The accord Carter announced on September 17 neutralized Egypt as a potential threat to Israel's survival, demonstrated that peace was possible between the Jewish state and its Arab neighbors, and changed the tone of Arab-Israeli relations across the region. Although broader peace talks in the Middle East have faltered time and again since then, the Egypt-Israel accord set a hopeful precedent and still represents the most important achievement in modern Mideast peacemaking.

During the next several months I made a number of foreign trips for the administration, sometimes on the issue of human rights and sometimes on America's strategic interests. Refining our foreign policy was often a matter of balancing one against the other, but we felt that, on the whole, we were putting a new face on American foreign policy. That's how I came to be involved in the crisis of the Southeast Asian refugees known as the boat people.

In the spring of 1979 we began hearing reports of a terrible humanitarian crisis in Southeast Asia. After the collapse of South Vietnam, the new governments of Vietnam, Laos, and Cambodia were expelling thousands of people who had sided with the West or opposed communism. In Vietnam, the policy had an especially nasty aspect because the government was expelling people of Chinese descent; it was really ethnic cleansing. Vietnam was expelling sixty thousand people per month, pushing refugees out to sea regardless of the circumstances. Newspapers had published the most horrific stories: Thousands of people had already drowned at sea, boats were being pillaged by pirates, women were being raped. One of the nearby recipient countries, Malaysia, had actually begun towing refugee boats back to sea, where they often sank or capsized. By June we were under pressure from several Southeast Asian countries, including Indonesia and Malaysia, to organize a permanent resettlement solution.

I was familiar with the Southeast Asian refugee problem. In the spring of 1978, as part of a tour to the Philippines, I had visited a camp in Bangkok, Thailand, where more than seventy thousand refugees, including a lot of women and children, were living in conditions of shocking squalor. I came home with those images seared in my mind, and I knew that, even without evil intent, the refugee system in that part of the world was stretched to the limits.

Carter's assistant secretary for Asia in the State Department was Richard Holbrooke, a gifted young diplomat who would later negotiate the Dayton Peace Accords for the Clinton administration and later still become Barack Obama's special negotiator for Pakistan and Afghanistan. Holbrooke called me one day in the spring of 1979, troubled about the boat people, and said our government was gridlocked. The navy, he said, didn't want to send in ships because it didn't see a military mission, and the Joint Chiefs concurred. At the State Department, a lot of career diplomats felt the refugee issue was an internal matter, not an international responsibility. Worse, the United Nations high commissioner for refugees, Poul Hartling, was the chief sponsor of that argument. The U.N. had held one conference on the refugees, in December 1978, but it had come to nothing. The top people at the U.N. were resisting any intervention, Holbrooke said, arguing that the refugee exodus was just the effect of poverty.

Holbrooke and I saw it differently. We thought this was a sinister and largely racist policy, putting people to sea in something that approached genocide and a form of revenge for their support of the United States during the Vietnam War. I made a few phone calls within the administration and on Capitol Hill, and shortly Morton Abramowitz came to see me privately. Abramowitz was a veteran diplomat with long experience in Asia and later president of the Carnegie Endowment for International Peace. In his view this was a scandal and a crisis. He said, "The U.N. high commissioner doesn't know what he's talking about. I know this area and I know what's going on. This is racism."

A week later, with Carter's assent, I called a meeting of the National Security Council. I asked Holbrooke to come over from the State Department, and we gathered in the White House Situation Room. It's a somewhat melodramatic setting, often used when a crisis is at hand, but I wanted to show that I was serious.

I went around the table, asking each representative to present his view on the refugee crisis. The State Department people raised the arguments that the U.N. high commissioner had raised—that we would be meddling in another country's internal affairs. Someone from the National Security Council brought up money; it would cost several million dollars to mount a rescue mission at sea and start resettlement camps. Someone else raised the political question, observing that it would not be popular to bring a large group of Southeast Asian refugees into our country. But the main opposition came from the Pentagon. The navy sent over an admiral who said, We are a military organization. We don't pick up people at sea.

Finally I said, "Look, are you telling me that we have thousands of people drowning in the open sea, and we have the Seventh Fleet right there, and we can't help them? Most of them are in jeopardy now because they worked with us during the war. How can we say we won't help these people?"

Quite apart from the humanitarian case, I saw an important foreign policy argument. We were in a position to create some stability in a part of the world that was highly unstable, with China, Vietnam, and Cambodia looking for any provocation to start hostilities. It was also a way to project the idea that the United States stands for international human rights even when that's not the convenient position. I concluded by telling the admiral, If you feel this is not part of your mission, then I think you need a change of mission.

After we broke up, I called Harold Brown, the secretary of defense—a good man—and made my case. He quickly said yes. I called Cy Vance, and he also came around. Now we had a united government. I asked for a few minutes with Carter in the Oval Office and said, "What argument do we have that this won't work?" He gave his approval.

Mounting a rescue, however, wasn't just a matter of redeploying our ships and rescuing people at sea. Someone would have to organize an international system of relocation camps so that we could take the pressure off the neighboring countries. Someone had to pressure additional countries for commitments to take refugees permanently. In June, Carter announced that the United States would double its intake of Indochinese refugees. A week later the Senate passed a bipartisan resolution asking the United Nations to call an emergency session on the crisis. Now we were in a position to go back to the U.N. and ask them for help. A few days later U.N. secretary-general Kurt Waldheim agreed to organize a second conference on the refugee crisis, in Geneva in July. More than sixty countries announced they would send delegates, and I felt we had made a great breakthrough.

On the eve of the Geneva conference I was traveling with my staff, giving speeches in support of SALT II, the new arms control treaty. A few days before the Geneva conference was to open, Ham Jordan called me to say that Carter had decided not to attend. He had just ordered a dramatic shakeup of his cabinet in response to that summer's energy crisis at home, and he wanted to remain at the White House. Then, the day before the conference opened, the White House called us in Philadelphia to say that I was to fly to Geneva, take Carter's place, and give the keynote speech. Without returning to Washington, I boarded *Air Force Two* with Jim Johnson, Gail Harrison, and Marty Kaplan, my chief speechwriter, and headed for Switzerland.

We had a lot of writing to do on that flight. Making the refugees' case inside our own government, to generals and cabinet secretaries who answered to the president, was one thing. Making our case to sixty other sovereign nations, many of them skeptical about the need for international intervention, was quite another. Yet the mission for which Holbrooke and I had been fighting would fail without international support. Marty and I worked through the night on the speech. In Marty's sheaf of briefing papers was a fascinating historical precedent that Holbrooke had stumbled upon. Forty years earlier, just down the road from Geneva at Évian, France, Western nations had met to discuss the refugee crisis facing Europe in the face of Hitler and the Nazis. The West had failed to act on that occasion—with horrific consequences for Europe's Jews—and Marty worked in the reference with tremendous rhetorical power. When we arrived in Geneva the next morning and stepped off the plane, I showed a copy of the speech to Elie Wiesel, the great human rights activist and Holocaust historian, who was part of the American delegation. He wagged a finger at Marty and said, "History will be watching you."

Wiesel was right, but I think history worked to our advantage that day in Geneva. In that speech I did my best to develop the case for international responsibility to these desperate people. I pointed out that China and Hong Kong had already taken in thousands of Vietnamese refugees. I said the United States was prepared to take tens of thousands more. And I reminded the delegates of the shameful chapter from Évian and the verdict that history might render on us: "Let us renounce that legacy of shame. Let us honor the moral principles we inherit. Let us do something meaningful—something profound—to stem this misery. We face a world problem. Let us fashion a world solution. History will not forgive us if we fail. History will not forget us if we succeed."

The diplomats who attend events like that have heard a lot of speeches in their careers, and the best we expected was polite applause and some nodding of heads. But this time the response was electric, and when I finished, people leaped to their feet for a sustained ovation. In the end, the governments attending the conference more than doubled the number of refugees they were willing to receive and pledged $160 million for the project. It's one of the few speeches in my life where I thought I changed the outcome of people's lives.

About a month after the Geneva summit I was in the South China Sea, completing a round of diplomatic visits to China and Japan. I choppered out over Manila Bay to the USS *Midway*, one of the carriers that carried out the refugee rescue, to greet the sailors and get a briefing from the commander. Mindful of the navy's initial resistance to the rescue mission, I asked his opinion. I've never forgotten what he said: "I didn't like the mission when I got those orders. I was convinced that it was inappropriate for the navy, and I thought it would demoralize my sailors . . . I was dead wrong." His sailors loved the mission. They had responded to desperate circumstances in the world's hour of need. They had rescued hundreds of people at close risk of death. They had provided a hopeful future to hundreds of people who had had no future at all. The commander added, "It's going to make a difference in the way those people think about America. Because when their life was at risk, they saw this ship with an American flag come up and these young guys go down and pick them up. They felt safe for the first time in months. The world looked better to them. It's hard to stay mad at a policy like that."

The crucial point about the boat people episode is that nobody could say our participation was rooted in geostrategic considerations or America's self-interest. America was standing behind the values of compassion, loyalty, and law. It allowed thousands of desperate people to start over in new places and build successful lives, including the large and thriving Hmong community in Minnesota today. It changed the way the world looked at America—after some pretty difficult years for us abroad—and I'm proud of it.

Despite a number of foreign policy achievements, by the middle of 1979 I felt the administration still had work to do in foreign affairs. Ronald Reagan, who was likely to be Carter's opponent in 1980, was beginning to take shots at us for giving away the Panama Canal and failing to stand up against communism. I thought Reagan was a shallow thinker, but I also thought it was important for Democrats to define a strong foreign policy—one that had learned from the hubris and incompetence of Vietnam but that would keep America safe while advancing our values in the world.

The looming opportunity was China. Richard Nixon's historic trip in 1972 had opened the possibility of a new relationship with Beijing, but we had taken few steps since to cement the relationship. Plainly China was ready for a new place in the world. In late 1976 Vice Premier Deng Xiaoping had ousted the Gang of Four, the heirs to Mao's absolutist vision of communism, signaling the reform direction he intended to pursue. Then,

at the end of 1978, Carter had signed documents to normalize our relationship with China. Yet all these were merely statements of intention,
and the Chinese were chafing for substance.

In the spring of 1979, at one of our weekly lunches, I proposed
to Carter that I make a state visit to China to accelerate the thaw. I
had been interested in China since my Senate days and, after Nixon's
trip, had made several efforts to make the journey, all discouraged by
the still-reclusive Chinese bureaucracy. I thought it was time to rebal-
ance our relationship with the Communist world, recognizing China
as a major power alongside the Soviet Union, and I thought we could
do a lot to encourage the political and economic reforms of Deng
Xiaoping. I was also frustrated at what seemed to be divisions in our
administration. Some of Carter's advisers were eager to advance the
U.S.-Chinese relationship, mainly as a counterweight to the Soviet
relationship, but Cy Vance worried that an opening to China would
alienate the Soviets and subvert our negotiations over nuclear weapons. Carter gave me the go-ahead, and this time I had the support of
both Vance and Brzezinski.

After my trips to Vienna and Jerusalem, I had a new idea about state
visits. I thought they needed to be more than ceremony and pomp. They
had to transact real business, and I had a theory that a state visit could
become a forcing event that would cause our own government to make
decisions and endorse new steps.

With the goal of a China trip in August, I convened a regular working group—Dick Holbrooke from State, David Aaron from the National
Security Council, and a number of distinguished academic scholars with
deep roots in China. We met periodically in the White House Roosevelt
Room throughout the summer to put together an agenda that would show
the Chinese we were serious.

But first, we had diplomatic tasks at home. A critical step would be
getting the State Department to declare China a "friendly" nation under
the Foreign Assistance Act. This would qualify the Chinese for financial
assistance on joint projects such as power plants and harbors, important
to a developing economy. I knew Cy Vance would be uneasy about this

step, so I paid him a visit and reassured him I had no intention of developing China as a rival to the Soviet Union. He told me, "I'll hold my nose and go along with this."

I also wanted China to receive financing from the U.S. Export-Import Bank, which arranges credit for foreign countries to buy American products. But I had to convince the budget hawks at the Office of Management and Budget that this would be acceptable to Carter. Critically, I wanted China to receive most-favored-nation status in trade relations, meaning it would qualify for the same level of tariffs as other major trading partners and would join our regular trade network. Carter was willing, but this step required congressional approval. So I met with Robert Byrd, the Senate majority leader and an old friend, whom I knew to be a supporter of the move. I knew I would have to tell the Chinese that Congress is independent of the White House and that we could not order congressional assent, but I wanted to be able to tell them that I had Byrd's assurance that it would be on the Senate calendar that year with Byrd's personal support.

In addition, we wanted to discuss military intelligence with the Chinese. After the Iranian revolution in February, we had lost a series of surveillance sites that we'd used to monitor Soviet missile bases. I thought we might replace them with sites in China. But this meant offering the Chinese a sign of our sincerity in sharing military intelligence, so I asked Defense Secretary Harold Brown to let me take maps showing what we knew about Soviet missile sites along the Chinese border. He agreed.

Finally, I put together a traveling team that would demonstrate we were serious: Holbrooke from State; Mike Oksenberg, a China expert from the National Security Council; David Aaron, then Brzezinski's chief deputy; and John Fairbank, the great Harvard China scholar who had spent years in Asia himself.

We arrived in Beijing on Friday, August 25, and at first the signs were not auspicious. Although Vice Premier Deng greeted our delegation at the airport, the ceremony was modest and the reception was chilly. Nothing indicated that this was the start of a major state visit or that an important dignitary was in Beijing. When we woke the next morning and left the official guesthouse to drive to our meetings, the streets were empty and the only signs of official welcome were banners near Tiananmen Square reading WELCOME TO THE KING OF NEPAL. After the months of intense preparation, I felt a sinking feeling. After a morning of preliminary formalities, we returned to the guesthouse and I took a walk in the garden (assuming the house itself was bugged) with Jim Johnson, my top aide. When we got a suitable distance from the house I asked, "What in the world is going on? Do the Chinese understand the significance of this visit?" Even the welcoming banquet at the Great Hall of the People that evening had a cautious tone, with Deng warning us that the Chinese-American relationship would improve only if the Americans made concrete steps.

But things changed abruptly on Monday, when my formal meetings with Deng and his delegation got under way. I didn't try to feed out our proposals cleverly, as if we were negotiating. I simply said the United States wanted a new relationship with China and that I had several points to announce up front: most-favored-nation trading status, new credits through the Export-Import Bank, relaxed controls on our exports to China, support for hydroelectric projects in China, and closer cooperation on military intelligence. I wasn't asking them to bargain away anything, I simply said we wanted a new relationship, and these were steps we were willing to take to achieve it. Then I had a military aide roll out Harold Brown's maps of Soviet missile sites along the Chinese border. That stopped the conversation for some time as Deng and his aides pored over the charts. I had deliberately designed the presentation so it didn't depend on eloquence; I would simply say what we had done and would do.

I don't mean to suggest that the visit was without friction from that point forward. Deng was prickly on statehood for Tibet and on the Dalai Lama, whom he dismissed as "an insignificant character." I assured him that the Dalai Lama was received in the United States as a religious leader, not a political figure. We also remained concerned about human rights and political freedoms in China, and I touched on that topic during my speech at Beijing University that afternoon.

But after that day, it was as if someone had flipped a switch in the relationship. To our astonishment, my speech at Beijing University later that day was broadcast on Chinese television—the first time any American political figure had addressed the Chinese people—without censorship and without prior approval of my text. On Tuesday morning, when we met for a second round of talks, Deng engaged frankly and easily, and as this declassified memo of our conversation shows, we even shared a joke about dealing with journalists:

> Vice Premier Deng: We will start our work when [the reporters] are finished.
> Vice President Mondale: I have some secret things I would like to tell you in their presence. They will never tell a soul.
> Vice Premier Deng: You cannot depend on that. (Laughter)
> Vice President Mondale: We have the nicest press in the world. I will tell you the truth later. (Laughter)
> Vice Premier Deng: You do not smoke, nor do you drink very much.
> Vice President Mondale: I have absolutely no vices. I will also tell you the truth later on that. (Laughter)
> (Press leaves the room.)

That afternoon, when we signed bilateral accords to promote cultural exchanges and cooperation on hydroelectric projects, Deng was joined by Premier Hua Kuo-feng, a rare joint public appearance. Then on Wednesday, after our formal talks concluded, Joan, Eleanor, and I traveled to the ancient city of Xi'an, home of the extraordinary exhibit of terra-cotta soldiers. Even more extraordinary was the crowd that greeted us. Officials estimated it at two hundred thousand, but I wonder if it wasn't closer to a million. People swarmed by the thousands along the length of our motorcade route, and at one point I even got out to work the crowd and shake hands. It was, before or since, the biggest crowd I've ever had. The overhead banners now mentioned that the vice president of the United States was in China.

Altogether, it was a high-stakes trip. But Vance and Brzezinski seemed relieved by the time we returned home, and Carter was delighted. Even the diplomatic reporters, jaded by too many hollow and ceremonial events, seemed impressed. "It did indeed seem that U.S.-Chinese relations had crossed the invisible psychological boundary that separates cautious first acquaintance and confident friendship," *Time* magazine reported.

Over the years that's proven true. Diplomatic and cultural exchanges could go forward. Business executives could close deals. The reclusive China that wanted nothing to do with the rest of the world became a country seeking notice and acceptance. American trade with China, which was tiny at the time, has mushroomed into hundreds of billions of dollars, helping to create a large middle class in Chinese cities while bringing China into the mainstream of the world community. Beijing itself signified the transformation. When I visited in 1979 it was a grim city where every pedestrian dressed in a drab gray Mao jacket and every street corner had a loudspeaker repeating the sayings of Mao. The city was desolate and joyless. I went back a few years later and the change was dramatic—bikes, cars, trucks; stylish women and men on the boulevards. It wasn't New York or Paris, but it had profoundly changed.

Political progress in China has been slower than the economic change, and slower than I would have liked. But I think we reinforced the moderates. Deng and the other reformers had gone out on a limb when they arrested the Gang of Four. We showed the Chinese people that this would produce tangible results—cultural exchanges, foreign investment, economic modernization, and so forth. Ultimately, Deng was able to utter that memorable line about his philosophy of communism: I don't care about the color of the cat as long as it catches mice. If it hadn't been for the Tiananmen Square tragedy, I think he would be remembered as a world hero. China has not moved forward as fast as we would have liked, but for the next thirty years, at least, there was no backsliding into the oppression and fear of Mao's time.

In the years since Carter and I left office, a number of foreign policy hawks have argued that we were naive moralists, a pair of idealists who didn't understand the way power works in the real world. I think it's exactly the opposite: There is power in our ideals. Promoting our values abroad enhanced our stature in the world, discredited and weakened extremist regimes who threaten us, and created more stable societies in regions that often lack stability. Our achievement in saving the boat people—making an issue of the immorality of the situation and organizing a response—made a big difference in the way the world regarded us and what we stood for.

As President Carter noted recently in a letter to *Foreign Policy* magazine, although we kept the peace for four years, our administration took many steps that strengthened the United States relative to the Soviet Union. These included establishing diplomatic relations with China and developing it as a counterfoil to Soviet influence; breaking Egypt loose from the Soviet sphere; supporting Soviet dissidents and helping to greatly increase the emigration of Russian Jews; and accelerating the development of advanced weaponry such as cruise missiles and precision bombs, where the United States held a huge technological advantage over the Soviets. We also reconnected the United States with human rights movements in Eastern Europe and Latin America, a step that had the effect of accelerating democracy movements in both regions.

Moreover, the countries that have adopted our ideals—nations in Latin America, Africa, and Asia—are more stable, more peaceful, and more likely to support us when we need their help. This is an important part of America's appeal.

I don't say that human rights was a simple message or that we never compromised. The old realpolitik politicians, including some good people at the State Department, were never persuaded. They thought you can't pass judgment on other countries, that you should just pursue your national interests. Others thought we were inconsistent—as when we negotiated naval bases with Ferdinand Marcos or arms treaties with the Soviets—and that if you are going to be for human rights in Vietnam, you've got to be for human rights everywhere.

I would only say that these are tough judgments, often confidential judgments, and you just have to make them as they come along, balancing the nation's various interests, and do what is principled and realistic.

I think we also developed a new language for Democrats in foreign policy. After Vietnam, many Democrats grew hostile to the Pentagon and regarded a strong military as a threat to human rights and peace. This is naive. There is great danger and much evil in the world. A small number of extremists are determined to kill Americans, as we saw on 9/11, and a larger group is hostile even if they do not pose imminent threats. A strong military is both a shield to minimize attacks from the extremists and a tool for getting a hearing from rivals. One of the hard realities of the world is that the deployment of a destroyer group or the repositioning of a fighter wing catches the attention of your enemies. I've always been proud that our administration never started a war or dropped a bomb. But I've also believed that our ability to do both helped us change minds, tame rivals, and promote human rights—as well as prevent deadly attacks on Americans.

Our record in office reflected this twin commitment to human rights and a strong defense. What's often forgotten is that our administration began a technological revolution in the country's weapons systems—the very systems that Ronald Reagan and George W. Bush would later use. Harold Brown, a brilliant secretary of defense, and his equally gifted undersecretary Bill Perry—both engineers by training—recognized the way that technology could be married to the needs of the defense establishment and helped our administration initiate the transition from electromechanical to digitized weapons systems. A glance at federal budget documents will show that increases in the Pentagon budget for which Ronald Reagan took credit actually began during our administration. Recently declassified Pentagon documents show that we began the development of today's advanced weaponry: stealth aircraft, cruise missiles, "smart" bombs, and pilotless drone planes. Brown and Perry were masterful strategists but also caring leaders: Their technological revolution was designed in part to create nonnuclear solutions to our security problems to reduce the risk of ever having to use nuclear weapons. You have nuclear weapons for deterrence, but you develop every possible strategy to avoid using them.

I mention this military history to challenge the false notion that we must choose between national security and human rights. The truth is that they support each other: A strong military dispels the notion that our foreign policy has gone soft, and the expansion of human rights builds stability in unstable places and sows democracy in autocratic regimes. I came of age in a time when the politics of national security were less divisive, when ensuring our country's security enjoyed bipartisan support, and when our leaders avoided the corrosive attacks on the patriotism of Americans who disagreed on policy.

For these reasons I was encouraged by Barack Obama's first months in office. He ordered an end to torture as American policy and declassified the odious Justice Department opinions that authorized it. We have never had a president with such a mastery of constitutional principles, an intellectual who was president of the *Harvard Law Review* and a professor of constitutional law at the University of Chicago. He understands the challenges of upholding our system of laws at a time when terrorist attacks remain a frightening possibility, and he has correctly rejected the false choice between liberty and security.

Obama has, nevertheless, tacked to the middle on issues where presidential leadership is needed, specifically in the matter of so-called state secrets. He has been much more prudent than President George W. Bush in using this tool to block legal challenges to government behavior, yet he did invoke the state-secrets defense to block a lawsuit by an American citizen wrongly arrested and tortured, and to frustrate litigation alleging unauthorized wiretaps by the U.S. government. That is a cop-out. Congress is quite capable of shaping legislation, as it has in the past, that both protects us from our enemies and prevents the abuse of our liberties by unwise and rash leadership. President Obama's talents are uniquely suited to reaching this crucial balance.

My argument to the cynics is this: Be honest about balancing America's priorities in the world. If for strategic reasons we have to soften our position on one of the moral questions, know what we are doing, recognize at times we will weigh one priority against another, and explain that publicly. Carter was never afraid to do that, and I think people appreciated his honesty.

But if you give up the battle, if you simply allow your national self-interest to subordinate all other values, you slip into a Hobbesian world of evil motives and worse behavior. That's why we did so much damage to our standing in the world with the Bush-Cheney torture camps and the black sites around the world. Suddenly you create an international spectacle of America renouncing its most basic values. You have to stand for democracy and human values, for a government that answers to its people and obeys the law. That has always been our strength as a nation, and Carter put the authority of the government behind it. As Dick Holbrooke later observed, "Mondale and Carter believed that, without being a missionary, you had a mission. Ever since their administration, people have argued how big a role human rights plays in our foreign policy, but they have never doubted that it is a core part of the agenda."

I would argue today that by projecting America's moral authority, Carter not only brought about a better world, he left us stronger as a nation. Not immediately, not in everything we tried. But looking back, you see that where we started fights—with the Soviet Union over Afghanistan, with the Philippines over democracy, with Chile over torture and repression, with South Africa over apartheid—within ten years those regimes were gone. I don't say we did it alone because many of those revolutions had internal sources, too. But our making the case for human rights, and making it publicly, put pressure on those regimes and accelerated the domestic movements for social and political reform. Andrey Sakharov and Nelson Mandela, among other champions of liberty, later said they took strength from hearing Carter emphasize human rights. They realized that they were not alone in the world.

11

America in an Age of Limits

I N THE LAST week of June 1979, Carter was in Tokyo for an economic summit with Helmut Schmidt, Margaret Thatcher, Valéry Giscard d'Estaing, and other Allied leaders. OPEC had raised oil prices twice that year, jolting the world's major economies, and the summit included a long discussion of conservation strategies. On June 28, Carter called to say the meetings had been productive but grueling, and on the way home he and Rosalynn planned to stop in Hawaii for a few days. We all felt he deserved the vacation. The entire administration had been working extremely hard for two and a half years, without much applause from Congress or the public, and we were all starting to feel the strain.

Back home, however, a crisis was developing. OPEC's decisions had pushed oil prices up a staggering 30 percent over the previous six months, and gasoline prices were soaring. Across America, gas stations were beginning to see long lines again, and even a few shootings. Carter's poll numbers were sagging, a lot of anger was coming from the Hill, and public sentiment seemed to be that we were adrift.

I went upstairs to Stu Eizenstat's office that afternoon to get his thoughts. We decided the problem was urgent—OPEC seemed to be stronger than we were, and the nation was fraying at the edges. In a spot like that, the only weapon the American people have is their president. Stu sent a cable to Carter, urging him to come home directly.

Stu and his staff had been working on a new energy speech for some weeks, and my first instinct was that Carter should speak to the nation immediately upon his return. We thought he could describe what he had achieved in Tokyo, and what other world leaders were doing, and give the public some confidence that we had answers—not solutions to all their problems, but some answers. Carter received Stu's cable and returned to the White House on July 2, exhausted from his trip but ready to move ahead on the energy question, and held a series of meetings with the staff and the speechwriters. He told Jody Powell to schedule a televised speech for July 5, then headed to Camp David to work on his text.

The next day the White House operator phoned and connected me to a conference call with the president. To my shock Carter said he wanted to postpone the speech. This worried me—I was afraid it would make him look indecisive. But Carter was determined and persuasive. By that time he had already given four national addresses on energy, going back to his first months in office, and he said he didn't want this one to be just another speech. "They've heard it all before and they are not going to be any more enthusiastic now than they were before," he told us. Instead, he wanted to hole up at Camp David for several days, call in experts and advisers from all walks of life, and do some thinking about what the nation needed and what he might say.

That next week would produce the address that became the signature of Jimmy Carter's presidency, the famous "crisis of confidence" speech. It was perhaps the defining text for his theory of the trusteeship president, the leader who would protect the country's best long-term interests whatever the short-term political costs. But it also led to the only serious falling out that Carter and I had in four years.

I could understand Carter's exasperation. He had been talking to the American people about energy since the earliest days of our administration, and it was not clear if they were listening. He had brought up conservation in the first weeks after we took office, and I remember being startled by his intensity. We all remembered the first energy crisis—the OPEC oil embargo of 1973, which caused oil prices to triple and created the first lines at gas stations. The federal government simply had no effective response. Nixon tried "odd-even" days at the gas pump, while experimenting with price controls, but never came to grips with the prospect of ongoing supply disruptions. The winter that we took office was extremely cold, with fuel-oil shortages in the Northeast, but Carter was looking beyond the present moment and conceiving long-term strategies. He gave his first major energy address just three months after we took office, in April 1977, and said, "We must not be selfish or timid if we hope to have a decent world for our children and grandchildren. We simply must balance our demand for energy with our rapidly shrinking resources. By acting now, we can control our future instead of letting the future control us." It was prescient. World oil prices had settled down from the 1973 embargo, and two years would elapse before all hell broke loose again. He had proposed a new federal Department of Energy to promote conservation and develop alternative fuels, and he got Congress to approve it. A year later he came back with a second energy package—deregulating domestic oil prices and natural gas prices and establishing a national conservation program. These were big ideas—bigger than anything other presidents had tried and, in retrospect, bigger than anything the public or Congress expected.

As with so many other issues in our administration, conservation was deeply personal and completely sincere for Carter. A farmer from southern Georgia, he believed in acknowledging limits and accepting sacrifice. A man of faith, he felt a religious obligation to preserve God's creation. When he put on his sweater, it wasn't just public relations. He was telling people, Turn down the thermostat and conserve. He did the same thing in the White House. He put solar panels on the roof and a wood-burning stove in his office, and he ordered limits on thermostats in all federal buildings. I remember the hot Washington summers of 1977 and 1978—it would be ninety-five degrees outside and Carter would have the White House air-conditioning turned off. We would sit through cabinet meetings and it would be hotter than a bug and muggier than hell—all of us wiping our brows. He would sit right through it because he wanted to provide an example for the country.

It also exemplified Carter's belief that he had to rise above the usual politics and put the country's long-term interests first. He remembered the 1973 oil embargo and its disruption of the economy, and he wasn't going to forget it simply because most Americans had forgotten. He didn't like our country's dependence on imported oil—or any finite fossil fuel.

The public, I think, was mystified at first. Congress had passed one major conservation bill in 1975, with the first fuel-economy standards for cars. But the Ford administration never actually put the CAFE standards into effect, and before long oil prices settled down again. As a result, Americans were skeptical that this problem was real. In Congress, scapegoating oil companies was the preferred response; that was easier than asking Americans to change their habits or devising a long-term energy policy. The public did a lot of wishful thinking—that oil shortages would go away, that panaceas such as skipping Sunday church services would save enough gas. When Carter said this was a serious problem, a permanent problem, many Americans greeted the message with disbelief.

Carter was far ahead of Congress on conservation strategies, and I don't think we handled the politics well. Carter personally wrote much of his first energy bill, sitting at his desk and consulting Jim Schlesinger, who was his energy adviser and would become the secretary of energy. Carter kept the details close. He was afraid we would get pecked to death if members of Congress got wind of the details prematurely. He also felt that he and Schlesinger had come up with a solid plan that didn't need a lot of negotiation. He had good people testify, and he would certainly make the calls to lawmakers, but he hated to negotiate with the Congress. He didn't want to get into that trap where the special interests he had criticized so often could sit down as equals and corrupt the legislation. The result, of course, was that sometimes we didn't get anything.

On submitting that bill, Carter faced the usual fragmentation within Congress. Members from oil- and gas-producing states wanted one thing: deregulation, get out of our way, let us drill offshore and raise prices. Members from consuming states thought deregulation and higher prices were just a way of gouging their constituents. They were usually looking around for scapegoats or panaceas. Environmentalists, who should have been allies of Carter, were skeptical about our proposal for an energy mobilization board because it would have the power to sweep aside regulations, to accelerate the construction of refineries and nuclear reactors. Then of course the Republicans just wanted to create frustration to help them in the next election—which worked.

These factors all combined to create problems for our first energy bill, in 1977. Both houses quickly approved Carter's proposal for a new Department of Energy. But the second big piece, the phased deregulation of natural gas prices, got bogged down in one committee after another, one draining fight after another, as senators from consuming states battled it out with their colleagues from producer states. This struggle came to a head in the Senate, in October, with an eight-day filibuster by Jim Abourezk of South Dakota and Howard Metzenbaum of Ohio, and the Senate's first all-night session in thirteen years. At the end, we had a big shoot-out over the stalling tactics. I went to the Capitol myself and took the presiding officer's chair in the Senate. Working with majority leader Robert Byrd, I threw out a huge stack of obstructionist amendments with a series of rapid-fire parliamentary rulings because Senate rules required the presiding officer to reject them as nongermane, or "dilatory." That session left blood on the floor by the time we were done. Even old friends such as Jacob Javits and Paul Sarbanes were bitter. Not until late in 1978 did Congress finally send that part of the energy bill to Carter for his signature, and though we won in the end, it was eighteen months of looking as if we were losing.

In some respects, the energy legislation resembled the water projects in our first year. Viewed as a public trustee, Carter was doing the right thing. Viewed through the lens of Congress, where each state had two senators and widely varying interests, where you ran into the coal lobby and the gas lobby, it was painful. A leader who takes on energy politics finds a lot of animals are rooting around in the woods out there ready to pounce. Meanwhile, the poor consumer is just trying to pay for a tank of gas.

Carter didn't give up. He delivered three more major energy addresses and pressed for new legislation. We sent Congress incentives for biomass and gasohol, a plan to streamline the licensing of nuclear power plants, additional incentives for solar power, and, later, a proposal for a synthetic-fuels corporation.

Meanwhile, consumers saw no relief. In late 1978 oil-field workers in Iran went on strike, which caused chaos in Middle East oil production and sent prices up again. You could see the possibility of gas lines coming back.

Facing these new pressures, in 1979 we began looking at various regulatory solutions to the prospect of fuel shortages. We considered standby rationing, for example, and allocating fuel supplies to prevent spot shortages. But I became convinced, after listening to the economists who advised Carter, that the regulatory approach would be impractical. Regulations would merely create inefficiencies and black-market behavior, and even if they were workable, you couldn't pilot them through the snarls on Capitol Hill. Every member of Congress had an idea of what the country most needed from a national energy policy, and by some coincidence it always served the interests of his or her own district. If you came from Texas oil country, your solution was higher prices and more drilling. If you represented Minnesota, with its brutal winter heating bills, you wanted price controls on natural gas. If you represented Winnebago County in Iowa, you wanted an exemption for Winnebago vans, so that people could go on their long driving vacations. I saw that the government would inevitably seem arbitrary if we tried to do conservation by regulation. It would not succeed, for political reasons, and people would think their government looked ridiculous.

So we turned instead to market signals. At that time the federal government had statutory price controls on domestic oil, caps that set the domestic price well below the world price. This was nice for consumers, but it was terrible energy policy. It encouraged Americans to waste fuel and domestic producers to hoard oil and sell it through brokers to overseas clients. So, in the spring of 1979, we settled on deregulation of domestic oil and gas prices as our main tool to promote conservation. (Price controls had been extended in 1975 and were due to expire in 1979, so the only question was whether we would ask Congress to extend them again or let them expire.) We decided on a market mechanism so that people, in every facet of their lives and their personal decisions, would be think-ing about how to cut consumption. The simplest, most powerful market mechanism was price. This wasn't easy for someone like me, a liberal who had always tried to watch out for consumers, but I felt we had to have a plan based on economics and individual choice.

But I also felt we needed to introduce some fairness as we let prices rise. Gas prices were soaring—not because of anything the oil companies had done to earn the money—and it was hurting everybody, especially people of modest means who had no choice but to buy gas and drive their cars. So we proposed a windfall-profits tax. It would skim off profits that didn't reflect productive activity by oil companies, and produce revenue that we could recycle into conservation investments and rebates to con-sumers. Carter embraced the idea, too.

In 1979 we sent a big new energy package to Congress—deregulation of domestic oil prices, a windfall-profits tax, a synthetic-fuels corporation, an Energy Mobilization Board, and standby authority to ration gasoline. Every piece of that package created its own political problems, and every one got us into another thicket on the Hill.

So by the time Carter returned from Tokyo at the end of June, we were facing some deep questions about leadership and the national mood. He was cornered because he didn't have much clout on the Hill by then. He wasn't a great orator, and it wasn't his style to go out barnstorming. We were dropping in the polls. He was, I think, losing confidence in himself.

On July 2, that first Monday back from Tokyo, Carter put in a long day in the Oval Office, and we had a series of meetings on the energy message. But Carter soon saw that his staff was divided. Stu Eizenstat and I were hoping for something quick and upbeat and concrete—an address that would show voters we were taking action on the energy problem. But his pollster, Pat Caddell, and some others were saying this problem was some-thing bigger, a problem of national confidence. Their argument went like this: A public malaise is sitting like a dead hand across everything we do. This was not because of anything Carter had done, but because we'd had Watergate, we'd had Vietnam; we'd had repeated examples of mendacity and failure in American public life, and it had finally crept into America's soul and created deep doubts about the nation's ability to address grave challenges. I think Carter, as he listened to Caddell and started reading his materials, decided he couldn't come up with an adequate speech to address that larger set of challenges in the limited time he had set for himself. I think it was tough for him to see those polls come in and see public support slip away. He was, I think, hoping to rally public confidence and restore his ability to lead.

At the end of the day, Carter left for Camp David, and the next day he called us to cancel the speech and schedule a period for reflection at Camp David. It would later be known as the "domestic summit," a time for rethinking our strategy with the hope that we could turn things around and regain some momentum heading into the last year of our term.

In putting together the domestic summit Carter wanted to hear from people who could help him measure the public mood and understand it. He envisioned a series of meetings with mayors, clergy, educators—leaders from all walks of life. Among the people he invited were Bill Clinton, then the young governor of Arkansas; Barbara Newell, the president of Wellesley College; John Gardner, the founder of Common Cause; Lane Kirkland, head of the AFL-CIO; and Jesse Jackson. Part of this, I think, was public relations. He wanted to be seen listening to America, so the retreat might build interest in his speech, and in this it succeeded. When he finally came down off the mountain, people had an awful lot of interest in what Carter was going to say. For those of us advising Carter, however, that week was tense and difficult. I think we all knew that this was our last shot. If we couldn't somehow restore public confidence with this speech and this initiative, how would we ever get it back? I had already spent some hours with members of my staff reviewing what we had accomplished during our time in office and where we felt frustrated. I had even spent part of an afternoon away from the West Wing at a Chinese restaurant with Stu Eizenstat, talking through our most fundamental priorities and whether we were achieving them in the face of budget cuts and inflation. We had been at it nearly three years, we were all tired, and we were all a little bit frayed personally.

On July 5, I climbed aboard a helicopter with Stu Eizenstat, Ham Jordan, Jody Powell, and Pat Caddell and we lifted off to join Carter and Rosalynn in the Catoctin Mountains. It was a strange weekend. At Camp David you are in a lovely, serene setting, and it should be the perfect spot to clear your head and think productively. But we were also away from home and family, confined to a stuffy, windowless conference room in Laurel Lodge for hours on end, trying in an artificial quarantine to resolve some of the most fundamental questions about our country's future.

Over that first long afternoon we discovered an abyss separating some of us from others. Jerry Rafshoon, an able media adviser who was close to Carter, believed, probably correctly, that we had a crisis in the public perception of the president's authority. Rafshoon argued that we needed a speech that would make Carter look strong and decisive. In one memo he said 66 percent of the American people thought Carter was honest, and 63 percent thought he was smart, but only 40 percent thought he was strong—and the numbers were going down all the time. "Unless we can get people to think of you as a strong president," Rafshoon said, "we're done." I agreed with that. But how to do it was another thing.

Pat Caddell, a bright guy, came up to Camp David with a load of books under his arm about social psychology and public confidence. He also had a lot of interesting survey data and had spent hours culling through it to interpret the underlying public mood. He argued that the public was having a sort of psychological breakdown after several bad years in American politics. He thought Americans simply could not grapple with the gravity of a challenge as severe as an international energy crisis. Caddell proposed that Carter speak to the public about this failure of will and urge them to buckle up and deal with it.

I thought that was a dead end. I looked at the books Caddell had brought to Camp David, and they were the same texts I had read at the University of Minnesota years earlier. I knew the field Pat was introducing us to, and I said, "Pat, I've read all those books and they don't have a damn thing to do with the price of energy or the next election."

So now the lines were drawn: one camp with Caddell seeing a psychological breakdown, and another camp with Stu and me saying this wasn't a crisis of spirit, but about real problems and solutions. We sat down around a big conference table—ironically, the same table we had used for the Israel-Egypt negotiations the previous year—and spent most of the afternoon arguing this point.

By late afternoon I was pretty upset, and probably for the only time, I broke with Carter. We had gone round and round and I wanted to make my case directly.

I said, I don't believe this problem is in people's heads. When one of our constituents is sitting in a gas line, getting shot at by some hothead, when a father can't feed his family because of the price of food, these are not psychological problems. These are real problems. People can't get gas. Their paychecks are getting smaller. They're worried about their heating bills. If you go out and travel this country, people will tell you these are real, hard, day-to-day frustrations.

Second, I argued, you can't blame the American people for the problems they face. We were elected to be a government as good as the people, yet now we're proposing to say that we need a people as good as the government. You can't sell that.

I probably got a little angry as I finished my case, something I can't remember ever happening with Carter and me, and I probably made an ass of myself. But I was afraid that this would be the end of our administration. I felt that if the public thought our leadership consisted in criticizing the American people, we wouldn't be believed and we would never have a chance to get back on our feet.

By the time I finished, Carter realized how upset I was. We'd been in this argument for several hours, and he knew I was worried about the future of our administration. He suggested we go out for a walk around the grounds.

Several accounts have been written about that walk, some of them accurate and some not. I know that some versions say I threatened to resign that afternoon, but that's not true. I admired Carter and I would never have quit his administration. We concentrated on the speech and the confidence of the public. I said I knew the field—the American people had real problems and only the president could lead us out. I said that we might not get our way with Congress, but if we were at least seen to be fighting for the things that count, we could make a difference. We walked for half an hour or so, and when we got back, I was in better shape. I think Carter was just trying to calm me down.

Before we returned to Laurel Lodge Carter brought up a second subject. He said he agreed with Caddell that voters had begun to feel our administration was drifting and that he had to do something decisive. Thus he planned to make some changes in his cabinet. He didn't specifically say he was going to ask each secretary to resign, but he said he felt that shaking up the cabinet would demonstrate leadership and show how seriously he viewed the moment. At this, I argued with him again. I said he had a talented cabinet, and that the healthy debate among his advisers should be seen as a sign of strength. I particularly said he should keep Joe Califano. I knew that Joe had strayed from the administration in opposing the creation of a federal Department of Education, but I thought Califano was a gifted secretary of health, education, and welfare, and that he was strong where we needed to be strong, in the case of a Kennedy challenge. I asked Carter, "Why don't you reprimand him, but ask him to stay?"

When we got back to the lodge, the others were still debating the speech. Finally Stu proposed a compromise that would simply pair the problem of public confidence with answers to the energy challenge. I had no objection to a speech that would touch on the public mood, that would call on Americans to rouse themselves to action, as long as it also spelled out specific solutions.

In the end, we went with the hybrid that Stu proposed. Carter did a lot of work on the draft himself and came up with an excellent speech that touched on the crisis of confidence but was grounded in the need for real solutions. He finished his consultations, came down from Camp David, and delivered the speech on July 15.

That speech became one of the defining moments of Carter's presidency, for both his supporters and his detractors, but it has also been widely misinterpreted. It came to be known as the "malaise" speech because that's how one of the commentators described it. But Carter never used that word. He talked carefully about the public mood, the nation's "crisis of confidence," and he urged people to confront energy shortages with the same unity of purpose that Americans had shown in previous times of crisis. His detractors have also come to say that the speech was a flop. But that's not true either. His approval numbers shot up instantly, and polling later showed it to be one of the most popular speeches Carter ever gave. The day after he delivered it, I was out on the trail again, traveling up the West Coast and through the Midwest, giving speeches on arms control and the energy legislation. When you're in front of an audience, you can feel the public mood, and I could tell that his speech had produced a dramatic, positive response. I think people were ready for a tough message and ready for leadership on a tough issue.

Then, two days later, Carter announced the cabinet shake-up, and our momentum instantly came to a halt. He asked for the resignation of every cabinet member and accepted those of five: Joe Califano at HEW, Jim Schlesinger at Energy, Brock Adams at Transportation, Mike Blumenthal at Treasury, and Griffin Bell, the attorney general. I was giving a speech in Tennessee when someone handed me a note. I thought, Oh-oh, what do I do with this?

I know what Carter was trying to do. He had tolerated a good deal of dissent in his cabinet, and some in his circle of advisers felt the public read this as a sign of indecisiveness. I'm sure they thought the cabinet shake-up would be a show of steely resolve, the action of a chief executive in charge. But this announcement out of the blue caught the public by surprise and completely shattered any confidence emerging after the energy speech.

I think our administration never recovered from that week. Congress was caught by surprise. Wall Street was rattled. The general public seemed flummoxed. The Republicans said Americans weren't depressed about America, they were frustrated with us.

I've always thought that was unfair. I don't think the problems facing America fundamentally flowed from the president's personal style. I think these were real, complex problems hurting real folks, and we just weren't able to propose neat, confidence-building solutions.

What stands out in retrospect is Carter's devotion to principle in the face of a vexing challenge. He had the courage to front-load the pain and back-load the pleasure on the most serious issues. He was willing, even determined, to talk about shared burdens in solving the country's problems. That's not the way politicians usually operate. We had set about enacting a responsible long-term policy—deregulation, conservation, alternative energy—but it had little short-term payoff. When that's your program, it's going to require deft salesmanship. I thought Carter did a good job, but the public didn't think so. It's ironic because voters will say in surveys that they want principled leadership and they will criticize politicians for short-term thinking. Reporters and opinion writers say the same thing. But just try it in the real world and see who wins the next election.

I'm sure Carter was torn by that. Does he do the right thing? Does he continue to be that valiant trustee of the American people, or does he start shooting angles that get him through the next election? Those are tough choices for someone in public office, and they were tough for us.

I think, however, that Carter's energy policy looks better and better as time passes because of his integrity and foresight. The strategy he set out was exactly what the nation needed. Later, when oil prices spiked again, in 1990 and again in 2008, causing great hardship and economic disruption, a lot of people recalled the Carter years and rued the lost opportunity. When they thought about our dependence on imported oil, when they began to see the evidence of global warming, when they thought about all the wasted years when we could have been developing renewable energy and fuel-efficient cars, I think they looked back and asked, Now where is that leadership?

I don't condemn people for being reluctant to take painful steps in difficult times. Living in a nation that had a history of unlimited bounty, Americans did not have to worry about conservation. If you asked them to accept limits, they asked for different solutions. That's exactly what Reagan did when he took office: He said we had plenty of energy reserves and we were in trouble only because we lacked the power and confidence to produce enough. Of course Reagan had to frame it that way. If federal conservation programs had succeeded, they would have undermined his theology that government never works. Carter and I tried to make public solutions work. We talked about what it takes to mobilize people to make sacrifices when they aren't sure the threat is real, especially when it's not a time of war or a matter of national defense. We talked in those terms—the moral equivalent of war.

After those grueling months I spent a lot of time thinking about the challenges of leadership. I believe a leader can convince Americans to make sacrifices when it's necessary. I believe that the American people can be moved and persuaded. You have to believe that or you go crazy. But the tougher the issue, the tougher the challenge.

Stu Eizenstat, a brilliant guy with a mordant sense of humor, used to joke that our administration had a knack for masking its victories as defeats. Nowhere was this more true than in energy policy. It is received wisdom today that Carter's "malaise speech" was a failure. But Americans understood that the nation faced an energy crisis, and they welcomed a call to action from their president. Beltway pundits accused us of mishandling our energy legislation in Congress—a charge that was true from time to time—but failed to note that we passed more energy and conservation policy than any other administration for the next thirty years.

Despite our frustrations Carter identified one of the dominating issues of our time, energy dependence, and fundamentally changed the nation's approach to it. Until our administration, energy policy was scattered across fifty different federal agencies, none with much power. After our administration, a cabinet-level Energy Department produced thorough and accurate analyses of the nation's energy consumption and produced coherent conservation strategies. Before our administration, Congress had passed a law to improve the fuel economy of American cars, but the government hadn't actually put any standards in place. We enacted those regulations, the CAFE standards, which ultimately raised the fuel efficiency of American vehicles by 40 percent. The National Energy Act of 1978, which Carter pushed through Congress with single-minded intensity, tripled federal funding for solar energy research, created loans and tax credits for homeowners to insulate their homes and install renewable-energy heating and cooling systems, set national efficiency standards for electrical appliances, provided $100 million for schools, hospitals, and local governments to install energy-conservation technology, and imposed a gas-guzzler tax on inefficient vehicles to encourage gasoline conservation. The country's first important steps on alternative energy, including wind, solar, and geothermal power, all started under Carter. Finally, we deregulated the price of domestic oil and began the decontrol of natural gas—steps that were painful for Democrats, but that probably did more to change the national energy equation than anything else we did. By the time we left office, we had cut oil consumption by 2 million barrels per day, reduced America's dependence on imported oil by 20 percent, and triggered such a surge in domestic oil and gas production that the country had a surplus of natural gas.

Inside the Beltway, especially in the heat of the moment, politicians are judged by whether they win or lose. I understand this: You can't accomplish much if you don't win elections. Given the choice, I would rather win than lose. But I think we judge our leaders by other standards: Do they understand the nation's long-term interests? Do they tell us the truth, even when it's difficult? Do they lead the country in a responsible direction, even when it's painful? Do they leave our country better off in the long run? Carter understood those standards, and I think history judges him kindly for it.

12

Hostage Crisis

B Y THE END of our third year in the White House, we'd had a lot thrown at us: double-digit inflation, a second global oil crisis, regular battles with Congress. But I don't think anything prepared us for the ordeal that started on November 4, 1979, the day we were notified that Iranian radicals had stormed the American embassy in Tehran and taken our people hostage.

The phone call I received early that morning from Cy Vance set the stage for what was perhaps the most agonizing year of my life, a chapter that came to define the Carter presidency in the minds of many voters, and a diplomatic conundrum that may have cost us our chance at reelection. It presaged 444 days of frustration and national humiliation, pain and suffering for our hostages in Iran, and a dismal national experience that deepened America's doubts about itself, but especially its doubts about us.

Yet the hostage crisis carried lessons that remain useful today. It revealed the limits of Western military power against foreign extremist movements, as well as the tension between public expectations in a time of crisis and a leader's judgment of what is possible and prudent. These remain instructive because that ordeal was the first Western confrontation with a new radical Islam, a force that was not well understood at the time and probably isn't fully understood today. It also exposed the difficulties of international cooperation against an extremist threat. Our ability to press for a peaceful, effective resolution with the radicals turned in part on the willingness of other Western nations to help us bring pressure on Iran, and we never got the cooperation we needed.

Finally, it was also an extraordinary study in the clash between domestic political pressures, the demands that a president take action and appear strong, and the country's long-term interest in prudence, diplomacy, and long-term security needs.

I would argue that, considering the ultimate resolution of the crisis, we did a good job in an impossible situation. I know many Americans didn't see it that way at the time and don't recall it that way today. But to put it in perspective: Every one of our hostages came home alive; we didn't start a war; we didn't invade a country; we didn't commit troops to a long and deadly conflict; we never resorted to the use of military power that could have killed our hostages and other innocents and armed the radicals with anti-American arguments and resentment. Viewed against the events of the subsequent three decades, I think that record holds up well. But of course insiders always think they did the right thing. I know of few episodes in my career where the public perception differs more from that of the people who were making the decisions.

One of the most vexing aspects of the hostage crisis is that, had we known at the beginning what we knew at the end, we might have done things differently—or at least made our decisions more quickly. By the end we realized that the Ayatollah Khomeini, the first powerful Islamic radical that the West had seen, was content to string us along month after month while he nurtured his own political fortunes in Iran. But for the first many weeks we hoped that the crisis would be quickly resolved—that the Iranians would come to their senses or that one of the traditional tools of diplomacy would prove effective. So we took the decisions one by one as they came to us.

From the beginning, our administration had differences of opinion on how to approach the revolution in Iran. Cy Vance, a respected diplomat, a lawyer who had many years in the Defense Department, consistently opposed the use of military power or harsh rhetoric. He supported economic sanctions, and he ultimately came around on other measures, but we always knew that he opposed the military solution. His argument was that the hostage-taking was essentially a political problem—that as soon as the Iranian radicals decided that holding the hostages no longer served their political goals, they would let our people come home. Vance thought that if we employed force, we would only escalate the trouble and maybe get our people killed. In retrospect, he was right about most of that.

Brzezinski, on the other hand, always hoped for some way to vindicate our national honor, show national strength, and retain a multinational bulwark against broader international threats to our national interests. He thought we should stand up to uncivilized, abusive behavior and restore America's stature in the world. But I don't think he, or any of us, ever came up with a military option that would have forced the Iranians to return our hostages early.

I was caught in the middle. I knew nothing about Iran or radical Islam, but I felt I could learn, take the counsel of experts, and help the president sift through his options to arrive at practical answers—answers that would be in tune with the public's expectations but also in accord with the counsel of seasoned military and diplomatic advisers.

Perhaps the first crucial decision came even before the Iranian students stormed our embassy, even before the Shah's government fell. By the fall of 1978 we could see that the Iranian revolution was the real thing. The anti-Shah strikes and demonstrations were drawing hundreds of thousands of supporters, and the mullahs were organizing. In November the Shah appointed a martial law government in an effort to restore order. In December the Muslim fast day of Ashura was marked by massive antigovernment protests in Tehran. We were getting mixed opinions from our embassy staff, but even so, we knew that the Shah's government was in danger of collapse.

The question was whether we should intervene to support him. He had long been an ally of our country, a steady foe of Soviet expansion in the region, and a major supplier of oil to the West—but he also used police-state tactics we considered unacceptable. Now he was caught between trying to speed up his country's political liberalization—his White Revolution—and cracking down on the protesters.

Even from our distance, in our first White House meetings on the crisis, we could tell that the Shah didn't know what to do. He was anxious about the demonstrations and kept looking for a signal from us. Zbig argued for strengthening the military command and having it hold Iran together while the government evolved toward something that would satisfy the public demand for democratic reforms. But when we looked closer, we could see no realistic way of doing that. In early 1979 Carter sent General Robert Huyser to Iran to make an independent assessment of the government and the military. Huyser was not encouraged. He reported that the various branches of the Iranian military had no tradition of cooperation because the Shah wanted to keep them in isolation from each other, and we could do little to instill collaboration.

We were also troubled by memories of Mohammad Mossadegh, the Iranian prime minister who was overthrown, with American assistance, in the 1950s. Mossadegh had become prime minister as a result of free and fair elections; this had been *their* government. Yet we had helped topple him because we feared he was a socialist. Those were the heydays of the CIA, when we thought we could go around the world and pick our own governments. We did that all over the globe, with terrible long-term consequences for democracy, human rights, and our own standing in the world. We understood that the Mossadegh experience had been a tremendous assault on Iran's sovereignty, and it remained a scar on the Iranians' psyche. Worse, many of the Iranian principals who were trying to help us create a transitional government in early 1979 had been Mossadegh supporters, and they were all repudiated by the ayatollah's hardliners whenever they tried to work with us. So Carter and I were wary of any intervention that might look as if we were again trying to play puppet master. After all, this was the president who had turned the Panama Canal back to the Panamanians, after many other presidents had failed in the attempt, because he believed that respect for the sovereignty of other nations actually strengthened our standing in the world.

In January of 1979 the Shah fled Iran, presenting us with the next major decision: whether to admit him to the United States. We had received warnings from Bruce Laingen, the American chargé d'affaires in

Tehran, who was a distant relative of mine from Minnesota. He cautioned us about Iran's student radicals and their hostility toward the United States. Laingen feared that if we allowed the Shah into the United States, these radical kids might seek revenge. Within weeks of the Shah's departure, the Ayatollah Khomeini returned from exile in Paris and was welcomed as Iran's next leader. This only made Laingen more wary. But Zbig had conducted meetings with government officials in Iran. He had assurances that they would protect our embassy. They had protected it once before from a student raid, and we believed that they would do it again. Zbig also felt it would be a stain on our national honor to turn our backs on the Shah in his moment of crisis.

The Shah went first to Egypt, then to Morocco, the Bahamas, and then to Mexico, where we interceded to find him a home and adequate medical care. This gave us time to consider our decision, but it probably worked against us. If the Shah had simply come straight to the United States on leaving Iran, the episode might quickly have passed. It would have seemed routine and it wouldn't have attained the symbolic power— at least for the Iranians—that it ultimately did.

By the summer of 1979 I wound up thinking that we should admit the Shah, and I wrote Carter a memo to that effect. I was angered that these fanatics in Iran, and Khomeini in particular, could tell America who could be allowed into our country. Even though the decision posed some risk to our embassy personnel, the more I thought about it, the more I found it an outrage. Much of the foreign policy establishment, including influential thinkers such as Henry Kissinger and David Rockefeller, also argued for the Shah's admission on the grounds that he had been a loyal U.S. ally over the decades.

Within a day or two Carter called a meeting in the Cabinet Room. We typically had foreign policy breakfasts there, and he would assemble the full foreign policy team—Vance, Brzezinski, Harold Brown, CIA director Stansfield Turner, General David Jones from the Joint Chiefs of Staff, and Ham Jordan, whose judgment Carter trusted. Carter had a keen sense of the politics and had told me more than once, "I won't have the Shah playing tennis in America while our people are at risk in Iran."

But he also understood the argument for loyalty to a long-standing ally. He went round the table asking our views. By this time, most of us had come around to Zbig's position. When we finished, Carter thanked us and seemed to think through the arguments. Then he said, "All right, if we let the Shah come in here, and if they take our people hostage, as some of our advisers are warning us, and I convene this group again a month from now, what is your advice going to be?" The room fell silent. Carter said, "I thought so." So we didn't do it.

In September, we were informed that the Shah was ill with cancer, a secret he had kept from everyone except his family. Then even the skeptics came around. We all thought, For God's sake, he's got a right to come here to get medical care that might save his life. We had another series of meetings, and in late October we announced that we would let the Shah come to America. A few days later, the embassy was overrun and we were in for what proved to be a long ordeal.

Americans who lived through that episode will never forget it; those who didn't might not understand the searing effect of the images we saw on television every night. The takeover began during a street protest, one of countless demonstrations in Tehran during the period. As thousands of demonstrators streamed down the road past the American embassy, a smaller group of student radicals broke off and stormed through the embassy gates. They expected to be evicted in short order, either by embassy guards or Iranian police, but hundreds of other demonstrators quickly poured into the compound, and they soon discovered that they were national heroes. Within minutes the crowd had overpowered the embassy security detail, and the compound became the scene of one appalling image after another: student radicals setting the American flag on fire and waving it from the embassy's roof, demonstrators shouting anti-American slogans against the backdrop of giant posters of the bearded ayatollah, and, worst of all, the next day, the radicals parading our people around the embassy grounds, bound and blindfolded, while ferocious crowds shouted angry taunts. These scenes were repeated night after night for weeks, and as we watched them on the evening news, it's hard to say what was more galling: the knowledge that our fifty-three people were in physical danger every moment, or the frustration at our powerlessness to punish this appalling violation of international law and human decency. The crisis even spawned its own TV show, *America Held Hostage*, a nightly news update that chronicled every day of the ordeal and eventually evolved into Ted Koppel's *Nightline*.

For the first few weeks, we expected a quick resolution. The students who seized our embassy seemed to be a rogue group acting independently of the government. We thought Khomeini would probably intercede and free the hostages, or at least talk to us about finding some way to negotiate a settlement. It's important to remember how opaque the situation was. Radical Islam was still something quite new in the world, and our grasp of it was tenuous. Khomeini's true motives, his true attitude toward us, and the nature of his bond with the Iranian people were hard to understand.

Soon, however, it became clear that Khomeini would not oppose the students and was perhaps using them to consolidate Iranian public opinion behind him. We began looking at our options. I think the public misunderstood Carter here. The perception is that we were paralyzed or indecisive or simply naive about our prospects. None of that is true. We were not schoolchildren with some irrelevant sense of virtue. Carter was consulting daily with the best military minds and some clear-eyed realists, with no shortage of hawks in his circle of advisers. Brzezinski's top aide on Iran, Gary Sick, was a gifted professional, a former navy officer, and deeply knowledgeable about the history of American involvement in Iran. Harold Brown, the defense secretary, was a former secretary of the air force and a genius. David Jones, chairman of the Joint Chiefs of Staff, was a former bomber pilot and had been through national security emergencies in the past. In the days just before the Shah fled Iran, for example, we reviewed a plan to use the Iranian military and police to maintain order in the streets while the Shah organized a transitional government, even though this had the potential for substantial bloodshed. We were not dreamy idealists.

In the early weeks after the embassy fell, Carter embargoed Iranian oil imports, froze billions of dollars of Iranian assets held in the United States, and began organizing multinational economic sanctions against the country. Then we began considering a long list of military options. One plan was to bomb a power plant near Tehran. The military experts told us this would turn the city dark for days, and the Iranians would understand that their recklessness imposed a price. We spent a couple of hours reviewing the plan before General Jones, the former pilot, brought us up short. "Let's slow down a bit here," he said. "I've been in the air force all my life. And I'll tell you this—there's no such thing as a perfectly aimed bomb. The generals will tell you that they can drop a bomb right on that power plant and nobody is going to be hurt, but that is not so." He said the air force simply couldn't guarantee that hundreds of innocents would not be killed, or that such an operation would not enrage the militants and endanger our hostages. Suddenly that option didn't seem as attractive.

We also looked at mining Iran's harbors to cut off shipping and put an economic choke hold on the country. That would be seen as more of a defensive measure than an offensive strike. We weighed that carefully. But it, too, had liabilities. Iran was one of the world's biggest oil exporters. What if we interrupted world oil supplies? Would it hurt our allies and disrupt the world economy? Would it trigger anger in Arab countries that might see it as more military grandstanding from the West? Crucially, would it actually exert any pressure on the Iranian militants to release our hostages or would it endanger them? That idea, too, lost its appeal.

In the backdrop to our deliberations was the *Mayaguez* hostage incident of 1975. In the wake of the Vietnam conflict, Khmer Rouge naval forces had seized a U.S. merchant ship off the coast of Cambodia and taken a number of American sailors hostage on a nearby island. President Ford had ordered a rescue mission using helicopters and gunships. We went in with guns blazing. Lots of Cambodian casualties resulted, and more than a dozen U.S. troops died. But we later discovered that the hostages had been removed from the island and released unharmed before we attacked. We finally resolved that crisis, but a careful review showed that our response wasn't properly planned or executed. General Jones had been involved in the *Mayaguez* rescue, and he was very skeptical as a result. In the end, the *Mayaguez* incident looked like a great example of what I would call a spastic national reaction—an entire country say-ing, By God, those people can't do that to us and we're going to get our revenge. It wound up doing vastly more harm than good.

So, although Carter called meeting after meeting, with one team of experts after another, they never suggested anything workable. Every mil-itary option ran the risk of killing a lot of innocent people, including our hostages, something that weighed heavily on Carter's mind and came up again and again in our discussions. We knew that any bloodshed would be on television around the world, which could trigger a regional Islamic reaction against the United States.

It's worth remembering that we were at a hinge point of the Cold War era. Soviet expansionism was still very much on our minds. Carter was a hawk when it came to communism, and so was I. We knew that the wrong step could strengthen the hand of the Soviets, who were always stirring around in the Middle East. We also knew that a mistake could strengthen Islamic extremism. We had no way of anticipating the wave of Islamic radicalism that would sweep the world in the next three decades, but we knew we were dealing with volatile social and religious forces that we didn't entirely understand, and we knew that we could cause tremendous long-term damage to American standing in the rest of the world.

World sympathy was still very much on our side, and on the side of patience, and the Iranians were paying a big price in world opinion. If someone had proposed a way of using military power in a responsible way to get our hostages home, I think most of us would have supported it. But we never found it. It came down to this: Would it free the hostages or only increase the risk to them?

Unfortunately, it's one thing to be working hard on a problem and making a series of what seem to be prudent decisions, but it's another to explain that to the American public at a time of anxiety and frustration. Americans had rallied behind Carter in the first few weeks of the hostage crisis. They were patriotic and his polls rose sharply in November and December. But now we were getting into February and March. We kept trying things—negotiating with the Iranians through some third party, or organizing United Nations sanctions—and everyone could see us trying, and everyone could see that nothing was working. We looked like ditherers. It seemed that every night the evening news showed footage of the student radicals taunting America—burning our flag, parading our hostages around blindfolded, hurling insults at our president. The American people were asking us to do something, demanding, What is wrong with you? Why can't you make it work?

Carter understood the political realities. He knew the public's frustration was rising. In late February or early March he asked me to go up to Capitol Hill and take a reading of the congressional leadership. I made some visits and talked to my old friends—fine, experienced members of the Senate and the House. Their reaction was, What the hell are you doing? This has been going on for months! A lot of them said, It's time for action—punch them out, drop something on them—and we'll all feel better about it. It was the *Mayaguez* mind-set; you can't think of what to do, so just do anything.

I went to see Carter after that and said, "You know, Mr. President, a lot of people on the Hill are telling me we ought to do something." He knew what I meant. He said, "I know it and I won't have it on my conscience."

The thing to remember is that Carter was a moderate at heart, not an ideologue. He had those small-town values—an honesty, a directness. He was trying to figure this problem out and get it right. It's not that he was unaware of the political price he might pay. He was fully aware of the steps he could take that might help himself politically and temporarily. He could have swapped American arms for hostages. He was obviously trying to resolve the standoff before the 1980 election, but he was not going to exercise American military might simply to gain some yardage with voters. Courage comes in many forms, and I think the political restraint that Carter exercised in those months was one of them.

So Carter hunkered down again and worked even harder to find a solution. He was always in the Oval Office—poring over memos, looking at maps, reading the briefing books, looking for a solution. He took the issue personally and worked tirelessly. By the end of the ordeal he could have earned a doctorate based on his knowledge of Iran.

By this time we were well into an election year, with Ronald Reagan beginning to close in on the Republican nomination and Ted Kennedy launching a full-scale challenge for the Democratic nomination. But Carter refused to go out on the campaign trail. He didn't want to seem to be using the hostage crisis to rally patriotism, and he thought it was unseemly to engage in politics while our hostages were sitting in Tehran. That was the way he wanted to work—show the American people that he was intensely focused on bringing the hostages home—and so Rosalynn and Joan and I went out on the campaign trail. In retrospect, I think he stayed in the White House too long. After a time I think the public began to feel he was Rose Gardening the campaign, avoiding his opponents, and it started to look like weakness, as if the Iranians had him tied down in the Oval Office.

Carter and I had several conversations about this. I would bring it up at our weekly lunches because Carter didn't like talking politics in cabinet meetings. He would tell Zbig or Cy or Warren, "You give me your best advice. I'll worry about the politics." Throughout that spring I kept telling him, "I think you've got to get out there. You've got to explain what you're doing and make your case to the American people." But I think by that time the hostage episode had taken a personal toll on him. You could see it in his face, the somber look that would come over him. It was draining him personally. At one of those lunches he told me, "They're not listening to me anymore."

By April, we had tried every diplomatic avenue. We had tried working at the United Nations with Iran's acting foreign minister, Abolhassan Banisadr. Then Khomeini fired him. Brzezinski had held secret meetings in Algeria with a representative of the Iranian government; but every time the Iranian delegates went home, the negotiations would leak, and Khomeini would immediately remove them from the government. Ham Jordan had been conducting talks with two intermediaries, a French lawyer and an Argentinean businessman, who had connections in Tehran and seemed interested in brokering a compromise. Through them, the Iranians actually agreed to accept a U.N. commission that would travel to Tehran, consider Iran's grievances against the West, and perhaps take custody of the hostages. Then Khomeini shot that down.

Meanwhile, we kept trying various approaches to Khomeini himself, which proved endlessly frustrating. It wasn't clear if he had any interest in negotiating, or if he was just using the crisis to consolidate Iranian opinion and torment us. It wasn't even clear if he was in full control of the country. He had to gauge the sentiment of moderate Iranians, and there were a lot of them. He had to worry about the other mullahs, who also had a lot of influence. Khomeini displayed a good deal of disarray and indecisiveness, too. But I also believe he was a fanatic who thought his opponents were wrong and should be punished for their evil. He hated us, he hated Carter, and we were a wonderful kicking post.

Meanwhile, we became frustrated in trying to round up support at the United Nations for sanctions on Iran. Most of our allies offered supportive rhetoric, but when it got down to jeopardizing oil supplies or other relationships of political or commercial value, they fudged. None of it was paying off.

This period of our administration gave rise to two theories about Carter's national security strategy that have circulated in the years since we left office. The first is that we deliberately provoked the Soviet invasion of Afghanistan in late 1979, knowing it would develop into a quagmire, distract everyone's attention, and hasten the collapse of the Soviet regime. The second is that we encouraged Iraq to attack Iran in the fall of 1980, hoping that a long, wasting war would bleed the Iranians and increase the pressure on them to release our hostages. Both theories are rooted in shreds of documentary evidence and both have an air of plausibility, but both, I am certain, are completely false.

The idea that we tricked the Soviets into invading Afghanistan sounds clever in retrospect, now that we know the invasion proved to be a catastrophe that sapped Soviet military strength for nearly a decade. But we could not have predicted that in 1979, and the invasion clashed with all our priorities at the time.

In December of 1979, when the Soviet invasion began, our top foreign policy goal was to win Senate passage of the SALT II arms control treaty. We had spent months negotiating the pact, and in late 1979 I was spending a lot of time on the Hill trying to line up votes for its ratification.

Carter was intent on finishing our first term with a more stable three-way relationship among the United States, China, and the Soviet Union. Ironically, the Soviets invaded Afghanistan on the very day we submitted the treaty to the Senate. The invasion destroyed any chance we had of winning Senate ratification.

The foundation for this theory seems to be a decision Carter made in July 1979, approving a CIA plan to assist Muslim tribal leaders who were fighting the Soviet-backed Communist government in Kabul. We didn't like Soviet meddling in Afghanistan, and rightly or wrongly we were looking for groups that shared our values. But the CIA program involved less than half a million dollars in aid and was all nonmilitary assistance—propaganda materials, for example, and radio scripts. It's a huge, unwarranted leap to conclude that the CIA plan was designed to provoke a Soviet invasion when we were, in fact, trying to discourage one.

Moreover, the invasion made Carter look weak, as though the United States were a helpless superpower standing by while the Soviets imposed their will around the world, and we knew that this would be a tough issue for us in the 1980 campaign. We quickly adopted sanctions against the Soviets—the grain embargo and our boycott of the 1980 Olympics in Moscow—which we executed at considerable political cost.

The Iraq-Iran War theory has a similar ring of plausibility. We did consider every option to punish the Iranian radicals and win the release of our hostages. This was not Sunday school. We did try to make life tough on the Iranians *after* the war began. But through the spring and summer of 1980 I attended all the White House meetings on the hostage crisis, and while this option might have come up in conversation, I can categorically say that it would not have appealed to Carter or to me.

The documentary basis for this theory is a memo delivered to Ronald Reagan by Alexander Haig, his secretary of state. Haig described a series of conversations he had held with Saudi leaders, who told him that our administration gave a green light to the Iraqis. But neither Haig nor the Saudis had firsthand knowledge of our conversations with Baghdad. The truth is we were caught by surprise when hostilities broke out. We knew the tension between Iraq and Iran, and we were watching that border closely, but we also knew their relationship was governed by a 1975 U.N. peace agreement, and we assumed it was in the interests of both sides to honor that. We had no sway with the Iranians at that time and little trust for Saddam Hussein's regime in Iraq. I remember Carter's shock at the news of the invasion, and Gary Sick, the top National Security Council aide for Iranian affairs, was with Brzezinski on the day the war broke out. They were both stunned.

The timing of the Iraq-Iran war also renders this theory implausible. In September of 1980, when Iraq invaded Iran, we were already negotiating for the release of our hostages, through intermediaries in Algeria. Negotiations were far along, and we were not looking for new ways to pressure Tehran to come to the table. Furthermore, the White House was not directing hostage strategy anymore; the Iranians seemed to chafe at everything associated with Carter, and we had turned the negotiations over to Warren Christopher at the State Department. If the Iranians thought we were trying to sick the Iraqis on them, that would have hurt our chances of winning the hostages' release and perhaps endangered their lives, concerns that were at the center of Carter's thinking.

Finally, the Iraq-Iran war turned out to be counterproductive for us. It took huge amounts of Mideast oil production off the world market, which aggravated energy shortages in the United States and worsened U.S. inflation. This is another theory that seems clever in retrospect but is completely inconsistent with the realities of the time.

In the spring of 1980, after five frustrating months, even Carter ran out of patience. So we came to perhaps the most agonizing decision, the only one that caused an open rift in the administration: whether to attempt a military rescue of the hostages.

As early as December 1979, Carter had ordered the Joint Chiefs to prepare rescue plans, and they had been giving him regular updates on how such an operation might work. One day in early April 1980, Carter called a group of us together and said he had decided the time had arrived. A few days later the Joint Chiefs sent over a briefing team, Carter assembled us in the Situation Room, and General Jones rolled out his maps of Iran. That afternoon we learned about Operation Eagle Claw. The mission would be a nighttime rescue using commandos and helicopters. Military transport planes would fly the commandos to a staging area in the desert south of Tehran, where they would rendezvous with eight helicopters. They would chopper into a base camp in Tehran by night, take cover through the following day with the assistance of CIA agents in the city, then storm the embassy and evacuate the hostages by helicopter the next night. The briefing must have gone on for three hours, and it covered every detail. On April 11 Carter convened another meeting. We all were there except Cy Vance, who was temporarily out of town. Carter went around the table asking each of us our opinion. My view, which was generally shared, was that we had tried everything reasonable—negotiations, diplomatic pressure, economic pressure—and that this was our last realistic shot at getting our people home. I said that if the military advisers felt it had a shot, it was worth trying.

But Carter wanted Vance's opinion, too, so on April 14 he called a second meeting. Before we convened, Cy asked me to step outside for a walk around the Rose Garden, and he said, "Please oppose this mission." I said, "Cy, I've already said I'm for it. What's wrong with it?" He said, "It won't work. These missions never work—something always goes wrong. The generals always say it will work, but they can never pull it off." Vance was convinced that a failed mission would only humiliate us internationally and harden the extremists against us and perhaps create new dangers for the hostages.

Cy was a highly respected and deeply principled diplomat. But I didn't think Americans could tolerate the passivity of his approach, even though it might have been the best thing to do on the merits. Moreover, the hostage crisis was beginning to be perceived as American diplomatic weakness around the globe. We assembled, we talked through the arguments, and on that day Carter gave the green light to Operation Eagle Claw.

Of many tense days we had in the White House, April 24 may have been the worst. Carter remained planted at his desk, taking regular updates from General Jones while others of us drifted in and out of the

Oval Office. The mission began like clockwork, with the C-130 transport planes arriving on schedule at the Desert One staging area. But almost immediately we began to get troubling updates: One of the eight helicopters was grounded en route to Desert One with what its crew thought was a cracked rotor blade. A second chopper flew into a sandstorm, causing such severe navigation problems that its crew aborted and returned to its base on the USS *Nimitz*. When a third helicopter experienced hydraulic problems on arriving at Desert One, the commanding officer, Colonel Charles Beckwith, recommended aborting the mission because, by prior consensus, it could not succeed with fewer than six helicopters. Carter agreed. Then, as they were preparing to leave, one of the helicopters collided with a C-130 refueling aircraft and crashed in flames. Eight of our people died.

We got the phone call about the deaths in the desert in the early evening. Carter and I were together in the small study just off the Oval Office, where he went when he needed peace and quiet, and that's where he took the call. I watched him on the telephone, receiving the news. He asked, "Are there any dead?" and he turned absolutely ashen. I think the weight of the entire crisis came down on him then—the gravity of so many wrenching decisions, the disappointment for our hostages, the knowledge that this had turned into an enormous failure—and now the loss of American lives. Yet he simply put the phone down, collected himself, and took charge again. He ordered Jody Powell to issue a statement immediately, gave assignments to the rest of us, and sat down to write an address he would give to the nation at seven o'clock the next morning. You couldn't fail to be impressed by him.

It fell to me that night to inform the congressional leadership. We had kept them completely in the dark because the Joint Chiefs had told us the biggest single risk to such a mission was a leak that would cause us to lose the element of surprise. So, well after midnight, I went to my office and had to call Tip O'Neill, Bob Byrd, and a few others at their homes—not only to tell them that we had planned this rescue mission without their knowledge or consent, but that in addition it had failed and we had lost eight of our people. They were beside themselves. The next day the newspapers were full of pictures of charred helicopters and dead Americans. A mighty nation had failed pitiably, and the responsibility landed on us, and everyone in the world could see it.

When I got home that night, it must have been three-thirty or four o'clock in the morning. I woke Joan up. I said, "Joan, I think we're all done. We'll never get past this one."

But of course the hostage crisis didn't conclude that night. It dragged on for more than eight additional months as we renewed diplomatic efforts to win the hostages' release. Eventually we did find a diplomatic channel that worked, thanks to the negotiating skills of Warren Christopher and Lloyd Cutler and a set of Algerian officials who volunteered to serve as intermediaries with Iran. It was a textbook case of resolving the irresolvable—we got our people out while protecting America's claims and interests.

Carter, however, took little satisfaction from the resolution. Throughout the ordeal he defined our success in terms of saving the hostages' lives, and he wanted desperately to get them home on his watch. He didn't get that satisfaction. On Inauguration Day 1981 we waited all morning in the Oval Office, with the plane and our hostages sitting on the tarmac in Tehran, hoping we would get the phone call that they had taken off. Finally we had to leave for Reagan's swearing in. The Iranians didn't let the plane embark until one minute after Reagan took the oath—a final humiliation. Even so, Carter never shed his feeling of responsibility to the hostages. His one request to President Reagan was that he be allowed to represent the United States in greeting the hostages on their release. That afternoon we boarded a plane for the air force base in Wiesbaden, Germany, and the next day Carter welcomed the hostages home.

Despite all our frustrations in that agonizing year, the hostage crisis was a chapter in American foreign policy that deserves study again today. Some will say it made America look weak and emboldened our enemies. Some have said it revealed a pattern of poor decision-making in the Carter administration. But I take a different lesson, one I think is more important than ever: a caution against the belief that the easy answer—the emotionally satisfying response—is the right answer to every crisis.

Crises of this sort confront nearly every administration, and every president, faced with such a dilemma, will be tempted to assert American military power and let someone else clean up the damage. There is a comparable impulse in public opinion—a tendency to think that if we simply flex our might, we will get our way. The truth is that some problems have no neat solutions. Some will linger for a long time no matter what we try. Some will leave our country frustrated. Every president faces an intractable problem sooner or later, and one of the president's greatest responsibilities is to sustain the public's patience and trust while guiding the nation to a responsible outcome.

This is perhaps what troubles me most about the Iran hostage crisis. The public perception is that we failed, that we didn't use American power, that we allowed a nation many Americans never heard of to push us around and humble America in the world. I believe that perception helped spawn what became known as the neocon movement in American politics. The neocons saw in this episode a nation that was tied down by the Lilliputians. They wanted a nation free from second thoughts, liberated from any obligation to get along with others—free of the wind factory at the United Nations, the endless diplomatic negotiations, delays, and irresolution. They thought that America, if it asserted its power, if it got away from these traditional entanglements, could have its way in the world and that people around the globe would finally respect us. That idea is appealing to some Americans, understandably, and it is dangerous.

I think this impulse helps explain why the second President Bush was able to rush into a war in Iraq. Americans were offended and frightened by the attacks of 9/11 and were susceptible to the appeal of retaliation. Carter could have resorted to the same tactic during the hostage crisis. He could have gone into Iran with a massive show of force, wrought a terrible revenge, and he might have been a hero at home—until Americans realized how many lives this could put at risk, how it might backfire against our own interests, and how it might damage America's long-term standing in the world.

The irony is that the original hero of the neocon movement, Ronald Reagan, understood these lessons. Reagan, though he talked a bold game, never succumbed to military recklessness on a large scale. He invaded Grenada, to be sure, but that was minor and short and easily resolved. In the big confrontations—Beirut, for example—he pulled out the instant our troops got in trouble. His advisers, old diplomatic veterans such as George Shultz, didn't want to play the neocon game. His successor, George H. W. Bush, felt much the same way. During the first Gulf War, he expelled the Iraqis from Kuwait, pursued them as far as Iraqi territory, and then called a halt to the hostilities. He knew the dangers of invading another country and the cost of reckless belligerence.

The neocons, in my view, drew exactly the wrong lesson from the Iran hostage crisis. The lesson is that when a country finds itself in such a crisis—and they will recur from time to time—before all else a president needs to rely on evidence and expertise rather than swagger and ideology. He must understand the nature of the threat and the political environment behind it, because these will allow him to solve the crisis at the smallest cost, in blood and money and reputation, to everyone involved. Carter understood these lessons. Gary Sick, who wrote a fine account of the crisis, *All Fall Down,* later said, "If I had been one of the hostages, Jimmy Carter is the president I would have wanted."

Finally, the president must be willing to do what's right for his country, even if it's wrong for his career. It is, in a way, the highest form of bravery. Carter understood this. He placed an absolute priority on protecting the lives of our hostages. But he also made sure the world came to grips with a horrible violation of international law, and he always held long-term American objectives in mind. He found a solution that allowed America to strengthen its relationship with moderate Islam, over time, and sustain the goodwill of the rest of the world. Viewed in the long term, his decisions did serve America's interests. We got our hostages home. We did not start a war. We spilled no innocent blood. We kept Western allies on our side and sustained the sympathy of moderates of the Islamic world. We marginalized the Iranian radicals; what had been a wealthy, highly Westernized society became a pariah state for two decades. We set an example for the Iranian moderates—of whom there are many—who for a time made important gains in their government. I kept telling myself that a time would again come when the Iranian people would think about their place in the international community, would seek acceptance in the world, and they would remember how they behaved and how America treated them.

I always said after the hostage crisis was over that we treated incivility with civility. We were confronted by an appalling abuse of civilized behavior, and we resisted the temptation to respond with its equivalent. We tried to be better people representing a better idea.

13

The Election of 1980

ANY CONVENTIONAL POLITICAL history would recount 1980 as the year Ronald Reagan defeated Jimmy Carter for president and launched the Reagan Revolution in American politics. For me, however, that election had a painful prologue and a long backstory. For 1980 was also the year when Ted Kennedy challenged Jimmy Carter for the Democratic presidential nomination. That struggle pitted a dear friend of mine against a president who had won my admiration and loyalty, put me in the middle of a fight over the future of the Democratic Party, and caused me to think that fate would always find a way to place me in battle against the Kennedys.

I had suspected Ted might challenge us as far back as the party's 1978 midterm conference in Memphis. With his famous "sail against the wind speech," Ted delivered an appeal for the loyalty of the party and a critique of our administration. I left Memphis wondering if he was laying the foundation for a White House run.

I got confirmation one evening in November 1979, the night before Ted announced. He called me at home and said, "Fritz, I'm going to run for president." I told him, "I'm very sorry that you're going to do this. I appreciate being told about it, but I want you to know we don't intend to leave voluntarily, and this is going to get rough. We can both say it won't, and we can both hope it will be nice and pleasant. But it won't be, and we're going to tear the party apart and it's going to be hard for us to win in November."

I knew Ted well by then, and I could understand his aspirations. The Kennedys had suffered through assassinations, heartaches, and disappointments. They believed they had been robbed of the chance to fulfill the promise of Camelot. The speech that Kennedy gave at the 1980 Democratic National Convention, when he said "the dream will never die," was not all hokum. A lot of people were carrying a torch for Jack Kennedy and Bobby Kennedy, and they saw it as a mission, even a duty, to get a Kennedy in the White House again.

But I wasn't going to give up and let Ted take the presidency away from us. I wasn't at all sure Kennedy could get elected president, and I certainly didn't think Carter deserved the challenge. I thought he was doing a good job in the face of terrible challenges: runaway inflation, severe energy shortages, and the first stirrings of what would become a nihilist, extremist Islam. I thought the country faced a lot of tough problems, and that Ted's challenge would rupture the party and lead to the election of Ronald Reagan.

Ted and I talked a little longer that evening, and finally I said, "We'll spend all our money and energy on internal struggles, and Reagan will be the beneficiary. I wish you wouldn't do it. I know you've decided, but I wish you wouldn't." When I hung up that night, I could see that the party was in for a wrenching contest, and that I would be squarely at the center.

I had known the Kennedy family for more than twenty years by that time, since before I went to Washington, and I took no pleasure in the prospect of political combat with them. I had greatly admired Jack Kennedy; I chaired his presidential campaign in Minnesota in 1960 and was proud that Minnesota delivered its vote for him and helped tip a close national election his way. I thought his inaugural address the following January was one of the finest political speeches of our generation. I believe that the stirring phrase he used—that America would "pay any price, bear any burden" to advance the ideal of liberty—was an enduring source of inspiration to the country.

Four years later, as a young senator, I got to know his brothers. Bobby and Ted and I collaborated on investigations into child poverty, migratory labor, hunger, Indian education, and other issues of disadvantaged Americans. My legislative record in the Senate reflected a commitment to those issues that was almost identical to Bobby's and Ted's. In addition to cosponsoring legislation, we worked together constantly in mustering votes, leading Senate debates, rousing public support—whatever was needed to pass the Great Society agenda. I found myself working with either Bobby or Ted or both almost every day. We were young, energetic progressives in the Eighty-ninth Congress, caught up in a thrilling time.

Yet we seemed fated, time and again, to wind up on opposite sides in big national contests. In 1960 I had worked on Humphrey's campaign for the Democratic presidential nomination, a heartbreaking and exhausting effort, in which Hubert could never quite catch up with the money and depth of the Kennedy organization. I was in Hubert's corner again in 1968, this time against a Robert Kennedy campaign that combined extraordinary charisma with a sense of inevitability—until its tragic conclusion. Now it was 1980, and I was fending off a third Kennedy while campaigning with a president whom I greatly admired.

By late 1979 the Kennedy people were pretty cocky because they had polls showing that Ted could handily beat Carter in the series of Democratic state primary elections. They also had polls showing that he could beat Reagan in the general election. Quite apart from the polling results, Ted found Carter hard to take. He was from the South. He didn't use the language of the traditional Northern liberal that was so basic to the Kennedys—and to me. I think Ted genuinely differed from Carter in his view of the presidency and his sense of the Democratic tradition. Carter was a problem solver. Kennedy was a more instinctive, emotional politician; he figured that if you were president, you hired people to do the detail work. He saw himself as the keeper of the grail.

I thought then and think now that Ted's instincts served him poorly that year, with consequences that were tragic for the country and for the causes we believed in. If you are a senator, you have the luxury of looking at the country's problems from a distance and from a regional perspective. You have the advantage of timing your involvement in the big issues, of disregarding some topics and emphasizing others, of shaping an approach so that, strangely enough, it takes care of your own state. I knew this—it had been my life for twelve years. But we've got fifty states in this country, and a president has to deal with all of them. That was the exacting challenge that Jimmy Carter had faced for four years.

I also think Ted badly misjudged Carter's effectiveness as president. Like many Northern liberals, Ted focused on the progressive causes where he was disappointed, rather than stepping back to see the full picture of Carter's legacy. Like many in Washington, he saw Carter as an outsider and accepted the prevailing narrative that he was a frustrated chief executive. But I think the facts showed the opposite, a substantial record of accomplishment in our four years: the Camp David Accords and a lasting peace between Israel and Egypt; a sweeping overhaul of U.S. energy policy and a huge reduction in American consumption of imported oil; normalization of relations with China and a realignment of the U.S.-Sino-Soviet balance; the SALT II arms control treaty, which, though never ratified by the Senate, did slow the arms race for several years; and deregulation of major industries such as airlines and trucking, which had far-reaching results in making our economy more efficient and competitive. In addition Carter passed a long-overdue reform of the federal Civil Service; modernized U.S. weapons systems with innovations such as stealth aircraft and the MX missile; and won ratification of the Panama Canal treaties—a goal that had frustrated five previous presidents and produced lasting economic and diplomatic benefits. In fact, the *Congressional Quarterly* later concluded that our administration prevailed more than 75 percent of the time on recorded roll call votes in Congress, a record exceeded only by Lyndon Johnson and John Kennedy.

Moreover, I don't think Ted had come to grips with the way our country's economic circumstances and political landscape had changed since the era when he and I arrived in Washington. Americans no longer had the same faith in public solutions that they had when we created Medicare, Legal Services, Head Start, and the War on Poverty. The U.S. economy had downshifted since the 1960s, leaving people with less confidence in the nation's prowess and the government with fewer resources to solve problems. The magnificent social vision Ted and I shared when we came of age as senators might be enough to rally the community of Democrats, but I didn't think it was enough to win a national election— or provide an answer to Reagan's conservative message.

Above all, I worried that Kennedy's internal challenge would weaken our administration and set up Reagan for victory in November, a victory that would undermine much of what Ted most valued and hurt millions of Americans for whom we had worked together.

Even years later, I think Ted misjudged Carter's place in history. I read, and greatly admired, his book *True Compass*, but I saw some of its pivotal episodes differently. As much as I admired Kennedy's long struggle for national health insurance—a cause in which we fought side by side—I think he misread the nation's circumstances and mood in 1980. If our administration had proposed a huge new national health program that year, at a time of frightening budget deficits and inflation, the Congress wouldn't have touched it and the public would have regarded it as an act of political desperation. We made an earnest effort to meet Kennedy halfway, with tireless work by Joe Califano and Stu Eizenstat, proposing a health-insurance system that would be phased in incrementally as the federal budget permitted. I think Ted erred in rejecting that compromise. I think he also misjudged Carter's final energy speech. While Ted was one of our great orators, with a gift for touching people's hearts and aspirations, I think he missed the way that Carter, with his honesty and directness, connected with the American people that night. The polls certainly showed it to be one of Carter's most effective speeches, with a degree of honesty and political courage that is seldom seen in American public life.

In the summer of 2009 I attended the magnificent memorial service for Ted, and I mourned his death deeply. When he finally dropped his presidential ambitions, after 1980, he concentrated on the Senate. He buckled down as he never had before. He took on the biggest issues, he mastered the details, he attracted the best staff. Everybody loved Ted and wanted to work with him, and prominent Republican senators found that they valued collaborating with him on the major issues of the day, including education and immigration reform. He was beautiful to watch—defending the undefended, giving his voice to the voiceless, truly becoming a master of the Senate. He is now rightly remembered as one of America's greatest senators and public leaders. He was, in the end, a giant and a great champion of the causes we both held dear. But Carter, too, was a brilliant, courageous leader and a strong president. He is a profoundly honest and decent person, a deep thinker, and a man of conviction, and I'll always look upon him as a strong president who served his nation with distinction and honor. I only wish their paths had not collided that year.

About the time Kennedy entered the race, the *New York Times* published a gloomy but perceptive editorial, and I think it captured our dilemma: There was no money to do the things we wanted to do. Carter had figured this out early in our administration, and it didn't take long for the rest of us to face up to it. But Democrats resisted the idea. Kennedy had the old-time music, the old-time programs—and no money to pay for them. It was all going to be paid for out of economic growth. But there was no growth. We were mired in slow productivity growth and stagflation. I didn't abandon my hopes that we could complete the agenda of social reform in America, including health care, but I also knew that the federal government was broke. Kennedy and I had it out in Memphis, and I wish the fight had ended right there. But it didn't.

It became my job, early in that campaign, to go out on the trail and do battle with Ted. Through much of the spring, while Carter handled the hostage crisis, Rosalynn and I were his proxies. I appeared at a lot of forums with Ted, carrying the torch and fending him off. It was no fun, and it led to one or two ugly moments. At an event in Iowa, Kennedy came after us for ordering the grain embargo against the Soviets. This was hard for me. Kennedy's position was my position; I didn't think the grain embargo would hurt the Soviets much, but I knew it would hurt American farmers and turn the farm states against us. But I was supporting the president. At a press conference I said something about Carter putting patriotism over politics and said Kennedy should support the president at a time like this. I regretted it immediately. I was tired and I shouldn't have said it. Ted took offense, and I took it back right away, and by the next morning he had accepted that. But it was bruising.

After the really tense appearances, I liked to get back to Washington, go home with Joan, and unwind over cheeseburgers and a glass of wine. Joan never critiqued my speeches the way Lady Bird Johnson is said to have graded LBJ. I was intense enough as it was. But Joan was an unfailingly perceptive adviser who could cut to the heart of any issue, and from time to time she would correct my Elmore grammar. She was also a wonderful and tireless campaigner.

In the end we fought Kennedy off, but the battle hurt us. We had hoped to wrap up the nomination early with a string of primary victories and show that Kennedy's campaign wasn't going anywhere. But we couldn't pull it off. We won the Illinois primary in March by a big margin, but then lost the New York primary a week later. So the fight dragged on until June—when we won Ohio and West Virginia—and it distracted us from preparing for the fall election. Ted had every right to run, of course, but he stayed in the race too long. That struggle divided the party, wasted weeks of staff time, sapped our fund-raising efforts, and introduced poison into what should have been a triumphant season.

Worse, Kennedy's challenge signaled a bigger problem for us, a demoralization among the traditional Democratic groups. Carter had been elected as a different kind of Democrat, and everybody in America knew that. But all the traditional Democratic constituencies were thinking, When he gets in office, it will be just like it was before.

Early in our term, at a national meeting of the Urban League, Vernon Jordan gave a speech suggesting that Carter was not completely delivering on the black agenda. Carter was an old friend of Jordan's, but he wasn't going to stand for that, and his response was pretty tough. He said essentially, I'm doing what I should do as president, and I'm not going to be pushed around this way. What had been a strong relationship during the 1976 election soured a little. I encountered similar problems in the Jewish community. Even though Carter had almost single-handedly achieved the Camp David Accords, and the Egyptian-Israeli peace treaty was this country's greatest achievement for the security of Israel, a lot of people felt Carter wasn't strong enough for Israel or was pro-Palestinian. In the end, we did pretty well in the Jewish community, but again Carter failed to get the credit he deserved with a group that should have been a natural ally.

I also spent a lot of time in that campaign shoring up our relationship with the labor movement. They knew me, I had campaigned with them, and I think we had some trust. Doug Fraser, the United Auto Workers president at that time, was a wonderful man and one of my best friends. But he was one of the stalwarts who went for Kennedy. He wanted national health insurance. I said, "Doug, you and I have been together on national health insurance for years. But we haven't done it, have we? How are people going to be persuaded that this can be done in this environment, without huge tax increases, which will drive us back into a recession again?" He didn't have an answer for that, but emotionally he just preferred Kennedy, at least until the primaries were over. That's the way it was with many Democrats all year long. Their hearts were somewhere else.

The common dilemma with all these constituencies is that Carter was stuck in a trap of frustrated expectations. These groups had achieved much of what they wanted in the 1960s and 1970s. The country had seen that tremendous high tide of social progress, and groups organized around each of the programs that we created during the Kennedy and Johnson years. If you put your hand on Head Start, for example, you'd find a lot of people who knew exactly what it meant to them and what sort of budget they expected from Washington. We faced countless similar constituencies, each with reasonable arguments but inflexible positions. I had talked about this with my colleagues in the Senate—you could accomplish so much, and still people wanted more. Those habits were realistic in the 1960s, when economic growth produced growing federal revenues without the need for tax increases. But suddenly hard times came along and we couldn't deliver that way anymore. It's a remarkable phenomenon—Carter was a spectacular conservationist, but the environmentalists weren't happy with him. He was good—very good—on civil rights, and yet the black leadership was often frustrated. He had submitted the best labor legislation in a generation, but the labor movement thought wrongly that we hadn't tried hard enough. A lot of hopes were dashed, and people took a while to get the disappointment out of their systems.

I was right in the middle of this feud—out on the campaign trail, trying to put the family back together. I was the guy they would call when they were mad. Teachers, mayors, governors, environmentalists, whoever. I started out trying to keep them happy, and at the end I was just trying to keep them less mad.

Despite the frustration it caused with the traditional Democrats, Carter's trustee philosophy was a noble idea and might have worked if we had been able to hold the political center. But by midsummer I was starting to have doubts about that, too. The Iran hostage situation had turned sour, and that spring I had seen public patience eroding. We picked up political strength early in the crisis, in the first few months of 1980. People always thought Carter was sincere. They knew he was smart. They knew he was working on a solution. But that support dissipated by the spring and early summer, especially when Reagan began saying all we had to do was get tough with the Iranians. When the rescue mission failed and we lost our troops that night in the desert and the hostages seemed to be pinned down endlessly, popular support melted away.

Meanwhile, the economy seemed to be worsening by the week. Consumer prices rose 13.5 percent in 1980 and the unemployment rate was approaching 7.1 percent. When numbers are that bad, people see it and feel it, even if they don't ordinarily read the business pages. Art Okun, a fine economist who had been one of Lyndon Johnson's advisers and gave us advice from time to time, had developed what he called a "discomfort index" to measure how the economy felt to average people. You simply added the inflation rate to the unemployment rate, and whenever that sum got above twelve, he said, it's trouble. We were approaching twenty-one.

It's not that we hadn't been trying to tame inflation. Early on, Carter saw the risk and tried any number of measures to give us a leaner economy. It was difficult stuff: cutting the federal budget, deregulating the airlines, and decontrolling energy prices. But these were strategies for the long term. The payoff came six years later, when inflation pretty well evaporated. Next Carter appointed Alfred Kahn to be his inflation czar. An able economist from Cornell who had been in charge of airline deregulation, Kahn wrote memo after memo on inflation strategies. We had whole committees of economists, the best experts in the country. But there were no recommendations. They would suggest another study group, or they would propose something that Congress had no intention of passing.

Faced with these frustrations, Carter could have turned to gimmicks—an independent commission to issue rosy forecasts, for example, or temporary wage and price controls of the kind Nixon had used. But gimmickry was not in his genes. He always chose to face the facts. About this time, Kahn sent Carter a memo summarizing one more task force report with gloomy conclusions—concerning efforts to control oil prices—and asking if he should release it to the press. I still have a copy of that memo, and Carter's reply is plainly legible, written in his strong hand on the upper right-hand corner: "Fred: Bite the bullet. Tell the truth. Let the chips fall. Try to shape headlines with your comments. Improve the system."

After more than a year of firing blanks on inflation, we had lost the confidence of Congress and the public. Finally, in August 1979, Carter had turned to Paul Volcker as our nominee for chairman of the Federal Reserve Board. Volcker was going to be the hammer, the one who finally nailed down the lid on inflation. Volcker was not well known to the public, but he had perfect credentials: He had held key positions in the Treasury Department under Kennedy, Johnson, and Nixon and had a good reputation on Wall Street. I helped vet him for Carter and I came to see that he was well respected, but I was uneasy. He had a strong independent streak. That's exactly what you need in a central banker, someone who will stick to the task and ignore the politics, but it wasn't necessarily good for us. Volcker's idea was that the Fed should take a new approach to inflation, a strategy known as "targeting" the money supply, advocated by a conservative school of economists known as monetarists. If you held the nation's money supply to a growth rate of, say, 3 percent per year, then the economy and prices could grow no faster. Close off the monetary spigot, and you would shut down inflation. It was an experiment, closely watched in the financial community, and Volcker didn't tell us that interest rates were going to take off or that unemployment would rise sharply as a consequence. He didn't get to any of the bad news. He just said we're going to close off the money and the economy will have to comply. It did wring inflation out of the economy eventually, but it also helped wring us out of the White House.

Between fending off Ted Kennedy and battling inflation, we probably didn't turn our full attention to Ronald Reagan until the spring of 1980. In the early going we weren't sure what to make of him. At the start of his campaign I thought he was wobbly, unsure of his facts and vague in his positions. Outside California, people thought of him as an old movie actor who had taken a lot of right-wing positions. They wondered, Can this guy, the oldest presidential candidate ever, actually govern? He had taken all sorts of wacky positions over the years, and for a time we told ourselves that once the American people got a good look at him, they would realize that he was an extremist. Yet we had our warnings. On one of my trips to California that spring I paid a visit to Jesse Unruh—"Big Daddy" Unruh, the former Speaker of the California State Assembly. He had run against Reagan for governor in 1970 and lost. I went to see him and said, "We're going to be running against Reagan. What should I do?" He said, "There's nothing you can do." I said, "What do you mean?" He said, "Just get ready. You are going to be surprised."

We did spend a lot of time looking at Reagan's record, and we knew he had made a remarkable series of nutty statements—comments that were frightening coming from someone who actually hoped to hold public office and should have made him suspect as a candidate. He kept saying there was more oil in Alaska than in the rest of the world combined, and that all we had to do was drill. He made up anecdotes about the welfare system—welfare queens driving Cadillacs, for example—and kept using those examples even after they were shown to be false. He said things about missiles that were just science fiction, and everyone with any expertise knew it. He had opposed every important civil rights law adopted by the Congress. He was one of politics' great creative thinkers because no matter what the problem was, he had his own set of facts with no bearing on reality. Then he kicked off his campaign in Philadelphia, Mississippi, the town where three civil rights workers had been murdered in 1964. I thought that would upset a lot of people and cause some to question his judgment. He made a lot of mistakes, detail mistakes, in his campaign operation and in his public statements. But voters were in a mood to forget the details and move on.

Then there was Reagan's economic program—the supply-side theory that you could cut tax rates and actually collect more revenue. I had been on the Finance Committee in the Senate. I'd heard these ideas floating around Capitol Hill. No one took them seriously, even on the Republican side. It was voodoo economics, as George H. W. Bush famously said while running against Reagan for the Republican nomination. And we were right: Congress adopted the supply-side tax cuts in 1981, and they never produced the revenue that Reagan promised. We ended up with a decade of massive deficits. But at the time, people bought the idea. His ideas were simple and people found them appealing.

That election season also saw the debut of a new form of politics, the culture wars. Reagan's campaign made effective use of so-called family values themes, and I remember wondering why Americans were so attracted to the rhetoric of the religious right. I asked our campaign staff to pull together some focus-group data, which showed that some voters didn't trust Democrats to understand and preserve their values. A lot of people felt that the Northern liberals looked down on them—their values, their families, their small towns, their churches, their prayers. George Wallace had tapped into this resentment, regularly referring to these pointy-headed liberals trying to tell "us" what to do. Nixon tapped into it, too. He thought the elites looked down at him because he had come up the hard way, and with his speechwriter Pat Buchanan he knew how to stoke the resentments in Middle America.

These forces found new vigor in 1980 with the religious right. If you read the sermons of some of the evangelical preachers or spent any time listening to them on television, as I did, you saw that they all had a slightly paranoid, "we'll show them" subtext. I remember listening to Jerry Falwell and being disturbed. I wasn't bothered by people invoking their faith. I was raised in a religious family. I'd like to believe that our faith informs our public judgments. But the religious right took it too far: When some-one like Falwell claimed to be judging others on God's behalf, I had to object. None of us has that kind of relationship with the Higher Being. If you are a person of faith, your actions speak for themselves.

These social resentments were also showing up in mail to the campaign headquarters. A lot of letters demanded that we take a stronger position against abortion, that we do more to protect "family values." People felt under siege, they wanted us to do more for them, and a lot of it was mean. I think that was a big reason why the South, Carter's great strength, collapsed on us. They didn't trust what we were doing up there in Washington.

That was the election in which these cultural issues moved out of the fringes and into the mainstream of national politics. Several giants of the Senate were voted out of office that year, including George McGovern and Gaylord Nelson, and the cultural right played a role in every one of those races. Moreover, great old Democrats weren't replaced by Republicans like the ones I had known in the Senate—an Ed Brooke or a Jack Javits—but by a new style of Republicans, people who lauded the rich and ignored the poor. They were a different crowd, and they introduced a mean and divisive tone into American public life.

By late summer I could see that Reagan was getting his sea legs. He started to seem more self-assured and more likable. He gradually built his standing with voters and, with a series of negative television commercials, slowly chipped away at our administration. Of course, he had the old actor's mastery of the camera. He had a steady, positive bearing, which appealed to people at a time of great uncertainty about our economy and our standing in the world. Nothing troubled him.

In contrast to Reagan's easy self-assurance, Carter was becoming exhausted and, I think, privately dispirited. He had worked tirelessly on the most difficult issues. He had tackled the Panama Canal treaties: the sheer drudgery of negotiations and politics, and he got it done. He had achieved Camp David: a hundred different moving parts that could have fallen apart. He pulled it all together and got it done. He had won the

White House that way, by sheer effort and discipline and attention to detail. People gave him no chance to be nominated in 1976, but he was. People thought he was in trouble with Democrats in 1980, then he beat Kennedy.

All through that spring I urged Carter to get out of the Oval Office and onto the campaign trail. My advice was probably wrong early on; I think the public respected the president for putting the hostage crisis ahead of campaigning. But then, as things went along and Carter wouldn't leave the White House, public support began to ebb. Voters were starting to say, What's he doing? What is going on?

I think a part of Carter was always more comfortable behind that desk working on the issues—cutting through the details, digging into the depth of the challenges, and mastering answers by sheer drive and grit—than out on the campaign trail. I told him at one of our lunches, "If we are going to do this, you've got to get out and speak." He said, "Yes, you and Humphrey like to do that." But it wasn't his kind of politics.

As a result, I became the circuit rider—sometimes the campaign strategist, always a party leader, and a uniter. Those were eighteen-hour days, seven days a week. It never let up and it eventually became discouraging. When people think you are losing, you can see it in their eyes. There's a kind of hollowness or fatigue. They are nice to you, they are on their feet cheering. You can't prove that they are not excited, but you can tell. I told Ham Jordan I was running the largest free mental-health program in America, because, in the middle of stagflation, high oil prices, the hostage crisis, my job was just going around trying to make people feel better about things.

Nevertheless, the polls showed a close race. Voters were attracted to Reagan's optimism, but they appreciated Carter's decency, integrity, and hard work. They were unhappy with us, but they weren't sure Reagan was ready to be president.

The real turning point, I think, came on October 28, the night of the presidential debate. Carter and Reagan had only one debate that year, with no vice-presidential debate, so this was the voters' one chance to take stock of the candidates. Carter showed up looking tired and drawn.

You could see it in his face, the drain of the campaign and the strains of the hostage crisis. Reagan looked cheery and confident. On substance, if the contest were judged by college debate rules, I would say Carter won that debate. But at the gut level, it was different. On the questions that mattered—did people feel good about Reagan as a person, could he be a president—he came out of the debate with all the answers breaking his way. Over the next week Reagan solidified a five-point lead in the opinion surveys. Then, right at the end, his polls took off. He was getting presidential crowds. When an extra ten thousand people show up for a campaign rally, you know something is happening.

On Election Day, Carter and the campaign staff got an early call from Pat Caddell. He had the latest polling numbers and said, "It's over. We've lost." Election Day is a long day in any case, because after months of frenetic activity there is nothing to do but wait, but Pat's call made it even longer.

That evening I was at the Hilton Hotel in St. Paul, where Minnesota Democrats had often gathered over the years, and Carter was in Atlanta. He called me about 8 p.m. to say that the outcome was clear and he was drafting his concession statement. He was businesslike, as usual, and he said he wanted to call Reagan, give his statement, and get it over with. I agreed, but I'm afraid we weren't thinking carefully and that early concession statement was a mistake. The polls hadn't closed on the West Coast, and surveys later showed that after our announcement a lot of Democrats simply stayed home, which probably hurt many of our congressional candidates.

I spent the rest of the evening making phone calls, most of them in consolation. I lost a lot of buddies that night—Gaylord Nelson, George McGovern, Birch Bayh, Frank Church. It was as if someone had turned out the lights and locked the door on a house where I had happily lived for a long time.

That election marked the beginning of a sea change in American life, a tectonic shift in American politics. Reagan helped bring it about, but it reflected something much bigger. After all the years of reform and social change—the New Deal and the Great Society, the civil rights movement and the War on Poverty, the consumer and environmental regulations we put in place, the women's rights movement and the changes in the American family—people were exhausted and wanted a rest. They wanted their country to slow down a bit and let all these changes settle in. People had also grown suspicious of the Democratic solutions that we had adopted in such profusion, skeptical that those ideas were as successful or as affordable as we had advertised. Arthur Schlesinger once wrote that politics in America is cyclical, with movements that come and go, and that is my experience. I think Americans just wanted to take it easy for a time, and Reagan was a good apostle of that.

In addition to that sense of unease at home, people were frustrated with our leadership in a world that seemed to be changing quickly. We no longer had the economic preeminence that America had enjoyed since World War II, and we had entered a new period in international affairs with the rise of a new, frightening Islamic extremism.

People feared that America had lost its stature in the world, its reputation as a can-do nation. To cast a ballot for Reagan was to strike back at forces the voters resented. Ironically, Reagan didn't have any answers either. As a candidate, he kept saying we should do whatever it took to bring the hostages home. But he didn't say what that was. He described the Soviets as an "evil empire," but by his second term he was negotiating with them just as we had. He didn't have an answer on the economy either. He got into office and passed a major tax cut, then two years later he had to raise taxes again. America today is still dealing with the challenges that had emerged at the time of that election—radical Islam abroad and economic self-doubt at home—and I don't see that anyone has discovered a simple solution.

I'm sorry we lost to Reagan, because his victory ushered in a long retreat from everything I believed in. But I'm proud of the things we accomplished: a visionary energy policy, gains for human rights around the world, the restoration of integrity to Washington. On election night I said of our administration, "We told the truth, we obeyed the law, we kept the peace," and I think those words hold up well.

14

Mondale vs. Reagan

O N JANUARY 20, 1981, Jimmy Carter and I sat with a crowd of dignitaries on the West Front of the Capitol for the inauguration of Ronald Reagan. It's a thrilling occasion: a constitutional pageant taking place before your eyes and a sea of people stretching back along the National Mall until your eye reaches the Washington Monument and the Lincoln Memorial in the distance. But that was not a good day for Carter and me. We had been up all night monitoring negotiations with Tehran, with no results by the time we left the White House. The day was bitterly cold, and I could see the strain on Carter's face.

What pained me most about that ceremony, however, was Reagan's acceptance speech. I didn't begrudge the new president this chance to address the nation. He had won the election and it was his turn to lead. But when Reagan uttered the phrase "In this present crisis, government is not the solution to our problem; government *is* the problem," I was stunned. Reagan's central idea—the notion that government never succeeds, that only the unfettered market can solve our problems—I found profoundly misleading and destructive. I probably decided in that moment that I had to run against him in 1984.

The next day, I found myself out of public office for the first time in twenty years. We moved back to our old house on Lowell Street in Northwest Washington, and that felt wonderful. Joan and I loved it. Joan had helped organize a food co-op during our early years in Washington, and she was soon volunteering again. We discovered that, in our absence, a family of raccoons had taken up residence in the attic. They resisted our best efforts to evict them until Joan discovered that Ted's and Eleanor's rock music, played at sufficient volume on the second floor, caused them to move out. On our first day back home the neighbors all showed up in the front yard to help unload a truckload of firewood. The vice president's mansion can get pretty lonely. It's a beautiful home— big and gracious—but it often has an empty feel. I would be home for a weekend occasionally, and I would wander around the big place and stare out the windows. No neighbors. Just trees and a Secret Service agent somewhere out on the grounds. Lowell Street felt like home.

I also welcomed the break from the stress. The White House is total pressure, twenty-four hours a day, seven days a week. You have staff around you constantly, so that whether you are in your office, in a car, or on a plane, you are always working. The Secret Service agents, though wonderful people, are ever present, so it was hard to move around the way I could in the Senate, and hard to find private time with people. Our four years had been a time of tremendous emotional tension, with sheer exhaustion at the end.

Now I had time to read books again and think things over.

But I didn't spend a lot of time in soul-searching. I was restless almost before I knew it, and I knew I had no time to waste if I intended to run in 1984. I took a job with Winston & Strawn, an old Chicago law firm whose Washington office was headed by my dear friend John Reilly, and spent some time talking with people I trusted.

The question that came up repeatedly was, If Reagan is so popular, why run? I would say, I want to take this guy on. I tried to set aside my feelings from the previous year's campaign, but I was immediately offended by the way Reagan governed. I thought he was trying to undo the entire structure of social justice that we had worked for years to establish: civil rights, child nutrition, a vigorous labor movement, access to medical care, dignity in old age, the notion that as Americans we are a family. I still wanted to see what America could do if we tried to give everybody a chance. I felt the race against Reagan was essential.

In those first six months, however, it seemed that Reagan could do no wrong. The Congress and the country were in his lap. When the House and Senate passed his landmark tax cut in 1981, the massive reduction in income tax rates, it broke my heart. I knew that it could end, probably for my lifetime, the hope of serious social reform. There would be no money left. Quite apart from starving the government of resources, I worried that reducing taxes on the wealthy would allow them to pull away economically and separate themselves from the rest of society, and that's exactly what's happened. It severed precious bonds that hold us together as a nation, the idea that we have some responsibilities in common. It led to two Americas.

I also believed in making government more competent, a cause I had embraced in the Senate and a responsibility that Carter and I took seriously in the White House. Some branches of the federal government *were* ineffective—Carter had worked hard to reform the civil service and streamline the executive branch. Reagan seemed to gloat when government failed, and it became a self-fulfilling prophecy: He cut program budgets and appointed inept people to run federal agencies, and lo and behold, government failed.

I was then, too, concerned about Reagan's international belligerence, particularly with respect to nuclear weapons. I believed the Soviets were a clear threat, but I also believed we should talk to them. Our country had decades of bipartisan efforts to negotiate arms containment with the Soviets, and I thought we needed to sustain that. Reagan didn't.

I also felt deeply about accountability and being straight with the public. That's a Fourth of July oration, of course, but public trust is essential to effective government. All that was vapor to Reagan. Before long he was making irresponsible claims about his tax cuts and playing games with the government's economic forecasts. His first budget was full of rosy scenarios and magic asterisks, and when anyone pointed this out, Reagan just brushed it off with a smile and a shrug of his shoulders. I wondered how the country would ever restore fiscal responsibility under a leader who had so little respect for the facts.

I wasn't the only one troubled by Reagan's direction. After the dust settled from the 1980 election, Joan and I took a vacation in Vail, where we always loved to ski. Vail was also a favorite spot of Jerry Ford's, and I bumped into him one day while waiting for a chairlift. He invited me to ride up with him; I discovered what a warm and generous man he was. The Reagan administration was just taking shape at that time, and Ford remarked on some recent newspaper stories that declared Reagan was putting together a clone of the Ford administration. "If that's true," he told me, "I sure don't recognize many of them."

Finally, I thought Reagan was careless in his thinking. He said things about world oil supplies and Medicare that were simply fiction. He would read something in some fringe publication and then repeat it. But when a president says something, it has consequences. I understand why Reagan's gift for simplicity appealed to voters. He had an easy formulation for every problem that seemed to make sense if you didn't really think it through. But I had always believed that Americans are smart enough and responsible enough that you can tell them the truth, even if it's complicated. He didn't want to bother with that. One day he said during a news conference that when you fire a cruise missile you can call it back. He called them "slow fliers." Well, you can't call back a cruise missile. You fire them and they are gone. That's a pretty important distinction because the president controls the button. I reminded him of that in one of our debates, and he said, "Oh, Walter, I never said that." But he did, and it was on the record, and he didn't recognize the difference.

When I spoke with friends who were still in government, I heard remarkable stories about Reagan's weak grasp of the facts. Tip O'Neill described White House meetings where Reagan would read off cards, leaving everyone to wonder if he actually understood the things he said. One morning Tip and Reagan were at the White House talking about the foster grandparents' program, a great success at helping disadvantaged kids. Reagan was telling Tip that one of his relatives was a participant. Tip said, "But, Mr. President, you just vetoed the funding for that program this morning." Reagan refused to believe it.

Despite my differences with Reagan, however, I didn't feel I could simply go on the attack from day one. I thought a new president deserved a decent interval to show what he could do, and I wanted to stay out of the trench warfare for a little while.

I had another, larger reason for biding my time: I felt I needed to make a fresh start with voters. I knew that if I got into a campaign dwelling on the Carter-Mondale years, I was probably doomed because our administration wasn't remembered with much affection. All that heartache—the hostages, the rescue mission, the high interest rates, the gas lines. Our polls had been right down in the cellar. I did not intend to run away from our record and the values we stood for. No one would have believed it, nor would I have. I was proud of the things we had accomplished, but I knew I couldn't spend the campaign rearguing history.

I also knew I couldn't just play films of the old Fritz Mondale. I was proud of my years in the Senate, and I still am. I had achieved things that reflected my values and my hopes. A lot of that work still provided the foundation for what I wanted to do. But I needed a fresh agenda, a new way of talking about the old principles. Anyone who has run a few campaigns understands this—you have to hear the music that's playing in the country at the moment. People didn't want to hear about Hubert Humphrey or Jimmy Carter or how we did things a long time ago. I had to identify with people's concerns *now*.

With this in mind, I set about restocking my intellectual capital and making a fresh start on the big issues of the day. I asked several members of my old staff to help out. Jim Johnson, who had been at my side all through the White House years, took charge of the process. Jim had a consulting business down the hall from my new law office, and he drafted a series of strategy memos to position us for the midterm Democratic conference in 1982, for a formal campaign announcement, and then for the party primaries and caucuses. We set up briefings, lunches, conferences. We brought in economists such as Jim Tobin, the esteemed economist from Yale, Charlie Schultze, who had been Carter's chief adviser, and Bob Rubin, who would later be Clinton's treasury secretary; and foreign policy experts such as Dick Holbrooke and Bill Perry from the Defense Department. I dug into the scholarly literature, reading up on the Soviet Union, for example, and its leaders and how Western leaders might deal with them. I spent a lot of time reading economics, and I made several trips to the Middle East, Russia, and Asia.

I also gave a series of speeches that were a way of trying out these new ideas, reintroducing myself to America and trying to bust out of the cage I was in. After the frustrations of the 1970s and a couple of years of listening to Reagan, people were worried about their world. What was it that encouraged the Soviet Union to think it could invade Afghanistan? Why did the Iranians think they could take our people hostage and pay no price? What had happened to our economy that stagflation could take hold? I knew that all these anxieties were gnawing at people, and that's why Reagan's simple answers were so reassuring. But I knew the simple answers wouldn't work for long. I felt we needed to dig deeper and come up with answers that would work in a complicated, dangerous world. How do you square military power with multilateral diplomacy? How do you make our economy competitive again without simply driving down wages and destroying unions? I wanted to feel I had better answers on these issues than I had had when Carter and I left office.

Because Reagan had spent so much time deriding government, and because it was playing well, we talked about how we could restore confidence in the public sector. I brought in Bill Galston, who was teaching political science at the University of Texas, for fresh perspectives on that. I think people looked at liberals of my school as predisposed to use government, even though that wasn't true of Carter and me. It's true that we wanted to solve problems—in contrast to Reagan, who liked to pretend that the problems didn't exist—and sometimes this required the use of government.

I also wanted to find a new way to talk about the economy. Economic policy was going to be a problem because I knew that once the campaign started, all Reagan had to say was "How did you and Carter do when you were in the White House?" But I thought back to the last day we were in office, when Carter called a final meeting of the cabinet. He went around the table and asked each of us to say what we had learned in those four years. Harold Brown, the defense secretary, said, "I learned that if you don't have sustainable economics, you will not have a good defense. They go together. If we want to be strong, it begins with a good economy." I believed that. If you want people to feel confident about the country and about your leadership, if you want revenues sufficient to fund high-quality public services, if you want to be respected around the world, you must preside over a strong economy. Democrats had not been especially good at talking about that since John Kennedy, and I spent a lot of time finding a new way to approach it. I think Carter and I had standing on that issue after our nomination of an inflation hawk, Paul Volcker, as chairman of the Federal Reserve Board, and our efforts to deregulate oil, natural gas, and the airline industry. But people didn't remember that. When they thought about Jimmy Carter and Fritz Mondale, they remembered stagflation and gas lines.

I also thought Democrats needed a new way to talk about crime. That issue doesn't ride today the way it did then. We had delivered a great deal of social reform in the 1960s, but then the cities exploded. People thought one was related to the other. Democrats, some thought, became the party on the side of the criminals, while Republicans were on the side of law enforcement. Minneapolis—a progressive town, the town that launched Hubert Humphrey's career—had elected as mayor Charlie Stenvig, a former cop and a right-wing politician. You couldn't ignore the power of the issue. But I couldn't renounce everything I had worked on for thirty years. We had a long staff debate on that one, on whether we could say we wanted law and order with justice, if adding the word *justice* simply turned people off. That was the country's mood.

I also spent a lot of time learning about the Soviet Union. I had come of age in a generation of Democrats who were reliably anticommunist— Jack Kennedy, Scoop Jackson, Hubert. Yet I didn't buy Reagan's "evil empire" formulation. Carter and I had spent months negotiating with the Soviets to get SALT II, the next round of the arms-control treaties, and nearly got it through the Senate. Reagan opposed it and was saying a lot of uninformed and dangerous things about it. I agreed that the world is a dangerous place, but I thought Reagan wasn't doing anything to make it safer. It was a big reason why I challenged Reagan, a major issue that I pursued in the campaign—and one instance where I drew blood.

I also knew we had to talk about social policy, and that it was going to be especially tender for a Democrat. Reagan used a lot of disingenuous arguments, such as his fictional welfare queens, and he had surrounded himself with a crowd that produced a pseudoliterature purporting to explain that welfare didn't work. I thought it was mostly propaganda, but I also knew that people had grown skeptical about the War on Poverty, often for good reason, and I knew that I would have to figure out a new way of explaining the social programs I believed in. I was able to draw on the child-development work I had done in the Senate during the 1970s—about strengthening families and giving them the tools to take care of themselves. I thought if I could cut through some of Reagan's reckless simplifications, I could make a good case on the merits of investing in children.

After our last year in the White House and my time on the campaign trail, I thought I had a pretty good fix on the way voters were feeling about these issues. I had spent months moving around the country listening to people, and I knew what they were thinking. I knew the hard issues that we had to get well on, but I also knew the public's doubts about Reagan. I wanted to take a few months to freshen up and be seen differently, then see what would develop. By early 1983 we were starting to raise the money and assemble the staff for one of the best-organized presidential campaigns in modern history.

Before I could take on Reagan, however, I had to get past Gary Hart and Jessie Jackson for the Democratic nomination, and that turned into a long battle. Hart was talented, handsome, and well-spoken. He had come to the Senate a decade after I had, after working on George McGovern's campaign in 1972, and he claimed to represent the next generation of the party, a generation with new ideas. He wasn't well known nationally when he announced in early 1983, but he was a good campaigner and reporters liked him, and he gradually moved up in the pack and ahead of some strong older candidates, John Glenn and Alan Cranston. Jackson, too, gained traction quickly. He had good political instincts and appealed to a lot of people who felt disenfranchised by everything Reagan had done.

Hart's success didn't surprise us. Early in the fall of 1983, in an effort to test our prospects for the Democratic nomination, we hired the pollster Peter Hart to survey New Hampshire voters on a set of hypothetical Democratic candidates. We didn't name names, but we asked voters to evaluate candidates with the biographical and political profiles of John Glenn, Walter Mondale, Gary Hart, and one or two other Democrats who were looking at the race. By an overwhelming margin, respondents chose the "Hart" candidate: young, Western, and full of "new ideas." From that day on, we stopped assuming that I was the front-runner and realized that, in effect, we were set up to lose.

Hart's main line of attack was that I represented the old crowd, the special interests that hung around the Democratic Party, and that he represented the new generation. I never bought it, and I don't think his case ever went far with most Democrats. It's true that the party at that time *was* organized into caucuses—the unions, the teachers, environmental groups, women's organizations. They all met separately and separately endorsed a candidate, and every candidate sought those endorsements. I got almost all of them. That's the funny thing—only after Hart failed to win their endorsement did they become "special interests." Until that moment, they were the greatest people he had ever known.

Still, that charge drew blood for Hart, and we should have blunted it more effectively. It made me look like old politics, as if I were trading away the public interest for the special interests. In the second debate against Hart, on February 12, 1984, in Des Moines, I talked about the interests I served and how they *were* special because as a nation we have to achieve the goals they represent—a better education for our children, a cleaner environment, a decent wage for working people. But I didn't deal with the issue adequately. All the surveys showed that people were doubtful about those things and me, and that's a dangerous place to be politically.

As a result of Hart's attack and Jackson's candidacy, a nomination that we should have wrapped up early in 1984 remained in doubt well into the spring. The season started off, with the Iowa caucuses in late January, much as we hoped. We had a strong ground organization and a lot of voters who knew me. When the night was over, I carried 49 percent of the total, with Hart at 16 percent and Jackson, John Glenn, and a handful of others in single digits. "We took the gold and the silver," Peter Hart told reporters. "Everybody else fought over the bronze." But the New Hampshire primary came two weeks later, and I've always thought the people of New Hampshire are a contrary lot. Hart stunned us there, winning the primary with 37 percent of the vote to my 27 percent. It was a huge blow: It cast doubt on our organization and spawned a wave of newspaper columns arguing that Hart had replaced me as the Democratic front-runner. The next day, back in Washington, Jim Johnson and I called a meeting of the senior campaign staff, shut the door of the conference room, and said, We're not leaving this room until we can convincingly tell the reporters, and ourselves, what we learned in New Hampshire. A week after that Mike Berman, who had been on my staff longer than anyone else, drew the assignment of drafting a memo describing how I might gracefully withdraw from the race if it came to that.

The battle against Gary Hart forced us to rethink a question that had vexed me, and my entire staff, since the beginning of the campaign: how to define the core message of a Democrat running for president in the 1980s. I went into the campaign knowing that my speeches had to accomplish several tasks. First, they had to hold the party together and rally its traditional constituents: labor unions, women's groups, the civil rights community, urban leaders, environmentalists, and others. They represented core groups of voters, and a Democrat could not win a national election without them. Moreover, I had grown up with them, they were my friends. Their values were my values.

But I also knew that the Democratic argument was going stale. The country was changing and voters wanted us to offer something else. Humphrey had perfected the art of identifying core constituencies and putting them together into coalitions. We continued that tradition and enumerated the causes that motivated our coalition—the Equal Rights Amendment, Davis-Bacon labor law, and so on. But most Americans no longer associated with traditional institutions the way they once did—unions, mainline churches, fraternal associations—and they weren't sure who stood for their interests in a society that seemed to be changing rapidly around them. Union membership had plummeted since the 1950s and now stood well below 20 percent of the workforce. The suburban exodus had also changed America, draining away traditional loyalties to neighborhoods, ethnic roots, and urban political organizations, and leaving many people to ask, Who's on my side? I knew that I couldn't simply replay the 1960s.

Yet I was convinced that the things I felt deeply about—economic opportunity, a clean environment, a sense of community, a safe world for our children—still resonated with voters if we could find the right way to talk about them.

In an early draft of a campaign speech, in mid-1982, Marty Kaplan had tried to weld together the old and the new. He wrote, "It takes excellence to get to the top. But it takes government to break the chains at the bottom. It takes pride to keep looking for work. But it takes government to see that work is available. It takes sacrifice to make ends meet. But it takes government to make that burden shared fairly. Fairness won't just happen on its own."

Over the next year or so, we kept working on that approach, and by early 1984 we thought we had solved the riddle. The speeches would become more thematic, clustering my core values under broader motifs with wide appeal. I identified three: a competitive economy, a safer world, and a restored sense of social fairness. In a widely covered address to the National Press Club in January, I summarized the themes this way:

> First, we'll be deciding what kind of economy we'll have. Will America get its competitive edge back and lead the world economy again? Or will we saddle our kids with debt, second-rate jobs, impossible interest rates, and a falling standard of living? Second, we must decide what kind of people we are. Will we restore a sense of fairness and decency in American life? Or will it be the rich against the rest? Third, we must decide what kind of future we will have—if any. Do we live in a safer world than we did three years ago? Are we further from nuclear war? After a thousand days of Mr. Reagan, is the world anywhere less tense, anywhere closer to peace?

That became the core of my stump speech as the campaign picked up speed, though, as I reworked the text over the next few weeks, some of the lines came more directly from my heart. "We are not a jungle," I wrote. "We are a community, a family, a nation—and we need a president who causes us to care for one another again."

Because we were trying to unseat an incumbent president, and because I was so offended by the direction Reagan was leading the nation, the speech also had to develop a specific critique of his presidency: His budget deficits were leaving a huge debt for our children. His fiscal policy had driven up the value of the dollar, making imports cheap and imposing an "invisible tax" on our exports. He had abandoned the progressive principle in taxation, so that tax cuts were heaped upon the wealthy, while working families got only the slightest relief. Every president since Harry Truman, Republican and Democrat, had taken steps toward arms control, but not Reagan. In every speech, I tried to talk about a brighter future for America rather than looking back on some old glory days of the Democrats.

I also wanted voters to know that Democrats understood the social upheaval that was gnawing away at their sense of tradition and morality. As a preacher's kid and a regular churchgoer, I was offended that Republicans would presume to be the party of God, and I was not going to cede the discussion of values. In a speech to the B'nai B'rith, I discussed the importance of the separation of church and state, but I also touched on the need for moral leadership. "Change is not easy. Many Americans have been upset to see traditions questioned. They have watched durable values give way to yawning voids. I join those Americans in their legitimate concerns. I join them in condemning the explosion in drug traffic. I stand with them in anger at street crime. Low standards—whether they infect the classroom, the workplace, the government, or the street corner—are a threat to all of us."

In late February, after Hart won the New Hampshire primary, I felt I had to rethink my message. I didn't want a fight with Gary Hart because party unity was important to me and to our success in the fall. But I wanted to make clear where we differed, and our staff was reporting from the primary states that voters still weren't quite sure what Walter Mondale stood for. Hart had tried to frame the primary race as a contest between old and new; I now argued that it was a battle between compassion and coldness, between fundamental fairness and technocratic tinkering. I spent several evenings working on these themes with Marty, and the resulting speech, delivered in Tampa on March 6, turned out to be one of the most powerful of the campaign.

> We're about to decide whether we'll be a generous party and a caring nation, or whether we won't. . . . Mark me well, because today there's a new argument in this land—a new idea about the Democratic Party and where it should go. This new idea is the essence of the battle that we're in. The idea is this: If you fight for the values that the Democratic Party has always believed in, you're supposed to go on a guilt trip. But if you fight against them, you're supposed to be applauded. If you fight for better schools, you're old. But if you fight for big oil, you're new. If a worker wants a raise, that's greedy. But if a plant closes down, that's trendy. I don't accept it. And I won't cut my values to fit this year's fashion. It's not a campaign for new ideas and old ideas. It's a fight between what's right and what's wrong.

The Tampa rally marked a turning point in the primaries. You could feel the energy ripple through the crowd, and the response to the speech was electric. We got bigger crowds in the following days and we could all feel a new momentum. The political writers noticed it, too, because they started asking Hart tougher questions in an effort to make him specify his vision of the party.

Then, at a campaign staff meeting a few days later, we developed what would prove to be the knockout punch. We were campaigning in Columbia, South Carolina, and my campaign manager, Bob Beckel, flew in from Washington with a glint in his eye. He had been watching television with his girlfriend and saw a Wendy's commercial in which a group of little old ladies went into a fast-food place and got a hamburger that was all bun. Beckel described the ad, getting more excited as he went, and then shouted, "Where's the beef?" We all stared at him. We thought he'd lost his mind. Then he summarized Hart's "new ideas" platform and repeated the question: "Where's the beef?" By the time the meeting was over, the staff had started warming up to it. I told Beckel I would sleep on it and go to church the next morning and pray for him.

Hart and I were scheduled to debate the next night in Atlanta, and by that evening I had decided I would try the line. The crowd got it instantly; it drew a huge laugh and caught Hart completely flat-footed. Journalists also seized on the moment because it did seem to capture a weakness in Hart's candidacy, and I think he lost momentum after that.

On Super Tuesday, March 13, with five primaries and four state caucuses, Hart did well. But we carried Alabama and Georgia, with solid victories and results that came in early, and renewed our momentum. Over the next six weeks we scored a series of primary victories, and by late April we could see the arithmetic running in our favor. I called together the reporters covering the campaign and made a prediction: By 11:59 on the night of the last primary, in May, I would have the nomination locked up. It was a daring bet, but we put our delegate operation into overdrive, and in the last week of May we turned over a list of twenty-one hundred delegates to Rob Gunnison, a political reporter and chief delegate counter for UPI. We had done it.

While I was fighting it out with Gary Hart and Jesse Jackson, however, Reagan was gradually gaining momentum. By the spring of 1984 the economy had recovered from the 1980–1982 recession, and Reagan's polls, which had dipped into the thirties for a time, were recovering nicely. It was Morning in America and he was pretending that we didn't exist. By June, as we prepared to head to San Francisco for the Democratic National Convention, I had wrapped up enough delegates to win the nomination, but I was also twenty-five points behind Reagan.

I told the staff that during those few days in San Francisco we would have to do something dramatic while we had the nation's attention. That's when we started thinking about the choice for a running mate. Gary Hart had proved extremely popular in some parts of the country, and some friends told me I could unite the party by bringing him onto the ticket. But I had watched Hart carefully during the campaign. I didn't think he and I agreed on the key issues, and our personal relationship had become edgy. I decided to cast the net wider. During my four years with Carter, I had admired his methodical approach to big decisions, and I thought he had developed a good candidate-selection process in 1976— narrowing the field of running mates to a list of finalists, then inviting each of us to Plains for a personal meeting. It was transparent and open, which voters appreciated, and it enabled him to get a feel for the personal chemistry with each of us. But I also wanted to use the selection process to send another message, a message about opening doors. That's what my whole career had been about and now I had a chance to do it on a big stage. We used that stage to showcase talent from all parts of the party—Tom Bradley, the mayor of Los Angeles, Dianne Feinstein, the mayor of San Francisco, Lloyd Bentsen, a respected Texas senator, Henry Cisneros, the mayor of San Antonio, Martha Layne Collins, the governor of Kentucky.

Not everyone saw it the way I did. Several newspaper columnists thought the parade of candidates to my home in North Oaks, Minnesota, had been tokenism. Jesse Jackson was still feeling a little tender from the primary campaign, and he told reporters he thought it was a charade. Others saw a cliché about the Democratic Party—a black candidate, a Hispanic candidate, a female candidate, and so forth.

In the end I chose Geraldine Ferraro, and I was satisfied with the process. First, I thought she would be an excellent vice president and could be a good president. She had already developed a strong record in the House of Representatives. Tip O'Neill, who knew all the young members, said Ferraro would be the best choice. She'd been chair of the Party Platform Committee and knew the issues. She also brought a lot of political strengths to the ticket. The Democratic constituency was shrinking and the departure of the Reagan Democrats was killing us. I had worked hard in the ethnic communities to try to reconnect with them, and Ferraro's biography helped make that connection. She came from Queens, New York. She was a Catholic and a mother. And she had a lot of fire.

I also knew that I was far behind Reagan, and that if I just ran a traditional campaign, I would never get in the game.

Joan, too, urged me to choose a woman. As usual, her analysis was straightforward but penetrating. In her view, a female running mate was not so much a symbol or a breakthrough as a natural progression in American politics. Joan thought we were far enough along in the movement for women's rights that the political system had produced plenty of qualified candidates, and she thought voters were ready for a ticket that would break the white-male mold. She also believed the women's vote had a considerable new and unappreciated strength that we could tap.

Finally, I thought that putting a woman on a major-party ticket would change American expectations, permanently and for the better. Picking Ferraro was symbolic in that sense, but a symbolic gesture with consequences. Skeptical voters would see what an effective woman candidate could accomplish. Young women could see new horizons open up. Everyone would see how America had changed in our lifetimes, and more doors would open.

The second key at the convention was my acceptance speech. I knew this would be a crucial chance to reintroduce myself to a lot of Americans—and maybe my last chance if I didn't get it right. It would be the most important speech of my career. We went through a lot of drafts and a lot of themes. One that wound up in the speech, famously, was this: "Let's tell the truth. Mr. Reagan will raise taxes and so will I. He won't tell you. I just did."

A lot of people have told me that was a mistake, and I notice no one else has tried it since. But I thought it was right at the time and I still think so today. As a question of public policy, voters had to confront the need to raise revenue. The federal deficit in 1983 had exceeded $200 billion, a record, causing the highest real interest rates in history and creating huge debts for our children. It was hard to explain to people that, in effect, their taxes had gone up a lot, only they were paying in the form of higher interest rates, soaring trade deficits, and an explosion of payments on the federal debt.

Then, as a matter of political style, I have always believed that voters respect honesty. We had spent a lot of time during the early stages of the campaign actually drafting a federal budget that was honest and balanced—an exercise that has seldom been repeated in subsequent campaigns—and I knew it would require higher revenues. Explaining that plainly to voters was a gamble, but I knew I would feel better about myself because I was telling the truth.

Finally, I thought that summer that people were having trouble seeing me as a leader. I thought that if I stood up and actually cut through the propaganda and gave hard answers, people would say, This kind of honesty represents leadership.

The taxes line had one additional rationale. I knew that Reagan was quietly planning a tax increase after the election. We had learned through friends in Washington that the Treasury Department was working on a tax bill, a plan with a big tax increase. So part of my motivation was to call Reagan on it. We learned later that, immediately after my speech, Reagan's campaign contacted Treasury and someone burned that document. So I told the truth, and I think people knew I was telling the truth. Whether that actually hurt me at the polls, I don't know. I did what I thought was right.

When we came out of San Francisco, we were gaining on Reagan in the polls. People loved Ferraro. Her pick brought tremendous energy to the convention and put us solidly back in the spotlight. Mike Berman, who had friends inside the Reagan campaign, said their tracking polls showed that the night I announced Ferraro, we actually pulled even with Reagan, or even a point ahead.

But anyone who's ever worked in politics knows that even when a campaign looks smooth and well oiled from the outside, it can be pretty bumpy on the inside. And that's when we hit our first bumps.

On leaving San Francisco, Gerry and I traveled to Minnesota for a stop in Elmore, then to her home in Queens, and back to my home in the Twin Cities to sit down with the staff and map out a campaign timetable. I thought our time together would be comfortable and relaxed, a chance to get to know each other better and come to one mind about the weeks ahead. It didn't quite work out that way.

On our first night I called a planning meeting, and my staff came in with a pretty complete calendar. Jim Johnson was a highly organized guy, and he set up some big flip charts to go through the schedule day by day. Gerry's first reaction was "Why is all this written in ink? Don't I get any say in this?" I think she felt they got a little arrogant with her, and she wanted to put them on notice that she wasn't going to be dealt with that way. It turned into a pretty rough meeting, and I was startled. I understood the way she felt because I had had felt much the same way when I signed up to run with Carter. I had been an independent senator, calling my own shots, and suddenly I was the second man. It's as if the doors close on you, you're trapped in someone else's space, and part of you says, "Wait a minute, I had a good life here—where'd it go?" On the other hand, we had a big job ahead of us and we needed to tackle it with a lot of discipline. Finally I stepped in and said why don't we just stop there and take the night off and get back together tomorrow. By the next morning everyone was feeling a little bad and was ready to make amends. Gerry was ready to go to work, and from then on she campaigned magnificently.

Then we hit another bump. Ferraro and I had agreed before the convention that she and her husband, John Zaccaro, would release their tax returns. John was a successful real estate developer, and people would be curious about his finances. We had vetted Gerry and John fairly carefully before the selection, but it had been a hectic few days, and we probably looked more carefully at her public record than at John's private finances. Sure enough, even before we left San Francisco, my staff got a fax from Charles Babcock, a fine political reporter at the *Washington Post*. Someone from the *Post* had gone up to New York City to take a look at the buildings John managed and found that a few of his tenants were in disreputable publishing businesses. Within a few days of the convention, a flurry of stories about his business and his tenants appeared, and all of a sudden everything blew up.

For a few days, Gerry said that John had decided not to release his returns, and that only made things worse. We hired a team of accountants to scrutinize John's records and try to clear the air. They found his bookkeeping was imperfect, but with no sign of wrongdoing. But reporters didn't want to hear about anything else, and people leaped to the worst possible conclusions. The whole picture looked bad, and we couldn't fight through all the noise. We were in a free fall. I didn't think I could order Gerry to release the returns; I thought she had to make a decision herself. Finally, after a couple of days, she called me to say they were going to release the documents. I said that's good, but if you do, please hold a news conference, make every document available, and stay there as long as the last reporter wants to ask a question. We helped her put together a news conference near Kennedy International Airport, where all the press could attend and the networks could pick it up. An accountant and a lawyer led off, going through every possible aspect of John's finances and taking one question after another. Then Gerry took the podium and gave a superb statement. The press conference lasted almost three hours, and when it was over, one of the reporters from the *Post* leaned over to Mike Berman and said, "That's enough. We're done with this story." That put it to rest for the reporters and the public. But we lost precious days and paid dearly for that.

Meanwhile, Reagan was holding one perfect campaign event after another and steadily gaining momentum. He seldom held big rallies or gave substantive speeches. It was all perfect miniatures, carefully scripted visits that produced thirty seconds of great television and made people feel good. Sunrises, sunsets. Picket fences and puppies. Morning in America. It only deepened our frustration to watch his strategy go over so well on TV while we were spinning our wheels.

In the first week of September we had a meeting of the campaign's senior staff. The newest polls showed Reagan with an approval rating over 60 percent, a figure that hadn't changed significantly all year. We wanted to find a point of weakness, an issue where the public had serious doubts, so we drew up a list of possibilities: fairness in society, his trigger-happy attitude toward nuclear war, the two-tier economy, his age and mental acuity, and his bellicose approach to foreign affairs. For the next six weeks we tried each one—with television commercials, as a focus of my speeches, as a theme for campaign events. By mid-October, none had made a dent in Reagan's popularity.

During this period I even agreed to a session of media coaching. I always joked that I didn't like TV, and it didn't like me. Some of the training was helpful, but most of it seemed pointless. I thought if I worried about how to hold my head in front of the camera and how to look winsome, I would look like a phony and feel like a phony. My theory was that if I spoke from the heart about issues I understood, voters would respond.

We also tried a new format for some of the campaign appearances, something more personal and humanizing—but seldom to good effect. The low point was probably a stop in Wisconsin, a visit to a paper mill where I was supposed to meet the workers as they came off their shift and talk about their struggles in Reagan's economy. We arrived late and stood there for about five minutes before we realized we had missed the shift change and nobody was going to come. Then the plant manager came out and gave me a couple rolls of toilet paper as a gift. The TV cameras were rolling and the exchange wound up on the national news.

The irony is that, although you are running for the most powerful job on earth, you are virtually helpless once you hit the road. You are constantly on the move from one appearance to the next, trying to stay on schedule, giving your speeches, trying to stay current with developments in the news and your opponent's campaign. But the campaign is being managed by others back at headquarters. When it's eleven o'clock, you have to show up where they have you scheduled. If there's a problem—you arrive late, or the wrong people are there—you don't learn about it until you bump right into it.

I thought I had a strong case for change. I thought I had some better ideas for our country. I wanted to make my arguments and have them remembered. Then you go to a toilet-paper factory, you are an hour late, and you get rolls of toilet paper, and that's the story for the day. It's frustrating.

That was our brief attempt at remaking Walter Mondale. I wasn't good at it and I thought it was a waste of time.

This tension over campaign tactics finally came to a head in the middle of September. The campaign had brought us to Tupelo, Mississippi, during a swing through the South. We brought in the whole team and had a big staff meeting. I knew what my staff wanted. They wanted me to embrace the new techniques—sitting in people's living rooms, posing for pictures in the sunset—and take on Reagan at his own game.

Before the meeting, I sat down by myself. I pulled out a legal pad and looked out the window for a while, then wrote down the things I stood for, the things I had been fighting for my entire life. Then I went out, called the meeting to order, and told the staff: I don't know anything about this other style of politics. It's not where I've ever been in the past, and it's not where I am now. I've only got this one shot, this one time to make my case for the things I believe in. What I'd like to do is be myself and try to persuade people that I have a few ideas that would put our country on the right path, and let it rest right there. Because if I do something else, I won't know who I am anymore.

After the Tupelo meeting, the campaign changed again, and for the first time in weeks it felt great. I got in front of the familiar crowds and I gave them my best. I felt liberated and was campaigning the way I knew. A few days later, speaking to students at George Washington University back in the capital, I said:

> I have been advised to ignore issues—to choose slogans over substance. My answer is no. There is a big distance between Pennsylvania Avenue and Madison Avenue. I have been counseled to cut loose from my history—to desert the forgotten Americans I have always fought for. My answer is no. I would rather lose a race about decency than win one about self-interest.

A couple of weeks later, at a rally in Columbus, Ohio, we sharpened the edge:

> This election is not about jelly beans and pen pals. It's about toxic dumps that give cancer to our children. This election is not

about banners and balloons. It's about old people who can't pay for medicine. All year, the Republicans have been grave-robbing. They quote Roosevelt. They praise Kennedy. They even paid tribute to my old friend Hubert Humphrey. How dare they? You don't honor Franklin Roosevelt by gutting Social Security. You don't honor John Kennedy by breaching the wall between church and state. You don't honor Lyndon Johnson by giving tax breaks to segregation academies.

Fay Joyce, a reporter for the *New York Times*, was following our campaign in those weeks and detected the shift in tone. She wrote about the energy that seemed to surge in the final weeks of the campaign: "In the streets of Chicago last night, 75,000 marched behind him, bearing flares against the fading light." She got it right: Adversity had produced a different kind of campaign.

Then a remarkable thing happened. Reagan and I had agreed to two debates, the first scheduled for October 17, less than one month before the election. The polls showed that I was twenty points behind, or more. I thought Reagan might pull out of the debate because, without working hard, he was just going to coast back into office. But he didn't pull out, so the event was confirmed for Louisville. I prepared for days, reading huge briefing books, considering sample questions, and honing the message to key phrases. Even so, I was nervous because Reagan was the master communicator and everything was riding on this night.

Broadcast time finally arrived, and I went out on the stage. By that point in a campaign you are completely exhausted. You've been working eighteen-hour days, moving constantly, trying to sleep on airplanes, and you would rather crawl into bed than walk out in front of the lights. But your adrenaline kicks in, and, I suppose, your competitive juices. When Reagan came out on the platform, we shook hands, and I noticed something was wrong with him. He didn't seem alert—not tired exactly, but not all there. Paul Newman, an old friend of mine, was sitting in the audience and saw it, too. He told me later, "I looked at him and I thought he wasn't going to make it."

As the debate got under way, I watched Reagan's performance carefully. Reagan was a simple guy, and he always used the same little set of speechettes. But that night he mangled them. Same stories, but mixed up and in the wrong order. Lots of statistics, but jumbled together incoherently. Later in the debate he even started forgetting some of his lines. He was lost. It was actually a little frightening. One of the reporters on the panel later told me I should just have yielded my time to Reagan and let him ramble.

As the debate drew to a close, Reagan was holding the lectern and looking pale. His final statement was almost incoherent. When I came off the platform, my people were buzzing about it. My press secretary, Maxine Isaacs, came up to me, thrilled. But I said, "I'm worried about him. Something's wrong." I told my staff not to talk about it, even though all the reporters were asking what we thought. Reagan's performance underscored the point I was trying to make: He was not engaged and in command of the issues. But it had never been my style of politics to jump on something like that. We all have bad nights. People saw Reagan's performance and didn't need my commentary on it.

Quite apart from Reagan's physical performance that night, we also scored on substance. We knew that Reagan used certain signature lines over and over, and we prepared for them. Months earlier, during the primary campaign, I had been on the road with David Lillehaug, a Minneapolis attorney and a member of my campaign staff. We were flying to Maine one night and I said, "We need to start preparing for debates with Reagan. What do you remember about his performance against Carter?" David said, "He used that line 'There you go again,'" I said: "Yup. Exactly." Reagan had used the line effectively when Carter warned voters that Reagan was an extremist who would dismantle valuable government programs. It made Carter sound like an old, fretful liberal, and we thought Reagan might use it again. Sure enough, in the Louisville debate he did. I brought up the federal deficit and predicted that, despite his rhetoric, Reagan would have to raise taxes after the election if he won. As if on cue, he responded, "Oh, there you go again." I turned toward him immediately and said, "Do you remember the last time you said that? It was four years ago. Carter warned in the debate that you would go after Medicare if you became president. You didn't want voters to believe him, but as soon as you got in office, you tried to cut Medicare. People remember things like this." Reagan's campaign staff saw instantly that I had drawn blood, and the next day they issued a statement that, no, he would not cut Medicare. It was one of the few times I was able to slice through that famous Teflon armor.

In a memo to my campaign staff the next day, the pollster Peter Hart summarized the public's reaction:

> Walter Mondale scored a major victory in the debate, though it was not the win that we expected—it was not based on voters agreeing with him on several individual issues but instead on the big points. Mondale gained with voters on the following points: they perceive him as a strong leader, more knowledgeable, stressing new ideas for the future and leveling with the people about what needs to be done.

I scored on Reagan that night, and I think it had an effect on his administration. It certainly had an effect on the way voters looked at us. The next day we went to Cincinnati and then up to New York for a big parade. The polls were swinging nicely. We got huge turnouts, a thrilling response from the crowds, and enthusiastic press coverage. The next week was great.

The second debate came two weeks later, in Kansas City, and if I could have done as well that night as in the first debate, we would have had a much closer contest. But as we prepared, I couldn't seem to focus as well. I didn't feel comfortable going onstage, and I had bags under my eyes that broke records. Liz Drew, writing in the *New Yorker*, noticed it. In the first debate, she observed, I was far more gracious toward Reagan. My summation was positive, and people were more receptive. In the second debate I was more the prosecuting attorney, making terse debating points. It wasn't a deliberate strategy, but debates seldom follow a script. You prepare as best you can, but when the moment comes, you have to answer the questions posed to you, follow your opponent's responses, and go where the debate takes you.

All the technique, however, probably didn't matter in the end because that night Reagan got off one of the great lines in the history of presidential debates. After the first debate and a series of newspaper stories about his performance in Louisville, his staff guessed that his age and acuity would come up in the second debate. It did, in one of the first questions, and this is how Reagan replied, "I will not make age an issue in this campaign. I'm not going to exploit for political purposes my opponent's youth and inexperience." He pulled it off well. I had to laugh. I thought about responding, pointing out that I actually had more government experience than he did. But I just laughed and let him have the moment. But I knew in that moment that we were in trouble. The joke completely disarmed people's doubts about his age and his capacities and allowed them to think, "He's okay." They wanted Reagan to be okay and now they could believe it.

In the next day's polls people mostly rated that debate a wash. But I think what happened was that Reagan looked competent again. He reassured Americans that he could do the job, and that night the race was basically over. When we got back to the hotel I told Joan, "I think that's it. I think we're done."

About two weeks before the election, I saw a poll in which 60 percent of unionized Chrysler workers said they were going to vote for Reagan. I was stunned. Just five years earlier, Carter and I had helped arrange the federal loan guarantee that saved Chrysler from bankruptcy. I helped get the package through Congress and helped persuade the president to sign it. A whole community of people in those Chrysler plants still had pensions and good jobs because we had moved decisively to save the company. Yet they were going to vote for Reagan, an antiunion president. That same week I was on the phone with Owen Bieber, then president of the United Auto Workers. He said, when you come to Detroit, I want you to come out in support of a trade bill we want. And I said, "What difference does it make? I just found out that all the Chrysler workers are voting for Reagan."

In those poll numbers, I saw that something fundamental was happening in American politics. I knew the labor movement well—I had been with them my whole life. Democrats had always counted on labor. We had always been with them on their issues, and they had turned out volunteers and money and votes for us. But America changed in the 1980s. We sometimes think that union members are different from other Americans. They're not. The same things that were gnawing on the general public were gnawing on them: Could they pay their bills? Did the future seem promising? Were they confident in their leaders? All the old alliances were shifting.

After the debate in Kansas City, the campaign was dispiriting in ways that are hard to describe. We would be working like hell, on the road constantly, twelve or thirteen events a day. We'd get good crowds and deafening cheers. Then, at the end of the day, someone would show us a poll in *USA Today* and we would be down twenty points. It was hard to take, but we just had to take a deep breath and go on.

But something about those last days was also liberating. I could throw away the strategy memos and the media coaching and go out in front of people and speak from my heart. "This is a season for passion and principle," I said in one of those fall speeches. "This election is about our values. The Republicans say they're for family values. But families don't disown their weaker children. What would we think of parents who taught their kids to think only of themselves? I won't permit this crowd to steal the future from our children without a fight. I won't let them put ice in our soul without a struggle. They have a right to ask for your vote. But I'll be damned if I'll let them take away our conscience."

I'm grateful for that chance to make my case to America. I spoke what was in my heart. I gave voice to the politics I had grown up with and the values I believed in. But it wasn't enough to change America's mind that year, and on November 6 Reagan carried forty-nine states.

On Election Day Joan and I voted early, then I drove to downtown Minneapolis for a favorite ritual: breakfast with some old buddies who loved to talk politics. My old friend Warren Spannaus joined me, as did former governor Wendy Anderson and other colleagues who were veter-

Mondale vs. Reagan

ans of countless campaigns. It takes a while to downshift from the pace of the campaign trail, and you're more exhausted than you realize. But I could finally relax for an hour or two. Then I drove out to our home in North Oaks, but I was too restless to sit still, so I wound up taking a couple of long walks with Jim Johnson.

By early evening, I was in downtown St. Paul at the Hilton, where we had rented a suite to have some food with old friends and watch the returns come in. When I arrived, the suite was empty, and Maxine Isaacs was just setting up the television monitors. She turned on the television just as the CBS broadcast began. Dan Rather was sitting by a map of the nation, every state they could call lit up red and the word "landslide" on Rather's lips. I looked at Maxine, shrugged, and said, "We did our best."

A night like that is hard on you. The room is packed with friends, from your oldest associates to the staff of your latest campaign. Everyone is wrung out, hopeful, and emotional. I know it was hard on Joan and our kids, but as always, they were wonderful. There are a lot of tears, a lot of broken hearts. People believed in you, hoped to see the changes you fought for. They've worked hard, they've given it everything they've got. Then you can't deliver for them. About 9 p.m. John Reilly, my old pal, came over and said, "I'm sorry, Fritz. You didn't deserve this."

But at those moments, you can't quit. The candidate is the one who has to give everyone a lift. I sat with Marty Kaplan, sketching out a few thoughts for a concession speech, then headed across the street to the main rally and said:

> A few minutes ago I called the president of the United States and congratulated him on his victory. He has won. We are all Americans. He is our president, and we honor him tonight.
>
> Although I would rather have won, tonight we rejoice in our democracy, we rejoice in the freedom of a wonderful people, and we accept their verdict. I thank the people of America. They've listened to me. They've treated me fairly. They've lifted my spirits, and they've added to my strength. If there's one thing I'm certain

· 305 ·

of, it is that this is a magnificent nation with the finest people on earth.

I've been around for a while, and I have noticed that in the seeds of almost every victory are to be found the seeds of defeat, and in every defeat are to be found the seeds of victory. Let us fight on.

The America we want to build is just as important tomorrow as it was yesterday. Let us continue to seek an America that is just and fair. That has been my fight. That has been our fight in this campaign. I'm confident that history will judge us honorably, so tonight let us be determined to fight on.

After the election I didn't sleep well for a month. I would wake up in a cold sweat wondering what I might have done differently. I kept a stack of books next to our bed, and I would read until I could get back to sleep. Finally, a few months later I went to see my old friend George McGovern. He had lost pretty badly to Nixon in 1972, and I thought he might have some advice. I said, "George, how long does it take to get over this?" He said, "I don't know. I'll tell you when it happens."

More than once since that election I've been asked why I chose to run. We had hit a cycle in American life when the things I believed in, the very reasons why I had entered politics, were just not selling well. Democrats such as I had spent our public prestige on the proposition that if we really went to work, we could produce a better society. We changed life for a lot of Americans. But many people felt that we hadn't entirely succeeded, and they were, I think, tired of trying. We had opened the Pandora's box and people didn't want to look inside anymore.

Those were transitional times for the liberalism I believed in. Mine was a progressive agenda, but was also tough. I don't know that I was the best person to carry that message. But I did the best I could. I found a way to earn the support of millions of people, but I did not find a way that got me close to being elected.

My friend Haynes Johnson, a wonderful journalist and social observer, later called that election the ratification of Reaganism. Haynes was probably right. People had had four years to get a good look at Reagan, to leave behind the *Bedtime for Bonzo* caricature and think of him as their president. They felt good about it. Ronald Reagan was not a deep thinker, and I don't say that with any malice. He was a nice man—he and I never had any unpleasant moments. But if you got him in a room and made him explain how he arrived at his views and what he read to get there, you wouldn't find much. Give him credit for having some kind of clever directional mechanism. He didn't know much about government, but he did know how to sustain public confidence. He recognized that the country needed a period of rest and recuperation. He understood that voters want to like their president, to have a leader who makes them feel good. He had that practiced optimism, the ability to convey confidence that everything would work out. He was selling Morning in America and I was selling a root canal.

But I'm sorry Reagan won that election. I think it set the stage for many years of retreat from economic justice, from hope for civil rights, from progress on the environment—even from a responsible approach to taxes and the federal budget. With time and experience, a lot of people have come to see that Reagan's great experiment didn't deliver. We wound up with colossal budget deficits and he had to retreat on the tax cuts. We lost a decade in the effort to promote energy conservation. That's the decade when the gap between rich and poor became a chasm.

I would also argue that Reagan's popularity has been exaggerated in subsequent years by people who want us to believe that we're living in Ronald Reagan's America. The pollster Arthur Miller of the University of Michigan, based on surveys early in Reagan's presidency, observed, "It should be abundantly clear that Reagan did not have a mandate for most of his policies at election time and had not yet succeeded in establishing a popular consensus. The administration's repeated claims to such 'mandates' can thus be seen as part of its attempt to in fact create such a consensus." Reagan's fans have airbrushed history, but you have to remember that by his seventh year in office he was starting to disappoint people, his numbers were falling, and his promises were starting to fizzle. He had to back away from his assault on Medicare and Social Security because

Americans believed in those programs, and after the 1984 election he quickly changed his mind on arms control and held four summit meetings with the Soviets—policies that George H. W. Bush embraced and continued after succeeding Reagan in 1989. Even Reagan's promise to shrink government was mostly a fraud: Federal spending measured as a share of the economy was actually higher in his administration than it was during the Carter years. On civil rights, on the environment, on economic opportunity, I think Americans were closer to me than to Reagan. But it's hard to argue with a landslide.

I think the prevailing view of that election, however, the "landslide" narrative, obscures something else important that happened in 1984, something with enduring consequences. The irony of that race, the mistaken irony, is that I was often depicted as an old-style liberal leading a Democratic Party of the past. I think 1984 proved the opposite. After two decades, the internal reforms we adopted in 1964 were coming to fruition: We had a woman on a major-party presidential ticket for the first time. We had an African-American candidate who contended competitively for his party's presidential nomination. We had a convention whose delegates fully mirrored the diversity of America, and a party where all Americans could participate with genuine power and influence.

This was not a party of the past, this was the party of the future. This was a party that recognized the fundamental changes occurring in America with respect to race and gender, that rewrote the rules of politics and opened doors that will never be closed again. Columnist Tom Wicker of the *New York Times* saw as much. Writing from San Francisco, he observed, "What happened to Mrs. Ferraro and Mr. Jackson here may also be the most dramatic evidence yet that the modern Democratic Party has become a new instrument in American politics. . . . A step has been taken, a door has been opened. The order of things—not just transient events but the human environment in which events take place—has changed."

What happened in San Francisco in the summer of 1984 didn't merely lift Geraldine Ferraro and Jesse Jackson to extraordinary heights; it didn't merely create new opportunities for a cohort of women and people of color in politics. It changed the expectations of every generation that followed them and allowed them to see America as a different and more hopeful place. Young women, young people of color who might otherwise have assumed they had no place in the upper tiers of American society, now understood that they did. The rights to participate in politics and society were no longer abstract; they were connected to the power to assert them.

Wicker, himself a great chronicler of the civil rights movement, observed in San Francisco, "In the long future power will be more avidly sought by and more widely distributed among those who in the long past could only suffer its consequences."

As I have argued from my earliest days in politics, this wasn't merely a breakthrough for women and people of color, it was a gain for all America. A nation is stronger when it can tap all its talents, and when all its citizens feel they have a stake in its success. Wicker's colleague Flora Lewis noticed the same thing that summer, writing, "America has grown up enough to be able to consider a woman, a black, perhaps a member of any of the minorities besides WASPs, as a possibility, without automatic shock. That is a solid achievement. It is a gain for all Americans, not just because it offers a new source of pride for special groups. But because it enlarges the resource of talent on which the country can expect to draw leadership."

The Mondale-Ferraro ticket was treated as a breakthrough in American politics, and it was. But that ticket, and the convention that embraced it, was also the fulfillment of a long struggle, a milestone on a long march toward an America that is fairer, bigger, more inclusive, and stronger. The strides we took that year affirmed that America is capable of progress. They flushed old poisons from our system and replaced them with new ideals. They reminded us of who we are as Americans and whom we have always aspired to be.

15

An Alliance in Asia

I HAD BEEN OUT of public life for the better part of a decade in November 1992 when Bill Clinton was elected president. Joan and I had moved back to Minneapolis, the kids were close by, and I had more time to relax with the family and participate in community life. It felt good to get close to Minnesota politics again and the DFL Party that was my native soil—and even to wonder if there might be another generation of Mondales in politics. We bought a house near Lake of the Isles in South Minneapolis, and I became the family's chief dog walker. The dog and I both needed the exercise.

A part of me, however, missed public life. I knew I didn't want to run for office again, but I did have an interest in international affairs, and I'd always been fascinated by what an ambassador does. I thought, Now we've got a Democrat back in the White House, let's see what develops.

It so happened that Brian Atwood, an old friend from the Carter administration, was a member of the Clinton transition team. Brian, who had worked in the State Department and later ran the U.S. Agency for International Development, was helping vet candidates for foreign-policy positions, and he was now pushing my name for some sort of diplomatic post. The first spot that occurred to them was Moscow. Brian called me, and without thinking about it too much, I said yes. I wanted to perform some more public service, and I thought this would be a fascinating way to do it. A few days later Clinton called me and we talked. I said hold the phone a moment and put Joan on, and she talked to Clinton for a while. Before the conversation was over, we had agreed to take the assignment.

But that night Joan and I talked about it again, and in the morning I said, "Joan, I don't know if I want to go to Moscow. I don't know if it's right for me." She said, "Really? Well, you'd better let them know." It was hugely embarrassing. Clinton was supposed to announce my nomination in the next day or two, as part of a foreign-policy speech at Georgetown University. When you're a new president, you want a smooth transition and a set of orderly announcements, especially on something delicate such as America's relationship with the Russians. So this was tricky. I got on the phone, trying to reach Brian and Warren Christopher, who was another old friend from the Carter days and was Clinton's pick for secretary of state. I also called Mike Berman, who was still in Washington, and asked if he could get Clinton's chief of staff on the phone in a hurry. I finally got through to Warren Christopher later that day and said somewhat sheepishly, "Warren, I don't know how to say this, but we thought about it overnight, and as important as it is, Moscow just doesn't quite fit." Fortunately, they got word to Clinton before his speech, but it was a little too close for comfort. I told Joan, "That's it. We'll never hear from them again."

Then a few weeks later Brian called back and said, "How about Tokyo?" I was thrilled, but I was also surprised. I wanted to be a little more careful this time around. I told Brian, "Maybe. But don't put my name in yet. I fumbled this the first time and I would understand if I didn't get the assignment."

Joan and I talked it over and we felt that Tokyo was quite a different prospect from Moscow. Joan knew a lot about Japanese culture because of her career as an arts advocate and potter. She also knew a lot of Japanese history through a branch of her father's family, the Oldfathers, who were Presbyterian missionaries in Japan at the turn of the century. Edwin Reischauer, the great scholar and American ambassador to Japan, was an Oldfather; his dad had founded the Tokyo Women's College and was close to Joan's father. Joan also knew Reischauer's wife, Haru, who was Japanese. Haru became a good friend and, after we took the assignment, would often come over to visit us at the embassy. For all these reasons Joan felt Tokyo would be a better fit for us than Moscow. A few days after my second conversation with Brian, I got another phone call from Clinton and I told Joan, "We're going to Tokyo."

I was not a specialist on Japan, but I had been there several times while in the Senate. I was also influenced by Mike Mansfield, an old friend whom I later swore in as ambassador to Japan in the Carter administration. Mansfield used to say that the U.S.-Japan alliance is the most important bilateral relationship in the world, bar none, and I believed that. At that time our economies were number one and number two in the world and accounted for 40 percent of global output. Our relationship could do a lot to promote trade and prosperity in the developing nations of Asia. The alliance also gave us a chance to build stability in a region that didn't have a lot of stability, yet was vital to our interests. We had fought three wars in forty years in that part of the world, something we did not want to do again. Asia does not have a NATO, and is not going to have one anytime soon. But it does have grave tensions between North Korea and South Korea and between China and several of its neighbors. The presence of the American fleet helps assure that sea-lanes stay open, which is vital because Asia survives on shipping and trade. I think the rest of Asia respects the U.S.-Japan relationship and likes the fact that we're over there to calm things down. As Joseph Nye of Harvard once observed, "Security is like oxygen—you don't notice it until you begin to lose it, and then it's hard to think about anything else." So I thought the post would give me a chance to learn more about a pivotal part of the world while helping to build an international relationship I considered crucial.

As I prepared to go to Tokyo, I understood that history would be important, so I spent a lot of time reading about Japan and our relationship. We had a legacy from World War II, an informal bargain promising that we would maintain military bases there and the two nations would form an alliance to preserve stability in the region. But it wasn't a symmetrical partnership. At the time of the deal, Japan was impoverished, flattened by the war, and Americans harbored a lot of Cold War fears that the Japanese could be susceptible to Communist blandishments. The resulting arrangement, known as the Yoshida Doctrine after Japan's postwar prime minister, called on the Japanese to emphasize economic development and political stability, while the United States guaranteed regional security. In a famous "change in course," the American government, which had been pressing for major constitutional and political reforms immediately after the war, instead encouraged the Japanese to simply pursue economic prosperity, even if it meant using the United States as a market for their exports. Thus we were implicated in a lot of the economic policies that cropped up as trade disputes in the 1980s and 1990s because for three decades we had encouraged the Japanese to do whatever was necessary to rebuild their economy.

When I took the assignment, however, the relationship had grown tense. We were running a large trade deficit with the Japanese and we were in the middle of a big shoot-out over access to their markets. Japan had rapidly rebuilt from the rubble of World War II and had developed a modern middle class with advanced education and a powerhouse economy. Books such as Ezra Vogel's *Japan as Number One* and Clyde Prestowitz's *Trading Places* had become extremely influential in Washington, New York, and cities of the industrial Midwest. Americans were feeling a lot of self-doubt, and it often flared in hostility toward Japan. During one of the trade debates in Congress, a few members actually took a Japanese TV set down on the floor of the House and smashed it. Japan was shocked. In some American cities, you could get heckled if you drove a Honda or a Toyota. Americans had a lot of pride wrapped up in this rivalry, and a lot of anger, and an American president, if he wanted to be successful, had to deal with it.

As a result, when I went to Tokyo, the pressure was intense to open Japanese markets to American products. Many felt that Japan restricted access of American products to its markets, and Clinton had spoken during the campaign about driving a harder bargain for American workers.

My predecessor, Michael Armacost, a talented ambassador, had tackled this issue and had earned the nickname Mr. Gaiatsu, from a Japanese word meaning "external pressure." I had a lot of respect for Armacost, and he was respected in Japan. Armacost and Bush had at one point been trying to promote numerical import guidelines, so that the Japanese would guarantee a certain percentage of their markets to American products. The Japanese complained that the United States, a bastion of free enterprise, now wanted to rig the Japanese market using "managed trade." They had us in a nice vise there. In fact, all we wanted was to open up the Japanese market a little so we could compete, but in Japan they certainly got the better of that argument. I talked to Clinton about it. I think he wanted a reduction in the trade barriers so we could get into the Japanese market, but he didn't want a big fight over it. He wanted a few basic accomplishments that would be understood by the average American worker, and that became our guiding principle.

Our point man in the trade talks was Mickey Kantor, the U.S. trade representative. I had known Mickey for years—he had started out as a Legal Services lawyer in the Office of Economic Opportunity and had developed into a seasoned negotiator. I would discuss priorities with our negotiators each time they headed into a new round of talks on a certain industry. I would sometimes go by myself or with them to see the principal negotiators on the other side. I also had a regular monthly meeting with the vice minister of foreign affairs.

But I hadn't taken the job to be a bully or to spend all my time negotiating market share for auto parts. I felt my responsibility was to keep the trade talks in a broader perspective. One of the great challenges in a job like that is to press a country to open up without seeming to be a scold—to go through these public spats over autos or semiconductors without poisoning the rest of the relationship. During one of my long breakfasts with the vice minister of foreign affairs, he said, "Your goal is to make us more like you. Is that what you want to do?" I said no, and I meant it.

I came to realize that we could not expect Japan to adopt our model of open, competitive consumer markets. I went over there thinking they could just open up. But the Japanese have a number of traditions that give them pause about the competitive free-for-all that most Americans accept as the norm. I think most Japanese put a higher emphasis on economic stability and social harmony and on a stable and proud Japan. They don't have the same uncritical affection that we have for the free market.

They also had a different idea of their nation and its place in the world. Someone on my embassy staff called it the Switzerland Position. If they had to choose between being a big, rich world power as against retaining the cultural essence of Japan, they would rather be Switzerland and forgo the role of player in world affairs.

This dynamic came up time and again as we discussed market access. Rice exports were a good example. At that time it was almost impossible to export American rice to Japan, even though it cost barely 12 percent of the price of Japanese rice. Some Japanese would respond to the consumerist argument, but I think the majority, at least those who made the decisions, put greater weight on the dependency problem. Japan had suffered starvation during the war. No nation ever gets over that. They would rather have expensive Japanese rice that they could count on than less expensive imported rice that might not be there when they needed it. We argued that you're more secure if you're part of an international trading system with multiple suppliers. But that dependency issue still hangs around. Japan has few natural resources. It doesn't have oil or iron ore or natural gas. Everything the Japanese do, they have to do by their own grit and genius.

A typical struggle was our negotiation over mobile phones. The Japanese, for all their advanced technology, had a peculiar cell phone system. A lot of the country didn't have towers, so reception was spotty. The phones themselves cost a couple of thousand dollars apiece. We argued that they should open their markets to our products to create a more competitive industry to benefit the Japanese consumer as well as our trading relationship. Motorola was a participant there, and it had superior technology, but it was struggling unsuccessfully for more market access. We argued that we could provide better phones, much more cheaply, for mutual gain.

We had a big blowup over it. I finally put in a phone call to Ozawa Ichiro, a leader in the coalition government assembled by Morihiro Hosokawa. He understood our arguments and wanted to make a deal, and we worked out an arrangement to open up the cell phone market. Within two years, they had moved toward a more open system and the price of phones came down dramatically. The Japanese didn't actually wind up importing a lot of cell phones, but they did develop a healthy market with genuine competition. I tried to use that as a lesson. "Look," I said, "you benefited from this. The phones are better. The prices are lower. The service has improved." They said that we were pushing them around and making unreasonable demands.

While I tried to understand the Japanese point of view, I also found other aspects of the country's politics frustrating. During my years in the Senate I had spent a lot of time thinking about government accountability, about how a government responds to the will of voters and the long-term interests of the general public. During my years in Tokyo I found the responsiveness of the Japanese government both fascinating and mystifying. Power was disaggregated there. The center, that is, the elected leadership, had little power. The prime minister and political ministers, even though they were theoretically elected to do the will of the people, seemed to have less power than the bureaucrats. Helmut Kohl, Bill Clinton, John Major, François Mitterrand—leaders in the West at that time—all could do business with each other. Within certain political and constitutional constraints, they had the power to deliver on their goals and promises. But their Japanese interlocutors could not. A good case could be made that Clinton should have been meeting with administrative vice ministers when he traveled to Japan—the career bureaucrats—because they were the ones who set the agenda.

As a result, a lot of our work was slow and frustrating. But now and then we had breakthroughs that, I think, changed the relationship between our countries with long-term consequences. When the auto talks bogged down, for example, I went to see the CEOs of Honda, Nissan, and Toyota. Those meetings were tense, and for a time I got targeted in the Japanese press much the way Armacost had been—a tool of American industry to bully Japan. But that was fleeting.

I think I finally got through during a series of meetings with Shoichiro Toyoda, then the president of Toyota, and a Toyota executive named Toshiaki Taguchi. Tag, as he was known by friends, had run Toyota's North American operations and was an old friend of mine. Taguchi and Toyoda understood that we had to get a relationship that served both nations. They told me that they had misunderstood this earlier in their careers and wanted to make a clean break. When we finally did get a deal, Toyoda announced that Toyota would open several plants in America and buy more components from American suppliers. Toyoda told me, We have to end up someplace where the Japanese and the Americans feel good about each other.

During my first two years in Japan we negotiated seventeen separate market-opening agreements covering important industries, including cell phones, finance, semiconductors, and insurance, and while the final auto agreements were a disappointment, I think we took some of the tension out of that issue over time. The Japanese, in my view, gained a new understanding of American needs, and I think we improved the sense of fairness in the relationship. You certainly don't hear the protectionist rhetoric or see the kind of animosity toward Japan today that we heard in the 1980s and early 1990s.

Although I was seven thousand miles from Washington, my time as ambassador also allowed me to get a good look at Bill Clinton, a leader who dominated American public life in that decade and a Democrat who found a way for our party to retake the White House.

When I took the Tokyo assignment, I had known Clinton for nearly twenty years, since a trip to Arkansas in 1977. I was there to speak at a dinner honoring John McClellan, one of the powerful Old Bulls of the Senate. The master of ceremonies introduced the various Democratic officials in the audience, and when he said, "Hillary and Bill Clinton, our new attorney general," the place absolutely exploded. I remember thinking, What's this all about?

After that, Clinton came to my office in the West Wing several times, and I was always impressed. He had a brilliant mind and great empathy for his constituents, and clearly was part of the answer if Democrats were to get on track again. We became friends, and later when I was running for president, he was supportive. Every time the campaign took us through Arkansas, Bill and Hillary would show up and help.

Naturally, I was curious about the way he would perform as president, and having watched him up close, I believe he may have been the most talented politician I ever saw—and I include Humphrey in that list. Like Carter he grew up on the worst kind of politics for a national Democrat—the politics of a poor, rural, Southern state—but like Carter he broke with the old racist strategies and brought change to his own state. On the national stage, in a period when voters were skeptical about progressive values, he had an uncanny ability to get moderate voters, even estranged voters, to listen to him and trust him.

I think the test of Clinton's great talent is that he rode out eight years in office with the political tides running against him—against liberal values at home and internationalism abroad. Through his political skills, his strategic sense, and his unrelenting energy, he exercised extraordinary public influence to keep pressure on the Republicans and to get the best possible compromise for progressive government.

That said, I don't think his will go down in history as one of the great presidencies because, after Republicans won control of Congress in 1994, he was playing defense for six years. After that setback he changed strategy, making Republicans the issue and keeping the heat on them. He still had the power of the veto, which he used to block their most egregious ideas, and he developed an uncanny political ability to turn issues, such as the 1995 government shutdown, against them and keep them on the ropes. They were furious, of course, because they appeared to have the issues, they had control of the House and the Senate, yet this interloper kept the public on his side and tied the Republicans in knots. He frustrated them again and again and left office with the highest approval ratings of any two-term president.

Clinton's legacy is, of course, marred by the personal habits that brought down so much criticism on him. When the Monica Lewinsky scandal broke, I called him and said, "Mr. President, you've just got to apologize to the American people. You've got to make it clear that you feel terrible about this. The public has to be persuaded that you know you've made a severe mistake and you want to correct it. That's all you can do—that and being a good president." I believe he heard that advice from everyone, and that's what he did.

I was also curious about the direction in which Clinton would lead our party. In some respects he was heir to the tradition that Jimmy Carter and I began. He had those Southern sensibilities that Carter had, that ability to connect with conservative Democrats, and he hewed in our direction on such issues as restraining federal spending, streamlining the government, and maintaining a strong military. Like us, he governed at a time when the old Democratic arguments were falling apart. He differed from Carter mainly in his personal style of politics. Carter was the trustee, the hardworking executive trying to rise above politics. Clinton had different instincts—he was out there trying to touch every voter, determined to succeed by winning people over through that personal connection. But he was unrelenting.

What I admire about both men is that Carter and Clinton, while governing in conservative times, with the political tides running against them, nevertheless tried to get the best deal they could for social justice, for education, for health care, for the environment. Both stood strongly against discrimination, both strengthened the federal judiciary, both were internationalists. They did the best they could in the times in which they served.

By the start of my second year in Japan, I thought it was time to take a breather on economic issues and reassess the relationship. We had accomplished a lot in the trade negotiations, but I thought we had pushed the Japanese about as far as we should. I talked with my staff in the embassy and had a conversation with Warren Christopher, then I sent a cable to Clinton. I said I thought it was time we changed the subject with the Japanese.

My timing turned out to be good because almost immediately we moved into a sequence of three crises that would test the U.S.-Japan relationship in a completely different way, raising questions we hadn't examined since the end of World War II.

In June 1994 North Korea announced that it was leaving the Nuclear Non-Proliferation Treaty, expelling foreign weapons inspectors, and planning to reprocess spent nuclear fuel to separate plutonium, a key ingredient in a nuclear weapon. We had laid down a red line that if they started reprocessing nuclear fuel for weapons-grade material, it would not be tolerated, for it would mean they were a rogue nation with the threat of nuclear weapons.

About a week later Warren Christopher asked all the U.S. ambassadors in Asia to meet in Honolulu to discuss the crisis. The United States had substantial forces stationed in South Korea, and the South Koreans had a huge army, so we were in a position to back up any threat with military action. But during the Honolulu conference, I was pulled aside by Jim Laney, our ambassador to South Korea. Laney was a wonderful guy, a former president of Emory University, and a close friend of Jimmy Carter's. He had also spent years in Korea before going to Emory, and he knew the region. Laney said, "Let me talk to you. This is what will happen if we start a war with North Korea. They have massive forces along the border, including a lot of artillery. They will kill more than a million South Koreans. They will destroy Seoul and they will kill several thousand American soldiers. That is inevitable. We will win, but it's very hard to see how this could work out to our advantage." Laney made the rounds during those couple of days in Honolulu, working on all of us to drive home the consequences of a military confrontation at the North Korean border.

The Honolulu meeting was one of those moments—not unlike the Iran hostage crisis, not unlike the period after 9/11—when the United States has to weigh its military options carefully. We have the most powerful military in the world. We can prevail if we move with force. A tremendous temptation in domestic politics is to use force and show the world who's boss. But you have to step back, consider the costs, and ask if another way may be less destructive in the long run, even if it's less satisfying in the short run. I thought that's how we needed to proceed with the North Koreans. But we would also need the Japanese working with us because they wielded such economic and diplomatic influence in the region.

Jimmy Carter volunteered to serve as an informal ambassador. He traveled to Pyongyang, met with Kim Il Sung, and negotiated an agreement whereby Japan and South Korea, working with us, would provide the North Koreans with assistance for a peaceful nuclear energy program in exchange for their agreement to shut down their nuclear weapons program and permit the return of international monitors. I went to South Korea myself, with Lieutenant General Dick Myers, the commander of U.S. forces in Japan, to help facilitate the arrangement. It hasn't been perfect; we have to keep our eye on Pyongyang. But it took the North Koreans out of the nuclear weapons game for several years, and it avoided a second Korean War.

That agreement defused a crisis, but it also exposed some fault lines in our relationship with Tokyo. As we thought through the hypotheticals of a military confrontation with North Korea, we had to assess how Japan would respond to regional security challenges under their existing laws. If South Korea were attacked and the war produced a stream of refugees, for example, could they be received in Japan? If we needed to protect international shipping lanes, or do minesweeping exercises, what role could Japan play? If we needed to mount a military operation in Asia, could we get fuel and other supplies staged through Japan? Could we use their airfields and ports?

All these questions came into play, and it became clear that we lacked good answers. The Japanese were fully aware of the North Korean threat. They lived close to it every day, and after the South Koreans, they would pay the biggest price if hostilities broke out. But because of the constitutional structure they had put in place after World War II, the answers to these questions were not clear. Japan does have a substantial navy, army, and air force, but their roles are strictly limited. The Japanese constitution, written with heavy U.S. influence in the aftermath of the war, banned the right of belligerency and the use of force to settle international disputes. The constitution has been interpreted as allowing self-defense, but not the right of collective self-defense—that is, going to the aid of allies. Until recently, the Japanese Defense Agency did not even have ministry status—it was merely a branch of the prime minister's office.

The Korean showdown challenged that deeply embedded formulation. The Japanese liked having us in the neighborhood, and since the

1970s they had agreed to shoulder a big portion of the expense of maintaining our military bases there. But now, with North Korea and China growing steadily as overt military threats, the stakes were higher, and the Japanese role would have to expand. I remember one of the top Japanese officials, an old friend of mine, pulling me aside and saying that if we got into a conflict where Americans died in the defense of Japan, under circumstances in which Japan would not help, that would be the end of our alliance. The domestic American backlash would be too powerful. "We never want that question to arise," he said.

But this was a delicate business. The Japanese had been living for fifty years under the assumption that the United States would take care of regional security. We had been right in the center of shaping their new constitution at the end of the war. Our military forces were embedded all over Japan, particularly in the early years. So we couldn't suddenly tell them how to rewrite their constitution. I tried to transmit my understanding of these tensions back to Warren Christopher and Bill Perry, Clinton's defense secretary, so that we could begin working on a new set of guidelines for the U.S.-Japan security relationship. It was a little like serving as a midwife: We couldn't do the job for the Japanese, but we could understand what they were going through and help them along as we could. So we started talking.

Then, in September 1995, crisis number two erupted. I had been back in the United States on vacation and was just returning to Tokyo. My deputy chief of mission, Rust Deming, met me at the airport with a batch of memos and news updates. One of them detailed an appalling crime in Okinawa in which three U.S. soldiers had kidnapped a twelve-year-old Japanese schoolgirl and raped her in a rented car. It hadn't broken as a major national news story yet, but the details were horrific and the implications were awful.

Anyone who knew our military installation in Okinawa knew it was a room full of gasoline waiting for someone to strike a match. We had forty-two bases on the island with more than twenty thousand personnel. All of them were living and conducting exercises right up against Okinawan civilian neighborhoods. Lots of noise, lots of helicopters and fighter planes taking off and landing at all hours. Off the bases—lots of bars and night-life. The base commander told me once, "How would you like to be mayor of a town of twenty thousand people, most of them nineteen-year-old kids cooped up under pressure and a long way from home? How trouble-free do you think a town like that is going to be?" And unlike our bases on the main islands, which were were generally located on public land—usually old installations of the Japanese imperial forces—a lot of our Okinawa facilities had been private property, simply seized during World War II, and some of the people wanted their land back.

I decided we couldn't excuse what these three young men had done. I talked to the Marine Corps commander on Okinawa and he agreed. "I don't defend this," he told me. "Marines are here to protect people, not to do this sort of thing." We would give them attorneys and make sure they got due process and a fair trial. But he said, "I don't think we should spend a minute trying to make excuses."

On September 20, Lieutenant General Dick Myers and I went down to Okinawa and met with Governor Ota to express our apologies and extend our sympathies to the girl's family. The next day, back in Tokyo, I met with Foreign Minister Yohei Kono, a close friend, and apologized again and asked his advice about a way to handle the trial that would seem fair to the Japanese. I didn't ask anyone's authority back in Washington, I just did it. In Japan, acknowledging your mistakes and showing remorse is a big part of being forgiven and maintaining honor. Quickly, President Clinton, Defense Secretary Bill Perry, and the commander of U.S. forces in Japan apologized, too.

On September 29, when a formal indictment came down from the Japanese justice system, we transferred the three servicemen to the custody of Japanese authorities. This wasn't an easy decision. Their families back in the United States claimed the men were being railroaded by the Japanese police. But we were not going to fool around with this. The evidence was clear, we had enough confidence in the Japanese justice system, and we knew we had to change our image over there. A few weeks later, when a U.S. Navy admiral brought up the incident and said the sailors could have "bought a girl" for the price they had paid for the rental car that night, Bill Perry saw that the admiral took early retirement immediately.

I think our response helped some, but I also suspected that the episode wasn't going to end with our apology. Over the next few weeks huge protest rallies took place in Tokyo and on Okinawa. Polls showed a sharp drop in public support for the Japan-U.S. alliance. Within days it became obvious that Japanese outrage over the behavior of three U.S. servicemen was evolving into something much bigger, a broader debate about the American presence in Japan and the outdated nature of the relationship. Elected officials began saying the Americans should get out of Japan entirely, and that if Japan ever needed us, they could call us back. I knew we had to do something substantive and long-term to change the relationship.

On October 3 I went to see Foreign Minister Kono again. Clinton was scheduled to visit Asia in November for a meeting of the Asia-Pacific Economic Cooperation forum, to be followed by a summit meeting with Prime Minister Tomiichi Murayama in Tokyo. I didn't want the Okinawa incident to overshadow that meeting, or to spoil what we had hoped would be an upbeat conclusion to our trade negotiations. The Japanese press had already raised legal questions about the Okinawa case, in particular whether the Status of Forces agreement governing our bases in Japan gave U.S. servicemen too much protection from the Japanese courts.

The rape was quickly becoming a flash point in internal Japanese politics. Governor Ota of Okinawa was now threatening to withhold his signature from leases on land used by the U.S. military, a stance the public applauded. Prime Minister Murayama had to defend the U.S. presence and even threatened to simply sign the leases himself. But Murayama was himself on shaky ground with voters, and I did not want an American scandal to wind up taking the blame for his political troubles.

Meanwhile, the protests continued. On October 21 a rally in Okinawa drew more than fifty thousand people and was endorsed by every political party on the island. I was completely sympathetic to the Japanese popular reaction. But I also knew enough about politics to fear that public sentiment over one incident might snowball into a much larger protest against the United States, undermining the overall relationship in ways that none of us wanted.

What happened next gave me new perspective on those Japanese bureaucrats whom I had, a year earlier, regarded as impediments to change. I watched the press coverage closely as the government figured out a way to respond to the rape. Clearly, the bureaucrats at the Ministry of Foreign Affairs were scared by the political pressure to jilt the United States. In the subtlest ways and comments, they tried to preserve the relationship against pressure from politicians in Okinawa. They suggested that we modify the procedures governing legal custody of U.S. servicemen without rewriting the entire Status of Forces agreement. They began to hint at working with the Americans on a base review, but one that would carefully be prescribed, not a wholesale "get out" document. It seemed to me that they were trying to lance the Okinawa boil without sending the patient home in an ambulance. When in late October Murayama, under intense political pressure, announced that he would ask Clinton to make major land returns during the summit in November, an official from the Ministry of Foreign Affairs told Rust Deming, Pay no attention.

Nonetheless, I felt it was time for us to make a major public gesture, to investigate if we could hand back some of the land we were using in Okinawa and consolidate our forces on bases where there was less friction. On October 24 I was invited to attend a meeting at the Japanese Foreign Ministry to discuss the future of our Okinawa bases and the way the Japanese government wanted to handle the issue. I had been consulting with Bill Perry on this issue during the previous few days so that I could speak for him, and I agreed that day with Foreign Minister Kono to establish a bilateral panel to be called the Special Action Committee on Okinawa, or SACO.

Around the first week of November I went down to Okinawa and spent a lot of time going over the various installations and reviewing how they operated. I met with local officials and elected leaders. I also met with our military commanders to review the tensions and their military needs. Even though I was convinced that we could and should consolidate our facilities, it was not going to be simple. Bill Perry believed that the U.S. force level in Japan at that time, some forty-seven thousand troops, was about right. His argument was that any abrupt troop reduction would invite trouble from the Chinese and the North Koreans and create anxiety among the Western-leaning nations of the region, which could ultimately lead to an arms race in Asia. Meanwhile, back in Washington, Clinton was caught in a nasty budget standoff with Newt Gingrich and Republican congressional leaders. Clinton feared this standoff could trigger a shutdown of the federal government—as it did, a few weeks later—and he canceled his trip to Japan. That only made the situation more delicate.

About two months later Bill Perry returned to Japan and asked me to meet with his staff on the ground. I told them, "Please don't look at this as a negotiation. If there's any land you can do without, any facility, now is the time to put it on the table because this is our last shot." With their advice and cooperation we crafted a proposal with major concessions. We agreed to transfer an army port in Naha to another location. We agreed in principle to close down our helicopter base in Futenma and put the choppers somewhere else in Okinawa. We closed a communications base and several other facilities. We also changed our interpretation of the Status of Forces agreement so that if an American soldier was charged with a heinous crime, he would be turned over to the Japanese authorities before he was formally indicted. It was painful, but it was necessary and productive.

On April 12, 1996, just a few days before Clinton was due to arrive for the postponed summit, Prime Minister Ryutaro Hashimoto approved a new plan for Okinawa. We agreed to consolidate several of the Okinawa installations, give up the facility we used at Futenma, and return nearly one-third of the land to Japan over the next five to seven years. But we also agreed that we would not cut U.S. troop levels in Japan, an important statement about the continued U.S. military commitment to Asian stability. Four days later Clinton arrived in Tokyo, and on April 17 he and Hashimoto signed a new security declaration embracing the changes we'd negotiated and setting forth a new post–Cold War rationale for the alliance.

But meanwhile the third security crisis had erupted. In March, China abruptly declared that it planned to test-fire missiles over the Taiwan Strait, an announcement that produced headlines all over the world and sent a shudder through every country in the region. I think the maneuver was intended to influence Taiwan's upcoming elections and put a chill on independence talk among Taiwanese candidates. But this remarkably irresponsible act had international implications. The Taiwan Strait is an international waterway, a crucial shipping lane used by dozens of nations. If the Chinese closed a portion to conduct their tests, they were, in effect, saying it was their territory.

The most alarming prospect was that if hostilities broke out between China and Taiwan, we could get pulled into the conflict. The Japanese were uneasy about China's ambitions—military, economic, and territorial—and I'm sure they were wondering if their most important ally shared that unease. If the United States was going to be impotent in the face of a provocation like this, if Japan's great ally couldn't deliver in a time of great tension, then where would Japan be?

The following weeks gave me a new appreciation for Bill Perry. Within days he flew to Tokyo and asked us to set up meetings with representatives of the Chinese government. Perry was angry. He had served on Okinawa as a young officer and had a good feel for Japanese interests. When he arrived in Beijing and sat down with the Chinese emissaries, Perry let them have it. He said the strait was a widely used commercial shipping lane. He said those were international waters and that the missile test was intolerable. At that point, one of the Chinese generals said that this was just an innocent missile test and they had every right to do it under international missile treaties. Perry wouldn't have it. "General," he said, "I don't believe that. Nobody who knows a thing about missile treaties believes that. And I don't think you believe that either."

When Perry got back to Washington he briefed Clinton on the meeting, then ordered a navy aircraft-carrier task force into the waters east of Taiwan—one of the largest military fleets in the world. He gave the Chinese full warning—told them exactly where the ships were going to be and assured them it was not a belligerent act. Then, a day later, he sent a second carrier task force over. I think the Chinese got the point: They wound up firing a couple of missiles but backed down from the brave talk, and there weren't any more missile launches after that.

About four months later we had a meeting with Clinton and Prime Minister Hashimoto in Los Angeles. "When you sent that carrier task force over, we were impressed," Hashimoto said. "When you sent the second one over, we were really impressed."

As we neared the end of 1996, I knew it was time for Joan and me to get back to Minnesota. I was homesick. I wanted to see our kids, spend some time being a grandfather, and reengage in the civic life of my home state. I also had a big backlog of hunting and fishing trips to catch up on.

But saying good-bye was not easy, for Joan and I had grown very fond of Japan. A week before we left, we threw a farewell reception at the ambassador's residence, and hundreds of guests turned out. Many were Japanese leaders who had become friends as we worked together. But at least half were there to pay their respects to Joan. In her work as a potter, in exhibiting Japanese art at the residence, in hosting dinners and traveling around the country, she had taken such obvious pleasure in knowing the Japanese people that she had become an ambassador in her own right, and I was proud to see how much she had achieved while we were in Tokyo.

Quite apart from the many friends we gained, I think I learned important lessons about Japan and the relationship between our countries. I believe our handling of the three security crises rebuilt trust between Japan and the United States, but the larger point I took away from those tense months in Tokyo is that these episodes were only the first pages in a new chapter of Asian history. To have a presence in Asia, in alliance with Japan, is one of the biggest advantages we have in the world. If the Japanese feel they have threats in the neighborhood, as they do with North Korea and China, they tend to scrutinize our alliance. They wonder if it's still serving their interest or if it's growing obsolete. For our part, we have to be careful what we press Japan to do. If we aren't careful, the Japanese leadership begins to look like our lapdogs, and politicians can't live long on that. I think we made some progress on these issues during my tenure, but it's not something America can take for granted.

The North Korean nuclear program, for example, remains a funda-mental challenge to regional security. The Chinese continue to build up missile operations along the Taiwan Strait. They're building quieter submarines that can threaten any vessel anywhere at sea. The challenges we confronted in the mid-1990s will only be more difficult the next time they erupt. I don't know when they will happen, or what form they will take, but given the history of the region, I fear that military or diplomatic hostilities will break out there again.

Even in Japan, some of the brushfires we thought we'd doused con-tinue to smolder today. In 2009 the Democratic Party of Japan took power, ending nearly half a century of dominance by the Liberal Demo-cratic Party, in part on pledges to reduce the influence of the entrenched ministry bureaucrats and in part on promises to establish a better balance in the relationship between America and Japan. Significantly, one of the coalition's campaign promises was to scale back, or even eliminate, the American military presence on Okinawa. Before long the Obama administration found itself negotiating many of the issues over Futenma that we thought we had settled more than a decade earlier. I'm confident that these difficulties will be resolved, but it would be tragic to see what Joe Nye has called a "second order" issue threaten the larger and crucial Japan-U.S. relationship. The friendship is too important to our two coun-tries and to other countries in the region. It's not only how we and the Japanese look at our relationship privately, it's how other countries in the region regard it, as a source of stability and development for the region as a whole.

Asia is the fastest-developing region in the world. It has lots of moving parts and lots of new people at the table. But the United States is prone to out-of-sight, out-of-mind thinking. It's too easy for Americans to forget about some part of the globe when it's not in the news or, worse, to assume that it doesn't matter. If we're not careful, we can seem a little imperious, and our friends around the world notice it before we do. That doesn't work in this world. Asia has a growing self-respect; it won't be taken for granted. How we handle those relationships will be an important test of whether we can get through this next chapter of Pacific history without blowing up the world.

Every autumn while I was in Tokyo I would host Thanksgiving dinner with a group of American students, many of them from Minnesota, and it was probably my favorite regular event. Meeting students always made me feel hopeful. They have energy and goodwill and a willingness to accept differences. They have a drive to learn that's exciting to be around.

Preparing for one of those dinners, I did some reading and came across a quote from Albert Camus, about those who are "allergic to hope" and unable to see a new day even after it has dawned. I suppose I've been guilty of that from time to time over these years. You can get pessimistic, to borrow another Camus metaphor, after spending so many years trying to push boulders up mountainsides.

I suppose that in those students I saw myself—the kid at Macalester College putting up posters and running around Minnesota on his weekends, working for Harry Truman and Hubert Humphrey and thinking he could make a difference. I hope I've made a difference. I hope people will look at my time and understand what I stood for. Sometimes I think that we adults, those of us who think we are in power, do little more than rearrange the furniture on the deck. It's these young students who will be able to chart a better future.

After Joan and I returned from Tokyo in late 1996 I thought I was done with public service. I had decided some years earlier that I would not run for office again, and Joan and I liked leading the life of private citizens. For several years we did. I resumed practicing law at Dorsey and Whitney, a large international firm headquartered in Minneapolis, organized a public affairs fellowship program at the University of Minnesota, and took a renewed interest in the DFL politics of my home state. New faces were appearing on the scene in Minnesota, including my son, Ted, who ran for governor in 1998, and Paul Wellstone, a magnificent progressive whom I greatly admired.

In the fall of 2002 Wellstone was locked in a tough race for his third term in the Senate. His opponent, Norm Coleman, was a shrewd, if highly flexible, politician and a popular mayor of St. Paul. But Wellstone had an extraordinary grassroots political organization and a huge store of affection among Minnesota voters, and the polls showed him with a slight lead as they entered the final two weeks of the campaign. On Friday morning, October 25, I was at a Wellstone fund-raiser in Minneapolis with Ted Kennedy. Ted told me that Paul couldn't be there because he had, at the last minute, decided to attend a funeral in northern Minnesota. The reception was winding down when one of the campaign staffers approached Ted and me and asked us to step outside the room. "Something's happened," the staffer said. "We've been told that Paul's plane crashed." After we recovered from our shock, Ted suggested that we head over to the Wellstone campaign headquarters on University Avenue to be with the staff and family, and that's what we did. There, a few hours later, surrounded by dozens of staff members and volunteers, we learned that the crash had killed Paul and his wife, Sheila, along with their daughter, Marcia, and two members of his staff. It was an afternoon of tears and disbelief.

That night Joan and I were home when the telephone rang. It was Jeff Blodgett, a gifted young strategist who had run all of Paul's campaigns and was handling the 2002 race as well. Jeff had been one of Paul's closest friends, and I could tell that he was reeling emotionally. Yet he was calling to ask a favor: He wondered if he might pay me a visit the next morning and bring a representative of the Wellstone family. He didn't make a mystery of the mission: "We are going to plead with you to run in Paul's place."

This was a tough decision for Joan and me, and under ordinary circumstances I would have said no. I felt it was time to turn things over to the next generation of Democrats, and Minnesota had plenty of good young candidates who had the future in front of them. I wasn't sure the voters of Minnesota would remember me, and I knew that eleven days wasn't enough time to start a campaign.

But these were not ordinary circumstances. Norm Coleman stood for everything I opposed. Although he had run for mayor as a Democrat eight years earlier, he had switched parties midtenure and was now running as a George W. Bush Republican. Karl Rove and Dick Cheney had personally intervened in the race, asking another Minnesota Republican to step aside so that Coleman could run for Senate. They thought Coleman would be loyal to their program and they were right: He was running on a Bush platform of tax cuts, neocon rhetoric, free-market fundamentalism, and the war on terror. Worse, a Coleman victory might give Republicans control of the Senate, and I feared that would unleash the worst impulses of the Bush-Cheney administration. Finally, with just eleven days to Election Day, I thought no one else had a chance to beat him. Joan took a deep breath and agreed.

On Saturday morning I drove to my office at the Dorsey law firm with David Lillehaug, who had been my traveling campaign aide in 1984 and later became U.S. attorney for Minnesota. Jeff Blodgett arrived with David Wellstone, Paul's son, and Rick Kahn, a close friend of Paul's and his campaign treasurer. His eyes red with grief, David Wellstone made a personal request that I enter the race. He was crestfallen that his father's voice would be silenced, and he conveyed the family's view that I was the only candidate who had a chance to hold the seat. Blodgett, who was by now a friend and a strategist I greatly admired, said he would put himself and the Wellstone campaign operation at my disposal. Lillehaug said he thought this was the only hope the party had of retaining the Senate seat. By this time I had already had phone calls from Ted Kennedy and Pat Leahy encouraging me to enter the race, and Tom Daschle, then the Senate majority leader, had assured me of a spot in the Senate leadership. I knew there was no time for equivocation, and by the time we finished, I had made up my mind. I had the elements I needed: a unified party behind me, a personal request from the Wellstone family, and the Wellstone campaign operation waiting to go. I said yes.

Despite the urgency of the situation, we could not launch the campaign immediately. The state was still in mourning, and the Wellstone family was trying to organize a public memorial service for early the following week. We decided that we wouldn't make a formal announcement or start campaigning until after the service. The story of that event, held in the vast basketball arena at the University of Minnesota, is now well known. It drew a huge turnout: Bill and Hillary Clinton were there, as were Bob Dole and about half the U.S. Senate, Democrats and Republicans. It started off as a beautiful tribute to Paul and the people who died with him, but speech by speech it gradually began to take on a political tone, and by the end it had turned into an unintentional rally for Democrats. I was sitting with the Senate delegation, and I could feel people squirming. The Republicans who had come to honor Paul felt tricked and abused, and one by one they began to walk out. No one had planned this—had the organizers really controlled the program, they would have kept away from politics—but some Republican officeholders felt offended and independent-minded voters felt the party was trying to exploit Paul's death. The news coverage was universally critical for the next twenty-four hours, and polls showed that 25 percent of undecided voters tilted toward Coleman after the event. I don't blame anyone—it all happened in an emotional rush—but I think that's when we started to slip.

On Wednesday, with six days to go before Election Day, we formally launched the campaign, paying visits to editorial boards and starting a bus tour of the state. But it was a miserable six days. All the issues of that campaign, in Minnesota and across the country, were Republican issues. The Bush White House was still in its early bloom, and Bush had high approval ratings. The administration was pushing the war on terror, starting to make belligerent noises toward Iraq, and politicizing the effort to create a Department of Homeland Security. Coleman understood the political mood of the country and used it to great advantage. He described himself as a post–9/11 candidate and boasted of his ties to the White House. In retrospect, I think my age also worked against me. I was seventy-four years old. It was eighteen years since I had run for office, and half of the state had never had a chance to vote for or against me. Coleman exploited the issue adroitly, never making it personal or disrespectful, but always mentioning the need for new ideas and fresh energy in Washington.

Then, too, I think I was not yet a good candidate. In an ordinary campaign you start out eighteen months before Election Day, and you spend some time moving around, talking to voters, reading the mail, and listening to your opponent. You try to understand what's on people's minds and how you want to talk about their concerns. You give a lot of speeches and try out a lot of themes, and gradually you figure out what works and what doesn't, framing your issues and working up your music. I had none of that. I had six days, and it was the first time I ever campaigned in the dark. Then, too, there was a simple logistical issue. Because the Wellstone plane crash was still so raw in people's minds, we decided to tour the state by bus rather than by air. Minnesota is a big state, and it's hard to cover in a week. We headed south to Rochester, then drove north to Duluth and across the Iron Range. By the time that swing was over, it was time for the only debate I had with Coleman, and I flew back to the Twin Cities. If I had had a good plane and a tight schedule, we could have hit twice as many towns. But we didn't.

On Monday, November 4, the day of our only debate, the polls showed the race too close to call. I thought the debate went well, but whenever I tried to pin down Coleman on the issues, he simply replied with a lot of comforting rhetoric about the need for bipartisanship and "new ideas in Washington." When the polls closed on Tuesday, I was down sixty thousand votes out of two million cast, and Norm Coleman won by 50 percent to 47 percent.

That race was the only election I ever lost in Minnesota, and it's hard to get over that. The state had changed since the last time I had run for office. The population had grown, and a big new exurban belt surrounded the Twin Cities. The Bush-Rove rhetoric about reducing taxes, downsizing government, and leaving people alone appealed in the new suburbia because many of the residents had moved away from the cities to find their own lives. Even in Minnesota, the message of the unfettered market had a lot of resonance. On Election Day we could see the results going against us, and by early evening I started to get a horrible feeling in my stomach. But mainly I felt bad for Joan and the kids—they had already been through this once, in 1984, and now they had to go through it again.

For all that, I have no regrets. I ran for the right reasons and made my case for the issues that mattered to me. The voters of Minnesota heard me out and treated me fairly.

That election, a blow for me personally, was also a blow for our country. Coleman's victory gave Republicans control of the Senate in addition to the House and the presidency. They now had it all. If there was ever a period when the country needed the Senate to serve as a check on a runaway executive, that was it. We now know the sorts of abuses and deceptions the Bush administration was committing in the name of the war on terror, and sadly the Senate did not hold the White House to account. I would have been just one senator, but I think I would have made a difference. A more vigorous Senate, with Democrats controlling the committees and setting the legislative agenda, standing up to the Bush administration, might have changed the course of those next few years, and I regret that we didn't have that opportunity.

16

Looking Forward

If you are going to be in politics, you have to be a soldier in the battle.

—Hubert Humphrey's farewell speech to the Minnesota AFL-CIO, 1977

I WRITE THESE WORDS from an office high above downtown Minneapolis. Below me sprawls the green and leafy city where I started in public life fifty years ago and whose enlightened, progressive politics have inspired me ever since. To the north, the Mississippi River curls away into the distance, an emblem of the magnificent, decent state I have been proud to represent.

Since retiring from public life, I have practiced law in Minneapolis and taught at the Humphrey Institute of Public Affairs at the University of Minnesota. The first job reconnects me with the civic life of a community I love; the second allows me to engage with young people, reflect on the way America has changed during half a century, and take stock of the challenges our country faces today.

I tell my students I've been a lucky man, taught by magnificent mentors, guided by a remarkable wife, surrounded by a wonderful family, supported by the kind people of this state—and able, I hope, to make a difference on behalf of the values I believe in.

When I began my life in politics, those values went by the name *liberalism*. But don't mistake the *ism* in that word. I never signed up for any ideology. I was just trying to live up to the ideals I was taught and the values I saw all around me.

I grew up in Depression America, a small-town kid from a place no one had ever heard of. My parents had no money and few prospects. I had no right to think that I might one day be a U.S. senator or a candidate for president.

But I was lucky to grow up in a loving family and a land of opportunity. My parents were compassionate people with a belief in public service. They instilled in my brothers and me a love of ideas, a sense of social obligation, and the idea that if you worked hard enough, you could achieve whatever you wanted.

When I left Elmore, there wasn't a lock on any door. People thought it wasn't necessary: We were all together as a community. If someone needed a hand, a neighbor helped. If anyone got in trouble, everyone else helped out.

For several years I traveled this country speaking for that kind of America. Its values were the same ones I had grown up with, as a man and as a politician: civil rights, social justice, inclusiveness and opportunity, tolerance at home, strength with patience abroad.

While I matured, however, the country changed. I had friends who heard me out, but the nation was no longer listening. Maybe I was looking at the low tide for the values I believed in. I believed that we couldn't solve our problems without an engaged government. But when you said the word *government*, people heard taxes and bureaucracy. I wanted to talk about poverty and opportunity, but people wondered why I wanted to give away things for free. I had an idea that we are a community, that we should solve our problems through common effort. But that was treated as old-fashioned, a kind of silly sentimentality that could only hold us back.

Then came the campaign of 2008 and the election of Barack Obama. People saw the economy coming down around their ears, their homes losing value, corporate executives walking away with millions of dollars despite disastrous mistakes in judgment. They saw America losing its way in the world and losing stature with our allies. They finally saw what people such as I had been saying for a long time: The market is not self-correcting. Belligerence is not foreign policy. Justice and opportunity do not prevail by themselves. People had worshipped the market, and now that god had failed. Liberalism, the kind I believed in, has a chance again.

But liberalism is still on trial, and nothing is to be gained by simply reenacting what we did four decades ago. During the "high tide" we expanded opportunity and redefined government's role in society. A lot of it was wonderful, overdue, and much needed. But we also overstated what was possible and failed to understand how much money and patience would be required.

The question for liberals today is how to use government well when government must be used: to educate our children, to protect our air and water, to defend our country, to enforce civil rights, to regulate the market and protect ordinary people from its excesses. These are things we all agree on. It's not ideological, it's practical. More than a century ago, Abraham Lincoln recognized this balance when he said, "The legitimate object of government is to do for a community of people, whatever they need to have done but cannot do at all, or cannot so well do for themselves, in their separate and individual capacities."

As a result of the cycle we went through, the liberalism that Barack Obama inherited is different. It understands that the world is a dangerous place and we have to protect Americans from attack. It understands that government must be competent and show voters results when it spends their money. It understands that without a competitive economy, you have nothing. It understands that decisions must be rooted in evidence, not ideology. All these things have to be working for us to grasp the renewed opportunity that's ours.

I say this because I've lived long enough to see a few cycles of American history, to see the ideals I cherish ebb and flow in the tide of public opinion, and to know that the problems America faces today are not anomalies. They are recurring challenges that will periodically test our most basic values.

Four decades ago, I lived through a war that divided our nation, destroyed a president, and drained the public's confidence in its leaders. Yet four decades later we found ourselves fighting a war in Iraq that was launched under false pretenses and conducted by leaders who had contempt for the public and the truth. In the Senate I helped expose a history of abuses by our intelligence agencies and write legislation to bring them back under the rule of law. Yet four decades later, we found ourselves with a president and vice president who spied on Americans in contravention of the law, trampled due process, and hid these activities not only from the public but also from their peers in Congress. I served with a president who changed the way Democrats think about economics, who struck a disciplined balance between fiscal restraint and federal compassion. I saw him replaced by a "conservative" president who used phony budgets to sell voodoo economics, transferred wealth to the rich, and paralyzed the government's capacity to deal with the nation's challenges.

I came of age in an optimistic America, a society that believed in opportunity and the value of common endeavor. Today, two generations have grown up in a flinty and anxious America, a nation where millions live without health insurance, poor children crowd into crumbling schools, and our young people take on crushing debts to get a college education—even while the rich pull farther and farther away from everyone else. I wonder what happened to that other America, a place of empathy and hope.

These four decades haven't changed my core beliefs, but they have sharpened and deepened my conviction about the values required to restore and sustain a country we can be proud to leave our children. As a closing note, I'd like to set them out here.

First, we must shake off the antigovernment dogma that has gripped our country for twenty-five years. We must remember that together we have an obligation, often through the use of government, to expand opportunity, invest in our people, protect the environment, and regulate the excesses of the market. We cannot project our values abroad unless we uphold them at home.

More than most Western societies, the United States relies on free markets and individual initiative, a tradition that suits our values and has helped us prosper over the decades. But the public sector has always been a partner to private initiative—from the passage of the Homestead Act to the building of the interstate freeway system. If we want a healthy population and a clean environment, if we want the best-educated workforce in the world, if we want an economy where everyone plays by the rules, government must play a role.

My home state of Minnesota is a fine example. In the 1930s and 1940s Minnesota was a poor state, a place richly endowed with natural resources but defined by low-wage industries such as farming and mining. In 1933 it became the first state to enact an income tax, with the revenues dedicated to improving public schools; one result was that during World War II Minnesota's military recruits had the lowest draft-rejection rate in the nation. Between the 1950s and 1960s Minnesota hugely increased its investment in public schools, community colleges, and state universities, and built a great research institution at the University of Minnesota. Within two decades Minnesota led the nation in high school graduation rates, student test scores, and the share of adults with college degrees. The formula worked: Minnesota became one of the ten richest states in the country, as measured by per capita income, with economic growth that far outpaced the national average. It achieved the nation's lowest poverty rate and the highest rate of health insurance coverage. Despite a reputation for liberal politics, it became home to more corporate headquarters than any other state of comparable size.

Jay Kiedrowski, a former banking executive and state finance commissioner who now teaches at the University of Minnesota, has written, "If our tax dollars are invested in the right public services, our competitive position is strengthened. Moderate Republicans and centrist Democrats collaborated to create a superior education system and built the infrastructure needed to sustain economic growth."

For three decades Minnesota was "the state that works," a place where political, civic, labor, and business leaders routinely put aside their self-interests and worked together to advance the common good. Progressive Republicans such as Luther Youngdahl, Elmer Andersen, Al Quie, and Arne Carlson poured money into public schools, understanding that they improved the state's workforce while expanding opportunity; pragmatic Democrats such as Wendell Anderson and Rudy Perpich reformed the tax system to improve the state's business climate and achieve a more equi-table system of public finance. Corporate leaders established the Five Per-cent Club of corporations that contributed that share of profits to public purposes.

In the past decade, however, the same divisive tactics that poisoned our national politics infected Minnesota. A Republican governor, Tim Pawlenty, broke with the progressive tradition of his predecessors, impos-ing a regime of no new taxes, dismantling health and education programs built through decades of bipartisan work, and adopting the scornful anti-government rhetoric of the national Republican Party. Eight years of this philosophy have done nothing to make Minnesota a stronger, more com-petitive state. Minnesota is no longer the healthiest state, nor the best educated, nor a place whose economy routinely outperforms the national average. These indicators may recover with time, but damage has been done—to the state's performance and, worse, to a civic culture that placed the common good above individual gain.

Minnesota has been an exceptional state, but countless other exam-ples show the dividends of public investment. When soldiers returned from World War II, they took advantage of the G.I. Bill and enrolled in college by the hundreds of thousands. It enabled an entire generation to expand their horizons in life, giving us the best-educated population in the world, and ultimately repaying the government many times over in higher productivity, income, and revenues. Similarly, we know beyond doubt that high-quality preschool programs improve the school perfor-mance and career outcomes of disadvantaged children. Economists Rob Grunewald and Arthur Rolnick at the Federal Reserve Bank of Minneap-olis estimate that money spent on quality early education earns a double-digit return, making it the best economic-development investment they have found.

At the foundation of all these investments lie our nation's public schools. We have been slipping against many other nations, and it's time we put the highest priority on restoring our edge. We should weed out teachers who are unsuited to the profession by periodic testing—for we cannot compromise on quality—but we must also identify and reward the best teachers. Countries such as Japan and Finland hire the best young teachers, pay them well, and show them the respect they deserve, while we tend to demean our teachers and our public schools. This might require painful choices; I have always supported union protection for our teachers, but sometimes union rules must have flexibility so that the best teachers of the best backgrounds are there to give our kids the best. Education also suffers from too much faddism. No Child Left Behind, for example, is a failed experiment. It has created a teach-to-the-test mentality that is dumbing down our schools while diverting resources away from history and the arts. Charter schools, an experiment where Minnesota was a leader and that was embraced by the Obama administration, are not the answer either. They bleed revenues from public schools without producing demonstrably better results, and, worse, can lead to separatism among our schools, diluting the shared public-school experience that has been so central to our nation's success. One thing works: good teachers in good classrooms. We should dump the fads and invest in what works.

Quite beyond investing in our people, government has a role in regulating the excesses of the private market. Before the Clean Water Act, factories and cities dumped raw sewage and industrial waste into our most beautiful rivers and lakes. And why not? The market told them it was free. Dirty air and dirty water became good business. Factories belched pollutants into our air for the same reason. We passed the Clean Water Act and the Clean Air Act—giving industry and cities the resources to treat their pollutants—and today the records of the Environmental Protection Agency show that our air and great rivers are cleaner than they were forty years ago.

As a young attorney general, I saw how swindlers would take advantage of an unregulated market to cheat people. Today we see it again on a massive scale, in Enron, in the Bernard Madoff scandal, in the frightening financial meltdown caused by unregulated investments in exotic financial instruments and risky mortgages. I have always argued that wise regulation does not subvert markets, it makes them stronger. Institutions such as the Federal Reserve System, the Federal Deposit Insurance Corporation, and the Securities and Exchange Commission make capitalism stronger and more stable. My friend William Galston, a fellow at the Brookings Institution and a professor at the University of Maryland, observed, "When the rules are inadequate, ill-conceived, or poorly enforced, markets malfunction badly, causing great damage. Regulatory institutions are not antithetical, but rather essential, to a well-functioning modern capitalist system."

This view has fallen out of favor in the past three decades, a time when it has become popular to say that government does no good. The skeptics forget that America's public universities are among the finest in the world and attract the brightest students from across the globe. They forget that Medicare—a public system using private doctors and hospitals—has the highest consumer satisfaction ratings of any health insurer and the lowest costs. No prosperous, developed country has achieved universal public education without government playing a role. No country has achieved first-rate health care, or strong transportation infrastructure, or pioneering scientific research without the help of government.

We have allowed public investment to decay tragically in the past three decades, and we have paid a price for it. The United States now trails most European nations in the share of young people who graduate from college, largely because of the crushing debts that students must take on. We trail them by an even wider margin in spending for early-childhood education, with the result that too many of our children enter public school unprepared to learn.

As a consequence of this retreat from public responsibility, we have created a two-tier society in which many of the rich have pulled away from everyone else, and millions of Americans, lacking economic security and decent health insurance, wonder what stake they have in a growing economy.

Our second task must be to restore the public's trust in politics. To those who say this is hopeless, I say history offers countless examples. Passage of the Congressional Budget Act of 1974 introduced new transparency to Congress's spending decisions and new rigor to its budget estimates; today any voter can go to cbo.gov and see how every penny is spent and raised and how federal spending has changed over the years. Public financing of presidential campaigns greatly reduced the influence of big money on candidates for our nation's highest office and, until the system broke down in 2008, gave us better, more constructive presidential campaigns.

Today, the greatest failing of government accountability comes in the way we finance political campaigns. A Senate race today can cost $20 million, forcing candidates into a never-ending chase for cash. The fund-raising ordeal demeans those who hold public office and repels those who might seek it. In the words of my late friend Robert Byrd, politicians have become full-time fund-raisers and part-time officeholders. Worse, the power of special interests paralyzes lawmaking. Issues of urgent public interest—climate change, health care reform, financial regulation—drag on forever because of the power and access of the narrow special interests. As a result, too many voters feel that laws are written for the rich and powerful, not for the average citizen, a prospect that only deepens their alienation from their own government.

In 2009, as Congress struggled to reform our health care system, address global warming, and regulate our financial markets, money poured into the committees that were crafting the legislation from the very industries affected. Insurance companies, medical professionals, and pharmaceutical corporations, for example, gave more than $20 million to members of the Senate Finance Committee and the Senate Committee on Health, Education, Labor, and Pensions. Securities firms and investment banks gave more than $4 million to members of the Senate Banking and Finance committees. Even if contributions on that scale produce no quid pro quos, the public can be pardoned for questioning the integrity of the system—and the loss of public confidence is dangerous.

Passage of the McCain-Feingold reforms in 2002 helped limit the influence of huge "soft money" donations and brought greater transparency to political fund-raising, but much remains to be done.

The recent Supreme Court decision authorizing unlimited corporate and union spending in political and judicial elections creates a dangerous new challenge to our democracy. For nearly one hundred years our laws have prohibited direct corporate and union contributions to political campaigns. For years the courts have held that Congress has the authority to regulate campaign contributions to prevent corruption and even the *appearance* of corruption.

The radical ruling in *Citizens United v. Federal Election Commission*—the astonishing conclusion that corporations enjoy the same constitutional rights as human beings—will permit corporate interests to reward their friends in high office and punish their enemies. No wonder John McCain remarked on the naïveté of the Court; no wonder Justice Stevens observed that the ruling was "at war with the views of generations of Americans."

The ruling demands an immediate response from Congress. At a minimum we need legislation mandating rapid and thorough disclosure of all political contributions, requiring approval by stockholders and union members before their money can be spent on political campaigns, and banning the intrusion of foreign-controlled corporations in American elections. The long-term goal must be a wiser Court that will reverse the 5–4 decision or a constitutional amendment to repair the damage.

Congress should also consider repairing and modernizing the system of public financing for presidential campaigns. One solution would be Minnesota's system: an immediate tax rebate to citizens for their campaign contributions. A second would be to increase the amount of public financing available to presidential candidates and tie it to the candidate's ability to raise small donations, much as Arizona does. A "multiple match" would strengthen the hand of small contributors and serve as a counterweight to the influence of big money. Both strategies are under attack—Minnesota's by a governor's veto, Arizona's by a bad court decision—but both would give us healthier politics.

Third, we must restore our respect for the rule of law. When terrorists attacked this country on September 11, 2001, Americans were afraid and so was I. But fear does not justify what our government did in response. Our president and vice president sponsored a pattern of deceit at the highest levels of our government, distorted intelligence about Iraq, and conspired to consolidate power in contempt of law and the Constitution.

They argued, as shortsighted leaders inevitably do, that laws and civil liberties are niceties we cannot afford in a dangerous world. We have heard this argument before. When anarchists sprang up in American cities early in the twentieth century, Congress responded with loyalty oaths and the Sedition Act. When fascism threatened from Germany and Japan in the 1940s, we interned Japanese Americans in what amounted to prison camps. When communism seemed to threaten our future in the 1950s and 1960s, the FBI and the CIA responded with illegal surveillance of Americans and harassment of loyal citizens.

The idea that respect for the law leaves us weak is a fraud. The law must be strong and it must be tough. There is no evidence that these tactics—locking up Japanese Americans, harassing antiwar groups, or subjecting Muslim detainees to torture—made us safer. Quite the opposite: They undermined support among our allies by making us look like hypocrites; gave our enemies a tool to recruit new extremists; and left the rest of the world wondering who stands for the rule of law and respect for civil liberties. As General David H. Petraeus has observed, "Whenever we have perhaps taken expedient measures, we ended up paying a price for it ultimately. Abu Ghraib and other situations like that are nonbiodegradable. They don't go away. The enemy continues to beat you with them like a stick."

If history has revealed our fallibility, it has also proven we can correct our mistakes. The Army-McCarthy hearings of 1954 showed Senator Joseph McCarthy to be a fraud and reassured the American people that their government was not infiltrated by Communists. The 9/11 Commission, equipped with subpoena power, leaders with integrity, and a talented investigative staff, helped Americans understand how our intelligence community had failed us in the months and years before the Pentagon and World Trade Center attacks.

This is why I believe our country needed a commission to investigate the legal abuses committed by our leaders after 9/11. I understand why President Obama asked the nation to look forward, not back, and why he feared that an inquiry might take on the appearance of partisan politics.

But a country cannot make a success of the future until it understands the mistakes of the past. As my friend Pat Leahy observed during Senate Judiciary Committee hearings on the matter, you can't turn the page until you have read it. In my view, a bipartisan commission of inquiry, created by Congress and the president but independent of the government, would take the issue out of politics, much as the 9/11 Commission did, and allow the public to see an investigation conducted with balance and integrity.

One great achievement of the Church Committee, still the best single example of this sort of rigorous investigation, was that it gave the nation a common, accepted set of facts from which we could debate the merits of the policies. The ultimate source of correction in a democracy is the ballot box. But voters cannot make this self-correcting mechanism work unless they have the facts. As James Madison wrote two centuries ago, "[a] popular Government, without popular information, or the means of acquiring it, is but a Prologue to a Farce or a Tragedy; or, perhaps both."

Some intelligence and some activities must remain secret to protect national security, as we learned on the Church Committee, so investigating military and intelligence agencies presents special challenges. But you can't leave the secrecy decisions to the executive branch and the agencies involved. You will always run up against enormous resistance from political figures who fear embarrassment, government operatives who want to hold on to their power, and agency officials who simply resist the idea of oversight from elected leaders.

My colleagues and I learned these lessons on the Church Committee more than thirty years ago. Those hearings were devastating to the argument that intimidation and abuse work. The committee penetrated the fiction and the fear and documented a hard story showing how a government that pursued these secret strategies wound up abusing the law, straying off course, and undermining its own mission. We're often told by people who violated the law that it was a courageous act to protect the nation. But many times these secret activities actually reflect the cowardice of people who are afraid to make their case to Congress or test their thinking in public debate. We wrote a law to restore accountability, and we found that those agencies were stronger when they operated inside the law.

In the years between appalling episodes of this kind, people tend to forget why the rule of law matters. Civil liberties become an abstraction; constitutional protections become a debating game for lawyers. People used to tell me there was no harm in secret taping and surveillance, that if you'd done nothing wrong, you had nothing to hide. They don't remember that our own leaders tried to destroy Martin Luther King Jr. and used the IRS to harass their political enemies.

Most Americans are levelheaded people with busy lives and little time for conspiracy theories. They think these abuses are anomalies that will harmlessly pass away. But I've been close to power, and I know the temptations a president faces. All presidents are told that if they break out of the ordinary constraints and resort to private government outside the law, they can accomplish what they want and accomplish it quickly. They are advised that military and diplomatic measures cannot achieve what three people in trench coats can—advice that is seldom true. When a previous administration has done something and got away with it, it sets a precedent. It's like a loaded pistol sitting on the kitchen table. It's too easy to reach for it.

More than two hundred years ago our founders understood this. They had seen the overreach of kings in Europe, and they understood that the same danger lurked here. Federalist Paper 51 has become gospel to me because James Madison understood not only the need for legal process but also the underlying human nature. He knew that "men are not angels" and that a nation cannot rely on humanity's better nature to constrain these abuses. It's why he and the other founders set up the delicate system of checks and balances, pitting ambition against ambition, so that public officials, if only to protect their own turf, would become a counterforce against abuse. It permits a government to act wisely, to correct mistakes. It was prescient, it was fundamental, and it has stood the test of time.

Fourth, we must restore our reputation in the world. When a president breaks the law, it doesn't merely endanger our liberties, it damages our stature abroad and our ability to project our values. Two decades ago, student protesters in Tiananmen Square held up miniatures of the Statue of Liberty in their battle for a more democratic society. They admired us.

They wanted to be like America. Something about the rule of law and the voice of democracy cuts across all societies, all cultures—people admire and seek its genius and integrity.

Through much of the past decade we made the mistake of thinking that our stature abroad rested on our might to the exclusion of our values. We celebrated hubris and arrogance and assumed, if we substituted swagger for judgment, the American military would have its way. Repairing that damage will require wisdom and hard work, but also the simple humility of recognizing that we need to understand the world we live in.

Understanding other countries might sound like a simple thing. But in Iraq, our leaders launched an occupation without comprehending what they were getting into. President Bush's assertion that the urge for freedom is universal had some truth. But I don't think he had a clue about the particulars of Iraq—the tribal loyalties that would influence elections, the bitter history of British colonialism that made Iraqis understandably suspicious of an occupying army, the way Islamic extremism and tension between Shia and Sunni had sundered their society. Our history is littered with episodes when the impulse for action overwhelmed our better judgment: the overthrow of Mohammad Mossadegh in Iran, the Bay of Pigs, the bombing of Cambodia.

I am not a pacifist. The world is a dangerous place, full of people who mean us harm. I came of age in a Democratic Party that battled communism because we knew that its totalitarian impulses threatened our ideals of liberty. I helped lead an administration that modernized our military, led the transition from mechanical to digitized weaponry, and pioneered some of today's most valuable weapons, including the cruise missile and stealth aircraft. But history teaches us that military power alone cannot keep us safe. If the fight against terrorism has taught us anything, it is that we must combine hard power with soft power and use what Harvard's Joseph Nye has called "smart power."

History also teaches the value of international cooperation. The gravest problems we face in the world—fighting terrorism, addressing global climate change, containing nuclear weapons, battling infectious diseases, building a stable global financial system—require international cooperation. Though the tests of diplomacy might sometimes leave us impatient, we are almost always stronger when we act in concert with those who share our values. The idea of treating other nations dismissively is toxic.

Today, a similar fear has muddied our thinking about immigration reform. Instead of recognizing that immigrants come to America because they admire our values and seek to make a contribution to our society, we have stereotyped them out of fear that they are coming here to exploit the system and subvert the American way of life. We nearly made the same mistake when I was a young senator. When we debated the Immigration Reform Act of 1965, which ended the old country-of-origin quotas and greatly broadened the geographic and ethnic makeup of our immigrant population, Senator Spessard Holland of Florida asserted on the Senate floor, "We have the complete right as a nation to safeguard ourselves and our own traditions and our own people." My good friend John Pastore, the son of Italian immigrants in Rhode Island, responded indignantly, "The bill is saying that it does not make any difference what the color of one's skin might be; if he can add to the glory of America, he will be welcome." We passed that bill and it opened up America to people from Asia, Latin America, and Eastern Europe. It changed the face of our country, fueled the growth of our labor force and our economy, and today we know it made our country stronger. It also made America the only truly multicultural major power on earth—surely one of our greatest attractions.

We are stronger in the world when other countries see themselves in our mirror. And the world is a better place when other countries reflect our best values of tolerance, enlightenment, respect for human rights, opportunity, and the rule of law.

Finally, we must restore civility to our political discourse. When I joined the Senate in 1965, Hubert Humphrey's first injunction was to treat my rivals as friends. The great civil rights legislation of the 1960s could not have passed if not for Hubert's practice of treating his Southern opponents generously, and many of my antagonists, senators such as Richard Russell and Bob Dole, always treated me fairly and respectfully. Yet generosity and dignity have all but disappeared from our politics today. When Congress debated welfare reform in 1996, members of the House

actually carried signs into the chamber reading DON'T FEED THE ALLIGA-
TORS—meaning poor children. When Barack Obama addressed Congress
on health care reform in September 2009, a Republican member of the
House, in an appalling breach of decorum, shouted, "You lie!"

A society cannot make progress in such an atmosphere. Years ago, the
great jurist Learned Hand wrote, "The spirit of liberty is the spirit which is
not too sure that it is right." Our greatest leaders—Washington, Jefferson,
Lincoln—have governed with an open mind and a magnanimous spirit.

This, too, is a chance for us to show the world a better example. Today
much of the globe is gripped by an angry fundamentalism and dominated
by people who fear change and vilify their enemies. Hopeful people
around the world look to us—our sense of tolerance, our openness to
change, our pragmatic tradition of solving problems, our acceptance of
diverse people into our midst. Countries that fear modernity, that cling to
dogma, that exclude women, that foment ethnic divisions—they cannot
seem to make progress and join the modern world. They look to us for a
better example, a society that tests assertion against evidence and debates
its differences respectfully.

Today the best example of America's better example is the election of
Barack Obama. It is proof that a nation can throw off a shameful past and
recover from its historical errors. It's a reminder that our country is capable of change—and a measure of how much it has changed in my lifetime.

When I attended law school at the University of Minnesota, we had
four women in my class, and they were considered peculiar. People asked,
Why would a woman want to be a lawyer? When I got my first job as a
lawyer, the firm had one woman attorney, Louise Saunders. She came to
me more than once and asked me to handle some of her clients. They
wouldn't work with a woman. We had a band of courageous women lawyers and they were pioneers.

I had grown up in a separate-but-equal Democratic Party, with what
amounted to a men's organization and a women's organization. The
women would meet socially and hold teas, and the men would run the
place. If you look at a picture of, say, the 1948 Democratic National Convention, you would see, essentially, a white male monopoly. There might

be one woman on the platform, and she would generally be there to introduce someone else. Terrific women worked behind the scenes, but the
men ended up in charge, or at least running for the public offices. When
I was in the Senate, I visited the University of Minnesota at Morris one
day and said it was nice to be there with the president and his lovely wife.
After my talk she came up to me and said, "Am I really that lovely to
you?" and I saw what an ass I was.

Now I look around and see a woman as Speaker of the U.S. House, the
first ever. A woman as Speaker of the Minnesota House. A woman nearly
became our president. The Minnesota Supreme Court, a few years ago,
had a female majority. The law firm where I work is headed by a woman,
Marianne Short, a magnificent attorney.

The women said, No more, and it has been a profound transformation.

My career has been about opening doors, and I believe we opened
doors in the 1984 campaign. Geraldine Ferraro got young women thinking about what they could do in politics. We didn't win that year, but
they saw the possibilities. They saw Ferraro debate George H. W. Bush
and beat him. They saw that a glass ceiling had been shattered and that
women could start thinking about higher possibilities. As I write these
words, someone right down the hall might be thinking about running for
president. It's been a tonic for America, and it's not going to go back.

As for race, the change has been profound. When I started in the Senate, it was an open question whether black Americans would ever fully
participate in our political system. Colleagues told me, You are playing
with fire, this is not the way it's supposed to be. Some would pull out
their Bibles and tell me that the races are not supposed to live and work
together. The year that we first tried to establish the Martin Luther King
Day holiday, a senator came up to me and asked, What in your background gives you standing to talk about civil rights? Why don't you stick
to your own business? He was a prominent and powerful senator at the
time. It was tough stuff, it was career-threatening.

Our country took more than two hundred years to confront this legacy, and when we finally did, with the civil rights legislation of the 1960s,
it was a remarkable lesson in the use of the law. The Voting Rights Act

represented an incredible exercise of federal power and encroachment on local government. We sent federal registrars right down to the precinct level. We had federal officers in Southern states to ensure that black citizens could register and that the voting was peaceful. We used force, with the support of the U.S. Supreme Court, to guarantee the one-man-one-vote principle, and suddenly the right to vote became a reality.

That was the compulsion side of the law. But good law must also be a teacher. It can set an example and change minds. I believe that was the broader accomplishment of the civil rights movement and the civil rights laws: We saw a transformation of people's minds and hearts, a profound shift in the way Americans look at race, and it all coalesced under Barack Obama. Americans saw him not as a black man who wanted to be president, but as a hugely gifted person who should be president—who also happened to be black.

As recently as twenty years ago, I wouldn't have believed that possible. We have opened doors for millions of Americans to participate in our democracy and our economy and, in so doing, have finally, after 250 years, redeemed our promise as a nation of justice and liberty.

Unlike the New Deal, this wasn't merely about spending money or expanding government. This was about dispersing power, about recognizing that the disadvantaged were not supplicants asking for a place in society but citizens who had the right to take their place. We didn't merely open doors, we gave all Americans the tools they would need to keep the doors open.

In the fall of 2006, not long after Keith Ellison was elected from Minnesota as the first Muslim member of Congress, I attended a meeting of Twin Cities religious leaders. An imam came up to me, thanked me for endorsing Keith, and said it made him hopeful about this country. He told me he had talked about the endorsement and the election with his son, and his son had said, I like America. Things happen here.

The point I want to underscore is that these movements didn't merely improve life for disadvantaged Americans, they made the rest of America stronger.

When I went to Washington, I could see the wreckage that segregation was causing in our country. We could never tap the talents of all our people. We sapped our emotional strength with divisive feuds. We had millions of citizens who were alienated from their own country, who could not support our system of government because they saw it was unfair. These were terrible burdens to carry as a nation, and they were self-imposed. When I was a young senator, the segregationists told me that racial integration would weaken the nation. No one believes that anymore. History has vindicated the effort to outlaw discrimination and expand opportunity.

By redeeming our national promise at home, we have increased our ability to carry hope and set an example abroad. Nothing is more toxic than relationships based on hate. It's the story of Afghanistan, Iraq, Yugoslavia. It's why hopeful people around the world look to us for an example. I think America's greatness can be found in its struggle to open doors. We can carry more weight today because we leveled the load across all of us. It's redemptive.

The reader who has stayed with me this far may note how often I have invoked the word *values*. I have used it to explain what motivated me in the public sphere, and what guided me in my private life. I have used it to account for the cycles in American history, some of them triumphant, and some tragic. As I have said in these pages, I believe that the values of the American people—our fundamental decency, our sense of justice and fairness, our love of freedom—are the country's greatest assets, and that steering by their lodestar is the only true course forward.

It is no mystery to me where my values came from. They are gifts from my parents, who derived them from their faith and lived them every day. They are the birthright of small-town America, of communities where people belong to and care for one another. They come from Joan, my compass and my rock; and my wonderful kids, who have taught me lesson after lesson as we lived this adventure together. They come from the generous teachers and mentors and friends I have been blessed to have; and from the ordinary extraordinary Americans I have been privileged to know as I've traveled our incomparably diverse nation; and from the people I have met around the world whose yearning for opportunity and dignity is the mirror of our own.

The values come from the ingenious architecture devised by our nation's founders—the clockwork of checks and balances, the guarantee of inalienable rights, the grace to appeal to the better angels of our nature, and the common sense to anticipate how short of our ideals we sometimes fall.

I was raised in a community of decent, optimistic people. They had risen to great challenges and conquered great hardships, and they believed that the hard work of good people could make America a better place. They thought politics means something and that you could change things if you tried. They understood that the burden is lighter when we lift it together, that the future is brighter when we face it as one. I suppose I grew up thinking that all America was that way, or could be.

Like everyone else, I have had my share of disappointments. But I have never doubted that those values also made me one of the luckiest of men on God's earth. For that, I will always be grateful.

More than forty years ago, at the start of my career in public life, I stood on the steps of the Minnesota Capitol and addressed a rally of civil rights supporters. I told them we were engaged in a struggle to change a nation and warned that the battle would be long. But I asked them not to lose hope, for I believed then—and believe today—that people of goodwill, engaged with conviction in a cause that is just, can leave the world a better place. I closed that day by quoting the Apostle Paul, and I hope that the inspiration I offered them has, in turn, been mine: "I have fought a good fight, I have finished my course, I have kept the faith."

ACKNOWLEDGMENTS

T HE IDEA FOR this book grew out of a series of seminars I taught with Professor Lawrence Jacobs at the University of Minnesota's Humphrey Institute of Public Affairs. I am indebted to Professor Jacobs and the institute's remarkable dean, Brian Atwood, for their inspiration and support.

Although this is in some respects a personal memoir, it is also a work of archival history, and it draws on the thousands of pages of documents that constitute the Mondale Papers at the Minnesota Historical Society. Robert Horton, the society's Publications and Collections Director, provided generous assistance in the early stages of this project, as did his talented research staff in the Weyerhaeuser Reading Room.

The manuscript itself was built from a series of in-depth interviews with David Hage, a superb editor at the *Minneapolis Star Tribune*, who served as my cowriter and became my comrade through three years of research and writing. From the start, David proved to be a gifted writer, but even more, a thoughtful and caring participant, and I am grateful for the attention he lavished on this project. I couldn't, and probably wouldn't, have undertaken this effort without him.

At the Dorsey law firm, I owe a special thanks to Marianne Short, the firm's remarkable chairwoman, for her understanding and friendship.

I've been privileged to work with many brilliant and dedicated people over the years, and many of them came to my assistance again when it came time to tell this story. They spent hours digging through their own files, offering insights on the key issues, shedding light on important episodes of our work, and reviewing early drafts of the manuscript. For their invaluable contributions I want to offer my deepest thanks to

Acknowledgments

Jim Johnson, Maxine Isaacs, Charles and Heather Campion (my friend who has traveled with me all over this country, and indeed, all over the world for years and yet remains a friend and source of acceptable jokes. Chuck and Heather continue to be an inspiration to me), Rust Deming, Bill Breer, Dick Moe, Mike Berman, Geri Joseph, Phil Byrne, Stu Eizenstat, Sid Johnson, Warren Spannaus, Gary Sick, Fritz Schwarz, Loch Johnson, Ellen Hoffman, and David Lillehaug. I owe a special thanks to Marty Kaplan, a master of ideas as well as words, who brought clarity and power to many of the themes in this book.

Others who worked by my side over the years and offered important insights for the book include Bert Carp, David Aaron, Richard Holbrooke, Bill Mullin, Rick Solum, Steve Engelberg, and Amy Klobuchar, now a stunningly effective U.S. senator. Tony Corrado, Jay Kiedrowski, and Bill Galston—brilliant scholars who helped refine my thinking on the key issues—shared their ideas generously.

One of the great pleasures in teaching at the Humphrey Institute is the opportunity to work with the brightest people of our next generation. Several of them offered crucial research help. The archival research would have been impossible without the guidance of John Farrell, who compiled the definitive index to the Mondale Papers while earning a graduate degree at the Humphrey Institute. Kyle Weimann, Sarah Treul, and Curt Yoakam also proved to be intrepid researchers.

My administrative assistant Lynda Pedersen, with the Dorsey law firm, has been an indispensable participant in bringing this book to completion, just as she was in my years in Japan, and in the years both before and after Tokyo. She is talented, thoughtful, efficient, and simply incredible. Researcher Johnette Johnson of the Dorsey staff saved us repeatedly in our hour of need.

For keen insights about the tone and structure of the manuscript, I want to thank Norman Sherman, a dear friend from the Humphrey days.

I also want to thank Al Eisele, Haynes Johnson, and Frank Wright, talented journalists who gave good advice in the early stages of this project, and especially Finlay Lewis, who wrote a superb account of my career in 1980 and shared graciously from his own archive of documents, notes, and interviews.

Jay Beck and his staff at the Carter Library in Atlanta were generous with their time and assistance, and Russell Riley of the Miller Center on Presidential History at the University of Virginia provided valuable advice on approaching oral history.

I owe a special thanks to Jay Mandel and Eric Lupfer at William Morris Endeavor, who understood this project from the beginning and found a home for it. And I am deeply grateful to the superb editorial team at Scribner: Susan Moldow and Nan Graham, who saw the promise in this book, and our gifted editor, Colin Harrison, who helped fulfill it.

Finally, a personal word of thanks to Joan's remarkable staff from the vice-presidential days, especially Bess Abell, Judy Whittlesey, Merrielou Symes, and Elena Canavier, who helped us reconstruct the many contributions she made, with their help, and the unique and spirited role she played in all the work described in these pages.

INDEX

Index

Index

Index

Index